THE MODERN MURASAKI

Asia Perspectives: History, Society, and Culture

ASIA PERSPECTIVES
History, Society, and Culture

A series of the Weatherhead East Asian Institute, Columbia University,
published by Columbia University Press

Carol Gluck, editor

Comfort Women: Sexual Slavery in the Japanese Military During World War II,
by Yoshimi Yoshiaki, trans. Suzanne O'Brien

The World Turned Upside Down: Medieval Japanese Society,
by Pierre François Souyri, trans. Käthe Roth

Yoshimasa and the Silver Pavilion: The Creation of the Soul of Japan,
by Donald Keene

Geisha, Harlot, Strangler, Star: The Story of a Woman, Sex, and Moral Values in Modern Japan,
by William Johnston

Lhasa: Streets with Memories,
by Robert Barnett

Frog in the Well: Portraits of Japan by Watanabe Kazan, 1793–1841,
by Donald Keene

THE MODERN MURASAKI

Writing by Women of Meiji Japan

Edited by

Rebecca L. Copeland and Melek Ortabasi

Columbia University Press   New York

Columbia University Press
Publishers Since 1893
New York   Chichester, West Sussex

Illustrations courtesy of the Nihon kindai bungakkan
(Library of Modern Japanese Literature).

Library of Congress Cataloging-in-Publication Data
The modern Murasaki : writing by women of Meiji Japan /
edited by Rebecca L. Copeland and Melek Ortabasi.
p.   cm. — (Asia perspectives : history, society, and culture)
Includes bibliographical references and index.
ISBN 978-0-231-13774-4 (cloth : alk. paper) — ISBN 978-0-231-13775-1 (pbk. : alk. paper)
1. Japanese literature—Meiji period, 1868–1912—Translations into English—
Women authors.   I. Copeland, Rebecca L., 1956–   II. Ortabasi, Melek.
PL782.E1M63 2006
895.6´409287—dc22   2006017786

Casebound editions of Columbia University Press books
are printed on permanent and durable acid-free paper.
Printed in the United States of America

CONTENTS

PREFACE

WHERE IS THE MODERN MURASAKI HIDING? Where the
Meiji Shōnagon? Eagerly I await your appearance. Nay, even more than
I, our very society longs for your arrival.[1]

Writing in 1890, author Shimizu Shikin (1868–1933) insists that the
inclusion of female voices is necessary to the reinvigoration of contemporary literature and indeed to Japanese society in general. At the same
time, the marginal presence of women writers despite this need frustrates
her. Ironically, while the women of the Meiji period (1868–1912) were still
largely disenfranchised as writers, courtly women authors like Murasaki
Shikibu and Sei Shōnagon, to whom Shikin refers, were being credited
with nothing short of having developed the earliest examples of a refined
and elegant Japanese literary language. Meiji scholars were reinstating
works such as Murasaki Shikibu's eleventh-century romance *Genji monogatari* (*The Tale of Genji*) as vital components in a newly emerging national literary canon. Though the brief heyday of women authors in the
Heian era (794–1185) was long past, their momentum having been undermined by the diminishing power of the court in the fourteenth century,
their works were now being held up as models of literary greatness.

That women writers during Meiji should have taken their cue from
the improved status of feminine courtly writing in the literary pantheon

is no accident. Shikin herself was well aware that the classical model had the potential to create a niche for contemporary women authors. In hope of luring out her literary-minded peers, she turns to history to invoke the names of those courtly women writers who had come to symbolize the society of their own period and, one could say, Japanese literary culture in general. In drawing such a comparison, she hoped that contemporary women writers would not only produce work of the same caliber but also be regarded with the same respect—as "modern Murasakis."

Shikin's comments accurately reflect a milieu that presented many barriers to women wishing to become professional writers. While there was an increased focus on women's education in the Meiji period, the pedagogical trends favored by the progressive government would come to have the goal of cultivating the *ryōsai kenbo* (good wife, wise mother) who would aid in the building of the modern nation—preferably confined within family boundaries. There was little room in the official social philosophy for the woman writer, a potentially public persona whose voice would be broadcast beyond the threshold of the home.

However, even though the "good wife, wise mother" ideology focused on limiting women's power to the household, its reliance on the idea of an educated woman with a positive role to play in her family's life had wider feminist potential. The ideology, which after all did accord women an important place in society, produced an unintentional byproduct: women's increased awareness of their importance to public affairs. This, along with the growing desire for individual identity that represented a larger cultural and political trend in Meiji, opened up a new intellectual space where creative women might launch their ideas. A result of this enlightenment was that educated women sought a voice outside the household. Like the mainstream (male) literary community in these years, which was struggling to develop a modern literary style, aspiring women writers too sought a new identity through which to express themselves, despite the additional difficulty of overcoming the limits imposed on their sex.

This anthology attempts to address Shikin's implicit concerns by making available in English translation an assortment of poetry, essays, short prose fiction, and drama by Meiji period women writers. Female authors were, as Shikin observes, rather slow to emerge during the purported civilization and enlightenment that characterized this period of Japanese history. Nevertheless, as the diverse authors represented in this anthology attest, it is hardly true that the Meiji "literary world [was] without female authors and . . . [was] one in which no woman [was] poised to emerge."[2]

Less easy questions to answer are what form and style came to characterize feminine literary expression and whether the contribution of the Meiji woman writer would simply be seen as a decorative garnish intended to make literary fare more palatable. While some authors did indeed embrace the comparison to historical literary figures, others experimented with contemporary writing styles and provocative content. Some of the authors included here were regarded as models of femininity; others, like Shikin, were considered renegade, whether for moral or stylistic reasons. Regardless of the judgments passed down by their male peers, however, a new generation of women writers was emerging. It is the hope of the translators that, by making the literary accomplishments of these pioneering women available for the first time in English translation, a new generation of readers may make their own judgments.

The editors wish to thank the many people who helped make this volume possible. Good translators seek input from a variety of sources, turning to native speakers of the target language to sound out sentences and test word choice and to native speakers of the source language to double-check for meaning, tone, and content. When appropriate, translators have acknowledged the assistance they received in their individual sections. The editors would particularly like to thank Jennifer Crewe, editorial director at Columbia University Press, for her encouragement and continued support of our anthology. The positive, thoughtful, and detailed responses of the anonymous reviewers greatly assisted us in revising our manuscript. We thank our contributors, too, for their high-quality translations and commentaries; the proof of their dedication is evident in every chapter. The lovely photograph on the cover appears courtesy of Nagasaki University Library, and the Nihon Kindai Bungakkan was kind enough to provide the images of the authors included with each chapter. Without Terri Viglietta, administrative assistant at Hamilton College, preparing the manuscript at its various stages would have been much harder; her assistance was indispensable. Clifton Ng supplied this volume with its excellent index. Last, but not least, we would like to thank our families, who supported us as we spent long hours bringing this book to fruition.

Melek Ortabasi

NOTES

1. Quoted from Rebecca Copeland's translation of "Nanzo jobungakusha deru no osokiya" ("Why Are Female Literati So Slow to Appear?") in *Lost Leaves: Women Writers of Meiji Japan* (Honolulu: University of Hawai'i Press, 2000), p. 7.
2. Ibid., p. 195.

THE MODERN MURASAKI

INTRODUCTION
MEIJI WOMEN WRITERS

Rebecca L. Copeland

Original woman was truly the sun! A genuine person. Now woman is the moon. She lives by the strength of others, she shines by the light of others and her pale moon face is as wan as an invalid's.

SO BEGINS THE OPENING MANIFESTO to the journal *Seitō* (Bluestocking), founded in 1911, the last full year of the Meiji period, by a group of young women interested in creating a forum for female self-expression. In linking woman with the sun, the manifesto alludes to ancient Japanese mythology, wherein the supreme Shinto deity was the sun goddess, Amaterasu, and militant, shamanistic female rulers took the throne. Somewhere along the line, however, this female strength was sublimated to a patriarchal order, and woman was relegated to a second-class position, her talents forgotten. From a literary perspective, the motif recalls the Heian era (794–1185), when Murasaki Shikibu and her literary sisters flourished, and female genius dominated the literary world. What had become of this female genius? Not content to let women blithely acquiesce to positions of subservience, Hiratsuka Raichō (1886–1971), the author of this manifesto and the editor of the journal, enjoins women to recover their original strength, to unleash their innate abilities. "We must now recover our sun which has been hidden for so long. 'Manifest your hidden sun! Your long-lost talents!' This is the cry that swells within us without ceasing. This is the thirst we find so hard to suppress, so impossible to slake. This, indeed, is the one instinct so central to our person that it overcomes all others."[1] And so she ignited a generation of women with her challenge. Not only did her journal serve as a vehicle for female creativity; it was the lightning rod that attracted and channeled new energy.

So spectacular were Raichō's achievements and so rich their influence that scholars have long accepted her lament over the loss of female luster and the silencing of the female voice; they have concurred that between the heyday of the Heian court and the explosion of the *Seitō* movement there was a dearth of female literary activity—if with a few bright exceptions. The medieval periods saw a female poet or two, an essayist here and there. And the early Meiji period (1868–1912) had the brief but brilliant glow of the literary talent Higuchi Ichiyō (1872–1896). Modern women's literature, it would seem, did not begin in earnest until the advent of *Seitō*, which presented the brilliance of Tamura Toshiko (1884–1945), Nogami Yaeko (1885–1985), Yosano Akiko (1878–1942), and many others. But there is evidence to the contrary. First, the premodern period was not as destitute of female talent as otherwise alleged. And the appearance of *Seitō*—or even of the exceptional Higuchi Ichiyō—would likely not have been possible without the contributions of many and varied talents that were already in evidence by the turn of the century.

This anthology showcases these talents, from feminist orator to cloistered daughter, from imperial tutor to household maid. Meiji women writers hailed from diverse backgrounds and made their mark in an impressive assortment of genres and styles: romantic poetry, political essays, Kabuki dramas, novellas, and stories. The works that emerged during the period, and the image of the woman writing them, were in constant flux, the terms of their evaluation shifting along with attitudes governing the reception of women in the public sphere. During the early part of the period, women writers were referred to as *keishū sakka*, or lady writer, a term that would prove to be as stifling as it was rewarding.[2] By the end of the era, they would be known as *joryū sakka*, a term that while less exclusive was nevertheless drenched in gender-based assumptions. Entering the public arena at a time when the boundaries of that space were highly unstable, the appellation of "lady" writer allowed a certain elasticity. The writer could step past the lines that had earlier demarked her limits and have a public voice as long as she continued to speak *as a lady*. Women writers of this early period explored new avenues of expression and embarked on new paths—some short and untenable, others highly successful. Like their male counterparts, these *keishū* writers were eager to craft a new language, one that shifted from neoclassical forms to a closer approximation of the spoken language. In addition, they sought styles and approaches that would meet the demands of a newly insistent modernity. The works that emerged at this time are marked by unevenness, experimentation, and energy.

Their audience was receptive. Works by women were marketable, to a large degree *because* they were works by women. Publishers and editors sought to capitalize on this interest by investing in women's writing. The editors of the newly established literary journal *Bungei kurabu* (Literary arts club), for example, collected works by thirteen women writers and produced a special issue on December 10, 1895, devoted exclusively to "*keishū* literature." Available just before the start of the New Year holidays, the special issue was a runaway success. As Robert Danly notes, the thirty thousand copies of its first printing were sold out immediately, and the journal "had to go to press a second time to meet the unprecedented demand."[3] Not only did the issue provoke a tremendous increase in sales for the journal, it also drew an increase in critical attention. The publication of the special issue was feted in most of the distinguished literary journals of the day, and leading critics reviewed the works. Literary historians, reflecting on the success of this issue, have termed 1895 "the year of the *keishū* writer."[4]

Motivated by the profitability of its first special *keishū* issue, *Bungei kurabu* attempted a follow up issue two years later on January 20, 1897. But the success of the first was not to be met in the second. Although the 1897 issue included women not showcased earlier, such as the impressive Shimizu Shikin (1868–1933), it had lost three of the brightest *keishū* talents: Tazawa Inabune (b. 1874), Higuchi Ichiyō, and the translator Wakamatsu Shizuko (b. 1864), each of whom had died in 1896. The devastation of this blow was exacerbated by the cautious conservatism that had grown increasingly pronounced in the wake of victory over China in the Sino-Japanese War (1894–1895). Women continued to write with dedicated vigor but failed to capture—whether intentionally or not—the vitality that had distinguished their works just years before. There would be no third special issue of *keishū* writers. Writing by women would dwindle henceforth, not to resume a similar level of activity until the first decade of the twentieth century.

By the early 1900s, with greater stabilization of a language for modern literature and greater inclusion of women (even if only perfunctory) in the literary circles dominated by men, women's writing enjoyed a resurgence. Beneficiary of the emphasis on universal education and a provisional leveling of social classes begun in the 1870s, a new kind of woman writer—known now by the term *joryū sakka* (female-style writer) began to test her talents. The advent of journals such as *Seitō* and *Joshi bundan* (Woman's literary world) offered a different kind of forum for women's writing, one that came closer to establishing the coterie atmosphere male writers had long enjoyed. While still mediated by male influence, these journals nevertheless provided the emotional sustenance and encouragement women needed to nurture their genius. Out of these associations emerged writers like Hasegawa Shigure (1879–1941), Tamura Toshiko, Nogami Yaeko, and Mizuno Senko (1888–1919), who would characterize the late Meiji/early Taishō literary scene.

Arranged chronologically, this volume offers a sampling of the rhetorical strategies and experiments these writers tested and adapted. The literary pieces selected for translation—characterizing the variety of genres and styles in which women were active—reclaim the diversity, the vitality, and the tenacity of the Meiji literary woman. Despite the unevenness of women's literary production over the Meiji era—the differences in language styles and narrative rhetorical devices and the distinctions among the writing women themselves—what unites their works are the topics addressed, the strategies for overcoming social and literary constraints, and the way their works were received. No matter how naive these writers may have been in their approaches to their art or how devoid of conscious political intention, the mere act of writing thrust them into the public domain and into conflict with ideas about new political spaces and evolving concepts of the family. In so doing, it made both the writer and her art commodities for public scrutiny. Because the author's personal life thus became entangled with if not her art per se then certainly the perception of it, each author's work will be preceded by a brief biography. The remainder of this introduction will consider the larger developments in the Meiji period that acted as important contexts for the encouragement and confinement of women's writing, with focus primarily on education, political participation, and the family. It will conclude with an assessment of contemporary critical reception.

ENTER THE MEIJI PERIOD

Most discussions of the Meiji period begin with the profound impact the Western world had on Japan in the late nineteenth century. Relatively isolated from contact with the West, the Japanese were stunned when confronted with Western power and its potential for dominating Asia. India had been colonized by the British, Thailand by the French. The Dutch were claiming the East Indies, and China, the once powerful civilization that Japan had emulated for centuries, was partitioned among the various Western potentates. Fearful of sliding down the same treacherous path, Japanese leaders soon recognized that, rather than resisting Western might or ignoring its threat, it would be far more sensible to strive to make Japan an equal power. The old shogunal system of government that had held sway for two hundred years was overthrown, and in its place the imperial system was restored. Rather than invoking a return to ancient systems, however, the newly reinstated imperial governance was meant to usher in an enlightened age, one that drew strength and authority from what was purported to have been an earlier era of just and unsullied leadership. Reform of the follies of the past and the installation of new approaches became the key to success; "civilization and enlightenment," *burmei kaika*, the slogan of fashion.

Eager to lead the country into the fold of the so-called civilized nations, progressive-minded politicians and intellectuals encouraged modifications that ran from the sublime to the mundane, from national governance to the local sewer system. Of note for this study is the fact that women were among the targets of reform. Captivated by rhetoric then popular among Western imperialists, reformers believed that the status of a nation's women was the measure of its civilization. While progress was afoot in Japan on many levels, Japanese women, or so these reformers were convinced, were far from modern. In order to redress this wrong, changes were encouraged. Women were required to modify their costumes, their cosmetics, their speech, the way they arranged their hair; some were even encouraged to learn the latest trends in ballroom dancing, all in an attempt to modernize or at least to earn the respect of foreign visitors. Japanese diplomats and politicians at the time were trying to amend the unequal treaties that had been signed earlier with Western powers. In 1883 an elaborate reception hall was built to entertain Western dignitaries and to impress them with the level of civilization Japan had achieved. Known as the Rokumeikan, or Deer-Cry Pavilion, the hall was the site of exquisite galas where Japanese ladies attired in Parisian gowns glided through the night on Western arms.

LOVE, MARRIAGE, AND FEMALE AUTONOMY

Certainly not all appeals to modernization concentrated on surface appearances. Nor were they invoked simply to produce a copy of Western models. Reformers were eager to stimulate change in Japan, but most wanted to do so in a way that retained quintessential Japanese elements. The Japanese woman, while upheld as a symbol of all that was backward in Japan, was also expected to stand for all that was elegant and pure in Japanese tradition. She was to become both a modern subject and a "repository of the past."[5] The female ideal crafted by early Meiji male intellectuals was to have enough education to make her an adequate conversationalist and companion for her husband and a resourceful household manager. But she was also to appreciate that her most important role in life was to provide a happy home.

Marriage and the role of women in the family became one of the most hotly contested subjects in Meiji Japan, and the initial participants in the debates were by and large men. Fukuzawa Yukichi (1835–1901), Nakamura Masanao (1832–1891), Mori Arinori (1847–1889), among others, banded together in 1874, the sixth year of Meiji, to form the short-lived *Meiroku zasshi* (Meiji Six magazine, 1874–1875).[6] Chief among the topics these men discussed was "the Woman Question." Most of the members of the Meiji Six had visited Western countries, and almost all were impressed by what appeared to them to be the natural and equal relations between the husbands and wives there. Spouses attended social functions together, conversed with one another with spark and wit across the dining room table, and interacted with apparent freedom in and outside family situations.[7] Western marriages, they deduced, were premised on mutual respect and mutual attraction. They were entered into voluntarily and were not determined by factors beyond the interests of the couple. And, most important, the Western marriage was considered a bond between two individuals and not an extended family. The happy image of marriage that Meiji men took back with them after their journeys through the West was one of a warm and equitable partnership between a man and a woman and brightened by the inclusion of children, all gathered tightly around a cozy hearth.

To a large extent, the image these reformers constructed of companionate marriages and male-female relations was informed by the Western romantic tradition, based on hurried observation, and was not grounded in any real understanding of contemporary legal codes. In most Western countries, women still lacked protection in marriage and were susceptible to inequitable divorce laws. Moreover, marriages were often the result of family pressure and frequently designed to advance family, not individual, interests. Still, the very concept of marriage as an equal partnership was an attractive notion at the time in Japan.

Whereas members of the Meiji Six deplored the fact that divorce was all too frequent in Japan, they recognized that, at least among the upper classes, these divorces were rarely initiated by a woman.[8] Occasionally, the wife's family might intervene and have a daughter brought home (regardless her own interest in the matter) if the family felt the marriage was no longer viable, whether for social or financial reasons. In such a case, the daughter might be placed in a more successful marriage. But divorces of this type were possible only when the wife's family had more political or financial clout than the husband's. More often, it was the husband or his family who severed the marital bond, and often for reasons that today would seem frivolous if not cruel. Women who did not produce male children, women who grew ill, women whose natal family members found themselves on the wrong side of the law, women who no longer pleased a husband or his parents could be sent back to their home with the notorious "three-line letter" (the formulaic language announcing a husband's intention to divorce his wife usually conformed to three lines). Some husbands did not even bother with this formality and, like the men depicted in "Hiding the Gray" (Shiragazome, 1897), by Kitada Usurai (1871–1900), or Shimizu Shikin's "The Broken Ring" (Koware yubiwa," 1891), simply left their wives behind in the countryside while they sought greater opportunity and often a new spouse in the city.

This is not to say that women could not sue for a divorce. But this alternative was not always preferred to marriage, no matter how horrendous. When educator and temperance advocator Yajima Kajiko (1832–1922) left her alcoholic and abusive husband and set out on her own, for example, her two nephews, Tokutomi Rōka (1868–1927) and Tokutomi Sohō (1863–1957)—relatively liberal men—were highly critical. In addition to the prospect of social stigma, a woman surrendered her property to her husband upon marriage. Any children born of the union were likewise considered the husband's possessions and could be kept by the husband's family if the woman chose to leave the marriage, an outcome that was all too common in contemporary Western countries as well. In Japan, the lack of claim a woman had to her offspring was especially true of male children. But if the husband refused to care for the children, the woman would have to find a way to provide for them and herself in a world where there were few opportunities for female employment, as Usurai so poignantly reveals in "Hiding the Gray."

One attitude that progressive Meiji men and women found regrettable was *danson johi* (revere men, despise women), which they attributed to an outdated feudal mentality. It was this attitude that kept many women from the educations they deserved, that remanded them to unequal rights in marriages, and that allowed for the systems of concubinage, prostitution, and to some extent son-in-law adoptions. Under contemporary law, a man was entitled to "own" a concubine, bringing her into the house with his legal wife, and often turning to the concubine when the wife was unable to produce a male heir. The offspring of such a union had, for a time, a legitimate claim to the family inheritance, thus further displacing the legal wife. Because jealousy was conveniently considered a female weakness, women involved in marriages such as these were expected to accept their situations without complaint. Such is the case of the beleaguered mother in Tazawa Inabune's "Godai-dō" (Temple of Godai), who, though recognizing that her husband's philandering with the household maid sets a bad example for her son, has no choice but to acquiesce to his behavior.

Similarly, men who spent money on the services of prostitutes were not penalized. And, unlike in Western countries, where dalliance with prostitutes was often conducted under the cover of darkness, so long as

Japanese men did not jeopardize the family finances with their activities, they were encouraged to disport themselves as they pleased with no fear of public reprisal. Wives, however, were vulnerable to legal punishment should they be caught in an extramarital relationship.

While not as harmful to women as concubinage, the system of son-in-law adoptions also undermined a woman's rights. Families that lacked suitable male heirs would frequently marry a daughter to an appropriate spouse who would then be entered into the legal registry as the son and heir (a situation depicted in Mizuno Senko's short story "Shijūyonichi" [For More than Forty Days]). The adopted son-in-law thus was entitled to the ownership and privilege accorded a son, and the daughter became a mere wife in her own natal home. This type of marriage, generally considered less attractive to the in-marrying man than it was to the daughter, nevertheless removed the woman from a position of inheritance.

Women orators like Kishida Toshiko (1863–1901) and Shimizu Shikin were outspoken in their condemnation of the unequal treatment of women. Both deplored the fact that women were regarded as property. Men down on their luck might legally sell their daughters, sisters, or even wives into prostitution, and the women had little choice but to obey. Should a woman not have the option of a respectable marriage—because she lacked wealth or backing—she could similarly be sold to a family as a concubine. Some were apprenticed as maids to families where they were little more than indentured servants and often expected to be sexually available to the men in the household. Indeed, although the central government declared a new and enlightened rule with the restoration of the emperor, very little changed for women. Women were, in the words of Mori Arinori, little more than slaves to their husband's wishes, "no different than chattel."[9]

In tandem with their abhorrence of the perceived pernicious habits still lingering in Japan, these women cherished an admiration for the concept of romantic love between men and women that was observed in the West. The notion that the love between a man and woman could circumvent the purely physical and unfold on a spiritual level was both novel and exciting. Kishida Toshiko (also known as Nakajima Shōen), for example, affirmed in her 1884 essay "Dōho shimai ni tsugu" (To My Fellow Sisters) that love was the most noble of human emotions, an emotion that Japan's current misogynistic character disallowed: "When a man and woman love one another equally and know a mutual compassion for one another; when they share in each other's sorrows and joys—then they are able to experience true passion and affection. . . . And yet, in today's society (particularly in Japanese society) the authoritative right to rule resides with men. And it is wielded with a demonic vengeance, tearing asunder the precious, joyous gift of love."[10] Shimizu Shikin, Kishida's contemporary, would similarly despair in her essays and stories that true love between a man and a woman—a love that bound the spirit as well as the flesh—was for most women little more than a wistful schoolgirl dream.

As the Meiji period advanced, women did what they could to rebel against the marriage institution. Of those represented in this volume, most were partners in marriages of choice. Three started out in arranged marriages: Shimizu Shikin, Kitada Usurai, and Hasegawa Shigure. But of these, only Usurai, who died within two years of her marriage, found the arrangement satisfactory. Shikin and Shigure were soon to follow their hearts and claim marriage partners more to their liking. Other writers selected their mates from the very beginning. Kishida Toshiko elected to marry Nakajima Nobuyuki, and Miyake Kaho (1868–1944) chose a union with Setsurei. A large percentage married fellow writers, often with unhappy results. Tazawa Inabune seemed the perfect match for literary star Yamada Bimyō (1868–1910), until his philandering sent her packing. Both Tamura Toshiko and Mizuno Senko found their marriages to writers rife with petty jealousies. Poet Yosano Akiko and husband Tekkan (1873–1935) shared a happier relationship.

More often than not women writers found themselves embroiled in scandalous relationships, frequently of their own initiative. Akiko, for example, pursued Tekkan when he was in a relationship with another woman who was pregnant with his child. Neither was Tamura Toshiko hesitant about involving herself in love affairs with married men. Hasegawa Shigure, having escaped her loveless first marriage, wed a man over ten years her junior, raising more than a few eyebrows in the process. Wishing to avoid the kind of scandal writers like these invited, Nogami Yaeko elected to marry a man whom she most likely did not love but whose occupation allowed her to live in Tokyo, where she would have greater freedom than if she returned to her country home and a spouse of her parents' choosing. Higuchi Ichiyō, the most successful of these writers in earning enduring fame, was also the only one to remain unwed. Lacking family backing, she failed to secure an appropriate spouse and died before her changing fortunes rendered her an attractive marriage prospect.

Given the significance of marriage to women at the time, it is not surprising that most of the writers in this collection turn to the subject, particularly to the importance of compatible marital relations, in their stories. In "Yabu no uguisu" (Warbler in the Grove) Miyake Kaho reminds readers to choose a marriage partner wisely. A match based on lust alone—though freely elected—is doomed to fail, a reality Tamura Toshiko's character in "Seigon" (The Vow) discovers all too late. Love marriages, though desired, are not that easy to acquire or maintain, Shimizu Shikin warns her audience of female students in her 1890 essay "Tōkon jogakusei no kakugo wa ikan" (How Determined Are Today's Women Students?). Men, once they have wooed and won a woman, are wont to stray. A woman who suffers such an indignity should not be forced to endure a loveless marriage. Like Shikin's narrator in "Koware yubiwa" (The Broken Ring), she can step out on her own. But unless her parents are willing to provide her with a room of her own—as in the case of Nogami Yaeko's Osetsu in "Kakiyōkan" (Persimmon Sweets), a woman had better be armed with appropriate knowledge so as to sustain her own independence. Far better to be versed in economics than song and dance, Kishida Toshiko advises.

Taken collectively, the pieces assembled here reveal a progressive tableau. Early works recount the optimism of a match self-selected, the exhilarating enticements of desire unleashed, or else the heroics of a woman able to stand up to familial and social pressure and chart her own course. As the era advances, however, we see the romance begin to tarnish. Love, though coveted, is not so easily acquired, and desire proves fickle. Focus shifts from the ideal of love to the toll of reality. Moreover, the physicality of the female condition, earlier only implied in modest innuendo, is foregrounded with graphic rigor. Mizuno Senko describes the physical ordeal of childbirth, whereas Yosano Akiko, while also known for her poems on childbirth, writes of the intense sensations of the female body in the throes of desire. Tamura Toshiko, not unlike Akiko, celebrates the pleasures of a woman awakening to sexual desire but also describes the trauma of a sexual encounter. Mapping the body with pleasure and pain, women writers in the latter years of the Meiji era emphasized the process by which the female body is both opened to physical awakenings and bound by cultural and political constraints.

EDUCATING THE MEIJI WOMAN

The longed-for companionate marriage, was thus almost impossible to achieve. Even men who respected women in principle found it difficult to live with a wife as an equal. And, for women, navigating the uncharted waters of their new roles was daunting. Both sexes agreed that true companionship, respect, and progress could not be achieved without adequate education. Education for women—as citizens of a new and enlightened rule—became one of the most important and frequently contentious topics of debate at this time. Impressed by what they had observed during their travels in the West, progressive Meiji intellectuals advocated for greater educational opportunities for women, arguing that by denying women access to education, Japan was keeping half its citizenship ignorant. Not only did this neglect women; it denied the nation access to a potentially rich resource. As one member of the Meiji Six noted: "The training of men and women should be equal and not of two types. If we desire to preserve an extremely high and extremely pure level among human beings as a whole, we should accord both men and women the same type of upbringing and enable them to progress equally."[11] The early years of the Meiji period therefore saw progressive intellectuals and government officials alike promoting equal education for the sexes. As E. Patricia Tsurumi notes, "during these two decades a number of determined girls and women experienced more gender equality in their education than was possible again until after Japan's defeat in the Pacific War in 1945."[12]

This is not to suggest that women had gone unschooled before the Meiji period. Women of elite families had always received training in Japanese poetry (as well as in sewing and other domestic arts); a smaller number studied and in some cases even taught the Chinese classics, thought to be the property of men.[13] Those families that could afford to allow their children time away from tending the fields in the countryside or the shop in the urban centers sent their children to "temple schools" (*terakōya*) where they learned the fundamentals of arithmetic and reading and writing—boys and girls, upper class and lower class, side by side. Alternatively, families set their children up with tutors, studying both Chinese and Japanese classics.

Regardless of class or location, most women were also instructed in the all-pervasive primers on appropriate female conduct. Largely Confucian in perspective, these primers, such as *Onna daigaku* (The great learning for women, attributed to Kaibara Ekiken, 1630–1714), exhorted women to acknowledge and accept their innate debased natures and to work to overcome the afflictions of their sex, namely, "indocility, discontent, slander, jealousy, and silliness"[14] by cultivating the Confucian virtues of "obedience, purity, goodwill, frugality, modesty, and diligence."[15] Above all, women were to recognize the "Three Obediences."[16] As daughters, they were to be obedient to their fathers; as wives, they were to submit to their husbands; and, as mothers, they were to sacrifice themselves to their sons.

It was this kind of education that Meiji reformers criticized. Believing it to be repressive and detrimental, many encouraged instead an education that would exercise the mind rather than fetter it. Kishida Toshiko, herself well trained in a rich cross-section of Chinese classics and Japanese history, criticized parents who prepared their daughters for very little but lives of drudgery and dependence. Poetry and pretty arts—traditional subjects for girls—are fine in small measure, she notes in her famous 1883 lecture "Daughters in Boxes," but in order to acquire minds that could think independently and with moral soundness, women needed more substantial training.

In the early years of the Meiji era, much of this training came from exceptional women. Miwata Masako (1843–1927) and Atomi Kakei (1840–1926), both of whom had been educated in the Confucian tradition, were quick to establish private schools for girls in Tokyo (these still exist today).[17] Shimoda Utako (1854–1936), Hatoyama Haruko (1863–1938), and Tanahashi Ayako (1839–1939) are among others who became active in encouraging women's education. Women were not limited, at this time, to separate schools. In fact, for a very brief moment in Meiji history, the conditions for women's education were so positive and the emphasis on equal opportunities so pronounced that women were able to attend public middle schools alongside their male counterparts. If a woman had enough determination, she could even receive the medical training sufficient to becoming a doctor.[18]

The Meiji educational system evolved over a period of time and—like much else during the period—went through stages of contradiction, optimism, and backlash before emerging in the last decade of the nineteenth century as rigid and state-centered. In 1872 the newly established Ministry of Education issued a law requiring sixteen months of compulsory education for children of both sexes and all social classes. The law was amended in 1880 to three years and again in 1907 to six.[19] Despite what would appear on the surface to be an encouragement of greater educational opportunities for women, what must be noted is the agenda that surged as a strong undercurrent: to produce women who would be of service to the state. The definition of this service would fluctuate with the fortunes of the state. The way women were educated, and why, are therefore important considerations in determining the influence of schooling on women writers in the Meiji period.

The first government-funded secondary school for women was the Tokyo Women's Normal School founded in 1875. Applicants that first year took a battery of entrance exams that tested them on their knowledge of Japanese history, Chinese thought, and Western science in addition to evaluating their ability to produce a good hand in Japanese calligraphy. Out of the more than three hundred who applied, only seventy-four were admitted.[20] Since the government failed to meet student demand for institutions at the higher level, private institutions and individuals worked to fill the gap. Christian missionaries from Europe and North America were quick to open schools for women. Mary Kidder opened her academy of higher learning for women in 1870. Five years later, it became the prestigious Ferris Women's Seminary, intellectual home to Kishida Toshiko and Wakamatsu Shizuko, among other prominent Meiji women writers. Kidder was soon followed by a host of other missionaries from a variety of countries and denominations, each sharing the same zeal to educate Japanese womanhood. The success of these mission schools did not discourage similar enterprises among Japanese educators, who created schools with curricula that ranged from Confucian classics to sewing. The most influential private school to emerge at this time was the Meiji Women's School, alma mater to Miyake Kaho and Nogami Yaeko, among numerous other women writers.

The Meiji Women's School was founded in 1885 by Japanese Christians who were alarmed by the growing proliferation of mission schools. Instruction at these schools was often in English and focused on Western history and literature at the expense of Japanese studies. Naruse Jinzō, who would later establish the influential Japan Women's College in 1901—which enrolled Tamura Toshiko among other future women writers—was to observe that Western missionaries erred when they tried to make "European or American women out of our daughters, and their educational efforts tended to produce undiscriminating westernization, which our society does not want."[21]

But not all were convinced that Japanese educators were any more successful in their efforts to train Japanese womanhood. Institutions like the Meiji School for Women were vilified as hotbeds of promiscuity, primarily because they advocated love matches instead of traditional marriages. Moreover, a number of its female students became romantically involved with the handsome young male teachers there, provoking considerable scandal. These scandals only inflamed earlier discomfort with liberal education for women. Many parents feared that too much education would "ruin" their daughters by making them unacceptable for marriage. This was the case for the mothers of both Higuchi Ichiyō and Hasegawa Shigure, who worried, along with an increasing number of government officials, about the "unsuitable consequences" of educating women.[22] And this concern operated as an undercurrent in a number of the works included in this anthology, notably the essays and stories by Kishida Toshiko, Miyake Kaho, and Shimizu Shikin.

The early years of the Meiji period, heady with hope, had produced female students who were shortly to step beyond the boundaries of the socially acceptable. Atomi Kakei notes in 1872 of the women she saw in Tokyo on their way to and from school, "There were some who had their hair cut and wore thin sashes like men; they did not wrap their books in a *furoshiki* cloth, but clasped them under their armpits, and then there were some who deliberately strutted along wearing long, striped *haori* jackets. . . . I thought that this was terrible and that I somehow had to reform girls' education."[23]

Not only did the liberal education produce women who dressed like men; it encouraged women to speak like men. Kishida Toshiko, Fukuda Hideko, and other women who traveled with the Freedom and People's Rights Movement began to make their support of women's education—and women's rights—the subject of public speeches, in forums that attracted larger and larger crowds. Government officials took note. And then they took action. As Tsurumi states, "the specter of women organizing and educating appears to have warranted an especially thorough eradication program."[24]

Shortly, government officials began to issue policies intent on curtailing these unsuitable consequences. Just as the social roles for men and women were to be clearly differentiated, so too their education. Girls were to be given instruction in sewing and domestic skills and were to be inculcated with ethical lessons that would more carefully reinforce understanding of their social roles. In other words, the girl student was to be trained specifically to acquit her duties as "good wife, wise mother" (*ryōsai kenbo*).

The Ministry of Education decreed in 1899 that the purpose of higher education for women was "to foster characteristics that make them develop into wise mothers and good wives. For this reason elegant and refined manners, and docility and modesty are qualities that must be fostered."[25] When Naruse Jinzō opened his private college two years later, his stated intent was to educate women "firstly as humans, secondly as ladies and finally as citizens of the nation."[26] But as Hiratsuka Raichō, one of his students, would soon discover to her great disappointment, the focus on the second of these charges far outweighed the other two.

Educators' determination to turn out good wives and wise mothers limited the options for women before they had even graduated. Rather than the eclectic blend of Western history and Chinese classics that many of the earlier schools had offered, now women were trained in the home sciences and, more important, Confucian ethics. A charge that had originated in early Meiji as an affirmative attempt to justify education for women had by the end of the period become a slogan for all that delimited and demeaned women in their quest for personal advancement. Should her situation afford, a woman's place was in the home, where she was to submit to her father, husband, and son. The Confucian notions early Meiji reformists had fought to eradicate were still very firmly rooted.

POLITICAL ASPIRATIONS

For many men and women, the advent of the Meiji period had promised tremendous possibilities. As the old structures of power were being dismantled and the rigid social caste system crumbled, new ideas poured in from abroad. It seemed Japan was poised for massive social, cultural, and political upheavals. But frequently the processes of change imagined with such enthusiasm and optimism concluded in frustration, as wheels that began rolling forward inevitably turned back on themselves. To an extent, this was the fate of education for women. At the dawn of the Meiji period, the prospect of an equal education was tantalizing. But by the end of it, though women from all walks of life had far more opportunities to attend schools than they had ever had in the past, the kind of education they were allowed did not live up to the aspirations of early Meiji idealists. The same may be said of advances in political opportunities.

In the early 1870s a number of former samurai, feeling disenfranchised by the recently created Meiji government, founded the Jiyū minken undō (Freedom and popular rights movement), intent on advocating for greater political representation among all the classes. One approach to spreading the word was lecture tours. Lecturers traveled for weeks at a time through cities and towns and backwoods hamlets voicing concerns about the unfairness of taxation without representation and the importance of creating new venues for political participation that would cross class lines. Crossing gender lines was an additional, though limited concern, and one raised primarily by the women who participated in the tours.

Foremost among these women lecturers were Kishida Toshiko, Fukuda Hideko, and Shimizu Shikin. Each participated enthusiastically and tirelessly, traveling far beyond her home and occasionally into venues typically off limits to respectable women. Wherever they went, their message was unwavering: women were not only entitled to equality in education and marriage but also to equal political representation. While the government was still in its nascent state, and before the constitution had been promulgated, hopes were high that women would be allowed to participate in the political process at all levels.

But with each step taken to create a more inclusive political system, the government responded with more stringent controls. Alarmed by the unrest lecture meetings fostered, government authorities, who had earlier been successful in creating rigid press laws, established in 1880 a detailed set of laws meant to curb political speech, known as the Public

Assembly Act. As Sharon Sievers describes the regulations: "Permits were required (three days in advance), and provisions were made for the police to attend such gatherings. No advertising of lectures and debates with political content was permitted, and military personnel, police, and teachers were not allowed to join political associations or attend meetings that featured political discussion. In practice, the interpretation and application of these regulations was left to the discretion of local police, who could arrest speakers, disrupt scheduled meetings, or refuse permits to those they judged disruptive of public order.[27]

Four years later, the Liberal Party, the political arm of the Jiyū minken undō, was dissolved and with it the only real platform women had had for political speech. To ensure their silence further, the Public Assembly Act was revised in 1890 under article 5 of the Police Security Regulations, and women—as a category—were added to the list of those barred from attending political meetings or joining political associations. Almost every avenue that women sought for political participation was blocked. It should thus have come as no surprise when in 1898, after nearly a decade of debate that had not included female representation, the newly promulgated Meiji civil code failed to advance the cause of women. Nevertheless, the former female orators and political agitators were stunned. Not only did the code not advance their cause, it set them back in time, confining all women under a patriarchal system that earlier had been expected only of the samurai, the most repressive of the four erstwhile classes. Sharon Sievers succinctly summarized the outcome: "The new code made the authority of the patriarch absolute, whether he was a Baron or a tenant farmer."[28]

THE MODERN MURASAKI

Barred from public speaking and largely lacking any other political platform, women turned, as Seki Reiko notes, "from the tongue to the [writing] brush."[29] Of course, women had been writing all along, at social gatherings and in private corners, in poetry circles, in intellectual enclaves, in the licensed quarters. The period following the restoration of imperial rule marked a conscious and deliberate effort on the part of both male and female reformers and educators to identify, encourage, and publish women's writing. No outlet was more important to this enterprise than journalism. Numerous journals and periodicals created space for women's literary expression, a practice that not only affirmed the importance of women's writing but cultivated an avid readership. Women, and men as well, who did not have immediate access to avenues of education found periodicals a welcome substitute. Journals and papers, though delayed perhaps by weeks or months, brought to eager readers in the countryside tantalizing news of urban innovations, new literary associations, and political movements. Similarly, these periodicals became important venues of expression for those on the fringes of social or political power. In this respect, one of the most important early journals was *Jogaku zasshi* (Woman's education magazine). Founded in 1885, the journal had dual goals of encouraging self-worth among a female readership while at the same time disabusing male readers of chauvinistic attitudes. The journal not only dedicated space to women's writing; its editor, Iwamoto Yoshiharu (1863–1942), openly solicited works from women and challenged those who claimed that writing was an activity better left to men. "I believe writing is an appropriate employment for women," he stated in 1886. "And I entrust this to them. The books we have nowadays are not good for female readers. And so it is that I hope women will emerge as excellent authors—to rectify this wrong.[30]

Iratsume (The maiden) was inaugurated in 1887 with the exclusive intention of promoting women's literary endeavors, particularly poetry. *Joshi bundan* (1905–1913), mentioned earlier, was immensely important in bridging the lacuna between *Jogaku zasshi*, which folded in 1905, and *Seitō*, the premier journal for women's literary efforts. Mainstream newspapers, such as the *Yomiuri*, offered women an opportunity to publish their works, and mainstream literary periodicals, such as *Miyako no hana* (Flower of the capital), *Taiyō* (The sun), *Shinchō* (New tide), *Myōjō* (Morning star), and the previously introduced *Bungei kurabu* frequently included works by women.

As is clear from the enthusiasm with which their writing was met, women were not without encouragement in their literary endeavors. To this end, male mentors were particularly influential. Male relatives—fathers, brothers, uncles—and occasionally male teachers, often encouraged these soon-to-be writers to pursue their craft. Brothers lent sisters copies of books or journals; fathers and husbands helped introduce daughters and wives to prestigious writers, who were in turn instrumental in editing drafts and helping introduce women to sympathetic publishers. Curiously, with some exceptions—notably Kishida Toshiko and Miyake Kaho—female relatives tended to be less supportive, and many, in fact, were prohibitive and discouraging. Mothers, probably better than fathers, knew all too well how unlikely it was that society would support a nonconformist woman. Moreover, it bears noting that mothers (and less so fathers) were frequently held accountable for the behavior of their daughters, as we see in Shimizu Shikin's "The Broken Ring." A wayward girl (that is to say, a woman unsuccessful in marriage) was thought to be the result of a poor role model.

The importance of the male mentor in furthering a woman's writing career, however, gave him a correspondingly significant role in determining the direction that career would take. The employment of the term *keishū sakka* is indicative of the way the power to define correlates to the privilege to confine. Generally daughters of affluent and privileged families, these *lady* writers received above-average educations. Most were conversant with Western ideas and were eager to participate in the modernizing efforts of their male counterparts. Denied other outlets for their voices, writing promised an appropriate medium for social protest and creative development. And yet, as a complement to the male literary enterprise and, more important, as *ladies*, *keishū sakka* were to avert their eyes from anything untoward and focus on the gentle, lyrical moments of their own pristine lives. Their lives, like their writing, were to be as pure and chaste as those that their Heian precursors were assumed to have lived.[31] Thus, when the seventeen-year-old Kitada Usurai made her literary debut in 1894, she was heralded as the Murasaki of the Meiji period—not because of any intrinsic elements in her style but because she was thought to be chaste and pure, tucked safely away at home with her writing brush and inkstone.

But, as these women were soon to discover, to be *modern* meant to engage current issues, to grapple with a new language, and to struggle to articulate a clearly defined subjectivity. In short, it meant to be all that the imagined Murasaki—chastely rubbing ink behind silk screens—was not. Women who experimented with language, who wrote in a forthright manner of social ills, and who invented characters who ventured beyond the sanctity of the sitting room were largely ridiculed as presumptuous, masculine, or imitative. Thus, when Miyake Kaho—for just one example of many—wrote of the exchanges between a "poison woman" and her lover, critics took offense. Either the scene had been written by a man, or this lady writer was no lady. Kaho was cautioned to "emulate the Murasaki Shikibu of old and not the Shikibu of the back alleys."[32]

It is interesting that in seeking precursors and models for Meiji women writers, critics would reach far back into the Heian era while ignoring those of the more recent Tokugawa era (1600–1868). Atsuko Sakaki suggests a political motive. "Women's literature from the Tokugawa period has been conveniently forgotten in order to invent the notion of women's liberation in modern Japan, and to uncritically and ahistorically bridge Heian court culture of the tenth to the eleventh centuries (epitomized by Murasaki Shikibu . . .) and modern capitalist culture."[33] Not only did this link to the Heian past erase the efforts of Tokugawa women of letters, creating the illusion of Japanese women as needing rescue from the tyranny of a feudal Confucian order, it also allowed supporters of early Meiji women's writing to craft an image of the woman writer as a perpetuator of native courtly traditions who was elegant and above all "feminine."

Japanese men of letters were being challenged by the reformist zeal of the transition to the Meiji period to restructure contemporary Japanese writing practices. The man of letters was a man on a mission. As writer and critic Saganoya Omuro (1863–1947) would describe in his essay "Mission of a Novelist," the writer is "a pursuer of truth, an acquirer of truth, a student of mankind, a master of human beings, a leader of men, an observer of society, a master of society, a social reformer."[34] By assigning the modern writer a social agenda of this dimension, Meiji critics invested modern letters with a seriousness of purpose it had not known in previous eras. And with this seriousness came privilege. Writing was to be—if only as an idealization—an occupation of intellectual merit and social purpose. It was not therefore to be the property of women. This assignment of values did not mean that women were to be removed from the sphere of writing. Rather, they were asked to serve as complements to their male counterparts in the literary arena—much as in the arena of the home—and to match the robustness of masculine intellect with the gentleness of feminine sensitivity. Most important, they were tasked with serving as a repository for the beauty and wonder of the native classical traditions as represented by Murasaki Shikibu and her contemporaries. In the process, Murasaki Shikibu—and the traditions she represented—was moved from her position in the literary mainstream to standing as the primogenitor of a female literary tradition, a smaller, more rarefied domain.

The transition also marked the evolution of a more clearly articulated distinction between the discursive literary practices of men and women. Briefly put, whereas men were enjoined to cast their gaze far and wide, to grapple with weighty social issues, and to endeavor to invent a literary language that would better represent the rapidly changing realities of the day, women were expected to confine themselves to a sentimental tone, a lyrical style, and, especially, a focus on the soft and subtle moments in a woman's quiet life. In sum, the woman writer was not to let her imagination soar beyond the parameters of her narrow base of knowledge but expected to turn what were believed to be her uniquely acute observatory skills on that which she knew best—namely, her family, in particular her children. It was argued that writing of this sort, while never, of course, comparing to a man's more robust intellectualism and social breadth, would offer an important counterweight by providing readers that which men could not approximate. Critic Akiyama Shun suggests that this prioritizing of the cerebral and the restriction of woman from it were less the expression of an inherent feudalistic misogyny than a calculated effort on the part of the "Meiji (male) elitist...to monopolize Western intellectual work."[35] Akiyama's observation reveals an anxiety on the part of male writers to authenticate their own literary practices by deliberately limiting female authors to an antique authority and thus excluding them from competition in the modern/Western/intellectual realms.

EXIT THE LADY WRITER

By 1900 the era of the *keishū sakka* had largely passed. But the closure of one era saw the opening of another, and a new kind of woman writer began to claim attention. Having benefited from the universal educational system and the leveling of class distinctions, she was not as averse to taking risks and facing scrutiny. Marked by sex but not by class, women writers from the 1900s on were largely referred to as *joryū sakka*—writers of the woman's style—a distinction that held its claim on women writers until the 1970s when it was replaced by *josei sakka*, woman writer. The change of terminology, however, did not diminish the insistence that women follow the same writing program that had been outlined for their predecessors.

In 1908 five male critics sat down to discuss contemporary women writers. What they ended up offering was a long splenetic complaint over the current state of women's writing.[36] Hasegawa Shigure, Ōtsuka Kusuoko (1875–1910), and Yosano Akiko—all contemporaries of the critics in question—are singled out for particular condemnation. What is interesting about this evaluation, however, is that the critics admit to having not actually read the works by the writers they rebuked. As in the earlier case of Kitada Usurai—who was acclaimed as the Modern Murasaki based on perception of her personal attributes and not an analysis of her writing—it was not so much what these women had written but the way they were perceived to have overstepped the very subtle bounds that defined them as women writers. Ōtsuka Kusuoko, for example, was known for creating middle- to upper-class female characters who uninhibitedly voiced their own desires. Her 1908 novella *Sora daki* (Incense burner) depicted the lust a married woman has for her attractive stepson. Her contemporary Hasegawa Shigure, now known, along with her friend Okada Yachiyo, as the founder and editor of the feminist journal *Nyonin geijutsu* (Women and the arts), which began in 1928, was at this time a rising playwright. Although written for the Kabuki stage, Hasegawa's plays resisted clichéd tragic endings and featured heroines who strove for self-fulfillment and independence. And Yosano Akiko ran afoul of expectations by dabbling in prose instead of focusing exclusively on poetry, a genre these critics find most becoming for women because of its association with the newly invented feminine tradition. None of the women in their midst suggested the quiet femininity that these male critics felt should be their mission. After waxing nostalgic for Higuchi Ichiyō and the writers of her generation, the critics offer the following:

> Because we need a literature of moderation, we need women writers. And yet, women writers these days, even though they are women and should observe moderation, are more and more apt to select wild topics and resort to bizarre characterizations after the fashion of [our male contemporary] Izumi Kyōka. They forget their innate qualities as women writers, and they make the mistake of rebelling against their essence. . . . When women writers imitate men it is always a disaster. Women writers have unique talents

that men cannot approximate. It is best for them to develop their uniqueness without trying to imitate men. . . . What we want is for women writers to pursue tenaciously that which distinguishes them as women.[37]

Whereas the authors of this 1908 essay could not have possibly anticipated such an outcome, they were shortly to be met by the inauguration of *Seitō* and another group who likewise wanted to restore to women their unique essence. But the essence these women sought was that of an original female strength. What is interesting about Hiratsuka Raichō's invocation of this female tradition, cited at the opening of this introduction, is that she means to restore to it the very female strength that earlier male-inspired enunciations of Modern Murasaki had elided. The era Murasaki represented had been more than just softly scented sighs emanating behind carefully drawn curtains. It had been an era of female genius: raw, at times ragged, and full of power. Raichō enjoins women to recover their primeval strength, to unleash their original talents.

True to its aims, *Seitō* offered a venue, into the early Taishō period (1912–1926), for the literary talents of many of the women represented in this anthology, such as Yosano Akiko, Nogami Yaeko, Mizuno Senko, and Tamura Toshiko, as well as to a host of others. But it also served as an important forum for political debate. Contributors to the journal ardently agitated for more equitable political representation. They roundly criticized current family law that classified married women alongside the "deformed and mentally incompetent" and perpetuated the patriarchal notions of female debasement summarily subsumed under the slogan "revere men, despise women."[38] From 1911 until its demise in 1916, the journal carried lengthy and controversial debates on prostitution, chastity, abortion, contraception, and marriage laws, debates that would continue well into the later Shōwa (1926–1989) period. The Meiji civil code may have rendered women incompetent, but Meiji women were not willing to surrender so easily. They were articulate, intellectually curious, and proudly conscious of their need to assert control over their own destiny—both physical and intellectual. Writing, whether or not they took up the brush in a conscious effort to protest, offered these women access to the ever-shifting spheres beyond the ken of family, home, and appropriate social roles.

NOTES

1. From the inaugural issue of *Bluestocking* (September 1911). The translation is from Rebecca Copeland, "Hiratsuka Raichō," in *Japanese Women Writers: A Bio-critical Sourcebook*, ed. Chieko I. Mulhern (Westport, Conn.: Greenwood, 1994), pp. 132–143.

2. In the early to mid-Meiji, the terms *"keishū"* and *"joryū"* (woman's style) were used interchangeably to define the works of women. But *keishū* was used with more frequency when referring to women writers collectively. By the end of the Meiji period, *joryū* replaced *keishū* in this regard as well, except when critics referred retrospectively to the women writers of the earlier age. This usage suggests that *keishū* was not simply a gender designation but incorporated certain class-related qualities that were no longer present in the women writing from the late Meiji onward.

    The term *"keishū"* was derived from China, where it had denoted talented women of the "inner chamber." See Dorothy Ko, *Teachers of the Inner Chambers: Women and Culture in Seventeenth-Century China* (Stanford: Stanford University Press, 1994). In the Meiji period, *keishū* writers were assumed to be women of privilege and were expected to behave accordingly. Because in Japanese the character *"kei"* denotes "bedroom" (*neya*), recent commentators have wished to imbricate the term *"keishū"* with a sexual connotation. When used in tandem with *"shū"* (talented lady), however, the (hetero)sexual connotation of "bedroom" is replaced by the single-sex sanctum of a woman's separate sphere: the "inner chamber" of the Chinese derivation.

3. Robert Danly, *In the Shade of Spring Leaves: The Writings of Higuchi Ichiyō, a Woman of Letters in Meiji Japan* (New Haven: Yale University Press, 1981), p. 149.

4. See, for example, Shioda Ryōhei and Wada Shigejirō.

5. Sharon Sievers, *Flowers in Salt: The Beginnings of Feminist Consciousness in Modern Japan* (Stanford: Stanford University Press, 1983), p. 15.

6. For more on the Meiji Six, see *Meiroku zasshi: Journal of the Japanese Enlightenment*, trans. William Reynolds Braisted, assisted by Adachi Yasushi and Kikuchi Yūji (Cambridge: Harvard University Press, 1976).

7. For more on the importance of male-female socializing, see Sally Hastings, "A Dinner Party Is Not a Revolution: Space, Gender, and Hierarchy in Meiji Japan," *U.S.-Japan Women's Journal*, no. 18 (2000): 107–132.

8. Divorce and marriage were as complicated in Meiji Japan as in contemporary Japan, if not more so. This introduction cannot possibly cover all the complexities. For a more detailed discussion, refer to Harald Fuess, *Divorce in Japan: Family, Gender, and the State, 1600–2000* (Stanford: Stanford University Press, 2004).

9. Mori Arinori, "On Wives and Concubines, Part Three," in *Meiroku zasshi*, p. 189.

10. As Nakajima Shōen, "To My Beloved Sisters," trans. Rebecca Copeland and Aiko Okamoto MacPhail, in *An Anthology of Meiji Literature*, ed. Robert Campbell, Charles Inouye, and Sumie Jones (Honolulu: University of Hawai'i Press, forthcoming).

11. Nakamura Masanao, as translated and cited in E. Patricia Tsurumi, "The State, Education, and Two Generations of Women in Meiji Japan, 1868–1912," *U.S.-Japan Women's Journal*, no. 18 (2000): 7.

12. Ibid., p. 4.

13. Ema Saikō (1787–1863), for example, was renowned for her *kanshi* (Chinese verse). See *Breeze through Bamboo: Kanshi of Ema Saikō*, trans. Hiroyuki Sato (New York: Columbia University Press, 1998). See also Patricia Fister, "Female *Bunjin*: The Life of Poet-Painter Ema Saikō," in *Recreating Japanese Women*, 1600–1945, ed. Gail Lee Bernstein (Berkeley: University of California Press, 1991), pp. 108–130. Tadano Makuzu (1763–1825) wrote poetry in addition to political treatises. See "Solitary Thoughts. A Translation of Tadano Makuzu's *Hitori Kangae*," trans. Janet Goodwin, Bettina Gramlich-Oka, Elizabeth Leicester, Yuki Terazawa, and Anne Walthall, *Monumenta Nipponica* 56, no. 1 (Spring 2001): 21–37; 56, no. 2 (Summer 2001): 173–195. See also Atsuko Sakaki, "Sliding Door: Women in the Heterosocial Literary Field of Early Modern Japan," *U.S.-Japan's Women's Journal*, no. 17 (1999): 3–38.

14. Mikiso Hane, introduction to *Reflections on the Way to the Gallows: Rebel Women in Prewar Japan* (Berkeley: University of California Press, 1988), p. 6.

15. Jennifer Robertson, "The Shingaku Woman: Straight from the Heart," in *Recreating Japanese Women*, p. 94.

16. Similarly, women were taught that they had no home in "three realms." As daughters, they lived in their fathers' homes; as wives, in the husbands' households; and, as mothers, they were to reside with their eldest sons.

17. For more on these early educators, see Sally Hastings, "Women Educators of the Meiji Era and the Making of Modern Japan," *International Journal of Social Education* 6, no. 1 (Spring 1991): 83–94; or Margaret Mehl, "Women Educators and the Confucian Tradition in Meiji Japan (1868–1912): Miwada Masako and Atomi Kakei," *Women's History Review* 10, no. 4 (2001): 579–602.

18. Tsurumi, "The State, Education, and Two Generations of Women," p. 17.

19. Ann M. Harrington, "Women and Higher Education in the Japanese Empire (1895–1945)," *Journal of Asian History* 21, no. 2 (1987): 170.

20. Tsurumi, "The State, Education, and Two Generations of Women," p. 8.

21. Harrington, "Women and Higher Education," p. 173.

22. Tsurumi, "The State, Education, and Two Generations of Women," p. 18.

23. As quoted and translated in Mehl, "Women Educators," p. 588.

24. Tsurumi, "The State, Education, and Two Generations of Women," p. 18.

25. Cited in Hane, introduction, p. 12.

26. Cited in Copeland, "Hiratsuka Raichō," p. 133.

27. Ibid., p. 32.

28. Sievers, *Flowers in Salt*, p. 111.

29. Seki Reiko, as cited in Takada Chinami, "Joken, kōen, seihyōden," in *Josei sakka shū*, ed. Takada Chinami, Nakagawa Shigemi, and Nakagawa Kazuko, Shin Nihon koten bungaku taikei, no. 23 (Tokyo: Iwanami shoten, 2002), p. 524.

30. Iwamoto Yoshiharu, *Jogaku zasshi* 32 (August 15, 1886): 23–34.

31. The chasteness of Heian-period writers is an imaginative invention. The portrait that Murasaki Shikibu projects of herself in her diary suggests that she might have been something of a prude. But her contemporaries Izumi Shikibu and Sei Shōnagon are known to have been involved with several men, behavior that at the time would not have been inappropriate for women in their positions at court.

32. Ishibashi Shian, "*Yabu no uguisu* no saihyō wo yomu," *Kokumin no tomo*, August 1888, p. 37, quoted and translated by Marianne Harrison in "The Rise of the Woman Novelist in Japan" (Ph.D. diss., University of Chicago, 1991), p. 93.

33. Sakaki, "Sliding Door," p. 4.

34. As cited and translated in Tomi Suzuki, *Narrating the Self: Fictions of Japanese Modernity* (Stanford: Stanford University Press, 1996), p. 24.

35. Akiyama Shun, "Ima joryū bungaku to wa nani ka: Sengo shi to no kanren de," *Kokubungaku kaishaku to kyōzai no kenkyū* 15 (December 1980): 124–127, as quoted and translated in Joan Ericson, "The Origins of the Concept of Women's Literature," in *The Woman's Hand: Gender and Theory in Japanese Women's Writing*, ed. Paul Gordon Schalow and Janet A. Walker (Stanford: Stanford University Press, 1996), p. 81.

36. The resulting publication was entitled "On Women Writers" ("Joryū sakka ron") and appeared in the May 1908 issue of the journal *Shinchō*, in the "Shitsunai gūgo (Conversations in a room) column. This column, which was initiated in January 1908 and continued throughout the year, brought together the writers Oguri Fūyō (1875–1926), Yanagawa Shun'yō (1877–1918), Tokuda Shūkō (also known as Chikamatsu Shūkō, 1876–1944), Ikuta Chōkō (1882–1936), and Mayama Seika (1878–1948). All five were regular contributors to *Shinchō*, offering prose fiction, critical and personal essays, and dramas in addition to their coverage of the current literary scene. The column also featured discussions entitled "The Writer and the Family," "The Writer and Society," "The Critic and the Critique," "Desire and Art—a Search for Harmony," and so forth. Ikuta Chōkō, of particular note in this group of writers, was recognized for his prominence as a translator of Western works (Nietzsche, D'Annunzio, Marx), his status as the driving force behind a salon for women's writing, and

his founding of the feminist journal *Seitō* (Bluestocking). Additionally, Oguri Fūyō was on the editorial board of *Joshi bundan* (Women's literary world), the journal inaugurated in 1905 with the express purpose of encouraging women's writing.

37. Oguri Fūyō, Yanagawa Shun'yō, Tokuda Shūkō, Ikuta Chōkō, and Mayama Seika, "On Women Writers," trans. Rebecca Copeland, in *Woman Critiqued: Translated Essays on Japanese Women's Writing*, ed. Rebecca Copeland (Honolulu: University of Hawai'i Press, 2006).

38. See Sievers, *Flowers in Salt*, p. 111.

MEIJI WOMEN'S POETRY

Laurel Rasplica Rodd

NOT MANY JAPANESE WOMEN are included among the ranks of noted writers of the Tokugawa period (1600–1868), but those few whose names *are* remembered are mainly poets. Several of these women who began their careers during the waning years of the Tokugawa continued to be active during the early Meiji era as well, producing *waka* and *kanshi* (poetry in Chinese) and often paintings, calligraphy, and pottery.

The courtly *waka*, or *tanka* (as it came to be known during the Meiji period)—thirty-one syllables arranged in groups of five, seven, five, seven, and seven—had been the most prestigious Japanese literary form since the compilation of the first imperial poetry anthology, the *Kokinshū* (Collection of modern and ancient Japanese poems), in the early tenth century. With its emphasis on elegant lyrical expression of emotion and sensitive response to the changes in the natural world, the *tanka* was seen by Meiji-era Japanese as a genre women could be encouraged to produce, one that connected them to the aristocratic ideals of Japan's classical past.

Late Tokugawa–early Meiji *tanka* poets were almost without exception adherents of the conservative Keien school of poetry founded by Kagawa Kageki (1768–1843). This school took as its ideal the poetry of the *Kokinshū* and the aesthetic articulated by its leading compiler, Ki no Tsurayuki (ca. 868–945), and encouraged the composition of poetry on set traditional topics (*daiei*). In his introduction to the anthology, Tsura-yuki had presented *waka* as the product of a natural impulse to lyrical celebration of emotional responses to the world. The *Kokinshū* contains poems composed on private occasions—to send to a lover or friend, for example—as well as more formal poetry produced for public court events on assigned topics. The Keien school particularly encouraged the composition of poetry on such traditional topics, and Keien school poets strove to weave the elements of oft-used rhetoric and images from the past in ways just slightly different from their predecessors in order to perfect the expression of received attitudes, perceptions, and emotions.

Among the women *tanka* poets who were active in the late Tokugawa period and continued to be prominent into the early Meiji era were such diverse figures as the Buddhist nun, potter, and calligrapher Otagaki Rengetsu (1791–1875);[1] the peasant and nationalist Matsuo Taseko (1811–1894);[2] the geisha Matsunoto Misako (1833–1914); and two women, Saisho Atsuko (1826–1900) and Shimoda Utako (1854–1936), who served at court and later became teachers of poetry, opening their own conservatories.

Meiji poetry conservatories served as finishing schools that applied the veneer of classical culture by means of a course of study based on the imperial poetry anthologies and the prose classics of the Heian era such as *Ise monogatari* (The tales of Ise, early tenth century) and *Genji monogatari* (The tale of Genji, early eleventh century). In the chaotic social climate of the early Meiji period, as many samurai and aristocratic families lost their livelihoods and farmers and merchants scrambled to improve their status and income, those who could afford to educate their daughters often chose to provide them with training in the prestigious traditional arts. As in Victorian England, women were assigned the role within the family of educating and humanizing. Women trained at these academies learned to produce classical prose, especially flowery travel diaries and essays, as well as classical poetry. *Tanka* in Meiji had come to represent the feminine tradition, and training in its composition was considered important for women.

The most famous of the Meiji poetry conservatories was the Hagi-noya, founded by the best-known of the women *tanka* poets of early Meiji, Nakajima Utako (1841–1903). Several important women writers, including Higuchi Ichiyō (1872–1896) and Miyake Kaho (1868–1943), studied poetry and were given an impressive grounding in the classics at Nakajima's Haginoya.

FIGURE 1.1 Haginoya Poetry Conservatory, February 21, 1887;
Nakajima Utako (1841–1903), center; Higuchi Ichiyō (1872–1896),
back row, third from left; Miyake Kaho (1868–1943), second row, fourth from left

A few Meiji women poets, such as Nakajima Shōen (also known as Kishida Toshiko, 1863–1901; see her speech, also included in this anthology) were known for their Chinese prose and poetry (*kanbun* and *kanshi*). Almost none is known for her *haiku*. One reason for this is the supposed disjunction between so-called feminine sensibilities and the *haikai* aesthetic of detachment and objective description.[3] In addition, *haiku* composition had grown out of the practice of *renku*, linked verse composed as a group activity, and such groups had traditionally been less welcoming to women. *Haiku* was popular during the Meiji period, but no poets of real distinction—male or female—appeared until Masaoka Shiki (1867–1902) encouraged the reform of both *tanka* and *haiku* in the 1890s. (He also gave the name *haiku* to the genre previously known by such names as *haikai* or *renku*.) Shiki's disciple Takahama Kyoshi (1874–1959), who continued to preach Shiki's ideal of *shasei*, or "sketching from life," formed a group of women poets to compose and exchange *haiku* in 1912 (just after the Meiji period came to a close, and therefore outside the bounds of this study). He also published the writings of women *haiku* poets in a new column he initiated in the magazine *Hototogisu* (The cuckoo). This group included Hasegawa Kanajo (1887–

FIGURE 1.2 Yosano Akiko (1868–1942), seated,
and Yamakawa Tomiko (1879–1909),
November 5, 1900

1969), Abe Midorijo (1886–1980), Takeshita Shizunojo (1887–1951), and
Sugita Hisajo (1890–1946).[4]

The Meiji craze for translations from Western literature (Longfel-
low, Blake, and Shakespeare were especially well represented) led to the
increasing popularity of *shintaishi* (new-style poetry): longer poems,
sometimes in free verse but often with alternating lines of five and seven
syllables, written on the model of these translations. *Shintaishi* poets
often used contemporary language, as opposed to the classical diction
of *tanka* or the elaborate and antiquated Chinese of *kanshi*. New-style
poetry thus allowed more direct, unaffected expression of aspects of
human experience and subjects foreign to the traditional poetic forms,
including current events, politics, philosophical and religious musings,
and lyrical outpourings of individual emotions about topics beyond the
set themes of the traditional *tanka*.

The 1890s saw the rise of new schools of *tanka*, too. Among the most
famous was the Shinshisha (New poetry society), founded in 1899 by
Yosano Tekkan (1873–1935), which nurtured the talents of a group of
impressive female romantic poets, including one of the greatest poets

of twentieth-century Japan, Yosano Akiko (1878–1942), and published their work in the journal *Myōjō* (Morning star). Two other women members of the Shinshisha, Yamakawa Tomiko (1879–1909) and Chino (Masuda) Masako (1880–1946), are often associated with Akiko as the "three talented women" (*san saien*) of *Myōjō*.[5] The three jointly published an anthology of *tanka* entitled *Koigoromo* (Robe of love) in 1905.

Many other women poets were inspired and mentored by Yosano Akiko and first published their romantic poems in *Myōjō*. These include Okamoto Kanoko (1899–1939), Ishigami Tsuyuko (1882–1956), and Yazawa Kōku (1877–1956).

Still other women, such as Ōtsuka Kusuoko (1875–1910) and Takeyama Hideko (1881–1915), discussed below, were inspired and encouraged by male poets and scholars, often their relatives, to reach beyond the traditional poetic approaches and topics.

The poets translated here are just a small sample of the women poets of the Meiji era. It is no exaggeration to say that virtually every woman writer of the era wrote poetry to some extent. Almost all received some training in the classics and in poetic composition. They were encouraged to study and compose poetry as part of their education, and many continued to compose throughout their lives, even those who later became known chiefly for their prose writings. The role of poetic composition in encouraging Meiji-era women to see themselves as writers and to find their own voices was truly fundamental.

SELECTED POEMS
BY MEIJI WOMEN

Translated by Laurel Rasplica Rodd

Matsunoto (Ogawa) Misako

Married at thirteen, Matsunoto Misako (1833–1914) was widowed at the age of seventeen and became a geisha in Fukagawa, a district of Tokyo east of the Sumida River in which the traditional entertainment quarters were located, after her natal family, the Ogawas, became impoverished during the Meiji Restoration. She later opened a poetry academy in Nihonbashi, the original business and commercial center of Tokyo, and in 1891 became an editor of the monthly poetry journal *Shikishima*. As with most Keien school *tanka* written on set topics and modeled on the *Kokinshū*, her verses tend to display intellectual cleverness and depend heavily on rhetoric for effect.

Love in a Dream (Yume no naka no koi)

In waking life
he's cold to me.
How strange that
only in my dreams
do I see his Truth.[6]

Hidden Love (Shinobu koi)

Unknown to others
we bound it—and ourselves.
There is now no way
to untie the maternity sash,
to dispel misunderstandings.[7]

Saisho Atsuko

Considered one of the best *tanka* poets of her day, Saisho Atsuko (1826–
1900) served at court as poetry tutor to the empress for many years and
then later became a teacher, opening her own conservatory. Her style so
conformed to the old-fashioned Keien rules that her work was termed a
primer for women's poetry. As is typical of the Keien style, most of her
very lyrical *tanka* are composed on set topics, although her originality is
sometimes revealed in slight modifications to them.

Welcoming the Mountain at the New Year
(Shinnen bōzan)

The clouds break—
and once again it's visible:
Fuji's soaring peak
blanketed with lovely snow
brightening the new year.[8]

Morning Mist (Asagiri)

As morning mists
begin to drift across
the broad heavens,
there too we can see
the colors of spring.[9]

Shimoda Utako

Shimoda Utako (1854–1936) served as poetry tutor at court for eight years and then opened her own conservatory, where she taught the conservative Keien style *tanka* she practiced. She came from a family of Chinese scholars and composed in a wide range of genres, including *haiku*, *tanka*, *kanshi*, other ancient poetic forms (such as *chōka*, long poems, and *imayō*, popular ballads), as well as the classical essay forms, *zuihitsu* (miscellany) and *kikōbun* (travel essay). She married in 1879, but her husband died five years later, at which point she turned her energies to education and social action, traveling to Europe and the United States between 1893 and 1895 to study Western educational practices.

> my pillow buried
> beneath a blizzard
> of blossoms
> moon of a night in spring
> cold fitful sleep[10]

> Geese While Traveling
> (Ryochū no kari)

> sleeping on a journey
> in the dead of night the sad calls
> of the wild geese
> echo and I yearn deeply
> for the town where I was born[11]

Nakajima Utako

Nakajima Utako (1841–1903) is perhaps best known as the proprietor of the Haginoya conservatory where several famous women writers of the Meiji period, such as Higuchi Ichiyō and Miyake Kaho, received their training. Like most of her contemporaries, she belonged to the conservative tradition of the Keien school of court poetry. The most famous

collection of her poetry, *Hagi no shizuku* (Dew on the bush clover), was
edited by her disciples after her death in 1908.

Clouds (Kumo)

gushing from the earth
they seem to billow toward me
in the blowing wind
they rise skyward
white clouds from the valley[12]

Old Age (Oi)

forgetful now
of every single thing
this aged body
yearns all the more for
that time so long ago[13]

Higuchi Ichiyō

Higuchi Ichiyō (1872–1896) was introduced to literature through the
study and composition of *tanka* at the Haginoya; she wrote nearly four
thousand poems in addition to essays, a lengthy diary, and the twenty-
one short stories for which she is best known. The Haginoya nourished
her classical knowledge and literary talents. After her father died and
she had to contribute to the family's income, she considered running a
poetry school, a more likely literary occupation for a Meiji woman than
prose fiction, but her hopes of inheriting the Haginoya came to naught,
and her early poetry, though appealing, was not of high enough quality
for her to make a name and a living as a poet. After she met and fell in
love with the writer Nakarai Tōsui (1860–1926), however, she produced
a number of striking love poems. For more on Ichiyō, her relationship
to Tōsui, and her journal writing, please refer to the chapter devoted to
her in this volume.

Loving Heart (Koigokoro)

if any should ask
after this heart that's lost its way
　on the path of love
just tell them it travels
the jet-black road of darkness[14]

mountain cherries
this year exquisitely fragrant
　and in their shade
as they fall, never to return,
I dream only of you[15]

the waves before the wind
rise and fall and yet
　what am I to do
in this drifting world
with a boat of a single leaf[16]

Wanting to Forget Love (Bōren o yokusu)

if only there were
no such thing as dreams
　in the jet-black night—
then I might forget that
one who's so cold to me[17]

One of a Group of Love Poems
(Koi no uta no naka ni)

It is that I am
so much in love? Is that why—
　whether spring mists
rise or linger on—I see
only your image?[18]

Love that Brings a Reputation (Nadatsu koi)

happiness
overflowed my enfolding
    sleeves and leaked out
carrying rumors about me that seem
to have risen to the skies[19]

Nakajima Shōen

Nakajima Shōen (1863–1901)—her birth name was Kishida Shun; she was also known as Kishida Toshiko—was invited to court in recognition of her knowledge of Chinese prose and poetry and at the age of seventeen became tutor to the empress. Even after she left the court and became notorious as the first female activist of the Popular Rights Movement, she continued to write *kanshi*, or poems in Chinese, as well as prose fiction and essays, publishing often in such journals as *Jogaku zasshi* (Woman's education journal) and *Bungei kurabu* (Literary arts club). Shōen's *kanshi* tend to be quite conservative in style and little distinguishes them from those produced in centuries past. Her "Reading the Writings of Wakamatsu Shizuko on the First Anniversary of Her Death" is modeled on traditional elegiac *kanshi* but celebrates the life and mourns the loss of Wakamatsu (1864–1896), the most prominent female translator of the Meiji era. For more on Nakajima's activities as a spokesperson for women's rights, please refer to the following chapter.

Reading the Writings of Wakamatsu Shizuko
on the First Anniversary of Her Death

What shall I do now that my mistress has disappeared?
Heartbroken, the spring wind of the second month crosses
    the heavens.
Who knows, at the base of the white flowering plum,
How many times, hiding tears, I read the writings she left behind?
Blossoms fragrant, birds singing, the sun begins to warm,
But my breast is filled with mourning for someone.

There is no spring within my gates, none on the road outside.
I'll not wear brocade sleeves and go off to visit famous gardens.[20]

Yosano Akiko

Midaregami (Tangled Hair), the first *tanka* anthology of Yosano Akiko (1878–1942), née Hō Shō, appeared in 1901, the same year Akiko married Yosano Tekkan (1873–1935), leader of the Shinshisha. Her poetry created an immediate sensation with its sensuality, intensity of expression, romantic ecstasy, and challenging and obscure language that combined classical diction with vocabulary and topics introduced by the romantic *shintaishi* poets and Christian missionaries. Several of Akiko's new-style poems, or *shintaishi*, including "Kimi shinitamō koto nakare" ("My Brother, You Must Not Die"), addressed to her younger brother at the time of the Russo-Japanese War, and "Yama no ugoku hi kitaru" ("The Day the Mountains Move Has Come"), published in the first issue of *Seitō* (Bluestocking), have become modern classics. Akiko attracted many poetic disciples and often lectured on the Japanese classics in addition to writing and editing both prose and poetry to support the eleven Yosano children. Known also for her essays on women's education, marriage and child rearing, social reform, and equal rights for women, she joined with other artists and liberal thinkers in founding a girls' school in 1922 and taught there until the school was closed during World War II. During her career, Akiko published twenty-four volumes of *tanka* and *shintaishi*, fifteen volumes of essays, numerous children's stories, a novel, plays, and groundbreaking translations into modern Japanese of the writings of Heian women authors.

> beneath the curtain
> of the night they whispered their fill:
> stars now descended
> to the world of men below—
> mortals with disheveled hair[21]

> in hot spring waters
> of the mountains my rounded

shoulders are reflected
drifting circles of white like
the moon of this dark night[22]

after the bath
rising from warm spring waters
    how cruel it is
to sully this soft skin with
the garments of this world[23]

her bloodtide all
aflame with her emotions—
    this young woman—
is it to go mad and die
that your poems would command?[24]

hands pressing my breasts
silently I kicked aside that
    curtain of mystery
deep crimson is the flower
that blooms within[25]

yesterday now seems
a world a thousand years
    or more ago,
but your hands on my shoulders—
ah, those I can still feel[26]

the peony she wore
in her hair turned to flame—
    the very surface
of the sea burned, so wild the thoughts,
the dreams, of the child of man.[27]

My Brother, You Must Not Die
(Kimi shinitamō koto nakare)

My young brother, I weep for you.
My brother, you must not die.
You, the last born,
Apple of our parents' eyes.
Did they teach you to hold a sword,
Teach you to kill?
Did they nurture you for twenty-four years
And send you to kill and die?
You are to carry on the name
Of a proud old house,
Merchants of Sakai.
My brother, you must not die.
Whether the fortress at Port Arthur falls
Or not—what does it matter?
Should it concern you? War is not
The tradition of a merchant house.

My brother, you must not die.
Let the Emperor himself go
Off to war.
"Die like beasts,
Leaving pools of human blood.
In death is your glory."
If that majestic heart is truly wise,
He cannot have such thoughts.

Ah, my young brother,
You must not die in battle.
Since this past autumn, your aged mother,
Widowed,
Has been pathetic in her grief.
Now she's sent her son away and keeps the house
    alone.
Even in this "secure and joyful" reign
Her white hairs increase.

Weeping in the shadow of the shop curtain,
Your young bride
Of but ten months—
Have you forgotten her? Do you not yearn for her?
Imagine her misery
If you to whom she would turn in sorrow
Were gone.
Oh no, my brother, you must not die.[28]

The Day the Mountains Move Has Come
(Yama no ugoku hi kitaru)

The day the mountains move has come.
I speak, but no one believes me.
For a time the mountains have been asleep,
but long ago they all danced with fire.
It doesn't matter if you believe this,
My friends, as long as you believe:
All the sleeping women
Are now awake and moving.[29]

Delivery Room Dawn (Sanshitsu no yoake)

Dawn outside the glass
Like a pale cocoon . . .
Something crawls on the delivery room walls
Silently pulling a beacon of branching coral
In a faint straight line.
Seeing it, I rejoice—
The butterfly of the feeble
Early winter day emerges.
Here a woman—
A woman who eight times evaded death—
A pale woman and
My daughter Ellen—tight-budded bush camellia,
    born of

My fifth birthing——and
A single jar of roses and
The light peach-colored day's butterfly
Bashful as first love—
All in the quiet, bracing dawn.

Dear, precious day! Now
Like one wounded in battle
I lie devitalized and drained.
But like the sunworshippers
I extend my hands to yours,
Oh sun, oh queen of dawn.
Oh sun, you too are afflicted by night and by
    winter.
In a million years how many times
Have you endured death's pangs to find reborn
That all-powerful heavenly flame?
In your trace will I follow
Though only eight times resurrected,
Though merely eight times, with screams, and
    with blood,
Have I crossed the valley of death.[30]

Yamakawa Tomiko

Yamakawa Tomiko (1879–1909) was one of the women members of the
New Poetry Society. Her *tanka* were collected together with those of
Yosano Akiko and Chino Masako in an anthology entitled *Koigoromo*
(Robe of love) in 1905. A rival of Akiko's for the attentions of Yosano
Tekkan, Yamakawa was betrothed by her family over her objections to
an older man who died two years later of tuberculosis. The disease killed
Tomiko herself a few years after that.

A bird cage
hanging on the lower branch,

I spend the long day
counting the number of the peach
blossoms before my eyes.[31]

Leaning on the rail—
do you still gaze in my direction
　　as the ship
on which I set sail
moves into the distance?[32]

Setting my brush
aside, burning my crumpled poems—
　　if only I—
I alone—could drift away
along with that rising smoke.[33]

Did you know, my love,
that the evening breeze which wafts
　　over the dew on
the lilies speaks to the blossoms
in the voice of the gods?[34]

From "Poems Written Thinking of My Father and Mother"
　　(Fubo o omou uta no naka ni)

If your sleeves,
so dear to me, should happen
　　to brush against blossoms
of the bush clover, try to keep
in mind this tumbling dewdrop.[35]

washing my brush
cleaning my ink stone
　　I write a letter
to someone to say the child
of the stars has come down to earth[36]

Chino (Masuda) Masako

One of the "three talented women" (*san saien*) of the New Poetry Society, Masuda Masako (1880–1946) began publishing her *tanka* in *Myōjō*
in 1900. Her *tanka*, which were much admired for their graceful expression and romantic sensibility, were collected with those of Yosano Akiko
and Yamakawa Tomiko in *Koigoromo* (Robe of love) in 1905. She married Chino Shōshō (1883–1946), a *Myōjō* poet and professor of German,
in 1907, the same year she graduated from Japan Women's College.
She continued to publish *tanka*, *shintaishi*, and short stories in various
literary magazines after her marriage, later joining the faculty of Tokyo Women's College. She was also active in the Bluestocking Society
founded by Hiratsuka Raichō (1886–1971) and published in its journal
Seitō (Bluestocking) beginning in 1911.

The Maiden (Otome)

Tractable and tame
is my black hair now;
Caressing it,
how I yearn for the return of
my young life, now gone.[37]

Beloved (Omowarebito)

Well then, just think of me,
my dear, as that person
who wept so
as the morning wind
blew cold in her disheveled hair.[38]

Teasing words—
meaningless words—oddly
wounded me.
This day has become
such a day![39]

Ishigami Tsuyuko

Ishigami Tsuyuko (1882–1956) began publishing fiction and poetry in *Fujin sekai* (Woman's world) in 1901. In 1903 she joined the New Poetry Society headed by Yosano Tekkan and began regularly publishing *tanka*, *shintaishi*, and fiction in *Myōjō*. She remained a loyal member of the Yosanos' literary circle throughout their lives.

Koita Bridge (Koitabashi)

As I crossed Koita Bridge
At first light, a rose, a single stem,
Swept by on the current.
That night I stepped out to wait for you,
Its fragrance pierced me, indescribably.

Now, I thought in pain,
I'll give up your name and my dreams, too;
Passing this night in sorrow—
Ah, rose—unable to hold back the future,
I hesitate alone on Koita Bridge.

To a Friend (Tomo ni)

Talking on the beach
the two of us together, today's
celebratory poems and
crashing waves striking
the drums of spring.[40]

Okamoto Kanoko

Okamoto Kanoko (1899–1939) began to study poetry with Yosano Akiko when she was seventeen, publishing *tanka* in *Myōjō* as well as in its successor journal, *Subaru* (The Pleiades), published by the New Poetry Society after *Myōjō* folded, and also in *Seitō*. Her first *tanka* anthology, *Karoki netami* (Little jealousies), was published by *Seitō* in 1911, the first year of the Taishō era. She published several more collections of poetry before turning her energies to the novels and plays for which she is best remembered.

Cherry Blossoms (Sakura)

Cherry blossoms—
when they bloom
    they give their all.
That's why I've risked my life
to gaze upon them.[41]

In the sunshine
by the house on top of the hill
where the cherries bloom,
a mother pig and baby pig
oink affectionately to each other.[42]

Yazawa Kōko

Yazawa Kōko (1877–1956) left school in 1891 at the age of fourteen and went to work as a telephone operator while continuing to study Chinese and English in night school. She later opened an English school in her home. She began to publish *tanka* in *Myōjō* in 1907 and was influenced by the romantic approach of the members of that literary circle. Her first volume of poetry, called *Kaete* (Cockscomb), appeared in 1910 but was banned for the overt expression of female sensuality in the love poems.

suddenly
far in the distance
an image floats up

and the person speaking beside me
is forgotten[43]

   not shunning
those who were unfeeling
    as stone,
not fleeing from those like fire,
that's the path I have traveled[44]

   like water flowing—
so naturally, unthinkingly, did I
    become a wife
become a mother
and now my regrets overflow[45]

   like the breeze
blowing across the cut reeds
    the voice
of one I love wafts
through my black hair[46]

Ōtsuka Kusuoko

Ōtsuka Kusuoko (1875–1910) began studying Keien school *tanka* and classical prose at the Tagizono academy of poet and scholar Sasaki Nobutsuna (1872–1963). Influenced by Mori Ōgai (1862–1922) and his translations from German writers such as Goethe and Heine, she also wrote romantic *shintaishi* and short stories. Her best-known *shintaishi*, "Ohyakudo mōde" (One hundred steps, one hundred prayers), which depicts a young wife pacing back and forth before a shrine to offer repeated prayers, was first published in the January 1905 issue of *Taiyō* (The sun) during the Russo-Japanese War. It is often paired with Japan's most famous antiwar poem, Yosano Akiko's "My Brother, You Must Not Die," which had been published just a few months earlier.

One Hundred Steps,
One Hundred Prayers
(Ohyakudo mōde)

With my first step, my prayers are for my husband,
with my second step, for my country,
with my third step, again for my husband.
Can a womanly heart be faulted?

Only a single country in the world
shines so beneath the morning sun.
Only a single man in this world
has plighted his troth to me.

So, if asked which carries more weight,
my country or my husband,
I can only weep, without an answer.
Can my hundred steps, my hundred prayers be faulted?[47]

Takeyama Hideko

Takeyama Hideko (1881–1915) was the younger sister of noted *tanka*
poet and critic Kaneko Kun'en (1876–1951), whose urbane and sophisticated style influenced her work. Beginning in 1902, many of her poems
were published in collections Kun'en edited. The elegant, lyrical style
on display in some of her *tanka*, such as those translated here, contrasts
with the strikingly florid romantic style she uses in others.

with prayer strips
in our hands he and I
    saw the wild geese off—
evening in autumn
at the Kamo Shrine[48]

when I turn to look back
the smoke from the incense

is faintly visible
and the offering flowers
sway lightly in the wind[49]

enveloped
in a color colder
than the water
the moon quietly
turns to autumn[50]

NOTES

1. For more information on Rengetsu, see John Stevens, *Lotus Moon: The Poetry of the Buddhist Nun Rengetsu* (New York: Weatherhill, 1994).
2. See Anne Walthall, *The Weak Body of a Useless Woman: Matsuo Taseko and the Meiji Restoration* (Chicago: University of Chicago Press, 1998).
3. The term *haikai* was originally used for nonstandard or comic *renga* (linked verse) sequences. The brief poems known today as *haiku* developed from the opening links of *haikai* sequences, also known as *renku*.
4. For further information about these poets and translations of their writings and those of other women *haiku* poets, see Makoto Ueda, *Far Beyond the Field: Haiku by Japanese Women* (New York: Columbia University Press, 2003). The suffix *-jo*, meaning "woman," is commonly appended to the pen names of female *haiku* poets.
5. Nishio Yoshihito, *Akiko, Tomiko: Meiji no atarashii onna—ai to bungaku* (Tokyo Yūhikaku shuppan sābisu, 1986), p. 180.
6. Utsutsu ni wa / tsurenaki mono o / yume ni nomi / hito no makoto o / miru zo ayashiki.
7. Hito shirezu / musubisometaru / iwataobi / iihodoku beki / yoshi dani mo nashi. Poems selected from Shioda Ryōhei, ed., *Meiji joryū bungaku shū*, vol. 1 (MJB1), vol. 81 of *Meiji bungaku zenshū* (Tokyo: Chikuma shobō, 1966), p. 7. According to p. 416 of this volume, both *tanka* translated here appeared in *Matsunoto Misako kashū*, a selection of Matsunoto's *tanka* published by her disciples in 1920.
8. Kumo harete / arata ni miyuru / fuji no ne no / miyuki ya toshi no / hikari naru.
9. Asagasumi / tanabikisomete / hisakata no / sora ni mo miyuru / haru no iro kana. Both poems from MJB1, p. 3. According to ibid., p. 415, they were collected in an anthology of Saisho's work, *Mikaki no shitagusa*, in 1888.

10. Tamakura wa / hana no fubuki ni / uzumorete / utatane samushi / haru no yo no tsuki.

11. Tabine suru / yowa ni sabishiki / kari no koe / waga furusato zo / koishikarikeru. Both poems from MJB 1, p. 22. According to ibid., pp. 417–418, they were collected in an anthology entitled *Kōsetsu sōsho* first published by Jissen Jogakkō in 1932.

12. Wakiizuru / kokochi koso sure / fuku kaze ni / tachinoborikuru / tani no shirakumo.

13. Nanigoto mo / mono wasure suru / oi no mi wa / mukashi nomi koso / koishikarikere. Both poems from MJB 1, pp. 12–13. According to ibid., p. 417, they were published in an anthology entitled *Hagi no shizuku* in 1908.

14. Fumimayou / koi no kokoro o / hito towaba / tada ubatama no / yamiji narikeri. From *Higuchi Ichiyō kashū shō*, ed. Yanesen Kōbō (Tokyo: Yanesen Kōbō, 2001), p. 7. The poem was originally composed in 1888 as one of "One Hundred Poems on Love."

15. Yamazakura / kotoshi o niou / hana kage ni / chirite kaeranu / kimi o koso omoe. From ibid., p. 13. This poem appears in Higuchi Ichiyō's diary entry for April 11, 1891.

16. Nami kaze no / ari mo arazu mo / nani ka sen / ichiyō no fune no / ukiyo narikeri. From ibid., p. 21. The poem was composed in 1892. Ichiyō's pen name means "single leaf," a reference to the miraculous vessel on which Bodhidharma, the Zen patriarch, is said to have crossed the Yangtze River before seating himself in meditation for nine years in the monastery of Shao-lin-ssu. See Robert Danly, *In the Shade of Spring Leaves: The Life and Writings of Higuchi Ichiyō, A Woman of Letters in Meiji Japan* (New Haven: Yale University Press, 1981), pp. 51–52, for an extensive discussion of Ichiyō's choice of this pen name.

17. Nubatama no / yume to iu mono no / naku mogana / tsurenaki hito no / wasurarenu beku. From ibid., p. 31. The poem was composed in 1892 as one of "Twenty Poems on the Topic 'Love.' "

18. Kaku bakari / koishiki mono ka / harugasumi / tachite mo ite mo / omokage ni miyu. From ibid., p. 35. The poem was composed in 1895.

19. Ureshisa o / tsutsumi amarishi / tamoto yori / morete ukina ya / sora ni tachiken. From ibid., p. 36. The poem was composed in 1895.

20. Higuchi Ichiyō and Itō Sei, *Higuchi Ichiyō shū: Fu Meiji joryū bungaku* (Tokyo: Kōdansha, 1962), p. 258. Wakamatsu died in 1896.

21. Yoru no chō ni / sasameki tsukishi / hoshi no ima o / gekai no hito no / bin no hotsure yo. This is the opening poem in *Midaregami* (Tangled hair, 1901). From Yosano Akiko, *Teihon Yosano Akiko zenshū* (TYAZ) (Tokyo: Kōdansha, 1980), 1:3.

22. Yama no yu ni / waga marogata no / utsureru wo / shiroki tsukiyo to / omoikeru kana. From TYAZ, 2:224.

23. Yuami shite / izumi oideshi / yawahada ni / fururu wa tsuraki / hito no yo no kinu. From TYAZ, 1:14.

24. Chishio mina / nasake ni moyuru / wakaki ko ni / kurui shine yo to / tamau miuta ka. From TYAZ, 1:308.

25. Chibusa osae / shimpi no tobari / soto kerinu / koko naru hana no / kurenai zo koki. From TYAZ, 1:12.

26. Kinō oba / sentose no mae no / yo tomo omoi / mite nao kata ni / ari tomo omou. From TYAZ, 1:54. Translation originally published in *The Distant Isle: Studies and Translations of Japanese Literature in Honor of Robert H. Brower*, ed. Thomas Hare, Robert Borgen, and Sharalyn Orbaugh (Ann Arbor: Center for Japanese Studies, University of Michigan, 1996), p. 409.

27. Kazashitaru / botan hi to nari / umi moenu / omoimidaruru / hito no ko no yume. From TYAZ, 1:152.

28. From TYAZ, 9:159–162. The poem was first published in *Myōjō* in September 1904. Translation originally published in Marian Arkin and Barbara Schollar, eds., *Longman Anthology of World Literature by Women*, 1875–1975 (New York: Longman, 1989), p. 189.

29. From TYAZ, 9: 288–89. The poem was first published in *Seitō* in September 1911. Translation originally published in Gail Lee Bernstein, ed., *Recreating Japanese Women*, 1600–1945 (Berkeley: University of California Press, 1991), p. 180.

30. From TYAZ, 9: 93–95. The poem was first published in the *Yomiuri shinbun* on December 13, 1914. Translation originally published in *New Leaves: Studies and Translations of Japanese Literature in Honor of Edward Seidensticker*, ed. Aileen Gatten and Anthony Hood Chambers (Ann Arbor: Center for Japanese Studies, University of Michigan, 1993), p. 170.

31. Tori kago o / shizue ni kakete / nagaki hi o / momo no hana kazu / kazoete zo miru.

32. Obashima ni / nao mo konata o / mitamō ka / ware ga noru fune wa / tōzakariyuku.

33. Fude orite / uta hogo yakite / tachinoboru / kemuri ni norite / hitori inabaya.

34. Shiru ya kimi / yuri no tsuyu fuku / yūkaze wa / kami no mikoe o / hana ni tsutaenu.

35. Hagi no hana / kimi ga tamoto ni / fure mo seba / koboruru tsuyu ni / kokoro kakemase.

36. Fude arai / suzuri kiyomete / hoshi no ko no / kudarikimasu to / hito e kaku fumi. These six poems are from *Yosano Tekkan, Yosano Akiko shū, tsuki Myōjō ha bungaku shū*, in *Meiji bungaku zenshū* (Tokyo: Chikuma shobō, 1968), 51:318–319.

37. Sunao naru / waga kurokami o / nazuru ni mo / wakaki inochi no / oshimaruru kana.

38. Saraba tada / hotsurege samuku / asa kaze ni / yoku naku hito to / oboshii-tamae.

39. Tawamure no / karuki kotoba no / fushigi ni mo / ware o sainamu / hi to narishi kana. All three poems are from *Yosano Tekkan*, 51:344.

40. Isogatari / futari ni kyō no / iwai uta to / nami ga uchiutsu / haru no kozu-tsumi. Both poems from ibid., p. 345.

41. Sakurabana / inochi ippai ni / saku kara ni / inochi o kakete / waga naga-metari.

42. Oka no ue no / sakura saku ie no / hiatari ni / nakimutsumi oru / oyabuta kobuta. Both poems from Okamoto Kanoko, *Ai yo, ai* (Tokyo: Metalogue, 1999), pp. 166–167.

43. Futo tōki / omokage ukabe / katawara ni / mono iu hito o / wasurekeru kana.

44. Ishi ni niru / hito o utominu / hi no gotoki / hito o osorenu / waga koshi-kata wa.

45. Mizu nagaruru / gotoku shizen ni / tsuma to nari / haha to naru ni wa / am-ari ni oshiki.

46. Karikaya ni / kaze fuku gotoku / mono omou / waga kurokami ni / hito no koe suru. All four poems from *Meiji kajin shū*, in *Meiji bungaku ẓenshū* (Tokyo: Chikuma shobō, 1968), 64:216–217.

47. From Higuchi Ichiyō and Itō Sei, *Higuchi Ichiyō shū: Fu Meiji joryū bungaku*, in *Nihon gendai bungaku ẓenshū* (Tokyo: Kōdansha, 1962), 10:258. Revision of a translation by Tomoko Aoyama. See Tomoko Aoyama, "Japanese Literary Responses to the Russo-Japanese War," in *The Russo-Japanese War in Cultural Perspective*, 1904–05, ed. David Wells and Sandra Wilson (London: Macmillan; New York: St. Martin's Press, 1999), pp. 60–85. Kusuoko's poem appears on p.71.

48. Nusa o te ni / kari o miokuru / hito watashi / kamo no yashiro no / aki no yuugure.

49. Mikaereba / ka no kemuri no / honoka nite / tamuke no hana ni / kaze soyogu nari.

50. Mizu yori mo / tsumetaki iro o / matoitsutsu / tsuki wa shizuka ni / aki to narikeri. All three poems from Higuchi and Itō, *Higuchi Ichiyō shū*, 10:305.

KISHIDA TOSHIKO
(1863–1901)

Rebecca Copeland and Aiko Okamoto MacPhail

ON OCTOBER 12, 1883, Kishida Toshiko (1863–1901) took to the stage at a local theater in Ōtsu to deliver the speech, "Hakoiri musume" (here translated as "Daughters in Boxes").[1] She cut a striking figure. Her hair arranged high atop her head in an elegant Shimada coiffure, her red crepe kimono set off by a black silk obi, "she was enchanting, just like the princess in a play."[2] Although her lecture began as an "academic address," her voice reached such a passionate pitch, according to her early biographer, Sōma Kokkō, that she was arrested on the spot and jailed for eight days.[3] Her crime: political speech.

The speech had been duly recorded by a policeman armed with ink, paper, and a quick hand—perhaps even proficiency in the new skill of shorthand (*sokkibon*).[4] The policeman was not just a casual member of the audience. Most likely he had been instructed to attend Kishida's lecture in the hope of catching her in a legal infraction. Kishida Toshiko had become something of a media sensation and thereby a potential threat to authorities. Young—she was just nineteen when she made her first speech—educated, articulate, respectable, and above all very handsome, Kishida spoke to capacity crowds wherever her speeches were announced. Her lectures, delivered with passion and poise, never failed to arouse her audiences. In fact, less than two weeks earlier, when she had spoken at a theater in Kyoto with three other women orators, an

FIGURE 2.1 Kishida Toshiko (1863–1901)

estimated two thousand people attended.[5] More than a few future female orators and political agitators cite Kishida as the stimulus that inspired their own activism.[6] Historian Sharon Sievers, whose work on Kishida is among the first in English, notes that, because Kishida's popularity and her association with the Jiyū minken undō (Freedom and popular rights movement) had earned her the suspicion of authorities, she had been tailed by the police ever since she began appearing on the lecture circuits in 1882.[7] That year, during a speech in Tokushima on the island of Shikoku, on June 24, the crowd had become so agitated that policemen had intervened. Kishida was hauled before the local authorities and warned. Her scheduled appearance the following evening was canceled. Between this lecture and her appearances in October the following year, she had spoken publicly only sparingly.

Whenever Kishida did manage to speak, she raised the issue of women's rights. Interestingly, however, it was not her advocacy of greater freedom for women that invited the ire of the authorities when she made her speech "Daughters in Boxes"; rather, it was their interpretation of her metaphorical language that led to her arrest. As the court records reveal, Kishida was assumed to have been advocating not a feminist assertion of selfhood but a popular revolution with her discussion of restrictive boxes and runaway daughters. Because of this interpretation, she was accused of violating the Public Assembly Act, enacted in 1880, which forbade anyone from making a "political speech" without a permit. Kishida had not applied for a permit.

Because she was the first woman brought to trial for the offense of "political speech," the proceedings on November 12 in Ōtsu were carefully watched and recorded. In two successive articles, on November 20 and 21, the *Jiyū shinbun* (Liberty times) published the speech that Kishida was alleged to have given, drawing from the account the policeman had read into record at the trial. Despite Kishida's objections to certain statements, the police record is the only transcription we have of her speech, and it is from the newspaper account that this translation of "Daughters in Boxes" has been made. Within days of the trial, however, the *Nihon rikken seitō shinbun* (Japanese constitutional party journal) provided the following details of the proceedings, in a series of articles spanning November 15–22, 1883, raising speculation as to the accuracy of the police record:

After listening [to the policeman's account of Miss Kishida's speech], the judge turned to the defendant and asked if she had in fact delivered the speech as it had been read aloud in court. The defendant confirmed that it was accurate in general, but objected to a number of misstatements. . . . She denied, for example, saying anything about: "the meshes of the law."

When the judge asked: "Then is it safe to say that the transcript of the speech, as read, is more or less identical to what you said?" the defendant responded, "yes." The prosecutor, however, noted that even though the defendant raised objections to some discrepancies between the transcript and her actual speech, the transcript had been recorded by a policeman who was in attendance when the speech was delivered and was himself under the supervision of other officials, and thus the transcript was a faithful copy of the original speech and could not be refuted otherwise. The prosecutor then proceeded with his argument.[8]

In his charges against her, the prosecutor contended that, when Kishida spoke of "daughters" and "flowers," she was actually referring to the Japanese citizenry. And her argument that the daughters/flowers were bound and boxed was meant to suggest that the government unfairly oppressed the people. He continued: "Then again, there is the line which reads 'God the Creator has endowed them with liberty' and another about being 'caught in the meshes of the law imposed upon them by the wattled fence.' Here we can infer that the defendant is drawing a comparison between 'the boxes' and the laws that govern newspapers, publications, gatherings, and so on. What the defendant in fact means is that these ordinances are restrictive and deprive people of freedom, and thus she is criticizing our current political structure." Moreover, the prosecutor complained, because the defendant described the way maids and menservants are employed to chase down runaway daughters and bring them back, she clearly intended to disparage policemen by comparing them to those in servile professions. "Let the record show that the defendant is guilty of two crimes: a violation of the Public Assembly Act and a disrespect for authority."[9]

What is ironic about Kishida Toshiko's arrest and conviction—she was fined five yen for her crime—is that, while she was in fact making a political statement, her agenda was not nearly as Machiavellian as authorities supposed; neither was the target of her criticism policemen or the Public Assembly Act. The "daughters" of Kishida's speech were not metaphors for the Japanese citizen. By daughters, she meant *daughters*: daughters of restrictive families, victims of misguided notions about female value, chastity, and rights. Her use of the phrase "daughters in boxes" referred to the practice, then prominent in her home region of the Kansai, of keeping the unmarried daughters of the middle and upper classes tucked away from the outside world, protected from dangers and degradation but also denied access to a meaningful education.

For Kishida, education was the most important treasure a woman could possess. She herself had benefited from an above-average education. Born to a well-to-do merchant family in Kyoto, Kishida entered the newly inaugurated municipal elementary school in 1869, notably three years before sixteen months of education was made compulsory for girls as well as boys. In 1876 she earned the highest score in a citywide examination and the following year matriculated into the Kyoto Women's Normal School as a member of its first class; unfortunately, she was soon to withdraw owing to ill health. Having earlier been summoned to demonstrate calligraphy in the presence of Prince Arisugawa, Kishida was shortly invited to enter court service in 1879, the first commoner so distinguished. It was Kishida's proficiency in the Confucian classics that brought her to the attention of the imperial family. Her primary role was to tutor Empress Shōken, who sought to create an artistic, woman-centered salon after the fashion of the great empresses of the Heian era.[10] Much as Murasaki Shikibu tutored her empress in the Chinese classics, so Kishida was to teach Shōken. She firmly believed that Confucian ethics offered women an important path toward self-discipline and advancement but could not long abide the sequestered life in the imperial court.[11] She tendered her resignation in 1881, citing health concerns. Sievers, however, speculates that Kishida was disenchanted with a court life "symbolic of the concubine system" and so far removed from the gritty reality she read about in the newspapers.[12] With her mother as her companion, Kishida traveled to Tosa to lend her support to the Jiyū minken undō and to seek a more active involvement in the gritty reality of life.

Undeterred by her arrest in 1883, Kishida continued to lecture until the Liberal Party—and much of the movement she had supported—collapsed in 1884. She transferred her energies to journalism and teaching. Although her contemporary Fukuda Hideko (1865–1927) claimed that Kishida's attitude changed after she married Nakajima Nobuyuki (1846–1899),[13] one of the founders of the Liberal Party, in 1884, her record of publication shows, if anything, a more determined and focused stance. Without question her most ambitious essay at the time was "Dōhō shimai ni tsugu" ("To My Fellow Sisters"), published in ten installments from May to June 1884 in *Jiyū no tomoshibi* (Light of freedom). Before her death from tuberculosis seven years later, she also distinguished herself as a novelist, translator, teacher, and poet. Following Nakajima to the Kantō region, where he was eventually to become the first president of the lower house of parliament, she took a job as a teacher at Ferris Women's Seminary in Yokohama. She also contributed regularly to Iwamoto Yoshiharu's *Jogaku zasshi* (Woman's education journal). It was here that she published "Zen'aku no chimata" (The crossroads of good and evil), her adaptation of Edward George Bulwer-Lytton's *Eugene Aram*, in 1887. In 1889 she contributed an original work, *Sankan no meika* (The noble flower of the valley), a "political novel" based on her own experiences, to the literary journal *Miyako no hana* (Flower of the capital). As diverse as her journalistic offerings were, it was in her essays, many based on her earlier lectures, that Kishida excelled.

"To My Fellow Sisters" is a case in point. Intent on advocating for the saliency of equal rights for women, Kishida avails herself of a clever rhetorical style whereby she introduces contrary arguments and then demolishes them one by one with sharply honed logic and snappy wit. For example, to the oft-cited argument that women cannot be entitled to equal rights because they are the weaker sex, she offers:

> Strengths and weaknesses, are these not relative concerns after all? If the difference between an aristocrat and a plebeian, between respect and degradation, were determined by the muscle of one's arm then the hierarchy among men would accord with the ranking list of the sumo world. An ordinary man cannot possibly best a sumo wrestler. By reason then the sumo champions Ume-ga-tani and Tateyama should take their place among the highest in the land and serve as Chancellor and Regent, and our aristocrats, with their delicately pale skin, should surely count themselves beneath the lowest of our low—the former outcasts. Where is the sense in such logic?[14]

To those who would argue that women were intellectually inferior, she suggested that women be given the educational advantages men enjoy. To those who insisted that women were not entitled to equal rights because they did not own property, she lashed back that the laws be rectified. And finally to those who claimed that according women equal rights would disrupt the harmony of the home, Kishida replied that, if husbands treated their wives with charity and fairness from the beginning, there would be no need for domestic squabbles. Whereas it is clear Kishida relished the rhetorical sparring she engaged in with her straw men adversaries, it was for her fellow political activists that she reserved her strongest criticism. While on the lecture circuit she stood shoulder to shoulder with men who clamored for equal representation among men but refused to acknowledge the need for similar standards for women. Many of these men were, according to Kishida's contemporary Shimizu Shikin, "hypocrites who stand before the government and coolly declare their liberal yearnings. But once they are home they lord it over their wives and children."[15] Kishida chastised these "hypocrites": "Alas, you men of society, pay heed. When you open your mouths to protest do you not cry out for advancement and clamor for reform? Why then when it comes to this single issue of equal rights do you suddenly clam up and cling with such affection to the customs of the past and yield so compliantly to the vulgarity of the present day? My beloved and cherished sisters, elder and younger, redress past practices, destroy contemporary customs, and awaken these heartless men from their deceptive dreams."[16]

Kishida devoted her life to encouraging her "beloved and cherished sisters" and awakening "heartless men." Whereas "Daughters in Boxes," as a speech and not an essay recorded by the author, is rhetorically not as rigorous as "To My Fellow Sisters," its place in Meiji women's history is profound. With this speech, Kishida stood before peers and authorities and challenged them to open their eyes to the cruel injustices endured by "daughters in boxes." With her own example she proved that for many daughters there were roles to play and battles to fight far beyond the confines of the box.

DAUGHTERS IN BOXES

Translated by Rebecca L. Copeland
and Aiko Okamoto MacPhail

LADIES AND GENTLEMEN, I am Kishida Shun. As I am easily given to illness and feeling unwell, I had thought to cancel my appearance this evening, but, not wishing to disappoint our organizer, I have come after all. I do worry that I may need to excuse myself midway, however. Ah, whom does heaven hate to make it rain so tonight? With the rain, the congestion in the streets outside could not have been worse. And yet, in this world of ours, it is through inconvenience that we come to appreciate convenience. The inconvenience of tonight's rain-congested thoroughfares may just be the conduit to tomorrow's easy passage. And today's lack of freedom just may become the catalyst for tomorrow's liberty. Heaven subjected Kishida Shun to this inconvenience tonight to allow me the pleasure of seeing so many of you come to hear my talk. Two words sum up my response to your dedication: abundant joy.

I cannot think of a single soul who enjoys listening to an academic address! Still, having made these speeches a woman's task, I have accepted speaking engagements far and wide. There are those who deplore my activities, saying that a woman who once dressed in brocade has now taken to the variety stage in a cheap bid to entertain. Naturally, I pay their criticism no heed. But let us consider the two ideograms used to write the word "entertain." Taken in turn, do they not mean "to raise" and "to achieve"? I may be the one who stands before you "entertaining" for the sake of our country. But that is not to suggest that I alone am gifted with extensive knowledge or blessed with abundant talent. Without you in the audience, this speech would go unheard and would be meaningless. Together we share in this exchange of knowledge, and together we teach each other, with the mutual goal of raising the level of learning throughout the land. Surely it is not inappropriate to say therefore that my "entertainment" benefits the country.

But, to turn to the topic of this evening's lecture, the expression "daughters in boxes" is a popular one, heard with frequency in the regions of Kyoto and Osaka. It is the daughters of middle-class families and above who are often referred to as such. Why such an expression? Because these girls are like creatures kept in a box. They may have hands and feet and a voice—but all to no avail, because their freedom is restricted. Unable to move, their hands and feet are useless. Unable to speak, their voice has no purpose. Hence the expression.

It is only for daughters that such boxes are constructed. Parents who make these boxes do not mean to restrict their daughters' freedom. Rather, they hope to guide their daughters along the correct path toward acquiring womanly virtues. Therefore it is out of love for their daughters that these parents construct these boxes. Or so we are told, but, if we look at the situation more closely, we cannot help questioning whether it is truly love that these parents have for their daughters. For do they not cause their daughters to suffer? I should like to gather a few students—perhaps only two or three—and make of them true daughters in a box. But the box I would construct would not be a box with walls. Rather, it would be a formless box. For a box with walls visible to the human eye is cramped and does not allow one to cultivate truly bright and healthy children. Sisters crowd each other, competing for space, and end up developing warped personalities. And so I intend to create a box without walls.

A box without walls is one that allows its occupants to tread wherever their feet might lead and stretch their arms as wide as they wish. Some may object and say: is your box not one that encourages dissipation and willfulness? No, it is not so at all. My box without walls is made of heaven and earth—its lid I would fashion out of the transparent blue of the sky and at its bottom would be the fathomless depths of the earth upon which we stand. My box would not be cramped, allowing its occupants such a tiny space that whenever they attempt to move, their arms and legs strike against one another, causing them to suffer. It may seem biased to say so, but constructing this box is above all a woman's task and an important task at that. A hastily made box will not do. A woman should carry with her into marriage a box filled with a good education. Upon giving birth to a daughter, she should raise her in the box she has herself carefully constructed. Thus she will nurture a bright daughter of good character. But if she forces her daughter into a box she has hastily constructed, the child will chafe at the narrowness of the structure and resent being placed inside. Far better to build the box before the birth of the child, for indeed a woman's ability to produce good children for the propagation of the family and to encourage domestic harmony depends on how carefully she has built this box.

I do not know anything about the world beyond my own small frame of reference, but I think it safe to say that all Japanese families raise their daughters in boxes. Certainly the kind of boxes we create and the way we raise our daughters in them vary in degree from household to household. Among these, I can identify approximately three different types of boxes. Of these three, which one would I select? I would select the one in which the parents value the teachings of the wise and holy men of the past and, through the lessons imparted in classics such as the *Great Learning for Women* and the *Small Learning for Women*, pass on to their daughters an appreciation for knowledge. Compared to the other two boxes, this one is far more cultivated. But then, which box comes next? Next, we have a box that upon the birth of a daughter is fitted with a secluded room deep in its interior; this is where the daughter is kept. The entrance to this room is barricaded by a long blind, and she must not leave the room. Nor may she lift the blind. And so she stays deep in her room behind her blind. The parents of the daughter in this box treat her not with affection; rather, they bring her only harm. And then, as for the third: in this box the parents refuse to recognize their responsibility to their daughter and teach her naught. They make no effort to shower her with love and instead expect her to obey their every word without complaint. The mother abusively wields her power over her daughter and is otherwise hateful in her treatment of her child. Such is the third box. Of the three boxes I have just introduced this evening, I consider the first commendable in its cultivation. But the second and third are not satisfactory and are not to be recommended.

Next, I would like to take up an extremely practical matter, and that is the way mothers today raise their daughters. There are some who argue, with exceedingly boorish logic, that learning is an obstacle to a woman's successful marriage. This argument is particularly specious. Women need learning. But if you think by learning that I am referring only to the *Four Books* and the *Five Classics* or the eight great writers of the Tang and Song—Han Yü in particular—or recitations of the great Chinese poets, then you are greatly mistaken. Nor am I advocating the composition of *waka* poetry or the extemporaneous recitation of short verses. A romantic ramble while enjoying the elegant diversions of moon or flower viewing does not to my mind constitute learning, either. Now, a daughter might display a natural talent for letters and be able to gladden her readers with her many compositions. Then let her become a writer. But those without talent should not waste their time in elegant diversions with moon and flowers or in dabbling with mountains and streams as though they were some revered recluse. No, what I call learning requires that a woman recognize, at least, the responsibility that she must shoulder as a woman; so long as she lives in this precious country of ours, she should refrain from squandering her talents. What I desire most is for a woman to prepare herself for marriage by assembling appropriate knowledge as the most essential item in her trousseau.

Eight or nine out of ten mothers in our society today believe that they have accomplished their duty if their daughters, once married, are not sent home in divorce. It does not even occur to them that their daughters might deserve higher goals. How can these mothers successfully accomplish their tasks when their expectations for their daughters are so low? What then is the appropriate way to raise a daughter?

What I deem appropriate is to allow daughters to study first and then have them marry. Education is the most essential item in a woman's wedding trousseau. And what are the subjects she should study? Economics and ethics. Although a woman lives under her husband's protection for most of her life, the day may come when he should die. Then she should fortify herself with her moral training and plan her future with her financial knowledge. Thus these subjects, when taken together, form the most important item a woman will bring to her marriage. Her kimono cabinet and bedding chest are vulnerable to theft and easily lost to fire. They cannot be trusted to last with absolute certainty. Even so, those who do not appreciate the fact that a daughter, too, should be educated, dismiss their maids and servants as soon as their daughter comes of age. Their rationale for this is that their daughter will soon be sent in marriage to a stranger's house, where she must know the ins and outs of cleaning. What better time to learn than now? And so they set her to work in the absence of the servants and maids. Truly, can we say that these parents know how to raise a daughter?[17]

Occasionally, parents will let their daughters study the arts, in which case they have them practice the tea ceremony or flower arrangement or *waka* composition or the opening line to a linked verse. Other than these accomplishments, they enjoy having their daughters learn the three-stringed *shamisen*. And so these parents take great delight in showing off their daughters in front of others and feel not the slightest twinge of remorse in pushing their daughters to these displays. Is it because these parents are themselves the product of ancient customs? How truly regrettable it is that they do not even think to consider the merits and demerits of their choices. Can they possibly produce talented daughters with training such as this? No, they cannot. True parents are those who impart to their children an appreciation of moral virtue. Yet these parents think they can educate their daughters by teaching them to dance and twirl. They train them to lift their arms, tap their feet, and bend their bodies as gracefully as a willow branch swaying in the wind and rain. But what models do these daughters follow with their lifted arms and lithe feet? And will even their own brothers be able to speak candidly of their sisters? Daughters who know a little shame will blush. Come now, can you parents actually claim to be innocent of the meaning of the song lyrics that you have your daughters sing? Do your daughters have no choice but to continue, cheeks burning with embarrassment?

Daughters taught to sing lascivious songs and display their bodies in suggestive dances cannot be comfortably placed in the kind of box where they would be trained in appropriate virtues, even if their parents should later wish to do so. Perhaps this point can be explained by comparing daughters trained in lascivious arts to flowers. When the cold of winter departs, the flowers welcome the warmth of spring. In the mountains, the purple buds begin to open and throughout the valley red blossoms laugh. Everywhere we turn there are flowers. Everywhere we go, the cherry trees bloom. When all the flowers are in full blossom, suppose we put one in a box. We set it beside an open window and surround it with lowered blinds. How the flower will envy the others. "Here I am in a box," it will say. "But the flowers on the plain bloom freely. They laugh freely. They spread their fragrant scents freely. But look at me, how miserable I am!" Up to this point, no box had been prepared for this flower, and now, just as spring has arrived, a box is built and the flower forced inside. Overwhelmed with grief and resentment, the flower slips from its box by the window and flees. Even as the parents try to capture the flower, it is blown by the wind and pelted by the rain, and those who try to restrain it are unable to do so easily. We humans are like this flower, are we not? Far better, I should think, to destroy the box that restricts the flow of air and denies freedom, and to do so immediately. For this is not a box designed to cherish a daughter but rather one that brings about her suffering. Daughters raised in these boxes grow sickly, their personalities warped, and so they run away. And yet, even though parents can see these boxes with their own eyes, they still do not recognize how detrimental they are, and they warn: "Daughter, dear, you must not leave this box for if you do, even you, a good person, will be corrupted." These parents do not realize how they warp their daughter by placing her in such a box. Such parents hardly warrant the title of "parent" in the true sense of the word. For true parents long to broaden their daughter's knowledge and seek the appropriate means to do so. In ancient times it may have been sufficient to keep daughters sealed in boxes this way. But now that our daughters know perfectly well that God the Creator has endowed them with liberty, we ought to be constructing boxes that permit them their liberty.

Consider this: the word "to parent" does not mean "to torment," and so parents today should take the interests of their daughters to heart when they construct their boxes and reflect on the merits and demerits, the pluses and minuses of their actions when doing so. Today's boxes, which torment daughters, are not constructed in their best interests. Similarly, there are a number of words in currency today that mean "daughter." One is created with the ideograph for woman on the left and goodness on the right. Another has woman on the left and wealth on the right. Both are used to mean "daughter." This may be why in the Kyoto region daughters from respectable families are addressed with the title "Miss," which is constructed with the latter word for daughter [woman plus wealth]. But regardless of the ideograph used to write the word "daughter," all daughters are also young maidens who should protect their womanly virtue by obeying thoughtful advice and by conceding what it is they should concede. But some people do not understand even these basic virtues and refuse to do for their daughters what it is they should do. How greatly mistaken they are.

At a time when knowledge progresses as it does now, learning and freedom should be encouraged. Without such encouragement, parents who put their daughter in the box they have built, believing that it is for her own good, are like a gardener who tries to grow flowers behind a fence. Flowers that are grown within a wattled fence are restricted beyond measure. Caught in the meshes of the law imposed upon them by the fence, they cannot freely bloom or spread their fragrance even if they do display a slight tinge of color. If we replace these flowers with the human spirit, imagine how restricted it would be! Many of you may know of a gardener who cultivates blossoms by limiting the space for their growth. See how he constructs his wattled fences. He cuts this branch here and snips those leaves there so should a tree wish to burst forth in blooms, it is prevented from doing so, and all because the gardener is as mindful of his fence as he is his flowers. Naturally, a gardener is not intent on damaging his flowers, since they are his profit, after all. But those who grow flowers are unaware of the feelings of the flowers they grow, and so they end up gazing at the faces of these oppressed blossoms without a second thought. Those who wish to grow beautiful, healthy flowers should try to appreciate the feeling of the flowers they grow and should set out their fences in a way that nurtures their proper growth. For to produce magnificent blooms, the gardener must imagine himself to be the flower he is tending. Yet what encourages gardeners to cause their flowers to suffer? Is it the promise of profit that leads them to treat their flowers cruelly rather than tenderly? Indeed, what a truly unfortunate, pitiful reason this must be for the flowers who must suffer for it.

But to return to the subject at hand, we humans are like these flowers. Therefore we cannot cultivate the human spirit to its full and brilliant potential if we restrict its freedom as would a gardener his flowers. To take the analogy further, let us compare these flowers to humanity and more particularly to daughters. If we enclose them in boxes, if we capture them when they try to escape and bind them in place, then just as the petals of the bound flower will scatter and fall, so, too, the bounty of the human mind will wither. And so I say to you, before you put your daughters in a box, try to imagine how she will feel once inside and thus construct the box to be as broad as the world is wide so that she might feel free. Should you do so, I guarantee that you will produce a true and virtuous daughter. But if you do not—if you force your daughter inside a narrow box and restrict her freedom—I have no doubt that your daughter will either escape or elope, and you will have to send your servants and maids out to search high and low to find her and drag her back. On the contrary, if the daughters in boxes today are allowed to feel as free as those outside the box, then the need to keep them tucked away in restrictive boxes loses its currency. And if we no longer need restrictive boxes, then daughters will no longer need to escape them, and servants and maids will no longer need to spend their time chasing after them. Their energy can be more appropriately applied to the management of the house, thus better utilizing household resources!

I had intended to address one more topic this evening. But owing to my illness, which I mentioned at the start of my lecture tonight, I am unable to continue. I hope to have an opportunity to continue at our next meeting. Until then, I solicit your kind understanding.

NOTES

1. Personal names at this time were highly unstable, particularly for writers. The author was named Kishida Shun at birth. The character used to write her first name, Shun, meant, appropriately, "excellence" and "genius" and could also be read "Toshi." In 1876 she appended the feminine suffix "ko" to her name, as was then the fashion, and went by Toshiko. She assumed a number of literary names, as was also common at the time: Shōen was one, Shunjo another. When she married Nakajima Nobuyuki in 1884, she took his surname and subsequently published as Nakajima Shōen. In this volume, we refer to the author consistently as Kishida Toshiko, although she introduces herself as Kishida Shun in the lecture we have translated.
2. The description of Kishida is from Sōma Kokkō, *Meiji shōki no sanjosei* (Tokyo: Kosei kaku, 1940), pp. 49–50.
3. She might have stayed in jail until her trial on November 12 but was released because of ill health on October 20, having served only eight days. She was known to have been of a delicate constitution.
4. See J. Scott Miller, "Japanese Shorthand and *Sokkibon*," *Monumenta Nipponica* 49, no. 4 (Winter, 1994): 471–487.
5. Sōma, *Meiji shōki no sanjosei*, p. 48.

6. Fukuda Hideko is one example, Tomii Oto another. See Sharon Sievers, *Flowers in Salt: The Beginnings of Feminist Consciousness in Modern Japan* (Stanford: Stanford University Press, 1983), p. 36. Readers of Sievers's pioneering study, which took its title from Kishida's speech, will no doubt wonder what has become of the "salt" in the translation here. The salt, however, was the product of old, worm-eaten research materials. Unlike the present translators, who had access to a photocopy of the relevant pages of the *Jiyū shinbun* (Liberty times), Professor Sievers worked from a yellowed original. The line that likened daughters to flowers grown by a gardener behind a wattled fence had been so compromised by ravenous *mushi*, that the wattled fence (垣 or *kaki*, in Japanese) looked like salt (塩 or *shio*). When she conferred with others, they confirmed her reading. And so the powerful image of flowers grown in salt took hold. As Sievers has noted in private letter: "By the time we got a better copy and accurate translation, the book was almost in press, and I had grown very fond of the metaphor. I can't say the same for some of my editors—who were afraid that librarians (and perhaps even booksellers!) would file it away in the horticultural section. Still, for me at least, the most important thing was really not a literal translation of that particular line, but the fact that 'flowers in salt' so powerfully conveyed the feelings of so many Meiji women I read."

7. Ibid., p. 41.

8. As cited in Itōya Toshio, *Josei kaihō no senkushatachi: Nakajima Toshiko to Fukuda Hideko* (Tokyo: Shimizu shoin, 1975), p. 46.

9. Ibid., pp. 47–48.

10. Atsuko Sakaki, "Sliding Door: Women in the Heterosocial Literary Field of Early Modern Japan," *U.S.-Japan Women's Journal*, no. 17 (1999): 4.

11. In her speech "Daughters in Boxes," Kishida notes the importance of familiarity with the Chinese classics. The *Four Books* are venerable Chinese texts that were selected by Zhu Xi during the Song dynasty (960–1279) to represent the foundations of Confucian thought. The *Five Classics* were believed to have been compiled and edited by Confucius to serve as the basis for Confucian practice. Kishida singles out Han Yü (768–824) in particular as an important model. Han Yü was a great poet and a master of Chinese prose who would become the first proponent of neo-Confucianism, which was widely influential in Japan.

12. Sievers, *Flowers in Salt*, pp. 34–35.

13. Hane Mikiso, *Reflections on the Way to the Gallows: Rebel Women in Prewar Japan* (Berkeley: University of California Press, 1988), p. 18.

14. Nakajima Shōen, "To My Fellow Sisters," trans. Rebecca Copeland and Aiko Okamoto MacPhail, in *An Anthology of Meiji Literature*, ed. Robert Campbell, Charles Inouye, and Sumie Jones (Honolulu: University of Hawai'i Press, forthcoming).

15. Shimizu Shikin, as cited in Rebecca Copeland, *Lost Leaves: Women Writers of Meiji Japan* (Honolulu: University of Hawai'i Press, 2000), pp. 165–166.
16. Nakajima, "To My Fellow Sisters."
17. The speech thus far is translated from *Jiyū shinbun* (Liberty times), no. 411 (November 20, 1883): 2–3, the first part of an article serialized over two successive days. The balance of the text is a translation of *Jiyū shinbun* (Liberty times), no. 412 (November 21, 1883): 2.

When the transcript of this speech was published, it was preceded by this lengthy passage:

Transcript of Miss Kishida Shun's Speech

The Court of Justice for Minor Offenses at Ōtsu held a public trial at ten o'clock in the morning on the twelfth of November 1883 to try the aforementioned Kishida Toshiko on the charge of having discussed politics during an academic address. The judge in charge of her case was Assistant Judge Doi Yotarō, the prosecutor was Hirakawa Tadashi, the court reporter someone named Ōtsuka, and counsel for the defense, Sakai Tamotsu. Over ten people were in the courtroom to observe the trial, during which time Miss Kishida's speech, which had been delivered on the night of the twelfth of October at Ōtsu Theater and recorded by a policeman in attendance therein, was read out loud. The policeman transcribed the speech himself, and it is not known how it will be amended by Miss Kishida when she speaks in her own defense or how her counsel will treat it during his rebuttal. Even so, Miss Kishida is the first woman accused of political speech in our country. Equally, it is the first time that a policeman has read into court record the transcription of a speech that he himself painstakingly recorded. To commemorate this occasion, the original transcript is published herein exactly as it was presented in court.

MIYAKE KAHO
(1868–1944)

Rebecca L. Copeland

MIYAKE KAHO is often referred to as the first woman writer of the modern period—a provocative distinction that nevertheless warrants cautious regard.[1] A naming of firsts assumes there were no women writers in advance of Kaho, and such was not the case.[2] Recent scholarship has shown that women wrote throughout the preceding Tokugawa period (1600–1868). Moreover, a variety of women published in periodicals before 1888, when Kaho published "Yabu no uguisu" (Warbler in the Grove). Kishida Toshiko's essays began appearing in 1884, for example, and in 1887 she published the little-known "Zen'aku no chimata" (The crossroads of good and evil). But since the latter was an adaptation of Lord Edward Bulwer-Lytton's *Eugene Aram* (1832) and not an original work, the distinction of "first" is typically pinned on Kaho.

The term "modern" also invites scrutiny. Although Kaho clearly reveals concern with contemporary social issues, as I shall discuss below, her early works stand, not surprisingly, with one foot rooted firmly in the literary past, a tendency not uncommon to other writers of this era, both male and female. "Warbler in the Grove," is recognized as Kaho's debut piece. It demonstrates an important debt to the character sketches of her contemporaries, notably Tsubouchi Shōyō (1859–1935), which were in turn redolent of the literary strategies of an earlier age. Notable in this regard is the language of the text—a mixture of clas-

FIGURE 3.1 Miyake Kaho (1868–1943)   FIGURE 3.2 Miyake Kaho in Western dress

sical narrative and colloquial dialogue—and the polyvocality of the text. The story lacks the unifying perspective of a main protagonist, preferring multiple perspectives and dramatic sketches to the narrative strategies of character development and psychological realism that are usually identified with literary modernity. Readers will find that scenes unfold with a dramatic flourish reminiscent of Kabuki theater. Information is often gained through eavesdropping, characters meet suddenly and under unlikely circumstances, and, most important, the narrative progression of the story is almost exclusively dependent on dialogue, which in the original is rendered in a playscript style.[3] The story that emerges thus is lively and robust, full of chatter and local flavor. However, the concerns that Kaho addresses—excessive Westernization, social responsibility, marriage, and education for women—were topics of contemporary debate.

Part 1 of this story is set in the Rokumeikan (Deer-cry) Pavilion, a lavish rococo-style building constructed in 1883 as part of a government-sponsored campaign to "demonstrate the high level of civilization in Japan and thus help persuade the Western powers to revise the unequal treaties imposed upon Japan."[4] Kaho, who came of age during the heyday of the Rokumeikan era, enjoyed the excitement and energy of the social functions held there. In her 1939 autobiographical essay "Watashi no ayunde kita michi—Omoide no hitobito" (The path I took—The

FIGURE 3.3 Woodcut of a dance party at the Rokumeikan

people I remember), she writes of rushing with her classmates to the beauty parlor, where they would have their hair arranged in fancy coiffures and their bodies fitted into luxurious ballroom gowns—with bustles and bodices—properly laced.[5] But by the time Kaho wrote "Warbler in the Grove," the era of the Rokumeikan was waning. Blind infatuation with Westernization, which for some was synonymous with the catchphrase *bunmei kaika* (civilization and enlightenment), had become the target of much criticism, and those who, like Count Shinohara in "Warbler," imitated Western customs with no real appreciation of the implications of their actions, were held up to ridicule. Intellectual leaders called for a more moderate approach to modernization, and Meiji youth were encouraged to learn from other countries but strive to retain that which would be of greatest benefit to Japan.

For Kaho and her peers, individual success was meaningless if it did not benefit the greater national good. Readers of "Warbler" will notice that men who seek only to benefit themselves do not fare well. Even the Western models of George Washington and Otto von Bismarck do not earn favor because their contributions, while impressive, did not better the world, or so Kaho's character Tsutomu argues. Successful characters lead lives that are productive and promising. The young Ashio becomes a prominent engineer, Saitō and Miyazaki are important educators, and Tsutomu—educated abroad, titled, and scion of a wealthy estate—is

FIGURE 3.4 Frontispiece for *Warbler in the Grove;*
Hamako, left; Hideko, right; and Namiko, lower center

poised to make significant contributions to the Japanese government. All
of Kaho's successful characters achieve their good fortune by virtue of
their own hard work. In this respect, they embody another important
Meiji catchphrase: *risshin shusse* (self-establishment and public advancement). Given the reforms in the governmental and educational systems,
it was assumed that access to success was available to all and any who
distinguished themselves with their hard work and the sincerity of their
endeavors.

Personal advancement and social responsibility were not exclusive to
men. Women of Kaho's generation felt equally called to serve the nation,
though the arenas in which they might operate were distinct. Educational reforms had provided women greater access to a variety of institutions of higher learning—some sponsored by the government, others
operated privately by either Japanese educators or foreign missionaries.
Kaho experienced the gamut of what the Meiji period had to offer. After enrolling her briefly in the local government-run elementary school,
her father moved her to the private Atomi Academy for Women, which
had been founded in 1875 as a finishing school for girls from wealthy
and aristocratic families. Here, Kaho was trained in calligraphy, art, and
arithmetic in addition to the Japanese and Chinese classics. She studied
traditional Japanese poetry, or *waka*, in Nakajima Utako's Haginoya, the

conservatory Higuchi Ichiyō also attended. Kaho studied the English language at the Sakurai Women's School (later known as Joshi Gakuen), run by the Japanese Christian Yajima Kajiko (1839–1922). After a brief sojourn at the Meiji Women's School, another private Christian institution, Kaho finally made her way to the highly competitive Government Normal School for Women (presently Ochanomizu Women's University) in the fall of 1886. It was while she was a student here that she wrote "Warbler in the Grove."

It is surely not surprising therefore that several of Kaho's female characters are "girl students," or *jogakusei*, and that much of her story, most notably part 6, seems intent on highlighting the positive nature of education for women. The "girl student" was not beloved by all. As Namiko notes in part 6, many were appalled by the sight of this new breed of woman strutting along public avenues with her books and knowing looks. At the same time, the girl student threatened to replace the geisha as the female sex object of choice in more and more stories, prints, and paintings. Unlike the courtesan, who was often employed for her tragic, as well as erotic, potential, the girl student was usually the target of satire, whether intellectually or sexually. Her appearance in what had heretofore been largely a male sphere clearly unsettled her male counterparts, whose only defense against this incursion was to belittle the offender. She was thus typically portrayed as either wantonly permissive or too bookish to be attractive.

Set against this context, Miyake Kaho's "Warbler" offers us a view of the girl student from the perspective of the girl student herself. To offset the negative images represented by her superficially Western character, Hamako, and the brazenly aggressive girl students of the 1870s, Kaho gives readers Namiko, who is both wise and attractive but also modest and generous. More significantly, Namiko recognizes the importance of marriage. Although several of her classmates vow never to wed, for Namiko, a woman's true calling is in marriage, but (and the distinction is important) in a marriage that is made willingly and out of a mutual attraction.

The marriage most central to the story is that of Shinohara Tsutomu. He had been adopted into the Shinohara family as a boy with the intention that he would marry Hamako and succeed to the family name. This practice of adopting a son-in-law was not unusual in families that lacked male heirs. Tsutomu's refusal of the modern Hamako in favor of the old-fashioned Hideko led many readers to assume Kaho was suggesting a return to traditional values.[6] But a careful look at Hideko's characterization reveals that, while Hamako's modernity is only a very thin veneer, Hideko's self-sufficiency and integrity embody the very values of Meiji's "self-establishment and public advancement."

Unlike Hamako, who studies violin, piano, and other subjects with no "practical" application, Hideko is gifted in Japanese poetry, which Tsutomu lauds as simple yet profound, requiring "an exceedingly refined sensibility." Her education, we are told, was acquired at the Shimoda Utako Academy for Women, a real institution. Formerly a tutor in the imperial court, Utako (1854–1936) opened her school for women in 1881, where she primarily taught the aristocratic elite in the Chinese and Japanese classics, poetry, calligraphy, history, moral ethics, embroidery, and so on. Kaho's character Hideko withdraws from the Shimoda Utako Academy when her parents die so as to conserve the family inheritance. She devotes her attention to knitting and with her skill and industry earns just enough to provide for herself and her younger brother, Ashio. Twenty-first century readers may find the mention of knitting a cliché for feminine domesticity. But in late-nineteenth-century Japan, knitting was an impressive new skill, imported (along with woolen yarn) from the West. A smartly knitted wool shawl, a trendy item at the time, could fetch a handsome sum. Hideko's piecework, while demure, is also surprisingly modern.

In many respects, the widow Osada offers an antithesis to the maidenly Hideko. Osada is also self-sufficient, being able to rely on the property left by her late husband. But, whereas widows were expected to live chastely, Osada uses her position to reel in the young bureaucrat Yamanaka. Kaho casts Osada as the "poison woman," or *dokufu*. This figure was typified in the Meiji period by the infamous Takahashi Oden (1850–1879), a murderess, who became synonymous with female excess and criminality.[7]

Miyake Kaho's portrayal of the lustful Osada and her reiteration of the speech of the lower classes earned criticism from some quarters.[8] Kaho was the daughter of a former samurai who was now a high-level government official. She had been afforded the best education money could buy and had enjoyed the privileges of the upper class. It was therefore thought unseemly that a young lady with Kaho's upbringing, who should have been a "daughter in a box" (see Kishida Toshiko's essay in this volume), would reveal such familiarity with society's riff-raff. These detractors aside, for the most part Kaho's story was well received.

Kaho claimed that she was inspired to write "Warbler" after reading *Tōsei shosei katagi* (The character of modern-day students, 1885) by Tsubouchi Shōyō, a long and intricately woven work portraying the varied experiences of a group of male students. Kaho was impressed by what she described as the naturalness of the work and declared that, if all one had to do to write a novel was record one's everyday experiences and observances, then she could write one herself. With her father's mediations, she sought Shōyō's support and encouragement, and her resulting story was published with his recommendation. The publication earned Kaho just over thirty-three yen, a sizeable sum at the time, when monthly salaries averaged twenty-five yen.

Kaho maintained that she knocked the work off effortlessly, but the resulting story nevertheless reveals thoughtful construction. Characters are more or less stereotypical, but to each positive rendering she offered a negative: the brazen Hamako to the demure Namiko, for example, or the sycophant Yamanaka to the sincere Tsutomu. Presented in twelve sections, the story also has a pleasant symmetry. A story that begins in the New Year at the Rokumeikan—site of Western excess—concludes in a Japanese-style restaurant at year's end. The narrative journey brings the surviving characters away from superficiality and back to sincerity; away from flirtatious infidelity and into marriage.

Finally, a word about the title, "Warbler in the Grove." The warbler (*uguisu*) was a regular denizen of traditional *waka* diction and associated with spring. The warbler in the plum blossoms was an early harbinger of spring and of all the human conditions associated with the season, namely, love, youth, and rejuvenation. The poetic association the title conjures is appropriate for a story—set in the first flowering of the modern period—that describes the budding of social consciousness among a group of men and women in the bloom of their youth. The fact that the warbler is in the *yabu* (bamboo thicket) and not on the plum calls forth associations with the wild warblers of the field (or grove, *yase no uguisu*), as opposed to the domesticated warblers caged and raised at court. In many respects, Kaho's young warblers are wild. Individuated and firmly resolved, they refuse simply to follow popular taste. Another connotation for the warbler in the wild is that of an especially talented and gifted person trapped within the wilds of mediocrity. Not an inappropriate association, perhaps, for Kaho herself.[9]

WARBLER IN THE GROVE

Translated by Rebecca L. Copeland

Part 1

MAN: Ha-ha-ha-ha-ha! Surely you *deux dames* have already selected your *danse* partners. I suppose I don't stand a chance![10]

WOMAN A: That's not true, not true at all. It's not that we don't want to dance with you. It's just that, when we do, you whirl about so, it makes our eyes spin. That's why we turn you down.

MAN: Well, if you haven't yet decided on a partner for *la valse*, please allow me.

He duly presents his ornamented *programme* and enters her name. "Until then," he nods and turns toward the dance floor. A group of young ladies closes in after him, leaving the two behind.

WOMAN A: Do you know that man?

WOMAN B: Yes. That's Mr. Saitō. He's been to my house before.

WOMAN A: Oh, is that who that is? I heard his name for the first time the other day while I was at my lessons. They say he is an attractive fellow. But he's rather brash, isn't he? And his laugh is so ridiculously loud. I think he's rather peculiar, don't you?

WOMAN B: But he's a learned man—and quite unaffected.

The two young ladies chatting with each other are far more beautiful than the others in attendance. Let us observe them more closely. One, barely sixteen, is fair of face. Her eyes are large, her red lips small and tightly pursed. Her cheeks glow with a natural charm, and she has a manner that attracts the admiration of others. The flower decorating her coiled coiffure holds nothing over her own natural beauty. Her waist may not be particularly trim, but she appears quite at ease in her Western dress. She keeps her gaze downward, her shoulders slightly rounded. But this only adds to her remarkable charm. The gown she wears is pink and of a fine fabric. From time to time, she flutters a fan with red tassels against her breast.

The young lady seated beside her appears to be two years her senior. Her nose is high, her brow lovely, and her eyes rather narrow. She has secretly used the very powder the maid cautioned her to avoid, telling her its lead base would damage her health, and as a result her skin is shockingly white. Her hair, twisted high atop her head, ends in a tumble of bangs. Crimped in curls across her forehead, they have a reddish tint. Her straw-colored gown, designed overseas, is bedecked with beads. And although she looks a tad uncomfortable, she has cinched her waist so tightly one fears she might snap in two. She stands proudly upright, her lower lip drooping slightly. "Because of her fondness for chatter," the stable boy has scoffed, behind her back. All in all, she is passably attractive. But nothing like the other young miss.

"Miss Shinohara, your elder brother [fiancé] should be returning soon, shouldn't he?" the first woman asks her friend.

"Yes, he has said he'll be back in the summer. But I'm not looking forward to his return. It'll spoil everything!"

"Why on earth? You should be happy. After all, you'll be able to ask him to help you with your schoolwork, will you not?"

"Don't be daft! I'm not going to school anymore, not since my father began to complain of a stomach ailment. And you know my mother can't manage a thing. I'm now busy directing the household."

"Oh? And what about your English lessons? Have you given up on them as well? But then I suppose that's fine for someone as talented as you are in English *parlance*."

"Why? I fully intend to continue my English study. Lately I've been taking lessons with—well, you must know him—Mr. Yamanaka? He's very fluent, you see. Oh, I've just been so busy. Every day—day in and day out—I study English. I'm frightfully burdened with household matters as well, but . . . I'm never too busy to attend a dance!"

"Even with your father ill? My parents always push me so to socialize, but I still find it uncomfortable. I just can't bring myself to dance with foreigners. Besides, with all my schoolwork I hardly have time to come to these parties. And then I don't even have a dance partner."

"Why are you so timid? No matter how listless I may be at home, the minute I arrive here I suddenly feel *active*. In the West, they call people who do not dance *fleurs du mur* [wallflowers, *kabe no hana*], you know. I'm afraid we'll have to count you among their ranks! Oh look, there's Mr. Miyazaki. It's been ages since he's come to one of these balls. He certainly is an accomplished gentleman. I hear he excels at most anything. Good looks and good-natured. Now that's a find, don't you think? I wonder who his partner is? She's so short. And look how horribly she wears her Western dress! Japanese people are just too short to be anything but pathetic in Western attire. And the way they dance! Just like herons plodding around in a muddy marsh. If their clothes don't fit properly, it's all the worse. I normally wear Western dresses all the time. My mother scolds me because the hem of my skirt catches on things, knocking them over. But I tell her that, in the West, people are not in the habit of leaving items scattered all over the floor as they do here in Japanese-style rooms. The fault lies with her. We're constantly arguing about it."

"You look very nice in Western attire. Mr. Miyazaki's younger sister does as well. She looks just like a European lady. At school she's praised for having the best style of all."

"Is that so? But doesn't his *soeur* have such uncommonly large eyes that she always looks affrighted? Is she very talented?"

"Indeed, she is only fourteen this year, but she is far more accomplished than her years."

"And what about you? Do you make a habit of wearing Western attire?"

"No, not often. I should think Western garments aren't convenient for most people. But everyone seems to enjoy dressing up in such finery whenever they step out for a day or evening on the town, and all anyone can talk about anymore is the latest Western fashion. You'll find people arguing over which shop sells the best ensembles—whether it's the Tanaka Clothier or the Shirogi Dress Shop. Personally, I prefer Western clothing, but since our school maintains the Japanese style, I can't just dress as I please, you know."

As they talk, the music ends, and the dancing subsides. Saitō and Miyazaki approach.

"Well, Hamako, if you please." Mr. Saitō presents his arm, and the young lady with her hair twisted high atop her head sets off with him.

"Hello, *Mademoiselle* Namiko," Mr. Miyazaki bows. "It's been a while."

"How have you been?"

"I'm rather tired this evening," he replies, only to add, "I wanted to thank you for all you've done for my younger sister. You're so kind to her, day in and day out, that she tells us she doesn't even want to come home on holidays!"

"Oh dear, I'm afraid I've not been any help at all."

And as they converse the music resumes.

"It's been so long since I've had the pleasure," Mr. Miyazaki presents his arm.

"May I?"

"Please."

Music, dancing, and a lavish buffet as well. It's not until one o'clock in the morning that the shouts of the carriage drivers fill the streets, carrying the revelers home to their respective residences. This is the night of the New Year's Ball at the famed Rokumeikan Pavilion.

Part 2

Turning into a small lane on the second block of Imagawa Kōji, we see that the third house down is of latticework construction. The street out front, swept spotless with a broom, stands out from the rest. The lattice door gleams with a luster all its own, so carefully has it been polished. The water remaining from the morning cleaning has been sprinkled over the entryway. Atop the granite stone at the threshold, two pairs of wooden sandals have been untidily cast off, a set of low-heeled student's sandals and a lady's delicate clogs.

From the second floor, a bay window overlooks the street, a wet towel dangling from the bamboo railing. Surely, this is no boardinghouse; it is clearly not a student's lodgings. If you were to guess, you might conclude that this is a home left vacant at its master's death. Or perhaps the master has merely set off on a trip somewhere, leaving a kind person behind to rent the place and keep an eye out for thieves? But, no, on further reflection, such a supposition seems far-fetched indeed.

The guest in the second-floor room pays not a single sen for his board and keep. He is twenty-seven or -eight. His nose and brow are finely proportioned, and, though he appears somewhat stern, there are those who find him attractive, remarking that he is stylishly handsome. With his striped *hakama* trousers of coarse silk thread folded at his side and his lunch box wrapped in a purple cloth, it is clear he is a civil servant on the fast track to success. Judging from the way the skin around his eyes is flushed, he must have just returned from the public bath. He places a mirror before the window and earnestly rakes his fingers through his hair. Suddenly, a coquettish voice rings out. "I'll give him the message myself!"

Footsteps sound on the stairs, and then a woman pokes her face into the room. "My, how handsomely you've cleaned up! I've brought a light for your tobacco."

With the fire pan in her hand, she plops down alongside the brazier, one knee drawn up slightly above the other. She is somewhere around thirty years of age. Her complexion is dusky, her nose high. The edge of the right sleeve of her black crepe kimono jacket has begun to fray. Her kimono is a fawn-dappled pattern, and her neckband is embroidered with thread dyed in Kyoto. The detachable collar is one she's washed again and again. Her thinning locks, so meager in places that her scalp peeks through, are gathered in a modest chignon, clasped tightly in place with a gold-flecked cinnabar-lacquered comb—of Master Shōmin's craftsmanship, it would seem. My, what a sneaky beast we have here! She places the burning ember in the brazier and then concentrates intently on fishing out the tobacco remnants from among the ashes. The way she speaks is much more coquettish than one would expect from a woman her age.

"Mr. Yamanaka, how much longer do you intend to stare at yourself in that mirror? Be a dear and look over here, will you? You know, just a few minutes ago . . . well, you must be feeling quite smug."

"Why?" the man asks.

"Why? Why because it looks like your ship has come in! Shall I tell you?"

"I'm all ears."

"Just a bit earlier I went to the bath, remember? While I was out, a very sharply attired rickshaw man—dressed in the impressive black livery favored by the rich—came by asking after you. When Okiyo told him you were out, he said he would call again later but that he definitely needed to see you. And off he went. Okiyo reported this to me just now as I returned. She said a young lady in splendid Western attire was seated in the rickshaw that he had parked just outside the lattice door. There can be no doubt about it—it had to be her."

"Who?"

"Don't play dumb with me, Mister!" the woman cajoles. "You know who! Miss Shinohara." Her voice grows louder and more nasal as she speaks.

"Oh, that cheeky devil," the man replies with disgust. "I haven't been to see her for some time, so she probably came by to ask about her English lessons. Her obsession with the West is a terrible nuisance. I can hardly stand to be near her, she reeks so like one of those vile foreign creatures."

"Oh, really? . . . and when have you been so near?"

"Don't be ridiculous. I go to the house every day for her English lessons, don't I? The whole time I have to sit there while she thrusts those wretched crimped curls of hers under my nose."

"Well, I suppose an attractive girl like that can't bear to be kept waiting. If you haven't been to see her for a few days, she must have grown restless. Can't keep a beauty on ice forever, you know." She laughs. "No, but seriously, I'm just worried about losing a young fellow like you. Surely you're not sneaking around behind my back? No hanky-panky going on, is there?"

"What? Should there be?" he responds impishly.

"You tell me."

"Absolutely not."

"Really? I wonder!" She laughs.

Pitter-patter-pat. Okiyo the maidservant bounds up the stairs and into the room. "Madam, the egg vendor is at the door."

"We don't need any today," the woman replies.

"But we have none left."

"We don't need any."

"As you wish."

"Here we go again," Okiyo grumbles to herself as she makes her way back to the kitchen. "Every time I climb the stairs, I have to turn around and go right back down!"

"Granny, she said we don't need any today," Okiyo reports to the old egg vendor.

"As you wish. Maybe next time, then."

"Well, take a seat and have a smoke."

"Thank you. I'll take you up on that offer. Whew! My, my, you sure do keep yourself neat and tidy—you and the Shinohara household staff. Very neat and tidy. But that young lady there, her Western clothes sure are peculiar."

"Oh! Do you stop in at the Shinoharas', too?" Okiyo's curiosity is piqued.

"I'd be lost without them," the old woman responds. "They're one of my best customers. Every day or so, they buy fifty to sixty eggs from me!"

"Then you must have seen the young lady. A pretty girl, is she?"

"No doubt she's a fine lady. But how I wish she'd dress her hair in a nice old-fashioned hairdo."

"That young lady and our Mr. Yamanaka . . ." Okiyo begins.

"You mean the fine gentleman who's staying here?"

"Oh yes, she's crazy about him."

"Well, is that why you said the other day that your mistress was acting strangely?"

"Indeed, she was acting strangely," Okiyo reflects. "In the evening—the day before yesterday—my mistress and Mr. Yamanaka went out to the theater. Close to one o'clock in the morning, they still had not come home. I was nodding off in my seat when finally I heard the sound of a rickshaw. When I jumped up to open the lattice door, I found them climbing out of the same rickshaw—and just as drunk as fish. Mr. Yamanaka, being a good-looking man as you say, and sugar-tongued as well, who wouldn't be tempted! Rascal though he may be, I can't help feeling sorry for him.

"His father was a second lieutenant in Saigō's army, and he died in battle. The year after that, his mother fell sick, and she died, too, leaving him without a soul in the world to rely on. The master of the house was still living then. He took pity on Mr. Yamanaka and had him help in the business. Just before he died, the master asked Mr. Shinohara to help Mr.

Yamanaka find a position in the new government. He can manage some English, and, being sugar-tongued and clever, it wasn't long before he began to rise up in the ranks. Now he's earning a salary of twenty-five yen![11] He is such a clever man, and my mistress, having been a fallen woman before she married my late master anyway, can hardly abide the chaste life of a widow. Oh, there's someone at the door!" Okiyo looks up quickly.

"All right. I'll be back for your order next time, if you please."

The old egg seller leaves. Okiyo peeks out the front door, and, just as she starts to head up the stairs, Osada, her mistress, makes her way down. "Who is it?"

"The young lady who called earlier," Okiyo replies.

"Well, show her upstairs. You need to be where you can hear should they call for anything. Stay in the next room, will you?"

Taking off her sleeve ties, Okiyo hurries after her. "What a strange eavesdropper I've become."

"What?" Osada asks irritably. "What's that you said about an eye-dropper?"

"What? No, I just said that's a strange place for me to leave my eye-dropper! Oh, there they are calling again at the front door. Can't you hear? I'm comiiiing!"

" 'Done up prettily, it invites scorn, the widow's hair.' " A passerby hums the cynical lyric. Indeed, a widow's behavior is sternly watched. According to the customs of the past, when a husband died, his widow—not wishing the world to think she'd been insincere in her vows to be as constant as the everlasting pine—hastily whacked off her trailing tresses with quick resolution. But then, as the days wore on, and her hair began to grow, did she not imagine fashioning a hairpiece from her former locks? Of course, an elaborate coiffure would by now be out of the question, would it not, but who could criticize her for a modern-style bun or a coiled chignon secured with a comb? Surely she could not avoid a tinge of regret—wishing she could but knowing she shouldn't. Knowing she shouldn't but wishing she could. . . . How much better it should be if widows were allowed to flower again and formally remarry. In the countries of the Occident, they say, women are not ashamed to remarry openly. Why should widows here have to suffer? Wishing to be thought as constant as the pine, they struggle to conceal their desires until one day a man comes along, and in secret they live together. These widows are like hardwood trees masquerading as evergreens. In no time at all, their brown branches are green, swathed tight in the parasitic growth of ivy vines—thus they counterfeit the name of chastity without truly retaining their color. But when their cheeks begin to glow like the scarlet leaves in autumn, how shameful it appears!

Part 3

Lofty, the towering mansion soars above the clouds. Imposing are the columns of the iron gate at the center of the surrounding brick wall. Without a doubt, this is the residence of a man of distinction. He is a count, they say, a former samurai from one of the southwest domains. In the years leading up to the Restoration, he served with an honor that far surpassed all others, and so, gracing the nameplate alongside his gate, is the designation "Noble of the Third Rank, " in black letters for all to see. It has recently been so affixed. And yet it wasn't so long ago that he was among those who advocated "Revere the Emperor" and preached "Expel the Barbarians." While in the midst of campaigns that took him hither and yon, he openly denounced the West and all its sundry countries. He despised their peoples as wretched fiends and reviled them as crafty villains.

He refused to change his tune, even after the advent of this new enlightened age. And so friends of his from his home domain, who now hold influential positions in the cabinet, decided it was time he, too, finally followed the trend of the times. With their encouragement, he traveled to the West under the auspices of a government appointment, and, while touring the countries there, he awoke to the error of his ways. When his yearlong sojourn in Europe concluded, and he returned to Japan, he was completely transformed into an advocate of the West. Believing native foods to endanger one's health, he now insists on Western meals. His house is built of stone with windows of glass. His clothes are fashioned of wool with sleeves as straight and tight as pipes. His maids and menservants are not allowed to dress in native garb but must wear Western-style garments. Indeed, in all matters great and small he adheres to the customs of the West. This is the father of Miss Hamako Shinohara—who appeared in part 1 of our story. His name is Michikata. He is fifty years old. He has no son—only this daughter, Hamako, on whom he dotes; he sees to her education himself. In all things, if it is Western, it must therefore be good. Having been instructed that young ladies in the West give themselves over to socializing, he has seen that Hamako busies herself with a smattering of this and a snippet of that—afternoons at the theater, evenings at soirees and dance parties. And as for schooling, she concentrates on two subjects only: *le piano* and *le violon*.

In any other family, the mother would be responsible for her daughter's training in household matters. But not in this case. Mrs. Shinohara is countrybred and unaccustomed to reading and writing. Hamako despises her. Should she ever try to counsel Hamako on this or that, her daughter refuses to listen, retorting that she has nothing to learn from an uneducated woman. And so it is that in the Shinohara family, Hamako rules the roost.

SENIOR MAID: Ohhh, what are you doing! The young mistress has not yet returned home. You've got no business sleeping!

JUNIOR MAID: Why? It's already past midnight, is it not? Even men don't stay out so late. And how many nights is it now?

SENIOR MAID: Are you going to start that again? If the master hears you, you'll be in for a scolding. In that place they call the West, having parties that last until the break of day is a regular event, it seems, and the young ladies don't get up before eleven or twelve in the morning. It's the way they do things, he's told you. He wants Japan to hurry up and do the same.

JUNIOR MAID: Well, if every household here did the same, it would be just fine with me. We could sleep all day for all I care. But the neighbors next door and those across the street get up in the morning, and we've got to, too. I'm always sleepy!

SENIOR MAID: Yes, I know. But we're not the only ones to suffer. The mistress is certainly unhappy with this Western style. Once she told me she was desperate for Japanese pickles with her meal, and I gave her some. But the houseboy must have overheard, because he ran around telling everyone she was cuckolding the master with Priest Pickle[12] as her paramour! Ha, ha, ha! But back to the young mistress … once she comes home, she won't go straight to bed. First, she has to go on and on about who she saw and what they said, and she always ends up turning the conversation to Mr. Yamanaka and making me listen to her latest romantic adventures. It's more than I can bear!

JUNIOR MAID: And to think of the young master off on his travels. He's to be the young mistress's husband, is he not? The master arranged it long ago. And there she goes carrying on like that!

SENIOR MAID: That's *enlightenment*, you dunce! You mustn't cling to your old-fashioned ideas. There is nothing the least bit harmful in a man and woman associating with one another. That's the only way to advance, or so the master always says.

From the window below they hear the horse carriage clatter to a stop and the sound of the groom as he calls out: "Welcome home, Young Mistress!"

Part 4

The sound of high-pegged wooden clogs clatters through the streets from Kudanzaka toward Horiden. The schoolboys wearing them must be on their way home from their lessons. There are two or three of them, each just fifteen years old or so. One carries a white canvas satchel tucked under his arm, on his head a woolen, hand-knitted beret. Although he does not appear to be of particularly humble origins, compared to the other lads he is a tad shabby. The padded jacket he wears, of common fabric, is a bit too gaudy and is soiled here and there. As is plain to see by the seams along the shoulders, the garment has seen considerable use.

△ : Today's *leçon* was certainly *difficile*!

□ : Not for me. Yesterday I had my *frère* go over the readings with me so I found it *très facile*.

○ : Me, too, I asked my father to help me. But, Ashio, you don't have anyone to go over the lessons with you, do you? You have to get everything from the lectures. All things considered, it is quite a feat for you to be so successful on the exams.

□ : Ashio, since it's just you and your older sister, don't you worry about the monthly tuition? Where does the money come from?

○: I can tell you that! Ashio's older sister is wonderfully resourceful. Just the other day, my father went to Ichiban-chō to see Mr. Miyazaki, who told my father that a young woman named Hideko rented one of his tenements. She was putting her younger brother through school, he said, by selling her knitting. And even though she has government bonds to fall back on, she never touches them.

□: Really! Is that true, Ashio?

ASHIO: How would I know?

○: Are you going home already? Well, I'll stop by for you tomorrow.

ASHIO: Suit yourself.

○ □: *Adieu!*

○ □: That's strange. Why do you think that rascal's trying to hide it?

Leaving their chatter behind, Ashio sets off up the hill with a vexed expression, grumbling to himself as he goes. Racing to Sanchōme-ya, he roughly rattles the lattice door open and thumps up stairs.

"Ashio, is that you?" his sister calls out. "You certainly are late today. I'm fixing rice to honor our mother's death anniversary. If you're hungry I'll fix you a nice rice ball."

"I don't want anything," Ashio says as he flings down his hat and lunch box.

"Oh dear, I almost forgot. As soon as I finish knitting this shawl I have to take it to the yarn shop in Kōjimachi. So please pull your desk out, and let's get to work on your lessons. Tell me what you learned today."

"You're right. . . ." Ashio softens. "Next month marks the third-year anniversary of our father's passing. You must want to get some extra money together so you can set out special gifts."

"Well, during his lifetime he enjoyed a status that entitled him to gifts from his acquaintances."

Within three years after they had left their country province and moved to the city, Hideko and Ashio's parents had died one right after the other. "We still have distant relatives back in the country, and we could always return," Hideko reminds her brother. "But if we did, both you and I would remain unschooled and illiterate. I'll do whatever I can to ensure that you make something of yourself here in Tokyo. And that means you have to study hard! That Mr. Miyazaki has been very supportive. He's generously lowered the house rent, and so I'd like you to take him some of the sweet rice cakes I've made for Mother's death anniversary."

"Hideko, how many savings bonds do we have?"

"Let's see . . . there are around fifteen hundred yen's worth. When Mother passed away, I used quite a bit on her memorial service. There's still a considerable sum left, and we need to leave it as it is for the time being. It will be an important resource to help both you and me get settled one day."

"But, Hideko, I'll soon be heading to university on a government tuition program. That's just three years from now. Why don't we take the money and use it so you can go to school, too? Wouldn't it be so much better if the two of us were both able to study?"

"Ashio, if we used all the money up now, then all that our father worked so hard to save would disappear, just like foam upon the water. Working at home the way I do, I can save from three to five sen every month. I tuck it away in our postal savings account. I have nearly two yen fifty sen saved up now, so if there's anything you want, I'll buy it for you out of that."

"There's nothing in the world that I want but for you to go to school, Hideko. You enjoy learning. And for you to have to spend every day, all day long, with your knitting makes me feel sorry for you."

"Nonsense," Hideko countered. "If you go to school and work hard at your studies and teach me what you've learned when you get home, then it's the same as if I went to school, too. Besides, if you feel sorry for me, then do your best to become an upstanding man as quickly as you can. With your present academic skills, surely you'll be able to enter university. The other day when I called on Mr. Miyazaki, he told me he had earned his bachelor of arts degree and was now an assistant instructor at the university. I told him about your aspirations and asked for his help."

"Ahh, this is such agony I don't think I can stand it!"

"Ashio, what on earth? You're such a little fussbudget; you get upset over the silliest things! What is it this time?"

"It's just that I seem such a sissy to pursue my studies with money my elder sister makes on her knitting. Sponging off one's sister is really unbearable. It wouldn't matter if I were relying on my parents—like all the other fellows do."

"Indeed, no one is as important as one's parents. Because ours are deceased, we can't perform filial acts for them, no matter how we try. Now, stop your complaining and go burn incense for them at the memorial altar. Oh, what a strange one you are to be giving way to tears about this. That kind of shortsightedness is uncalled for. Isn't that what we find in the *Essays in Idleness?* 'When the activity of the mind is constricted and rigid, a man will come into collision with things at every turn and be harmed by disputes.'[13] Isn't that what it says? A person who faces adversity bravely will have a future. Now, enough of your crying face!"

For a maiden still just seventeen, her face glows with a startling wisdom. But just the thought of her late parents and her brother's tangled feelings makes her sleeves grow moist. She turns her face this way and that to hide the tears.

"Tofu! Any tofu today?"

"Sister, the tofu seller's here," Ashio calls to Hideko.

"Tofu!"

"Sister, didn't you hear? The tofu seller . . ."

"I heard." Slowly dabbing her eyes, Hideko looks up. "None today, thank you."

Part 5

"Hello! Anyone home?"

"Oh, hello, Ashio." Mrs. Miyazaki greets the boy as she opens the door. "What a pleasant surprise, do come in. Ichirō is home today, and Mr. Saitō has also dropped in." A year beyond her sixtieth birthday, the old woman has her hair cropped short in a widow's style. Her plump cheeks lending her face a jolly air, Ichirō Miyazaki's mother is the owner of the tenement that Ashio and his older sister rent.

Ashio steps up quickly into the house and greets both Miyazaki and Saitō. Then, he turns again to the old woman. "Today marks the third year of my mother's death. We've put together sweet rice and bean jam cakes to commemorate the occasion. My elder sister made them herself, so I can't promise they're very good, but I've brought some by for you."

He hands her the tiered box of treats that he'd been carrying, wrapped in crepe cloth.

"Well, is it already the third-year observance?" the old lady asks. "My, my, how time flies. But just look at these cakes, Ichirō! Don't they look delicious?"

"Ashio," Miyazaki turns to the boy. "I hear you're really distinguishing yourself at school. Just now Saitō was remarking on your swift climb through the grades and praising you as a child prodigy."

Saitō is a teacher at the school Ashio attends.

"There can be no doubt that your late father's spirit is rejoicing from the grave," Mrs. Miyazaki adds. "Listen here, Mr. Saitō, this boy's older sister is quite praiseworthy. Their father left them his life savings in bonds that to this day draw at least eight or nine yen per month in interest. But reluctant to dip into this for fear of using it up, she takes in orders for knitted goods, cooks the daily meals, and pays this boy's monthly tuition, all with the money she . . ."

"Auntie, that's not true! She doesn't . . ." Ashio begins to protest.

"Ashio, are you trying to hide the fact that your sister takes in piecework at home?" Miyazaki cuts him short. "There's nothing to be ashamed of! You should be proud. People must eat by their own labors. Your sister is laudable. At least we are certainly praising her in this household, aren't we, Saitō?"

"She is laudable indeed."

"And that's not the half of it," Miyazaki's mother continues. "Because she can't go to school herself, she has Ashio copy out the lessons he's just learned the minute he gets home from school. And with her quick nature, she picks it up so fast, she's still able to help her younger brother with his lessons. Isn't that so, Ashio?"

"Well, yes, that's true. My success is all due to my sister."

"Really? Ashio, Saitō here tells me that you are much better at literature than most students your age. Well, you could say then that it's all on account of your sister."

"Yes, when my late father was alive, my sister went to the Shimoda Utako Academy all year round. She studied Japanese poetry and read books all the time. She passed what she learned along to me."

"I see. What about English?"

"Well, we've read through the fourth reader in the world history series."

"That's certainly impressive," Saitō chimes in. "No wonder you're such a child prodigy! My own specialty is chemistry, so I haven't had a chance to have Ashio in my class yet."

"Oh yes, but I've heard a great deal about you, Professor Saitō!"

"Well, if you're such a bright student, you'll become a government bureaucrat in no time!" Mrs. Miyazaki beams.

"Mother, you shouldn't say such things to a boy. You sow the seeds of misjudgment," Miyazaki chides. "Ashio, you do not go to school just to become a bureaucrat and draw a salary. You do so to become a man who can contribute to society. Students who graduate from the political science and law courses of the university become bureaucrats, but even so there are many among them whose scholarship pales in comparison to those who have graduated in literature or engineering. Don't you agree, Saitō? Well, as they say, the miller only draws water to his own mill. And that is why, Ashio, you should get the idea of becoming a bureaucrat out of your head and set your heart instead on doing something to benefit the world."

"Mention of bureaucrats reminds me of Yamanaka. How are things with him?" Saitō asks. "These days I hear he has an influential position with the government and is really flying up the ranks. But what a worthless fool he is—a panderer to the trends of the day. If you were to analyze the difference between him and us scientifically, then he is a mixture of seventy percent sophistry and thirty percent sycophancy! Ha, ha, ha!"

"And when you consider that his salary is over twice what you make, there really is no honor in being a bureaucrat!"

"Yes. These days, I hear, he's been turning up at just about every social event imaginable. And he even swaggers in the presence of the most senior officials."

"I hear he's been enjoying unprecedented attention from Miss Shinohara, who's been dragging him all around the city."

"I don't know if it's true or not, but I've heard the most outlandish stories."

"Well, don't believe everything you hear. He's a handsome man, and she's a spirited young woman—they're bound to raise eyebrows. But I am sure it is just idle gossip. Besides, it is clear he is fawning on her for his own advancement. But, come to mention it, didn't you get a second posting at the School for Women she attends, Saitō? I hear she's withdrawn from classes."

"She's withdrawn. All in all, her strongest subject was *le piano*. In everything else, her abilities were limited to superficial polish. I have no idea what will become of her next year at graduation. It's fine by me if she withdraws. She's at least continued her English, and Yamanaka sees to her lessons with great attention. I hear she's not half bad now. Of course, she has her father to thank for the arrangements. Because she socializes without any thought for decency, she's been the favorite target of school gossip. There's really no promising student in that school, anyway. Of course, Namiko attends the private academy."

"Yes, that's right. My younger sister is there as well, and she's constantly enjoying Namiko's kindness. I'm impressed by her maturity and generosity."

"Well, I'll be going," Ashio stands to leave.

"Oh, so soon?" Mrs. Miyazaki asks. "Please give my regards to your sister."

Part 6

Wedged into the Japanese-style alcove, beside the bedding closet, are a bookcase and bureau, bearing traces here and there of ink spills. A tin washbasin—with several towels folded neatly inside it—sits in front of the chest of drawers. Scattered alongside the basin are two or three long-handled combs and a wide-toothed one. Otherwise, the room is neat and tidy, with nothing out of place.

A student sits before the window holding a package the maid has just delivered. Running her fingers busily through her bangs, she tousles them haphazardly over the lovely widow's peak at her hairline. Her brow slightly furrowed—perhaps in imitation of Seishi, the frowning Chinese beauty—she gazes distractedly at the letter in her lap, forming the words with her lips as she reads. Just as she does so, another student enters the room.

TOMOKO:[14] Namiko, aren't you going home?

NAMIKO: No, I received this letter from my parents today telling me not to.

TOMOKO: Excellent! It'll be so much livelier in the dormitory with you here. If you happen to have an English-Japanese dictionary, may I borrow it, please?

NAMIKO: Here you are. And I just received these treats, won't you help yourself?

TOMOKO: Thanks! I'll call Matsuko Saitō.

She stands in the doorway calling, "Matsuko!"

MATSUKO: Whaat? Ohh, I'm so terribly sleepy today. Why, I was so
tired I fell asleep during the eight o'clock evening lecture last night,
and Shinako had to shake me awake. I came back to my room in a daze
and crawled into bed without even changing clothes! Ohhh.

Letting out a big yawn, she steps into the room, leaving the sliding
door agape despite her attempt to close it.

TOMOKO: Why, Miss Saitō! You must have been raised in a barn!
MATSUKO: Not I. I merely thought it too stuffy in here and am releasing
some of your "hot air," Miss Miyazaki!
TOMOKO: Well, you're never at a loss for words!
MATSUKO: My mouth may not want for words, but my stomach wants
for food! I'm starving. I'll take one of those treats.
TOMOKO: That's why I called you!
MATSUKO: You deigned to call; I deign to dine. Now, where is it?
Here? You received this from home? Well, let's have a look. Oh my,
castella sponge cake from the Fugetsudo¯ Confectionery, a packet of
peanuts—I'd say these must have cost at least five sen—and what
have we here inside this lacquered box? Ooh, all kinds of delica-
cies and white fish, too. A homemade specialty, no doubt, from the
kitchen of the Honorable Mr. Councilor's elegant wife. How kind of
your mother to have sent this to you, Nami. "Truly a parent's love is
deeper than the sea!"
TOMOKO: Matsuko! While you're jabbering away, I'll just help myself
to it all!
MATSUKO: Oh, I just remembered. Last night, I had the most peculiar dream. That darling Kabuki star, Fuku-chan, had turned into a
real woman and was engaged to marry my older brother. But I said,
"What are you thinking? You're really a man, and you're supposed
to marry me!" And then my brother was relieved because he's been
madly in love with a certain Miss Namiko Hattori ever since he laid
eyes on her at the New Year's Ball. "Too bad for you, Fuku-chan," I
said, and he grew quite angry!

TOMOKO: Here, Matsuko, this should shut you up!

She divides the sponge cake into pieces with a penknife.

MATSUKO: *Many, many thank yous. How you are kind.*

And snatching up a piece of cake, she continues, "And then, Miss Miyazaki . . ."

TOMOKO: Enough, now! You're such a free spirit, you don't care, but the rest of us . . . Anyway, enough, please!

MATSUKO: As you wish. My humblest apologies. Shinako will want to join us. I'll just be off to look for her.

And off she goes with a mouth full of cake.

TOMOKO: My, she certainly is a person of *mouvement rapide*!

NAMIKO: Well, she really resembles her brother . . . and is just as talented, too! There are any number of people like her these days.

TOMOKO: True. But I really dislike that cheeky friend of yours. The one who is always putting on airs. If she scores poorly on her composition assignment, she'll make a big to-do about how busy she's been. And she's so mad about the West that she's always going on about how the foreign residents here do this or that. It's almost more than I can stand!

When was it? The other day I memorized your composition. The one that went like this: "Misguided indeed are those who select from the teachings of the sages only what suits their own interests. And when a little ditty lodges itself in one's heart, who's to say it, too, is not instructive? Truly, if the ground where one plants a seed is not fertile, nothing will grow. If there is no one to hear, then whatever one says will go unheard." I hadn't told you that I so liked your composition I have made it a motto for myself.

NAMIKO: What a good memory you have. I'd forgotten all about it. But speaking of Hamako, her elder brother returned to Tokyo yesterday.

TOMOKO: Oh, isn't he her "H"?[15]

NAMIKO: Well, yes, he will be. But they're just engaged right now. Anyway, Hamako still refers to him as her elder brother.

TOMOKO: Can she really expect to marry—I mean, after the way she has misbehaved?

NAMIKO: How can you say such a thing? They are both very educated people. They haven't done anything untoward. You've been listening to gossip. All of us are now doing what we can so as not to be overlooked by the civilized nations. We apply ourselves tirelessly to those soirees. Of course, you and I have no idea what it is really like in the West. But to judge something as wrong simply because we do not understand it is absolutely offensive.

Whenever something is just the least bit different, people blow it all out of proportion. And when it comes to people who know nothing about the subject anyway, they invent the most incredible gossip, which they then pass along to everyone they know. Truly, there is nothing more terrifying than an unleashed tongue! I know it's not right to stay all cooped up with my thoughts as I do, but if it were all the same, that's what I'd do. I'd like to stay right here with all of you for as long as I could!

TOMOKO: Oh, so would I! I feel exactly as you do, Namiko!

Just at that moment Matsuko bounds back into the room with Miss Shinako Aizawa in tow.

SHINAKO: Ohhh, poor me!

TOMOKO: Whatever is the matter??

SHINAKO: This Matsuko is what's the matter! She snatched away the sweet potato that Miss Nishimura had given me—and just as I was planning to eat it. Here she came and stole it for herself! What a horrid person!

MATSUKO: But I was sent to tell you about the sponge cake!

SHINAKO: Really? Is there sponge cake to be had here? Well, then you can have my potato!

TOMOKO: Oh? So you're going to barter, are you?

SHINAKO: But I see no proof of your treasures! Matsuko, you must be a *menteuse*.

MATSUKO: Not I. It's not polite to call others "liars"!

TOMOKO: Let's get back to the reason we're all here! Please, help yourselves.

The girls eat with smacking sounds and then . . .

SHINAKO: Oh dear, if we're not careful, we'll eat it all up!

MATSUKO: Not to despair. Namiko will go home tomorrow. So what does it hurt to finish it off now?

NAMIKO: Yes. Please, eat it all. But I want to go over tomorrow's lessons, so if you'll excuse me . . .

SHINAKO: Namiko, do you have to? It's a holiday. It'll be all right to let it go just this once, won't it?

TOMOKO: Really, Namiko, if you study too much you'll damage your health.

MATSUKO: As for me, I never know a day of rest!

SHINAKO: I worry myself sick before an examination. For the last one, I was up until two o'clock in the morning studying, and even so I got a low score. It's not fair!

TOMOKO: But you're still impressive, Shinako.

NAMIKO: Female students are just not as relaxed about their studies as males. They rarely skip classes. And even if they are not encouraged to study hard, they do. They study according to their own abilities. But, of late, education for women has been so overemphasized that it is becoming a great problem. If women push themselves to such extremes in their studies, as Shinako does, they weaken their mental health and, as a result, will produce weak children.

SHINAKO: What a very silly thing to say. I have no intention of marrying!

TOMOKO: Don't say that, Shinako. It's better to marry—even if you do become a teacher.

SHINAKO: Impossible! What teacher would bend her knee to serve and wait on a man?

NAMIKO: Now, you see, that is why scholars of late are saying that women should not be given an education. They argue that it is better to keep women ignorant and unlettered because, if you give a girl even a smattering of learning, she'll become a teacher, and then she'll have no man as her master. Our nation will not propagate as a result, and so, they conclude, educating women is unpatriotic. I have heard that in the fifth and sixth years of Meiji [1872–1873] women behaved in an altogether outrageous manner. They strutted about in high-waisted *hakama*, their shoulders squared, spouting the most self-righteous nonsense. It must have been absolutely scandalous. I think things have improved considerably now, but then, when I hear how women are still treated with an absurd degree of respect in the West, I fear we may revert to our earlier behavior once again. Women today are faced with great responsibility.

Shakespeare writes of aggressive women and feminine men. Things aren't that different for us nowadays. Disagreeable, if you ask me! They say that Napoleon carried out his reform of France on account of his noble mother. Certainly, if women are not given an education, it is very unlikely that they will become noble mothers like her. But, when they are educated, they turn into offensive shrews. No, a certain person has said that a woman should select one subject and study it thoroughly, but in such a way that she avoids becoming overly proud. She must continue to respect modest feminine virtue if she is to produce brilliant children and grandchildren. In this way, she can create a new nation that can stand proudly among all the other civilized nations of the world.

MATSUKO: Oh, I do not agree at all, Namiko! Every time I hear these arguments, I feel terribly annoyed. No matter how hard a woman studies, once she marries, she finds it much too demanding to work outside the home as well. Not me. I shall remain single and become an artist. A painter. When it comes to the arts, all stem from paint-ing—all except maybe song and dance and composition. Painting is the "king" of art. Or perhaps I should use the *féminin* here? It is the "queen" of art. I shall definitely become a painter.

TOMOKO: Well, that's just like you, Matsuko, to aspire to something as fussy as painting!

NAMIKO: But Matsuko is the type to devote herself heart and soul to her endeavors. I'm sure she'll succeed.

SHINAKO: Well, you know, I'm devoted, too! The other day, I earned a high score on my science exam. So, I plan to become a scientist. What about you, Miss Miyazaki?

TOMOKO: When I graduate from school, I plan to marry and become a wife. You do, too, don't you, Nami?

NAMIKO: Well, let's see. I enjoy literature, so I think I'll marry a writer, and the two of us can go into business together.

MATSUKO: Well, won't that be a pretty picture! I'm absolutely, posi-tively certain I do not want a husband.

TOMOKO: Nami is going to marry my elder brother, Ichirō. And I think it is just wonderful!

"Hear! Hear!"

Still just innocent girls, they are unable to fathom the emotions of another with their maidens' hearts. Although only teasing, have they not inadvertently said something to hurt her feelings?

And so we come to the end of this scene.

"Clack, clack," the clappers clatter, sounding the lunch hour. "Let's go!" And with a pitter patter, they scramble out the door.

Part 7

Day and night the two-man hand-pulled carriages pass in and out of the gate. Without interruption, the houseboys and rickshaw delivery men scurry back and forth with boxes of Fugetsudō confections and baskets of fish. Inside, the house teems with activity. Must this not be the estate of Count Shinohara? His illness has not responded well to treatment, and *le docteur* shakes his head in exasperation. Visitors come and go, paying their respects. Into this chaos, Tsutomu, Count Shinohara's adopted heir, returns from his studies abroad. But just as the houseboy declares, "I'm so busy, I can't stand it!" as he relays messages here and there, the count's condition improves slightly. Throughout the household, high and low heave a sigh of relief. In no time at all, even Osan, the scullery maid, can be heard laughing.

As usual, Yamanaka stops in on the pretext of visiting the ailing count, but he takes the opportunity to duck into Hamako's room, where they engage in eager conversation. Tsutomu, who has felt somehow out of sorts ever since his return, is fretful and unable to relax. Sitting at his desk, his nerves on edge, he grows so utterly distracted that he begins to give in to delusions. A brisk walk would do him good, he knows, but he feels he should stay close while his foster father convalesces. He is not free to come and go as he pleases. In the meantime, he must endure the peals of laughter that burst intermittently from Hamako's room. It is enough to make him explode with anger! Glaring at the ceiling, he bites back bitter words and with a scowl curses his raging nerves. From time to time, he feels as if an evil apparition has materialized before his eyes. But just as it seems ready to pounce, a beautiful maiden is suddenly standing at his side. The visions come and go in an endless series of variations. So lost in thought, he can hardly discern his dreams from reality. Finally, in the hopes of finding some diversion to clear his head—if only for a while—he rises deliberately to his feet and slides open the *shōji* door, yawning twice, then thrice, as he steps down into the garden.

He walks aimlessly among the flower beds, careful to avoid Hamako's room. Strolling leisurely to the front of the estate, he comes across the carriage house, where he hears muffled voices and hushed laughter. The voices of the common people, so unfamiliar to him after his years in Europe, strike him as curious, and he stops to listen. The large hunting dog, knowing its master's step, runs out to greet him, head lowered and tail wagging. Commanding him to silence with a glance, Tsutomu kneels down alongside the beast and strokes its head while he listens.

RICKSHAW PULLER: Hey, the other day I got caught up in some really bad business!

GROOM: Why? What happened?

RICKSHAW PULLER: What happened? Well, I'll tell you what happened! That cheeky mistress of yours had me take her over to the widow's house. That's where Yamanaka—the fellow who's with her now—stays, you know. She invited him to slip off with her to Mukōjima. At first I thought it was all aboveboard. I'd heard the gossip about the widow and Yamanaka, so I never suspected he'd be running off with your mistress, too! What with blossom viewing being over and all, the streets weren't crowded. Before I knew it, that rascal Yamanaka leapt out of my rickshaw and into hers, and one, two, forget you! Off they went with the hood down tight. I ought to have gone on home, you know, with nobody to haul around after that. But try talking sense to the upper crust these days—you'd be better off reasoning with a bawling kid. So there I was tagging along behind them and feeling plenty stupid, let me tell you. They got out at the Uehan Japanese Restaurant, where they stayed for lunch and then some, I imagine. After all that, I figured I'd get at least a one yen piece. But here she came after a bit, as clever as you please, and handed me fifty sen. Not but half a yen—like I wasn't worth the whole effort—and with all I'd put up with. I was so mad, I couldn't stand it!

GROOM: Going to an old-fashioned Japanese restaurant, huh? That explains why she set out in kimono the other day—which she never does.

RICKSHAW PULLER: So does her feller know?

GROOM: Not a chance of that. We've been paid right and left to keep our mouths shut! It's a secret.

They speak with lowered voices, but when they see their ride approach, their voices suddenly grow louder. Tsutomu rises to his feet. Listening to their accounts has made him feel as though a lightning bolt had struck him between the eyes again and again. He is overcome with a desire to rush away, but he thinks the better of it and resumes his post.

GROOM: When you think about it, I suppose it isn't so strange. We cart these people off to fine establishments all the time. What do you think they're doing there?!

RICKSHAW PULLER: I suppose that's how it's done in the West.

GROOM: What? We're still not civilized, are we?! And here we've got our geisha trading in their long trailing sashes for those bustles that stick out behind them like the proud tail end of a bantam rooster! Times are a-changin', I'll give you that much. The other day, that big-mouthed son-of-a-gun said a good one. He said that we're now in a pleasure-seeking era. Flirting with ladies is the way in the West. Keeping a concubine's a thing of the past. Either way, you gotta have cash! With not so much as a sen between the two of us, looks like we're not going to be seeking pleasure anytime soon, huh? Ha, ha, ha!

As they indulge in their silly chatter, a cry rings out from the kitchen. "Mr. Yamanaka is ready to leave!"

Tsutomu beats a hasty retreat. His heart may be heavy, but his footsteps are light as he tiptoes back toward the garden.

Part 8

The sixth month, the Waterless Month, is so hot that metal coins would melt. A man of twenty-four or -five steps up to the lantern-festooned doorway of the pleasure-boat stand. His nose is straight, his skin fair, and his eyes, though not particularly notable, flash from time to time with a brilliance not unlike that of a bolt of lightning illuminating the stony recesses of a cave. It is true that his mouth is rather too small. But the defect is concealed by his neat moustache, which is in the shape of an inverted v. He stands taller than most men. His striped, light flannel suit, of matching jacket and trousers, is tailor-made. He carries a slender walking stick and sports a jaunty panama hat but has come equipped with a black umbrella, just in case.

"My, my, if it isn't the young master of Surugadai!" the woman at the pleasure-boat stall exclaims. "Such a long time it's been! Mr. Miyazaki let us know not long ago that you'd returned. Welcome home."

"I've been home now for about ten days," Tsutomu answers. "It being so hot today, I promised Miyazaki I'd join him for a cool breeze, and here I am. I'd like to engage one of your pleasure boats, if I may."

"And will you be needing some sake, sir?" she asks. "Some treats as well?"

"Three bottles of Stock will do and enough snacks for three.[16] We'll be stopping along the way and so don't need much."

As he says this, Miyazaki and Saitō appear.

"And we were hoping to arrive ahead of you!" Saitō says disappointedly.

The boat is now ready, and they step aboard.

"Five years is a long time," Miyazaki begins, "but now that you're home, it seems to have elapsed in the blink of an eye. I'm sure you have a lot of stories to tell us of your travels in Europe. And, knowing you, numerous accounts of the latest scientific discoveries as well. I've wanted to call on you and ask about your trip, but knowing that your father is ill and your household in turmoil, I've resisted adding to your burdens. I'm sorry to have waited so long to contact you."

"The same goes for me," Saitō chimes in. "How are things these days?"

"I've been hoping to meet with you—my old friends—and indulge in leisurely conversations. But my father's illness has kept me at home. Things have not gone as I'd expected. But over the last few days he's improved considerably, so I decided to invite you out."

"Tsutomu, you were kind enough to send me books while you were overseas, but being a poor correspondent myself, I only managed to send one response for every three letters I received from you," Miyazaki notes apologetically. "I tried to keep you current on events in Tokyo and wrote with the detail of a newspaper reporter. Each letter I sent invited criticism from you over the silly way we Japanese imitate anything and everything Western so obsessively you'd think we'd been hypnotized! Your pet theory on the matter struck me as quite ironic. Most people who travel to Europe become enamored of the West. You, instead, became disgusted! Your friends found this very odd."

"I guess it is strange when you stop to think of it," Tsutomu agrees. "I was in Europe for five years. It may seem an exaggeration, but all I learned during that time was what fools we Japanese are to invest so much in copying." Noticing that their ice has melted, he turns to the boat steward. "Say! Dock somewhere and pick us up a block or two of ice, will you?"

"By the bye, Tsutomu, ever since your return, we've been looking forward to your nuptials! But I suppose they've been put on hold until your father recovers."

"That's right," Saitō agrees. "I envy you your luck, Tsutomu. Your father's been promoted to the peerage on account of his past meritorious service. And your *mademoiselle* is smart as well as pretty. Of late, her English-language skills have improved, and she's accomplished at the piano! Moreover, she holds her own quite admirably at those dance soirees. In truth, you and she are a perfect pair, or so all your friends conclude."

"I suppose it must seem that way," Tsutomu says as he looks at his friends. "But it brings me no great joy to hear it. I'm troubled by this engagement. Since it's the two of you, I'll disclose my secret. As you both know, the Shinoharas have raised me since I was a boy of five or six, and it has been their desire that I marry their daughter and succeed to the family name. They've been most generous, even spending a small fortune on sending me to Europe for my studies. To turn around now and say that I despise their daughter would be unconscionable. And, if I backed out and walked away, I would seem the most ungrateful fellow alive. And so I've been wrestling with this problem. Here I am at a crossroads in my life. Fortunately for me, my father's illness has put the wedding on hold!"

"Well, this is quite unexpected," Saitō notes with surprise. "Your opinions have certainly changed since going to Europe. No, not just your opinions, I suppose. I guess there's just no accounting for taste, and here we've all been so jealous of your impending marriage. Wait, I know what you're up to! You made a pledge to a golden-haired beauty while you were in the West, which you so despise, and now you're awaiting her arrival!"

Tsutomu looks at his friend incredulously. "Don't be ridiculous. I did no such thing. I just don't want to go through with this marriage. I don't want to spend the rest of my life this way. But you're right about one thing. My opinions did change after I traveled to Europe. It was disillusioning to see up close everything that I had only imagined before from my readings. And it brought me to the conclusion that what humanity must rely on most is a proper sense of morality."

"Indeed," Saitō encourages him to continue.

"But when I got home, I found that my father was still as obsessed with the West as he had been before I left. All he could think to ask me about my five years abroad was, 'What kind of coiffure is fashionable now in Paris?' 'What kind of clothing?' I am interested in Western knowledge and technical skill. I have absolutely no interest in social customs. And I don't think this notion of men and women dancing together is altogether wholesome. It does have its purpose, I suppose, as a means for young people with a mind to marriage to meet one another. In this way, it is not unlike the midspring meeting in China. But neither custom is exempt from a sense of lewdness. Both are remnants of barbaric customs. And the requirement at these soirees that wives not dance with their own husbands is absurd. A married couple has pledged to be man and wife for a thousand generations. To see them dancing in one another's arms would be charming and sweet. But to require that they partner up with strangers is wretched. It is as if the world can find pleasure only in seeing a husband cuckolded.

"Moreover, these corsets women feel obliged to cinch about their waists with no thought to their health—all in an earnest effort to follow popular taste! In China, they bind feet to keep them small. What's the difference? . . . Once you start in on such things, there are a thousand examples. That is why I do not like the Western concept of morality. While I was sitting at my father's bedside the other day, he brought up the subject of Western customs. Before I knew it, I began my criticism of dance parties. He countered with the argument that they are a good way for young people to socialize. Not wishing to contradict a sick man,

I fell silent. And then Hamako piped in. 'Sending Tsutomu abroad has been to no avail at all,' she snorted with contempt. 'He still clings to such moldy old Chinese-inspired notions as the one that insists boys and girls be schooled separately from the age of seven.' That snort of hers cut me to the bone and left me sick with revulsion. At that moment, I knew that I could never marry her. But I owe my father too much to tell him that his daughter disgusts me! And so I have kept my secret. But my chest aches from the effort."

Saitō interjects, "Everyone agrees that she will make a fine wife for a bureaucrat. She's an able conversationalist, and even if she is a bit willful, it . . ."

"Well, you're right on that score. But the fact of the matter is I despise bureaucrats! They have absolutely nothing to offer the social good. I much prefer Benjamin Franklin to George Washington, after all. And you can't say Franklin was a bureaucrat. Certainly, Washington unfurled the banner of liberty in Boston and united the thirty some states.[17] And so he founded the United States of America, which now stands proud alongside its European counterparts. But the benefit of this endeavor is limited to one country. What did he give to the world? Franklin, on the other hand, discovered electricity, and as a result we can all now enjoy the telegraph and the electric light bulb. The benefits extend to hundreds of countries, and millions of people are the better for it. I can't think of another accomplishment that even comes close to rivaling this one. In our current era, I would choose de Lesseps over Otto von Bismarck. The latter tweaked France's nose and united the German empire under the authority of the king of his own home state of Prussia. Germany now leads the rest of Europe. But this benefits not the rest of the world. Ferdinand de Lesseps, on the other hand, dug the Suez Canal and opened a passage that has now made transport more convenient for the entire world! And when he has completed the Panama Canal, it will be truly wonderful, will it not? If the United States of America had never been created, it would not have made much difference to us in Japan. But how unfortunate we'd be without the telegram! And if the German states had never become an empire, Japan would not even have noticed. But without the Suez Canal, trade and transportation would be immeasurably inconvenienced. And the effect would not be limited to Japan but would be felt everywhere! And so I've come to the realization that becoming a bureaucrat is no great achievement."

Miyazaki nods in agreement.

"Therefore, I have no desire for a wife who is gifted in conversation. The wife I desire will not be unlettered and will naturally be endowed with wifely virtues. I should like her to be equipped with enough of an education so that she can acquit her duties efficiently. And I definitely don't want one of these combustible compounds known as a hussy, who is one part feistiness and the rest hot air! I would much prefer a wife who can knit to one who can dance! At least the former can earn enough money to assist with the family income."

"Family income!" Both Miyazaki and Saitō interject. "A member of the peerage doesn't need to be such a penny-pincher! Ha! Ha! Ha!"

They all laugh.

"Yoho!" The boat steward calls out. "Matsuya! We've reached Matsuya."

Clippety-clatter! The wooden *geta* sandals ring out along the bridge as the Matsuya waitresses run to prepare the tea.

"You're earlier than expected!" the proprietress calls out.

Part 9

Tsutomu Shinohara applied himself diligently to his studies at Cambridge University in England and succeeded brilliantly, earning a master of arts degree. On his way back to Japan, he took the time to travel throughout Europe, taking in the different countries. After a five-year sojourn, he has finally returned. While he was away, his foster father was promoted to the peerage, an unexpected honor that has brought the family immeasurable prestige. Among the many blessings to have graced the family in such abundance is the long-standing marriage contract between Tsutomu and Hamako.

Hamako's behavior of late has weighed heavily on Tsutomu's heart. Even while he was away, he had his suspicions. But now his feelings of misapprehension pile one upon the other. The conversation that he had accidentally overheard, the one between the groom and the rickshaw man, had caused his heart to shudder and shocked him to the very core. Now alert to Hamako's proclivities, he has begun to notice a wealth of other such misdeeds, and the seed of suspicion planted earlier has brought forth fruit. Hamako hardly bothers to attend her father's sickbed and takes every chance she can find to leave the house. Realizing he will never be able to accede to his foster father's wishes now, Tsutomu begins to consider more and more seriously the option of breaking ties with the family and moving out on his own. He has hinted to two or three of his closest friends about what is pressing on his heart. And yet he has been with Hamako since childhood. They have grown up together, comparing their heights at the well curb to see whose shoulders would outreach the other's. Hamako will not be easy to abandon. With her glossy black tresses and her flower-fresh face, with her delightful figure and her learning, talents, and intelligence, she is second to none. And yet hers is a beauty that does not appeal to Tsutomu. Even if he imagined their relationship might eventually deepen—as does the luster of a rough jewel that is slowly polished—he still could not muster any interest in the arrangement. But what of his obligation and duty to his foster parents, who have raised him since he was a boy? How can he justify disobeying them? And so he torments himself with his dilemma.

His foster father's condition is now so grave that everyone's attention is focused on his care. Michikata calls famous doctors to his side. He even engages Dr. Baelz,[18] who has recently arrived from Germany, to examine him. All apply themselves diligently to his treatment. He rallies slightly, and it seems the worst has passed. One day, Tsutomu slips out to enjoy the evening cool, but, by the time he returns, his foster father's health has faltered. Suddenly in a grave state, Michikata's life slips away the following day, and he heads off on a journey from which there is no return. Needless to say, Tsutomu and the others are filled with grief. Bereft of a fine man, who would not have felt regret?

Tsutomu succeeds to his father's name and estate, and, once the mourning period has passed, everyone from his foster mother to his relatives and friends begins to press him to move ahead with the marriage. With no further recourse, Tsutomu unburdens himself to his foster mother. Unable to refute the rumors, she insists that they are false nonetheless. By rights, Michikata's illustrious inheritance—his court title and his estate—belong to Tsutomu. But ever mindful of his debt to his foster father for raising him, Tsutomu bequeaths the assets of the estate to Hamako and sees to it that arrangements are begun for her to marry this Mr. Masashi Yamanaka. He sets them up in a house he has recently acquired—complete with an old man for a caretaker and maids

aplenty. He spares no expense on her provisions, and all who witness it
praise him for his generosity.

Once he has settled in with Hamako, Yamanaka becomes a million-
aire overnight, a fact he celebrates. But since he is an acquired husband,
Hamako is his lord and master. Even if she is talented and beautiful, he
finds no happiness with her and much prefers his earlier freeloader status
in the house of the widow Osada.

WOMAN: About our talk last night—now I understand your feelings.
And I finally feel reassured. But I had thought you'd tired of me because I was so old and had thrown me over for a fresh new treat! You
don't know how the thought tormented me.

MAN: Please understand, I got my job in government service through
the good offices of her father. Everything I have is thanks to him, so I
figured there was no harm in trying to curry favor with him. I worked
as hard as I could, and, while I was at it, I saw to his daughter's English lessons. And now you say I've offended you!?

WOMAN: You don't need to explain.

MAN: This isn't to my liking either, you know. But we need to stick to
the plan we hatched last night. We've come to the part where I have
to pretend to have nothing to do with you—just like the scene in *The
Subscription List* where Benkei pretends to be Yoshitsune's master and
gives him a good thrashing.[19]

WOMAN: Very well then, if that's how you feel, I'll reveal my true nature as the evil woman and play the role of Takahashi Oden! But
you'd better not change your mind. If you pull the rug out from under me, I'll look a fool!

MAN: It takes a cheat to know one! I suppose I'm now the one who's
being duped.

WOMAN: What a fine thing for you to say. Clearly, *I'm* the one who has
to watch out. Your wife's pretty, and we know you're a sucker for a
pretty face!

MAN: Don't be absurd.

WOMAN: So, are we square on this?

MAN: Of course. Now pay the gossips no heed.

He lowers his voice, and the two spend their time speaking to one
another in whispers. They are in the second-floor room of a house

of assignation known as the Shinkyō-rō, just to the side of Shinbashi Station. Sitting face to face, this man and woman are none other than Masashi Yamanaka and the widow Osada. Yamanaka pulls his watch out and studies it. "Damn! Time already!" And as he stands to leave, he says, "Will you be alright at the hot springs without me? You're not going to go running off with another man, are you?"

"Not unless it's you!" she coos. "By what karma, I wonder, would I be unfaithful? If you don't trust me, see me to my train. You'll find that my only companions are Okiyo and our tomcat!"

They flirt with one another all the way to the station.

"Ding! Ding!" The bells clang as the train departs the station.

Part 10

The rickshaw man in service to the estate diligently sprinkles water over the gravel path at the entranceway where the carriage is parked. Judging from its graceful appearance, one could mistake this residence for the home of a noble of at least the second or third imperial rank. But this is the house of Mr. Masashi Yamanaka, bought and paid for out of Hamako Shinohara's inheritance. From household affairs to social engagements, all the decision-making power resides with Hamako. Practicing the policy of "revering women,"[20] she gads about here and there as she pleases in her own personal rickshaw, while Yamanaka sets out for work every morning on foot, his lunch pail in hand. On the way home, he flags down a rickshaw and takes it all the way to the hill beneath the house, secretly reveling in the little luxury he steals from Hamako.

Having finished sprinkling all the water, the rickshaw man gazes absentmindedly at the evening scene, when just before his eyes, a rickshaw jerks to a halt.

"Pardon me young man," the woman passenger calls out. When the rickshaw man nods slightly, she continues, "Is this the residence of young Miss Shinohara? I heard there was a fellow staying here, and I was wondering if he were in now?"

"He went out; I don't know where," the rickshaw man replies. "You might ask around back at the kitchen door."

"Just beyond the wall and around back then? I understand. Thank you."

In the kitchen, Osan is cutting pickled vegetables. "Hello! Anyone home?" Hearing a woman call out, she opens the lattice grate. "Who is it?"

"I'm here from the Yamanaka residence. Thank you so much for the kindness you've shown my husband over these many weeks. I've just gotten back to town this morning and have opened our house, so please ask him to come on home as soon as he can."

"Well, *this* is the Yamanaka residence," the maid snaps, "and we are not expecting any visitors today!"

"Really? Then this isn't the house of young Mistress Shinohara?"

"No, it is indeed."

"Well, if you let me see her, I'm sure we can straighten this out. I'm Osada, Yamanaka's wife. Will you please go tell your mistress that I would very much like to speak with her?"

Osan rushes off to the inner rooms with a startled look. "Excuse me, Madam. There's a woman at the door, about thirty I'd say, who looks like the proprietress of a geisha tearoom. She says she wants to see you."

Hamako is sitting with her arm on the windowsill reading *Woman's Education Journal*. "What kind of person is she?"

"She's wearing an old *haori* kimono coat with a small family crest. Quite smart, really, and she was going on about all sorts of things that I couldn't make heads or tails of!"

"I wonder if that's Osada, the woman who looked after the Master earlier."

"I believe she did say her name was Sada Something."

"Well, then, it's she, no doubt about it. Please send her in."

"You'll see her?" Osan asks in disbelief. She leaves the room perplexed and returns momentarily with the visitor.

"It's been a long time," Hamako greets her guest.

"Please forgive me for not contacting you sooner. I had some business to attend to in Osaka that has kept me for some time."

"Is that so? I trust all went well."

"Thank you so much for all you've done, looking after my husband for me."

"Whomever do you mean?" Hamako asks.

"But you've been keeping an eye on my husband," Osada replies with assurance. "I was afraid he'd be lonely while I was away, so I closed up the house and had him stay here with you, in my absence. I'm ever so grateful."

"I'm terribly sorry. I'm not familiar with your current husband. To whom are you referring?"

"Oh, I see! What a clever joke," Osada laughs. "You know my husband! Mr. Masashi Yamanaka!"

"Whatever are you talking about? You are so amusing."

"Amusing?" Osada asks sharply. "How is that?"

"How? Oh, ha, ha, ha!"

With an intentionally serious expression, Osada continues, "Why are you laughing?"

"Why? Because Yamanaka is mine. He's my husband," Hamako replies.

"What? Yours? How can that be?"

"Stop it now," Hamako begins to grow frustrated. "You're not serious, are you? We were married quite some time ago."

"You were what? Married? Miss Shinohara, I am stunned. I would never in a million years dream that you . . ."

"Well, I understand your confusion. The wedding was all very sudden, and we haven't had a chance yet to make it official. But we did have a state ceremony, and I purchased the house for us out of my inheritance. The servants you see here also came over from my family's estate," Hamako explains.

But Osada is muttering as if she has not heard a thing Hamako has said. "I'm stunned! Your behavior is simply outrageous! It's wicked to deceive others."

"What? I've not defrauded anyone."

"Defraud, declawed . . . I don't care! You shouldn't seduce another woman's husband and then be so smug about it, Miss!"

Hamako glares at Osada in outrage, and Osada raises her voice all the louder:

"As soon as I returned from Osaka, I was going to have an acquaintance of my former husband's stand in as go-between, and we were going to make it official—Yamanaka and I. You picked a fine time to steal my husband away! Get Yamanaka out here now, and ask him yourself. He'll tell you. Go on. Bring him out!"

"Fine for you to say when you know he's not home. How dare you come into my house and abuse me like this, trying to embarrass me in front of my servants!"

"Well, aren't you the proud one! And what do you have to be so proud about, I wonder? You think just because you have money you can get away with doing whatever you please. You steal my husband while I'm out of town and act so smug about it. I cannot bear the shame any longer. Now, please, give me my husband."

"Steal!? Do you think you can get away with these slanderous accusations? I'm a member of the peerage, after all!"

"Well, very pleased to meet you, I'm sure! Peerage, porridge, pudding, and pie! Do you suppose the law will let a little princess such as yourself get away with stealing a woman's husband?"

"I don't know that I'm a thief. All I know is that Yamanaka is my husband!" And in exasperation Hamako begins to call out, "Help! Somebody come quick and throw this crazy woman out of my house!"

"Who are you calling crazy?" Osada retorts. "I may flatter myself, but I'm a scrupulous person. Let's settle this preposterous business. Please call in a policeman. Call anyone!"

And so their argument grows more and more vociferous. Sheltered all her life, Hamako has never even dreamed of engaging another in this sort of duel. All she can do is repeat the same arguments until finally, exasperated, she bursts into tears. Just at this point, her steward, Santarō, rushes into the room.

"I don't know what tearoom you're from lady," he says to Osada, "but you're plenty rude. Now, princess, stop your crying. Look, lady, the master is out just now, and I don't know what's going on here. You ought to leave and come back when he's in residence. I'll be sure to fill him in on all the particulars."

Osada quiets down. Realizing that she has accomplished her immediate aims and that the best policy now is to proceed cautiously, Osada allows Santarō to pacify her. Fortunately for all, she heads home, grumbling all the way.

Her voice quavering with tears, Hamako says, "Won't someone please go call for Yamanaka? Be quick!"

That night is not the only night Osada comes to visit. She comes the next morning and the next night, too! She heaps abuse on not only Hamako but the servants as well. At each visit, they refuse her admittance, saying the master is out.

Yamanaka's behavior changes drastically after this. Every three days or so, he spends the night out somewhere. Before Hamako even realizes what has happened, her bracelet, the ring she wore, and her other jewelry disappears. Finally, coming to her senses, Hamako has Yamanaka followed one day and finds him and Osada living together as husband and wife.

Playing on Hamako's desire, Yamanaka succeeded in tricking her into marriage and so embezzles her inheritance. Much of it he now squanders on pleasure trips with Osada—so brazen are they that they set out together in a single rickshaw, traipsing purposefully past Hamako's house. Hamako is mortified. She knows not what to do. Finally, realizing that she has received in equal measure what she herself had doled out to others, she is too embarrassed to go home to the Shinoharas or to let them know of her suffering. She instructs all in her employ, from Santarō to Osan, not to breathe a word to anyone. But rather than hiding the truth, Hamako seeks only to avoid it, and before long Tsutomu gets wind of what has befallen her. He launches a full investigation and discovers in the process that Yamanaka has borrowed an exorbitant amount of money against Hamako's house. When Yamanaka is found out, he hastily resigns his government post and makes off with Osada—whereabouts unknown.

Hamako, not wishing to return to her circle of acquaintances, accedes to the censure she receives; repenting her actions bitterly, she spends her days in tears.

Part II

"Come in and sit a spell! Have a smoke!" the teahouse women call out. At the souvenir shop on the corner, a customer haggles over prices. "We've got your tortoiseshell goods! Bamboo trays! Come in and take a look!" the hawkers cry. "Tortoise goods—good they are, for ten thousand years!" The voices ring out clamorously. It is a late autumn day in Takinogawa.

The crowds grow thinner as the maple leaves fall. At the roadside teahouse beneath the scarlet branches, two men linger. They are of no mean appearance. As they stand, one addresses the other. "Tsutomu, let's amble over that way a bit, shall we? Ever since your father passed away, you've been looking very wan. A brisk walk will do you good. You mustn't spend all your time sitting at home, you know. I expect you're feeling regrets, but you must realize that there was nothing you could have done to prevent it. Miss Hamako had her mind made up. I suspect she has her own remorse now. Yesterday I had some business that took me to Yokohama, and I called on her. She told me with tears in her eyes how ashamed she was and that she had now become a devout Christian. I tell you, she looked nothing like her former self!"

"Well, my younger sister is not completely to blame for what happened. The man involved was certainly imprudent. She may be truly repentant and have settled down, as you say, but she is still too embarrassed to face even her own mother! It certainly is a pity, when you think of it."

"That is understandable. You honored your obligations to your foster parents, but if you end up worrying yourself sick and dying of consumption or such—what kind of filial son would you be then? It may be strange for me to say this, but, because I am a very timid man myself, I used to grow anxious over even the most trivial matters. Saitō took it upon himself to convince my mother that Miss Namiko Hattori was the bride for me. Now when I get home, I have nothing to worry about. When I'm tired of slaving over my books, she plays the *koto* for me, or she serves me tea, or we discuss literature together until I have regained my spirits. I am sure your foster mother has the same in mind for you. It is only natural that you might be concerned. I don't mean to interfere, but I will be glad to help. Leave it to me—I'll introduce you to the next Mrs. Shinohara!

"To tell the truth, that incident with Hamako was pretty hard on me. I had thought of her as my wife for so long, and now all I can think of is how pathetic she is, how very pitiful. I really don't want to think of it at all. Ahh—this conversation has gotten a bit too serious, don't you think?"

"Shall we go then? Wait. What's this? Someone has posted a poem here. Do you see? It seems to be the comical opening verse to a longer link:

> The maple viewers;
> Red-faced, every one of them!

Ha! Ha! Ha! What fun! Well, no chance of finding an elegant *waka* poem in a place like this, is there?"

"Hold on a minute," Tsutomu says. "Look over there. I believe that is a *waka*. And it is written so prettily, even if in pencil.

> Maple leaves
> Capriciously you scatter
> Amid the wave of people
> Who sees your true color?

A strangely melancholy verse, isn't it? I wonder who might have written it? It's a first-rate poem; very refined, in fact."

"I say there, old woman," the man calls out to the tea stall lady. "I don't suppose you can tell us what sort of person left this verse? You have so many customers, after all."

"Which?" she asks. "Oh, that one was written by a young lady who stopped to rest here with a young fella of about fifteen, I'd say."

"A woman?" Tsutomu expresses surprise and then notes, "Well, of course, now that you mention it, it does betray a feminine hand—rather after the fashion of Ki no Tsurayuki.[21] Now, I've always considered poetry the highest form of art. I hear that among the Westernophiles these days, there are those who consider it nothing more than a plaything. But I don't agree. Composing poetry allows one to create verses that are simple yet profoundly meaningful—and it requires one to have an exceedingly refined sensibility. They really ought to demand the teaching of poetry composition in our women's academies."

As he speaks, they approach the other side of the river, where Ashio Matsushima is resting. He catches sight of the two gentlemen. "Look, Hideko, there's Mr. Miyazaki!"

"Oh, what a nice surprise," she exclaims. "It's been ages . . ."

"What a stroke of luck to have run into you here," Miyazaki states. "Are you two alone?"

"My sister doesn't get out much these days. I convinced her to join me today."

"Well, excursions like this are recuperative. Tsutomu, this is the one I've told you so much about—Hideko Matsushima. Miss Hideko, this gentleman is my valued friend, Mr. Shinohara. Why don't you draw a bit closer?"

"I'm very pleased to meet you," Hideko replies, after she has been coaxed forward. She glances shyly up at Tsutomu. His brow is distinguished; his nose high and thin. The shape of his mouth, while not unusual, has its charm. If he has studied abroad, the level of his scholarship must be exceptional indeed. And with his noble bearing—if he is a steadfast man, not given to fickle whims—it is not just his learning that proves attractive. She feels herself flush in spite of herself.

Tsutomu finds her far more genteel than he had been led to expect from Miyazaki's conversations about her. On her face, as fair as snow, her cheeks flush a maidenly pink. Her hair is pulled back in a neat, modern-style chignon. Her *kosode* kimono, ordinary if perhaps too subdued for a woman as young as she, is a silk crepe, soft with wear. And her sash is a lavender satin, lined with crepe. Atop it all, she wears a black shantung silk *haori* jacket. She is dressed with modest elegance. Tsutomu, who has long been lost to melancholy, takes pleasure in the sight of this flower whose beauty far surpasses the autumn leaves. And he, too, becomes as tongue-tied as she.

Ashio, unaware of what is transpiring, leaps up to wait on the gentlemen. "Here! Have a seat . . . please!" And, so encouraged, Miyazaki comes to sit beside them.

"Tsutomu, why don't you sit as well?" Miyazaki urges. "Miss Hideko, the leaves have fallen beneath that maple there; are you, per chance, the one who wrote this poem?"

"Really? Why do you ask?" she replies with a blush.

"Well, because I have never seen such a fine example of *waka* poetry. If you can produce a piece of this caliber, then your education has been more than adequate—even if you have learned at home. But like the maple leaves that "capriciously scatter amid the wave of people," you must not hide your "true color," unbeknownst to others. You would be like the thousand-li horse of the parable, whose potential would go undetected. Right, Tsutomu? It takes the trained eye of the critic to discern talent."

"Yes. You must not disparage your own talent or believe that whatever you do is unimportant. But, at the same time, you have to be careful to avoid self-congratulation. Resisting conceit is the mark of true scholarship. Don't you agree, Miss Hideko?"

"Indeed, I do! I study so as to learn more about natural principles."

"Miss Hideko has high aspirations!" Miyazaki smiles.

"Oh my, I've been so enjoying our conversation that I didn't notice how late it'd become. We'd better take our leave now. Shall we go, Ashio?"

"Yes, it's growing late. It wouldn't do for you young people to be out after dark," Miyazaki says. "Well, good-bye. But do stop by sometime. I'll have Mr. Shinohara come over and tell us more about his travels and the customs in the West."

"That would be lovely. Excuse us, then. Good-bye."

"Good-bye," Tsutomu waves.

"Good-bye," they chorus, parting from one another reluctantly.

Ah, a meeting of beauty and talent. The god of marriage could not have arranged a more fortunate match. Two hearts that yearn for the other reveal not their feelings; they part without disclosing their true colors. Even onlookers cannot help being moved.

"How about that! Did you find her attractive?" Miyazaki asks eagerly. "She seems to meet your requirements to a 't.' I don't believe there's another as splendid as she!"

"Yes, I suppose so."

"Well, I take your indifference as proof of your interest. What do you think? She's the thousand-li horse your discerning eye has sought, is she not!"

"She is certainly dignified!"

"None could suit you better!" Miyazaki blurts out and glances back over his shoulder to see two shopkeepers heading back to Takinogawa.

"Well, then, shall we make it Ogiya, the Fan Shop Café?" one shopkeeper says to the other.

Miyazaki claps Tsutomu's shoulder with a laugh. "I guess they're discussing their evening meal. Rather than the Folding Fan, I'd prefer the Frying Pan, ha ha! What do you say?"

Part 12

The Red Maple Pavilion, on a small hill in Shiba Park, was built to provide a setting for the banquets of dignitaries and the festivities of millionaires. In all of Tokyo, there is no other facility that compares to it. The construction is attractive, and the cuisine exquisite. Rickshaws and horse carriages have been arriving since four o'clock this afternoon for the evening's celebration. Now they are lined up outside the entryway. And so begins the wedding banquet of Count Shinohara and Miss Hideko Matsushima, with Mr. Ichirō Miyazaki standing in as go-between. If the late count were still alive, no doubt the nuptial celebrations would have been conducted in Western style at the Rokumeikan Pavilion or the like. But Tsutomu and his foster mother prefer it this way. Hideko is not yet familiar with Western manners, and, among their friends and family, most prefer sitting before a lacquered tray to standing around a table eating and drinking. And so, purposefully remaining behind the times, they host their party on woven rush mats.

Miyazaki turns to the wedding party. "To each of you, my heartfelt congratulations!"

"Thanks to your good offices, we have found a perfect bride," Mrs. Shinohara says. "I am greatly relieved."

Her words say one thing, but her eyes shine with tears of regret. And who could blame her?

Miyazaki's congratulatory speech is equally restrained. But once the festivities are under way, all assembled are buoyed along by the celebratory mood, taking turns to offer a congratulatory toast. Mr. Saitō, flushed from the sake, raises his voice enthusiastically. "Say, Miss Namiko, or, excuse me, I should say 'Mrs. Miyazaki'! You used to be such good friends with Miss Hamako. She'd be our guest of honor today if it hadn't been for that unfortunate business. It's disappointing, isn't it?"

"I suppose" is Namiko's only response. Not realizing that she feels constricted in old Mrs. Shinohara's presence, Saitō continues.

"You know, Tsutomu, that rascal Yamanaka had his nerve to carry off a stunt like that, didn't he? He did whatever it took to curry favor with the late Count Shinohara, and because Miss Hamako was his beloved daughter, he fawned on her—following the philosophy that the master's servant is the one who holds the keys. And thus, as a result . . . well, we know what happened next. But it couldn't be helped. You did the best you could, but he knew no shame. He aspired to become the prized son-in-law of a distinguished aristocrat, second to none! He should have left well enough alone and counted his blessings. Everyone, including myself, says as much. Gossip usually dissipates in seventy-five days. If he had bided his time, all would have been forgotten.

"But he was egged on by that wretched widow Osada. What an idiot! He committed an outrageous deed. Even so, he was not meant for the role he played. Rather than the villainous lover, he was more suited to the role of the weakling pretty boy. At heart, he was spineless. He didn't have a goal in mind at first. From the beginning, he just wanted to curry favor with the late count. He didn't set out to trick Hamako. That was the widow's doing. Her bed was cold, and, since her husband had been kind to Yamanaka, she used that to reel him in. Yamanaka might have seemed like a cad, but he was unexpectedly soft-hearted and easily swayed by that witch of a widow. And so he carried out his deed, marching to the beat of her drum. Strange creatures humans are. We're less likely to defend ourselves than we are to use our influence in following another's directions. Unintentional though it might have been, because he carried out such an evil act Yamanaka is a cad, after all. To exaggerate, he's just like Benedict Arnold. And if you ask me, so was Saigō Takamori.[22] Led by the political bullies of Satsuma, he was prompted by a loyalty that wasn't honorable. To cleanse away the brand of traitor, he lost that which he should have protected." And in a smaller voice Saitō adds, "And he ran off with his master's money to boot! But the widow is going to take him for everything he has, and, when she's done, she'll throw him over. Hamako's the one who deserves our pity. This should have been her day."

Saitō's is a speech hardly appropriate to the occasion! Those assembled exchange uncomfortable glances, but no one hazards a reply. For a time, they pretend to pay attention, and then, clap! clap! the merrymaking begins to carry them off. They commence to sing what songs they know.

"Marriage is a strange business," Miyazaki offers. "Even though I knew my wife for some time before we married, it was only afterward that I found out how truly wonderful she is! But you!" He catches himself. "For both of you, such an unexpected partnership!"

"Indeed. When you think about it, what has happened here is rather like the plot in a storybook, isn't it?" Tsutomu counters. "That we're even having this marriage celebration tonight is quite a stroke of good fortune."

Picking up on his final words, Saitō bursts out in a loud voice. "Hear! Hear! A toast to good fortune!"

And so, to conclude:

Ashio Matsushima enters university shortly thereafter. He studies engineering and, when he graduates, becomes the supervisor of a huge public works project. Now he is known far and wide. He marries Ichirō Miyazaki's younger sister.

Saitō's younger sister, Matsuko, and Shinako Aizawa go on to Teachers' Normal School and both earn names for their talent and education. As has been their lifelong wish, they have no husbands. And so perhaps will they live out their lives. But who knows what the future will hold!

The whereabouts of Masashi Yamanaka and Osada remain a mystery. Everyone suspects they ended up as Saitō predicted.

NOTES

1. Readers will also find this writer referred to as Tanabe Tatsu or Tatsuko, which was her childhood name. Like other writers of her generation, Kaho adopted a variety of pen names for her literary endeavors. Kaho is the one applied most consistently. Miyake is the name she began to use after her marriage to Miyake Setsurei in 1892.

2. Historian Margaret J. M. Ezell, for example, cautions against the naming of firsts because such appellations tend to deny the possibility of any precedents. See *Writing Women's Literary History* (Baltimore: Johns Hopkins University Press, 1993), pp. 41–42.

3. This playscript style, influenced by theatrical productions, was typical of literary works of this and previous generations. Speech is first attributed to unnamed characters, such as "Man" or "Woman A." When the characters are eventually named, their speech is listed under their name: "Shinohara" or sometimes, in abbreviation, "Shino." Occasionally, in dialogue among a group of minor characters, the different voices are represented by geometric symbols, such as circles, triangles, or squares. I have retained the playscript style in a number of passages to give readers a sense of what it was like, but to accommodate the sensibilities of modern readers I have used embedded dialogue for the majority of the story. Readers will also note the presence of French words in the translation. In the original, these words are rendered in *katakana*—the syllabary used to represent foreign loan words—and are meant to record newly imported English words. I hope the intrusion of the French will provide the same flavor as that of the English in the original, which to Kaho's contemporary readers would have appeared novel and chic.

4. Sally Hastings, "The Empress' New Clothes and Japanese Women, 1868–1912," *The Historian* 55, no. 4 (Summer 1993): 677.

5. Miyake Kaho, "Omoide no hitobito," *Fujin kōron* April 1939, p. 108.

6. Seki Ryōichi, "Yabu no uguisu," *Kokubungaku* 13, no. 5 (1968): 17–20.

7. Takahashi Oden was accused of murdering a used-clothing dealer when he refused to lend her money. The subsequent trial, which lasted more than two years, inflamed the imaginations of contemporary journalists, writers, and Kabuki playwrights. Oden was depicted in the media as an evil seductress shortly after she was executed for her crime and earned the name of "poison woman" (*dokufu*). Perhaps the most popular retelling of the Oden story was

Kanagaki Robun's *Takahashi Oden yasha monogatari* (The tale of the she-devil Takahashi Oden, 1879).

8. Ishibashi Shian, for example, suggests that either Kaho had a more worldly man write the "dirty parts" of her story, or she wasn't as innocent as she seemed. See "Yabu no uguisu no saihyō," *Kokumin no tomo*, August 1888, p. 37.

9. I am grateful to Professor Sumiko Shinozuka of Kyoritsu Women's University for bringing these associations to my attention.

10. This text is translated from "Yabu no uguisu," in *Gendai Nihon bungaku taikei*, vol. 5 (Tokyo: Chikuma shobō, 1972).

11. The average salary at the time was fifteen yen.

12. The humor here depends on a clever play on words. The word used for pickle, *takuwan*, refers to a very common radish pickle. If the same Chinese characters are read *takuan*, an alternative possibility, the rendering would refer to the Rinzai priest Takuan, who lived from 1573 to 1645. The houseboy misinterprets the mistress's desire to be for a priest, not a pickle. The punning only adds to the silliness of the situation.

13. Yoshida Kenkō, *Essays in Idleness: The Tsurezuregusa of Kenkō*, trans. Donald Keene (New York: Columbia University Press, 1967), p. 175.

14. The author does not give this character, Ichirō Miyazaki's younger sister, a first name. Moreover, at the beginning of this dialogue, she is referred to only as "student." The name is the invention of the translator and meant to facilitate readability of the dialogue.

15. "H" is schoolgirl talk for "husband."

16. Beer was not a native beverage but one that made its way into the country by way of Western visitors. In 1870 a beer brewery was founded in Japan by William Copeland; the product, Amanuma Biyazake, eventually became Kirin Beer. Stock Beer was introduced to Japan in 1886. Although it was presented as a domestic product, it was actually a German import.

17. "Thirty some" must be a mistake—either Kaho's or the printers—for "thirteen and some."

18. Dr. Erwin von Baelz (1849–1913), a German, was appointed in 1876 as professor for internal medicine at Tokyo Imperial University, where he taught until 1902. He was among a number of notable Western scholars brought to Japan at this time. In addition to his professorship, Dr. Baelz also became the private physician to the crown prince, Yoshihito (later the Taishō emperor), and a host of other important men and women. Baelz is largely credited with introducing physical education into the school curriculum. Many also believe that Baelz was responsible for the invention of judo and the modern martial arts in Japan.

19. *Kanjinchō* (The subscription list), derived from the Noh drama *Ataka*, was adapted for the Kabuki stage by Gohei Namiki in 1840. The play features

Yoshitsune's flight from his half-brother, Yoritomo, the Kamakura shogun, who wants to kill him. To make it across the barrier gate, Yoshitsune disguises himself as a porter and his loyal attendant, Benkei, who is disguised as a mountain priest, is forced to beat his "porter" to convince the barrier guards of the ploy.

20. Kaho is being facetious. The appropriate phrase is "revere men; despise women."

21. Ki no Tsurayuki (ca. 872–945), a prominent male poet, arbiter of poetic taste, and statesman, wrote the *kana* preface to the *Kokinshū* (Collection of modern and ancient Japanese poems, early tenth century), considered to be the first example of literary criticism in Japanese. He also wrote the *Tosa nikki* (Tosa diary, ca. 935), using a female persona, ostensibly in order to allow himself the freedom to write in Japanese (the "woman's hand") rather than Chinese, the language usually chosen for public documents written by men during the Heian period.

22. Saigō Takamori (1828–1877) was a key figure in the overthrow of the Tokugawa Shogun and the restoration of imperial rule. Angered when his hopes of attacking Korea were dashed, he resigned his post in the Meiji government and returned to Satsuma in southern Kyushu. Four years later, he led the Satsuma revolt against the government, which he found too far removed from traditional samurai values. His forces were defeated, and Saigō committed suicide.

HIGUCHI ICHIYŌ
(1872–1896)

Kyōko Ōmori

HIGUCHI ICHIYŌ is often described as a genius who made a meteoric rise from obscurity only to disappear as suddenly as she had appeared. She published most of her twenty-one novellas between 1894 and 1896 and died of consumption at the age of twenty-four while at the height of her success. Despite the brevity of her writing career, Ichiyō is today considered a canonical Meiji woman writer for her elegant yet candid depictions of lower-class everyday life in and around the Tokyo demimonde. Mori Ōgai (1862–1922) praised Ichiyō in 1896, saying that the characters in her story "Takekurabe" (Comparing heights, 1894–1896) "are not those beastlike creatures one so often encounters in Ibsen or Zola, whose techniques the so-called Naturalists have tried their utmost to imitate. They are real, human individuals with whom we laugh and cry." A skeptic of other contemporary writers' blind fascination with Western realism, Ōgai declared Ichiyō "a true poet" who excelled in depicting characters in a realistic light through beautifully flowing language.[1]

"Takekurabe," which is probably Ichiyō's most famous work, portrays a group of adolescents coming of age in a lower-class neighborhood adjacent to one of Tokyo's pleasure quarters. The story focuses on the bittersweet love between Midori and Nobu, two young teens. As they gradually become aware of their feelings for each other, they also

FIGURE 4.1 Higuchi
Ichiyō (1872–1896), 1896

FIGURE 4.2 A page from
her diary, *Shinobugusa*

realize that they must part ways to become a courtesan/prostitute and a Buddhist priest, respectively, in order to fulfill familial expectations. Ichiyō skillfully develops these two and a handful of other adolescent characters; she shows how varied educational, economic, and social-class backgrounds could be, even in a small lower-class neighborhood. She also shows how these differences lead innocent children to follow predetermined paths in life. To this day, "Takekurabe" is taught as one of the masterpieces of modern Japanese literature. It is also readily available through a variety of popular adaptations in the form of TV dramas, movies, *manga* comics, and anime.

Her diary (1887–1896), excerpts of which are presented here, was first published in 1912, sixteen years after her death, through the efforts of her younger sister, Kuniko, and a literary friend, Baba Kochō (1869–1940). It covers the last ten years of her life, during which she first aspired to excel in poetry and later became involved in writing prose. Ichiyō's diary (or *nikki*) is more than just a collection of personal memoranda and private accounts; it also functioned as a means for learning penmanship and composition.[2] Ichiyō began her diary entries at fifteen—soon after she entered the Haginoya (a private school for classical poetry in Tokyo)— and she kept at them until her untimely death. Filled with accounts of her literary activities, actual poems, and allusions to the literary work of her contemporaries and predecessors, the diary clearly served as a means for her to track and pursue her own cultural refinement, an activity strongly encouraged by her literary-minded father. Her diary is also a highly valuable source of information about Meiji society in general and more particularly about the literary works and figures of the 1890s, all observed through Ichiyō's critical eye. Additionally, the diary takes on the character of a practical daily record when Ichiyō becomes the official head of the household and starts keeping records of visitors to the Higuchis, their visits to others, daily income, and debts.[3]

Ichiyō was born in Tokyo as Natsu (she also went by Natsuko) to Higuchi Noriyoshi and Taki, whose families both had roots in the peasant class.[4] With hard work, considerable savings, and a brief period of good luck, her father, Noriyoshi, was able to buy his way into the rank of *dōshin* (a low-ranking samurai position) in 1867. But with the Meiji Restoration in 1868 and the abolition of the samurai-ruled hierarchical system in 1869, Noriyoshi and his family were able to enjoy the actual privilege and benefits of the samurai class for only a couple of years. Nevertheless, this moment of class privilege—brief though it was—continued to live on in the collective consciousness of the Higuchi family. Noriyoshi and Taki taught their children to take pride in their samurai-class status even though they were not wealthy.

When Ichiyō entered the Haginoya at fourteen, Nakajima Utako, a leading classical poet and owner of the school, recognized her talent immediately. Reticent but highly competitive, Ichiyō studied hard and constantly won the top prizes in the regular poetry contests at the school. In her early diary entries, she expresses pride in her literary superiority over her classmates, the majority of whom were from the former samurai class or the imperial family; they were also financially much better off than the Higuchis.[5] She also became increasingly critical of the closed, aristocratic world of composing classical poetry and reading Heian classics; she believed it a hobby of the rich and privileged, one that was divorced from the reality of a Japan that had been undergoing rapid changes since the mid-nineteenth century.

The diary also vividly portrays the struggles of a young woman placed in the unique position of supporting a family. By the late 1880s the Higuchi family was in crisis. The eldest son and heir had died of tuberculosis, the second son had been disowned, and the third had died while still an infant. Ichiyō's elder sister had married into another family. When Ichiyō's father died in 1889 after losing everything in a failed business venture, the seventeen-year-old Ichiyō assumed the burden of supporting her aging mother and a younger sister as the registered head of the family, an unconventional situation for a woman at the time.[6] Noriyoshi had tried to secure Ichiyō's future from his deathbed by enjoining a promising law student named Shibuya Saburō to marry into the Higuchis. But the young man soon reneged on his agreement (see the September 1, 1892, entry). Desperate, the Higuchi women began borrowing money from relatives and friends. Ichiyō began to work as a live-in apprentice to Nakajima Utako at the Haginoya in 1890, but her actual role was more or less that of a live-in housekeeper. In addition to this income from the Haginoya, the Higuchi women made small sums of money by weaving rattan soles for summer sandals and taking in laundry and sewing jobs at home.

Ichiyō felt she had found a new way to overcome her family's dismal situation when she saw the great success of her twenty-year-old Haginoya schoolmate Tanabe Tatsuko. Tatsuko, later known as Miyake Kaho, became famous when her novella "Yabu no uguisu" (Warbler in the Grove, also featured in this anthology) was published in 1888 with the help of leading novelist and scholar Tsubouchi Shōyō (1859–1935). Not only did the young woman win a reputation as a writer, but she also earned thirty-three yen and twenty sen as a manuscript fee, an impressive amount to Ichiyō, considering that the Higuchi women were earning only seven yen a month through tailoring and laundry work. Miyake's success would prove to be an important source of inspiration for Ichiyō.

The diary also treats her ardent but unfulfilled love for newspaper reporter and writer Nakarai Tōsui (1860–1926), the pathos of which has earned her the general public's sympathy. A friend of her sister introduced Ichiyō to Tōsui in April 1891, probably because Ichiyō was looking for a mentor who would teach her to write prose and also help her to break into the commercial publishing world. Tōsui's light and entertaining *gesaku* prose works were a good contrast to the highbrow poetry that Ichiyō was accustomed to, but she also understood that this popular genre was a way for Tōsui to support his family. Ichiyō began to visit the widower regularly for advice on becoming a professional writer. She describes him as a tall, handsome man with a gentle and sociable personality. In early 1892, with Tōsui's help, she finally had the opportunity to publish in magazines and newspapers. However, after finding out from Mrs. Nakajima and fellow pupils that people suspected her of having become Tōsui's lover, Ichiyō stopped seeing him on the advice of her poetry teacher. Some informed her that Tōsui was an infamous woman-izer and that he was in fact the source of the unsavory rumor. Although upset with him, she still felt ambivalent about this parting, clearly torn between a sense of morality and her affection for him.

Regarding both this incident with Tōsui and another rumor about the writer Kawakami Bizan (1869–1908), who visited her repeatedly and even asked for her photograph, Ichiyō expresses her frustration with the literary circle's gossip and speculation regarding her love life. Other en-tries tell us that a variety of literary-minded people (the vast majority of whom were male) visited Ichiyō or wrote to her after they read her publications. These entries reveal that many people in literary circles acknowledged Ichiyō's talents, despite the fact that she was a young woman. They also show, however, that many were curious about the young woman's association with men in the male-dominated world of Meiji literature. In several entries, Ichiyō observes the craze surrounding her with a cool, dispassionate eye.

By 1894 Ichiyō was in her prime. Leading writers such as Mori Ōgai and Kōda Rohan (1867–1947) expressed their interest in collaborating on stories. She was finally making enough money with her pen to sup-port her family. Yet she dismissed people who praised her as a mod-ern-day Sei Shōnagon or Murasaki Shikibu as not sophisticated enough to see the flaws in her work. She also believed that people extolled her talents mainly because, as a woman writer, she was a novelty, and she an-ticipated that the craze would soon die down. Before it could, however, she fell seriously ill, and after seven months of fighting tuberculosis, she passed away on November 23, 1896.

While Ichiyō sought Tōsui's advice on becoming a commercial writer for financial reasons, the diary reveals her dilemma over selling her artistic productions. Ichiyō's references to the comments of contem-porary writers and literary critics tell us that she was concerned about the debates over literature for pure artistic purposes and literature as a commercial entity.[7] In her entry about the repeated visits of her for-mer fiancé, Shibuya Saburō (September 1, 1892), she describes herself as wavering between writing as a means of earning a living and seeking a man's support so that she could treat literature purely as art. Feeling ambivalent, she continued to write stories, and, with the initial help of Tanabe Tatsuko (Miyake Kaho), began to publish in leading literary magazines such as *Miyako no hana* (Flower of the capital) and *Bungaku-kai* (Literary world). Ichiyō mentions how much she made with her writing. For example, in her entry for October 21, 1892, she mentions that she received eleven yen and seventy-five sen for "Umoregi" (In obscurity, 1892) from *Miyako no hana*.

Although people began to recognize her as a writer of great potential, the manuscript fees she had received so far were not enough to feed three people, especially with the debts that the family had already accumulated. In the summer of 1893, Ichiyō decided to stop selling her work and open a small candy and toy store. She thought that a store would bring in a more stable income and that she could then pursue writing free from the worry of having to make a living. She found a small house in the lower-class neighborhood of Ryūsenji, adjacent to the Yoshiwara red-light district. Ichiyō's mother was opposed to the idea of running a store because she considered it a disgrace to their samurai background; Ichiyō herself describes this move as a step down the social ladder. The business was a success, but the income was still insufficient to support the family, because they sold only small and inexpensive items to customers in a poor neighborhood. In October 1893 Ichiyō shifted responsibility of the store to her sister, Kuniko, and resumed her study of literature at the Ueno Library. In May 1894 she closed the store, and the family moved to Maruyama-Fukuyamachō, where she would live for two and a half years, until her death in November 1896. Perhaps ironically, in her last two years, Ichiyō established her fame by publishing in *Bungakukai* and several other major magazines and newspapers, such as *Taiyō* (The sun), *Bungei kurabu* (Literary arts club), *Yomiuri shinbun* (Yomiuri newspaper), *Nihon no katei* (Japanese families), and *Kokumin no tomo* (Nation's friend). The works she published, "Yamiyo" (Encounters on a Dark Night), "Ō-tsugomori" (On the Last Day of the Year) and "Takekurabe," which are considered among her best, were born from what she witnessed in the rather unsavory neighborhoods where she had lived.

Besides her private struggles, Ichiyō's diary also shows her search for a new literary language that would do justice to everyday life in a Tokyo deeply involved in rapid Westernization and modernization. At the same time, her style was indebted to certain pre-Meiji traditions and customs. Inspired by the elegant writings of Heian women but also aware of

FIGURE 4.3 A page from the special *keishū sakka* issue of *Bungei kurabu*,
December 10, 1895; Ichiyō is lower left

her contemporaries' efforts to reform literary language, Ichiyō sought
to rise beyond a world of literature that was only a cultural refinement
for young women. In 1893 the work of the Edo's most famous popular writer, Ihara Saikaku (1642–1693), was reprinted in its first complete
edition; many contemporary writers welcomed his earthy style of portraying Japanese life as an alternative to the Western realism sweeping
the literary world. Ichiyō read Saikaku around this time and added his
perspective to her own style. Combining her expertise in classical Japanese court literature, the *gesaku* tradition culminated by Ihara Saikaku,
and the literary languages her contemporaries were attempting to invent
was surely far from easy.

Given the revisions and reorganizations that the text underwent, one
can argue that Ichiyō's diary gradually became an expressly literary production. The entries are written with brush and ink in forty-four notebooks made of rice paper. Ichiyō took her inspiration for the title she inscribed on the front page of each notebook from the house in which she
lived when she wrote the entries. Later, when she prepared the diary for

publication, Kuniko would organize the entries using these titles, which include "Wakaba kage" (Under the shade of spring leaves), "Yomogiu nikki" (Mugwort diary), "Chiri no naka" (Amid the dust), and "Mizu no ue" (On the water), poetic allusions to the ambience of each dwelling.[8] The earliest entries (1887 to 1890) are more or less simple memoranda of the day's events, and we do not see particular literary efforts in style or formal structure, except for the *waka* poems that she occasionally inserts. In 1891, in "Wakaba kage," Ichiyō started employing language that combined an elegant, Heian style with a more contemporary voice. The entries have more narrative unity. Unlike the early memoranda, entries starting in 1891 have apparently gone through at least one revision. Critics speculate that Ichiyō wrote memoranda of her life almost daily and then rewrote them later, occasionally combining several entries into one story or later adding comments on the events to the entry.[9]

Because of this multilayered process of writing and reorganization, her selection of topics, and her decisions to shed light on certain events, Ichiyō scholar Wada Yoshie suggests that we should read the diary as a *shishōsetsu* (I-novel) rather than accept it as a collection of straightforward depictions about her life.[10] For example, we see Ichiyō's manipulation as narrator when she depicts her family in poverty, even though the Higuchi family was rather well off until her father's death. It is as though she wanted to draw contrasting pictures of a poor young woman with literary talent among a crowd of rich and spoiled girls at the Haginoya. Noguchi Seki, another Ichiyō scholar, notes that Ichiyō wrote the day's memoranda regularly with the expectation that they would help in later examinations of her past self.[11] Donald Keene wonders if she kept the diary "mainly for the practice it gave her in calligraphy" because such a skill was an important part of education for ladies in those days.[12] In any event, these ten years of diary writing correspond with a period that she began as an avid learner of classical poetry and concluded as a writer of prose intent on achieving literary and economic success. In a March 24, 1892, entry, she mentions a conversation with Mrs. Nakajima in which she tells the older woman that she is "writing in my diary every day. Some entries are written in *genbun itchi* [unity of speech and writing], others in classical style, and yet others are in the journalistic *bungo* style." She then asks for Mrs. Nakajima's advice, explaining that she wonders if "trying various styles might only be harmful to my writing."[13] Thus one can argue that the diary was more than a mere record of daily events; it was practice she assigned herself to seek the most suitable language for her storytelling.

In this period, Ichiyō also makes references to the various ancient and modern Japanese writings she read at the Ueno Library and in books she borrowed from her friends at the Haginoya. For example, she read classical works such as the *Nihongi* (Chronicles of Japan, written in Chinese, compiled in 720) and *Genji monogatari* (The tale of Genji, written by Murasaki Shikibu in the eleventh century) to more recent ones such as *Tsukinami shōsoku* (a collection of letters by Udono Yonoko, a pupil of the *kokugaku* scholar Kamo no Mabuchi from the late eighteenth century) and works by Ueda Akinari (1734–1809).[14] It seems that she attempted to combine the knowledge she obtained from reading with the materials she found in her daily life (especially in the Ryūsenji neighborhood) to compose literary works. The later works are clearly more mature and complex than the early works. Ichiyō recorded in the entry from July 15, 1896, that a literary critic, Saitō Ryokuu (1867–1904), had visited her and pressed her to answer his question: "To me, it is laughable that people think you wrote 'Nigorie' ["Troubled Waters"] with passionate tears and that they don't see the sarcastic smile behind it. Personally, I prefer to see irony instead of passionate tears. Please tell me [if my observations are correct]."[15]

We see from these entries that Ichiyō's struggle to become a professional writer was not just a woman's struggle in a male-centered literary society; she also confronted the particularly modern challenge of facing socioeconomic class and gender conflicts. Her motive to write stories was not simply to emancipate women from the oppression of men, as is often argued of women writers in early modern societies; it is more complex: she wanted to write because she knew her writing skills were much more sophisticated than those of her peers, whether male or female. But she also needed to write for practical reasons; she needed to make money in order to support her family as the registered head of the household. It is therefore somewhat ironic that a photograph of the young, quiet-looking, but strong-willed Ichiyō, a woman who spent much of her adult life struggling with acute economic problems, is now depicted on the new 5,000-yen bill launched in 2004. This makes her the first woman to appear on any banknote issued by the Bank of Japan, which was established in 1882.[16] She is representative of women who thrived (though briefly) without being discouraged by gender barriers and poverty, as well as a symbol of Japan's literary achievement in the early modern period.[17]

HIGUCHI ICHIYŌ'S
JOURNAL ENTRIES

Translated by Kyōko Ōmori

Entry from "Mugwort diary 1" (Yomogiu nikki 1),[18]
September 15–November 10, 1891

September 22, 1891

By dawn, the rain stopped. As the sun rose and the skies brightened, morning dewdrops glistened like beautifully strung beads on the tree-tops and brushwood fences. Mr. Inaba Hiroshi paid a visit, as did Mr. Iseri. In the afternoon, the books [of an annotated edition of *The tale of Genji*] I had lent to Miss Nakajima Kurako arrived in the mail. A letter was also enclosed. I finished the tailoring job for my teacher. Around sunset, the rain started again, and it poured throughout the night. I did not go to bed until almost midnight, but I must have dozed off from time to time at my desk. I wonder why I am so lacking in stamina. Having the desire to strive, I pick up my brush to write stories, or I read a book to understand it fully. Am I exerting myself to the utmost, or am I still not ambitious enough? My dull mind is getting even dimmer. As the days go by, the things difficult to understand get more difficult. Today, I forget the things I learned yesterday. I might as well just choose to do what a woman ought to and be a housewife, but I do not think I can do that, either. And yet it is impossible for me to be like a man—to educate myself for a job in society. I wonder what will become of me. I have an aging mother to support. I feel sad when I think of her, and I feel sorry for my younger sister, who has now reached marriageable age. When I ponder all these things, I feel that the entire situation is due to my lack of effort. The old Chinese proverb says, "When you are wrong, don't be afraid to change."[19] Still, it is not only tonight that I tell myself I will become a new person, starting tomorrow.

Undated Entry from "Forest undergrowth 1" (Mori no shitakusa 1), Late 1891 or Early 1892

It has been almost a year since I started writing, but I have published nothing so far. I have not even a single story that satisfies me. My family says I am wasting my days by being indecisive and constantly dwelling on the past. They say that even the most renowned and accomplished writers were never praised for their earliest work, and they remind me that criticism is what determines the value of one's writing. But here is what I think. Even though my stories may be trifling, I have taken up my brush with sincerity. Even if I write for clothing and shelter from the rain and dew, that should not be an excuse for dull, low-quality work that any reader would find boring. To be acknowledged as a novelist, I am determined never to write like frivolous and popular writers, whose works will be discarded after a single reading. In these dehumanizing, modern times of ever-changing values, what is popular today will likely be abandoned tomorrow. Still, if one writes but a one-page piece that appeals to the human heart and depicts human sincerity, how dare we say it has no literary value? I do not desire to live lavishly by dressing splendidly and dwelling in a grand house. I am attempting to establish a thousand-year legacy as a writer; why would I tarnish it with temporary extravagance? It is due to my sincerity that I write and rewrite over and over even a single sentence before I am ready for people's comments. However, even if my efforts come to nothing, and I end up wasting my paper and ink, so be it. I will resign myself to the will of Heaven.

Entry from "A pondering fern" (Shinobugusa), August 24–September 3, 1892

September 1, 1892

Early this morning, Kuniko visited our elder sister.[20] Nothing unusual. Mother went to Mr. Ishikawa Ginjirō's house in Kaji-chō to borrow money. I had a terrible headache, so I washed my hair with cold water and tied a towel around my head. Since I did not feel like working on my stories, I read *Bunshō kihan* [Basic writing] for a while. "Zeinan" [The difficulty of persuasion] in *Kanpishi* [by Han Feitzu] was deeply moving.[21] Mother borrowed fifteen yen from Mr. Ishikawa and returned in the afternoon. Later that same afternoon, she went to Mr. Yamazaki to repay ten yen. He repeatedly offered to serve as a mediator, suggesting that Shibuya Saburō could marry into our family or I could marry into his. Mother turned down the offer. We all laughed, saying how strange people can be. Mr. Shibuya himself visited me today, but I wonder what his intentions were. I felt that he was trying, in some strange way, to insinuate marriage but left it to me actually to mention it.

When Father was still alive, he had expectations of Mr. Shibuya and proposed that he marry into our family as my husband. Without giving any clear answer, Mr. Shibuya continued to pay regular visits, conversing with me in a casual, friendly way. He, Kuniko, and I would sometimes go to a *yose* theater together. At that time, Father was very interested in our marrying. When he suddenly passed away, he was convinced that matters had already been decided, more or less. I wonder whether Mr. Shibuya was still too young and unsettled in his thinking at that point. One day, Mother gently raised the issue, saying, "We would be grateful for an answer." Shibuya said, "I do not have any objections. I agree to the arrangement." Pleased, Mother replied, "Then we will ask Mr. Saegusa to be our official go-between." "Please wait a while," he said, "I must consult my father and brother"; then he went home. After that, for whatever strange reason, he sent Satō Umekichi to communicate his outrageous demands for an extravagant dowry. Mother was infuriated by the request and turned it down. "Then this arrangement cannot be fulfilled," he said and broke things off. From the beginning, I was not particularly enamored of the relationship. At the same time, though, I didn't hate the idea. Mother was terribly upset, so I tried hard to calm her down.

Many months passed in this fashion. And yet his visits never ceased. On the first anniversary of Father's death, he was mindful enough to pay us a visit. He has never missed the New Year's greetings. He made sure to stop by when he was departing for Echigo [Niigata] for his appointment as a public prosecutor. Thus we could not ignore him. When he wrote to us, we wrote him back and so continued the relationship. But what can he be thinking to visit us like this, seeming to want a renewal of our engagement? My family's fortune has gradually been waning, and we are no longer what we used to be. Our debts have piled up like a mountain. Moreover, we are forced to live only on my scarce income from writing. The shame and hardship from being despised and looked down on by society is not easy. By contrast, he is rising like the morning sun in a cloudless sky. His family is renowned for its wealth and seems to be becoming even more prosperous. His elder sister is married to a trader of raw silk, and I hear that the business makes a profit of three hundred yen a month. Shibuya himself has been conferred the rank of shō-hachi-i [upper eighth] as an honorable public prosecutor in Niigata and is said to be receiving a monthly salary of fifty yen. If I relied on him now, I would not disgrace Mother, my sister, my brother, and even my late father's name, and our family would be splendidly established. However, such prosperity would only be temporary. I have never sought luxury. What is the use of rankings? I will provide a comfortable life for Mother and a good husband for my sister; I am ready to sleep on the street if no one supports me. I would shave my head and beg for food. After all that has happened, I do not want to accept this man now. It is neither that I hate him nor that I am being stubborn and trying to endure out of pride. I just think this world's empty wealth and fame are deplorable, and I wish instead to follow the example of Ono no Komachi and follow the path of literature even if I fall low in the end.[22] I do not know if I will change my mind someday, but that is what I feel today. Suspecting that I may rethink my options at some point, I am writing this down. I felt very weary all day long today, so I spent the day doing nothing.

Entry from "Diary" (Nikki), September 4t–October 25, 1892

October 20, 1892

Beautiful day. Since I stayed up late last night, I was still in bed when the *Kōyō shinpō* [Kōyō news] was delivered in the morning. Kuniko rushed to open it and shouted, "Oh, the serialization of your 'Kyōzukue' [The sutra reading stand] has started this morning!" I hurriedly got out of my bed and looked, and I realized what Kuniko said was true. I had sent them the manuscript around the sixth day of this month. Judging from this success, I imagined they would not reject my manuscripts if I sent more, and the idea gave me peace of mind. But I am also embarrassed that I am writing fiction—the most difficult task in literature—and supporting a family of three with it, knowing only too well that I lack knowledge and have not received enough education. Is it that I am bold, or am I over-estimating myself? No one noticed when panic struck and I awoke in the middle of the night, my back cold with sweat. Nevertheless, if I do not rely on my writing, I will not be able to ease Mother's mind or gain back the family's reputation. I am lost among my thoughts.

Two entries from "Mugwort diary" (Yomogiu nikki), December 24, 1892–February 11, 1893

February 5, 1893

Satō Umekichi invited Mother on a visit to Suitengū Shrine. He treated her to a meal of grilled eel on the way home, and that made her happy. Because today is Sunday, Ashizawa came.

How disgraceful is love! It would be fine if, after committing one's body and soul, the relationship were to reach a happy ending. Love is something we cannot give up, however, and thus we agonize over it day and night, even when we are aware that it is doomed. We are not attracted to anything specific, such as a person's eyes, nose, chin, arms, or legs. Nor are we drawn to how or what the person writes or the way he talks, his voice or disposition. There is nothing in particular about the person that we long for, and yet we find ourselves pining fervently for him. This is where thoughtless and unwise people make a mistake and give in to a passing affair. Those who are thoughtful, sensible, and calm will make efforts not to give in to such feelings. Even when they are pining for someone, and the inside of their body is burning with passion, or when they are terribly lovesick, there are those who will still eventually wake up from the dream without completely falling in. Because women are faint-hearted, some of us become almost mad when we lose the struggle against love. Such things, however, happen only when the love is an immoral affair. If it is the case of a wife in a rightful marriage, people will envy such a passionate relationship, and society will praise such love. Those who are called women of virtue will keep such passionate love to themselves and will give priority to the accomplishment of the duties society expects of them. Whether it is between a parent and child or a lord and vassal, such love is desirable. But passionate feelings tend toward extremes—usually to a harmful extent. From what I have been hearing and seeing recently, it seems that even some respectable people are behaving improperly, and those are examples of just such extremes. I wish I could help them find the path of sincerity and honesty.

February 6

Cloudy. People say it will rain again. My writing is not making as much progress as I would wish. My head continues to hurt, and any ideas I had before have disappeared. Setting myself the goal of depicting the perfect image of a beauty, I close my eyes, face a wall, cover my ears, and sit in front of the desk. But heaven and earth become complete darkness, and neither her beautiful and flowerlike appearance nor her lovely birdlike voice is reflected on the mirror of my heart. When I push myself to seek out and portray a beauty, the purple erases the vermillion,[23] white becomes black, the reverse side appears on the front, and the evil appears together with the good. Unable to describe her fully with my writing skills, I lament repeatedly and feel resentful. I delete here and remove there. Just when I think it will suffice, the white disappears with the black, and, when I get rid of the evil, the good is nowhere to be seen. Does the beauty I am seeking really not exist in this world? Or perhaps I am a complete stranger to beauty even from my previous life, and my

mind's eye can only see the commonplace beauty of the spring flowers and autumn leaves. Or maybe there is no such thing as true beauty
in this world. I wonder. Or, again, what my eyes do not see as beauty
might be true beauty. Could it be that the nature of heaven and earth
equals beauty? Is true beauty something that no painting can draw, no
writing can depict, no utterance can describe, and no mind can imagine,
just as the air that fills the world can be neither seen nor touched but is
something indispensable for people to live? Could even what I am saying now also be beauty? Or is beauty in the eye of the beholder? Will
what I wrote as evil be seen by others as good? Then does that mean that
what I consider evil equals beauty?

I repeatedly turn these questions over in my mind, which wanders
around between heaven and earth. I am drenched with sweat from the
anguish. Exhausted from thinking, not even knowing whether it is day
or night, I now feel neither asleep nor awake. When will I be able to
discern clearly whether such a form of true beauty exists? Am I writing
for the sake of money? If so, why do I agonize so much? What I earn
for a manuscript page of four hundred characters amounts to merely
thirty sen. My family is more and more pressed by poverty. We can afford no fish or meat or new clothing. I have an aged mother and a sister
to support. Day and night, I have no time to feel at ease, but it is also
lamentable that I have to sell my writing despite myself. I bite the cap
of my writing brush in vain. How pitiful! What a painful and sorrowful
world is this!

Undated entry from "Diary" (Nikki), July 1–14, 1893

If one does not have a steady job, one will not have a steady mind. We
may long for a life of poetic elegance where we need only admire the
flowers and moon. Yet one cannot survive without food. Also, literature should not be what we do to make a living. It ought to be what
we do when we want to write freely as our thoughts drive us and our
mind instructs us. From now on, I will abandon the idea of writing for
a living. Instead, I shall start a business with an abacus in hand, counting each bead of sweat. Of course, I will forget the gatherings at the
Haginoya, where people hold cherry branches over their heads and en-

joy the elegant beauty of traditional poetry; they are merely yesterday's dreams that are already passing from my memory. I will strive to gather many small coins, so many sen and rin—so small and with their ripple marks on the back—instead of enjoying the ripples on the water in the old capital of Shiga. Although I will seek profit, I do not wish for the splendor of Mitsui and Mitsubishi. And yet I do not intend to be twisted and cynical about the world. It will be enough if the three of us, mother and daughters, can survive, living together like the cottonweed [known as "mother-daughter plant" in Japanese] on the wayside. If I have the time, I will gaze up at the moon and gaze on the flowers. If I feel interested enough, I will write poetry, compose some sentences, and produce novels. I hear, however, that thoughtless publishers say to writers such things as "This time, please give us a tale of double suicide. Or an elegant story about a poet will be fine. Overtly sentimental stories will not please readers. Anything too sensitive is not popular anymore. The subtle and profound beauty called *yūgen* is too difficult to understand. Historical fiction is fine. Political novels are also good. Detective stories are even better. Choose a topic from among those." Though I have not yet had too many bad experiences in this area, such foolishness from publishers should be stopped. I have made up my mind to open a candy store because I want to be liberated from such a world and free from any duties—at least in the world of literature.

On the other hand, in the twenty years of my life, I have never become used to socializing with neighbors. I have neglected to greet and chat with other bathers while at the public bathhouse. For an unsociable person like myself, it will indeed be a difficult thing to greet people on the street by exchanging the appropriate daily or seasonal greetings, to cope with customers' tough negotiations on prices, to buy goods at wholesale shops, and to pay close attention to our customers' moods. Come to think of it, business is full of hardship. In addition, our capital is almost nonexistent. I wonder what will happen—I am already at my wits' end. I try to think that a life is like a Bodhidharma figurine displayed on the shelf: just as it cannot fall over or stand up all by itself, we, too, are affected by larger forces. Ah, God of Creation, please lead me in the right direction!

> Whatever the cost, I shall live
> By crossing the floating bridge of dreams in this world[24]

Entries from "Amid the dust diary" (Chiri no naka nikki), November 27, 1893–February 23, 1894

December 1

Sunny. The eleventh issue of *Bungakukai* [Literary world] came in the mail. Oh, what a surprise, Miyake Kaho's story is in it. It is about the *koto* teacher Yamanoi Kōtō. Her writing is neat, fully mature, and without a flaw. Of the few women writers these days, she will be the one who will receive everlasting fame and be remembered in future generations. In addition [to her own talent], she also has a prestigious family background and a noble personality.

"Sakawa-gawa" (The Sakawa River) by Baba Kochō and "Aien" (Sorrowful fate) by Musei [Shimazaki Tōson] are also excellent works. But compared to "Aien," "Sakawa-gawa" is not quite successful. It is not a poem, but with its *waka*-like meter of five-seven, it reminds me of a *jōruri* puppet play. Speaking of experiments with new literary styles, literature has departed from the tradition of *waka* poetry that focused on the beauty of nature, but it does not yet seem to have adjusted to our modern civilization and enlightenment. Recent trends have brought us the so-called *shintaishi*, or new-style poetry. Of course, there are compositions by brilliant and well-educated people. But many of those by young people demonstrate complacency and have a pretentious style. I feel it is not unreasonable that older people point to such works and laugh at them. At the same time, I find that in this world of steam locomotives and steamships, we cannot hold on to the old tradition of thirty-one syllables as though we are riding slowly in a Heian period ox-drawn carriage. I hope to follow the changes in our natural world and depict the subtle images of nature and various aspects of human affairs in my writing. I am sure others share the same wish. But I wonder whether such a wish can be realized, unless by a genius. There is refined elegance in the secular world, and there is great vulgarity in refined elegance. But new-style poetry appears vulgar and *waka* seems elegant not only because of tradition. Modern poetry is inferior because it does not enter into the human heart or sing its truths; it does not match the broad-minded thoughts of the present era. Even if the words are vulgar, a poem's melody will naturally have dignity as long as there is elegance at its heart.

Indeed, the way of poetry is easy to learn but difficult to compose; its profundity is difficult to master.

An extra edition of the newspaper came at night. It reported that a vote of no confidence against Hoshi Tōru, the Speaker of the House of Representatives, was passed after it was submitted to the Emperor.[25]

December 2

The assembly has been in chaos. They are exposing one another's private affairs and disclosing secrets. How indiscreet it is!

At midnight, I close my eyes and think quietly about today's society, wondering how it will change in the future. If people knew what I was thinking, they might say that I am forgetting my position as a woman. They might think that a powerless woman concerning herself with society is like an ant or worm discussing the world. However, even mere women live in the same society and are exposed to the same stormy weather as men. Although born in a marginal corner of the country and raised there, women are still born in the land of Japan and are equally indebted to His Majesty. In that sense, women are the same as those ministers and leaders. How can I look at the increasingly imminent danger to my country as if it had nothing to do with me? People have become accustomed to a comfortable life and have gotten extravagant. Their hearts seek fancy customs from foreign countries and cast away our country's old traditions. Such frivolity has spread from small aspects in daily life to substantial arenas such as literature, education, and politics. It is as though the water is flowing down and carrying away the dirt and rubbish but does not know where to stop. Let's look at what has come of this situation. Internationally, the incident with Korea has become more difficult to handle.[26] We did not win the lawsuit against Great Britain over the collision and sinking of the battleship *Chishima* although our country stood in the right, and because of it we are made light of by other countries. There are many other international concerns as well, such as the need to amend the unequal treaties [with the United States, Russia, Holland, France, and Great Britain]. At the same time, when we look at domestic issues, people regard one another with hostility. The sacred assembly is disgraced by disputes among its members. Many people are seeking only their own profits and are no longer paying attention to national interests. The dirty water will not be cleaned in a day. What will be the future of our country in this flow of events? When we look outside, an eagle is sharpening its claws and a lion is snarling at us.[27] Looking back at what has happened to India and Egypt,[28] my body and soul tremble with fear. Even if I am called whimsical and naive by my contemporaries and laughed at by future generations, how can I—since I happen to have been born in this time—waste my life by doing nothing? I can only think about what I should do and try to do the right thing. It is embarrassing to say as a woman, but:

> In the blowing autumn winds,
> How can an *ominaeshi* plant escape the field?[29]

Entry from "On the water" (Mizu no ue), February 20, 1896—?

February 20

The sound of raindrops on the eaves and the clamorous cries of crows— these brought me back from the dream I was having at my reading desk. While I was counting the dates on my fingers and wondering if today was the twentieth of February, I gradually remembered my name and age, returning to reality. Today was Thursday—the day when people come to my house for literary lessons. Since the spring snow is falling very heavily, I thought the streets would be treacherous. I felt for those people, thinking they would be inconvenienced.

I was happy in the dream I was having; I was saying what I wanted, and people understood exactly what I was thinking. Once I awakened, however, I returned to myself in this world, where there are many things that I am not supposed to say or that I find difficult to express.

Resting my cheeks in my hands at my reading desk, I ponder things. Indeed, I am merely a woman. How can I ever realize any of my thoughts?

I am not certain if I have the aptitude for appreciating poetic elegance over secular life. I don't cherish the idea of abandoning this earthly world and hiding myself in the deep mountains. Nonetheless, there are those who say I am a misanthrope. I do not understand why. If I write something of little significance, they praise me with such commonplace expressions as "the genius of modern times," while I might just as likely hear slander from the same mouths tomorrow. How miserable! I am in a world where I cannot find any friend among the people I see every day. Since no one really understands me, I feel as though I have been born into this world all alone. I am a woman. Even if I have ideas and thoughts, how can I realize them in this world!

Entry from "On the water diary" (Mizu no ue nikki), May 2–June 11, 1896

May 2

. . . Of all the visitors I receive, nine out of ten come merely out of curiosity, because they find it amusing that I am a woman. That is why they praise and congratulate me as a "modern Sei Shōnagon" or a "modern Murasaki Shikibu," even when I only produce scratch paper. They do not have enough insight to fathom my deepest thoughts, and they only delight in the fact that I am a woman writer. Thus they reveal nothing in their criticism. Even if there are flaws in my work, they cannot see them. And when there are good things in my work, they cannot explain them. They merely say "Ichiyō is good," "she is skillful," and "her skills even exceed those of male writers, not to mention other female writers," and "indeed, she is good and talented." Besides such empty phrases, can they find no other words to say? Can they not see any flaws in my work to criticize? This is indeed a strange phenomenon.[30]

NOTES

All translations by Kyōko Ōmori unless otherwise indicated.

1. Mori Ōgai, Kōda Rohan, and Saitō Ryokuu, "Makoto no shijin" (A true poet), *Mezamashigusa* (Awakening), April 1896, p. 48. This translation is from Robert Danly's book of translations with critical essays, *In the Shade of Spring Leaves: The Life and Writings of Higuchi Ichiyō, A Woman of Letters in Meiji Japan* (New Haven: Yale University Press, 1981), p. 148.

"Takekurabe" has been translated into English multiple times, but the best-known translations are "Child's Play" (Robert Danly) and "Growing Up" (Edward Seidensticker).

2. Ichiyō's diary shares these characteristics with its courtly predecessors, which began to appear around the tenth century. For example, Heian courtiers read famous diaries that were circulated through their small circles, copied them with brush and ink, and wrote their own by observing literary conventions and alluding to topics that they learned from those who came before them.

3. See Nishikawa Yūko, "Diaries as Gendered Texts," in *Women and Class in Japanese History*, ed. Hitomi Tonomura, A. Walthall, and H. Walita, (Ann Arbor: Center for Japanese Studies, University of Michigan, 1999), pp. 241–256, a helpful overview of the tradition and significance of diary keeping in Japan.

4. It is said that her pseudonym, Ichiyō (written with the kanji characters "one" and "leaf"), comes from a Buddhist legend about a famous Zen patriarch, Bodhidharma, who crossed the Yangtze River on a boat made of a single reed, arrived at a meditation site, and sat for nine years until he lost his legs. Based on this legend, Bodhidharma has been a symbol of enduring hardship. It also happens that the phrase "*o-ashi ga nai*" (to have no legs) means "to have no money" in Japanese slang, which Ichiyō once noted humorously in explaining how she arrived at her pen name. Ichiyō repeatedly used the imagery of a floating leaf in her writing, alluding to her unpredictable life.

5. Ichiyō started studying among the rich at Haginoya in 1886 because her father, recognizing his young daughter's precocious talent in literature, wanted her to continue her education at least in *waka* poetry. Ichiyō had graduated from the fourth year of a private elementary school, Seikai gakkō, at the top of her class. Her mother, however, was afraid that too much education hindered young women from arranging good marriages, and this was the last time Ichiyō received formal education.

6. Normally, the eldest son would inherit the headship of the family. If there was no son in the household, it would fall to the eldest daughter. Almost never would a widow assume the role of family head.

7. For example, Oku Taisuke's column in *Waseda bungaku* (Waseda literature), nos. 24 and 25 (September and October 1892), entitled "Bungaku to kokō" (Literature as a means of livelihood), criticized the act of writing to make a living. Ichiyō mentions in her December 24, 1892 entry that she was embarrassed to read this article because it appeared around the time when she finally started receiving requests from publishers. Incidentally, Ichiyō scholar Suzuki Jun speculates that Ichiyō alludes more particularly to her job as *waka* poetry teacher at the Haginoya when she talks about "literature as a means of livelihood" (*Higuchi Ichiyō nikki o yomu* [Tokyo: Iwanami shoten, 2003], p. 43).

8. It is said that the entirety of what survived of the diary was published, but it is not clear if the pages missing from the original notebooks were removed by Ichiyō herself or by her sister and Baba Kochō.

9. The custom of rewriting daily entries into a reconstructed memoir can be traced back to tenth-century *nikki* such as *Kagerō nikki* (The gossamer diary), *Sarashina nikki* (The Sarashina diary), *Murasaki Shikibu nikki* (The Murasaki Shikibu diary), and so on.

10. Wada Yoshie, *Ichiyō no nikki* (Tokyo: Fukutake shoten, 1983), pp. 49–50.

11. Noguchi Seki, "Kaisetsu," in *Zenshū Higuchi Ichiyō: Nikki-hen*, 3 vols. (Tokyo: Shōgakukan, 1996), 3:343. For example, Ichiyō wrote the following passage in her diary: "This is not something I have prepared in order to show to others, but if in the future I look back on this account of my past, I am sure that many things will seem most peculiar and even demented, and if by some mischance other people should see it, they will surely say, 'This is the work of a madwoman' " (translated by and quoted in Donald Keene, "The Diary of Higuchi Ichiyō," in *Modern Japanese Diaries* [New York: Henry Holt, 1995], p. 291).

12. Keene argues that the diary writing was not for practicing modern prose on the grounds that Ichiyō primarily employs Heian language and classical wordplay (ibid., p. 288).

13. Higuchi Ichiyō, *Jō*, book 1 of *Nikki: Jō and ge*, ed. Shioda Ryōhei, Wada Yoshie, and Higuchi Etsu, in vol. 3 of *Higuchi Ichiyō zenshū* (Tokyo: Chikuma shobō, 1978), p. 120.

14. Ichiyō lists in her diary these and many other titles of books that she read. There is not much evidence, however, of her reading non-Asian writings except for the Japanese translation of *Crime and Punishment* and a few others.

15. Higuchi, *Jō*, p. 519.

16. It should be noted that there are two earlier cases of depictions of females on Japanese banknotes. The first was of Empress Jingū, on a note issued by the Meiji government in 1881–1883, but since she was a legendary figure from the second/third century, her portrait was an artist's creation. The second was of Murasaki Shikibu, on the 2,000-yen note issued in 1999, but since the main design was the Shureimon Gate at Shuri Castle in Okinawa, the Bank of Japan does not consider the small depiction of the legendary writer from the eleventh century on the reverse side as the first female portrait.

17. The following sources were consulted for the translation that follows: Yamada Yūsaku, *Higuchi Ichiyō*, Sakka no jiden, no. 22 (Tokyo: Nihon tosho sentā, 1995); Higuchi Ichiyō, *Higuchi Ichiyō shū*, ed. and ann. Kan Satoko and Seki Reiko, Shin Nihon koten bungaku taikei: Meiji-hen, no. 24 (Tokyo: Iwanami shoten, 2001); Higuchi Ichiyō, *Honkoku Higuchi Ichiyō nikki*, 3 vols. (Tokyo: Iwanami shoten, 2002); Higuchi Ichiyō, *Kanzen gendaigo-yaku Higuchi Ichiyō nikki*, trans. Takahashi Kazuhiko (into modern Japanese) (Tokyo: Adoree,

1993); Higuchi Ichiyō, *Gendaigo-yaku Higuchi Ichiyō*, 5 vols. (Tokyo: Kawade shobō shinsha, 1996–1997); Higuchi Ichiyō, *Zenshū Higuchi Ichiyō*, 4 vols. (Tokyo: Shōgakukan, 1996).

18. The term *yomogiu* (a place where mugwort grows) connotes a ruin or a dilapidated place.

19. Ichiyō is apparently quoting 過則勿憚改, a phrase from "To Learn, and Then" in *The Analects*, by Confucius.

20. Kuniko is Ichiyō's younger sister. Ichiyō lived with her and their mother, Taki. Kuniko visited their elder sister on this day because the latter was then pregnant and close to delivery.

21. The teachings of Han Feitzu are titled *Kanpishi* (*Han Feitzu*) in Japanese and are included in the famous Chinese textbook *Bunshō kihan* (Basic writing). *Han Feitzu* was a popular textbook for learners of classical Chinese writing in Japan during the Edo period. "Zeinan" (The difficulty of persuasion) is a section in the book.

22. Ono no Komachi was a poet from the ninth century. While very little about her actual life is known, she is legendary for her beauty, amorous poems, and her bitter end as a crazy, wandering hag, as poignantly portrayed in a Noh piece, *Sotoba Komachi*.

23. This expression is borrowed from *The Analects of Confucius*. According to *The Analects*, purple is a symbol of evil, and vermillion represents a man of virtue or justice. It is likely that Ichiyō learned this expression from the writings of Shimazaki Tōson (1872–1943), which Ichiyō read avidly.

24. This entry was probably inserted later as a preface to this section of the diary.

25. Hoshi Tōru (1850–1901) was accused of influence peddling and accepting bribes in 1893.

26. This is called the Bōkokurei Incident (1893). The Japanese government was at odds with Korea over the exports of grain from Korea to Japan.

27. The eagle is the United States, and the lion is Great Britain.

28. They were both colonized by Great Britain.

29. Its English name is goldbaldrian. In Japanese characters, *ominaeshi* is written as 女郎花, and its status as a "woman flower" goes back to Manyō poetry in the eighth century.

30. This is a partial translation of the entry.

TAZAWA INABUNE
(1874–1896)

Melek Ortabasi

LIKE MANY OF THE AUTHORS included in this anthology, Tazawa Inabune, born Tazawa Kin, had a regrettably short career. "Go-dai-dō" (The temple of Godai, 1896), included here, was one of the last pieces she wrote before her premature death at age twenty-three. She is noteworthy, though for her sheer tenacity and commitment to becoming an author. The ambitious Kin, born to a military doctor and his wife in Yamagata Prefecture, loved literature from the start. She pored over regional newspapers and sent off for literary journals from Tokyo to follow the work of her favorite authors. Her goal was to become part of the literary community she saw represented there. She left her hometown, Tsuruoka, for Tokyo at age eighteen, ostensibly to pursue a degree in the painting department at the Kyōritsu Women's Occupational School, but she never graduated. Given her strict upbringing and the fact that her father had certainly frowned on her literary interests, one may guess that getting to Tokyo (the center of the Japanese literary world) had always been Inabune's real goal.

In Tokyo, she immediately contacted Yamada Bimyō (1868–1910), a well-known male member of the Ken'yūsha literary coterie with whom she had already been corresponding. Having adopted the pen name Inabune while still in Tsuruoka,[1] she had been sending manuscripts to the journal Bimyō edited, *Iratsume* (The maiden). Bimyō, only six years

Inabune's senior, was a rising star in the literary world, known for his elegant style as an author and a man. While Inabune looked up to him as a teacher, the relationship soon became intimate.

Inabune had better judgment in choosing her literary mentor than did her contemporary Higuchi Ichiyō, since Bimyō was making a name for himself while Ichiyō's teacher, Nakarai Tōsui, already had a reputation as a hack writer. Ichiyō, however, broke off her friendship with Nakarai after hearing that rumors about the two of them were circulating (see the journal entries included in this volume for her feelings on the matter); Inabune was not so shrewd. Bimyō, while an innovative author, was also a confirmed playboy who did not appear to take the affair as seriously as did she. Nevertheless, after Inabune was called home to Yamagata by her outraged parents, Bimyō made the journey to Tsuruoka to ask for her hand. Some speculate that he settled on Inabune for her money; some insist that he had real feelings for her. In any case, the two returned together to Tokyo and were married at the end of 1895.[2]

While Inabune was following the example of most other female authors of this period in seeking to become someone's protégé, starting a relationship with her mentor did not serve her well. Furthermore, there were already two other women in Bimyō's household: his mother, "an unhappy woman who had lost her husband to a rival," and his paternal grandmother, "a willful and domineering woman who controlled the household."[3] Given this hostile environment, Bimyō's continued philandering, and the fact that the newspaper gossip columns reported gleefully on the difficulties in the relationship, it is perhaps no wonder that the marriage lasted only three months. With her husband's permission, Inabune, in bad health, returned home to her parents. According to the *Chūō shinbun*, a major Tokyo newspaper, it was only natural that such a fate should befall Inabune, who had, after all, "abandoned her parents and disregarded public opinion" in her single-minded commitment to love.[4]

In spite of the disappointment in her personal life (or perhaps because of it), Inabune was meanwhile becoming a more accomplished author. Her name first became known to the literary world with the publication of "Igaku shūgyō" (Medical training) in the July 1895 issue of the well-known literary journal *Bungei kurabu* (Literary arts club). This story, about a young woman who fails at becoming a doctor but succeeds as a *gidayū* ballad chanter, is generally regarded as a "well-written" piece

FIGURE 5.1 A page from the special *keishū sakka* issue of *Bungei kurabu*,
December 10, 1895; Tazawa Inafune (1874–1896) is upper right

with a narrative that unfortunately mimics Bimyō's taste for the outlandish.[5] She officially entered the ranks of the Meiji women writers when
her story "Shirobara" (White rose) appeared in the much-publicized
keishū sakka (lady writer) issue of *Bungei kurabu* alongside pieces by
Higuchi Ichiyō, Miyake Kaho, and Kitada Usurai, among others.[6] This
story, in which an upper-class young woman ultimately commits suicide
after being raped by her no-good suitor (who renders her unconscious
by chloroforming her), was criticized for its portrayal of graphic violence. Significantly, however, the criticism was personal: contemporary
critic Gotō Chūgai (1866–1938), for example, complained that the heroine, Mitsuko, was much too aggressive and furthermore that it was "not
clear where the portrait of Mitsuko ended and the author's began."[7] Accusations of mimicry and perversity continued to inform the discourse
on Inabune's work. "The Temple of Godai," published posthumously
in the November 1896 issue of *Bungei kurabu*, demonstrates this perhaps
more than any other piece.

The suave and handsome protagonist of "The Temple of Godai," writer Imamiya Yoboro (aka Hōtō Sanjin), is unquestionably reminiscent of Yamada Bimyō. Similarly, the young heroine, Itoko, who falls in love with him and chooses to help pay the price for his previous indiscretions, probably resembles in some way the naive young woman who went to Tokyo in search of literary fame. Certainly, most critics both past and present have chosen to read the story autobiographically, as has been the case with so many other writings by women. Shioda Ryōhei, referring to Inabune's ignominious return home after her failed marriage, asserts that the story boils down to "an attempt to resolve her present mental state."[8] Wada Shigejirō criticizes Shioda but ultimately makes the same argument for Inabune's psychological imbalance when he avers that the story "naturally reflects [her] interiority, which had been torn in two."[9] These recent literary critiques not only echo but actually reproduce the patter of the late Meiji gossip columns. But while "The Temple of Godai" no doubt has its origins in lived experience (as does the work of any author), it is not autobiographical.

Presupposing this sort of reading, perhaps, Inabune has her protagonist, Imamiya, protest the close identification of literary product and lived experience in the case of women authors: "These women writers are certainly pitiful creatures. Whenever they allow themselves to describe even a little of their own thoughts, they are immediately derided as hussies. Fearing just this sort of reaction, they avoid writing what they really want to, both hoping to be praised as feminine and lacking the courage to go against public opinion." Readers who choose to identify Inabune with the timid Itoko clearly overlook the fact that Itoko is rather single-minded about her love for the deeply flawed Imamiya, whereas her creator writes reflectively on the shortcomings of both characters. Clearly, Inabune had no problem going "against public opinion" here or in her other writings, where she boldly confronts violence, sexuality, and other such unfeminine vices.

Critics connect Inabune's work to male influence not only in terms of content but also in terms of style. For example, most agree that Inabune's early work closely resembles that of her mentor. Similarly, defenders of this later story tend to value it because it seems less dependent on Bimyō's advice. "Now far away from Bimyō's influence," Yukiko Tanaka writes, referring to Inabune's last months at home in Tsuruoka, "she was slowly finding her own mode of expression."[10] Wada Shigejirō goes even further by actually collapsing the distinction between content and style. After pointing out the break in tone between chapters 1–9 and 10, where Imamiya undergoes his change of heart, he asserts that this "flaw" in the work is actually an expression of its modernity: "when we see the relationship between this work and the author's self . . . can't we say that [it] has surpassed the qualities of the *gesaku* of the previous age, that is, the 'customs and manners' literature of the Ken'yūsha?"[11] In other words, though the too intimate relationship the author had with the content of the work caused a structural flaw, this close identification resulted in a truly modern expression of self.

Wada's left-handed compliment actually serves as an introduction to more general influences on Inabune, ones that also shaped her mentor. *Gesaku* is generally used to refer to the popular literature of the Edo period (1600–1868), which had fallen "into disrepute during the Meiji era," at least among novelists. This is not to say, though, that this "frivolous" style disappeared overnight; there were modern champions, such as the writers of the Ken'yūsha.[12] In any case, locating "The Temple of Godai" within a literary climate strongly influenced by *gesaku* writing is perhaps the most effective method of dismantling arguments for either autobiographical or Bimyō-influenced readings of Inabune's work.

"The Temple of Godai" has many features reminiscent of Edo-period writing. Most notable, perhaps, is the double suicide: Imamiya and Itoko choose to be together in death, thus absolving themselves and their families from the social shame that would be caused by their inappropriate relationship. This theme has been replayed in countless premodern and modern literary works. The lovers who may not consummate their relationship because of social or familial obligations are probably most famously portrayed in Chikamatsu Monzaemon's play *Shinjū ten no Amijima* (The love suicides at Amijima, 1721), in which a poor merchant ultimately chooses to die with a beloved geisha rather than stay with his wife. This battle between *giri* (duty) and *ninjō* (emotion), though deemed old-fashioned by some contemporary critics, continued to inform narrative structures throughout the Meiji period and beyond.

Another similarity with *gesaku* writing is the polyvocality of the narrative. While Imamiya is arguably the main character, the narrative switches perspectives regularly and features an impressive cast of characters. For example, the most important event in the development of the love story, where Imamiya and Itoko come up with a plan to elope,

FIGURE 5.2 Tazawa Inafune (1874–1896)

is never featured. We witness only the missive Itoko casts in Imamiya's direction when he is walking in the garden at her home; the next time we see them together, at the roadside inn, they already seem quite familiar with each other. One might say that the narrative arc is thus imperfectly formed, but that would ignore the historical and literary context of the story. The intervening (sometimes convoluted) scenes involving Fusao (Itoko's brother), Itoko's parents, and O-Tsuyu's plight, are somewhat episodic in nature but also provide a kind of symmetry: Fusao's loss of innocence and O-Tsuyu's downfall both comment on Itoko's fate. This parallel plot structure is a device the story shares with earlier Japanese literature and drama, as well as some contemporary works, such as Miyake Kaho's "Warbler in the Grove" (in this volume). Each character, and each subplot, adds its own flavor to the narrative.

The levity with which the narrator often treats these multiple characters, too, is more reminiscent of witty and urbane Ihara Saikaku (1642–1693), the doyen of Edo period writing, than the newer psychological style championed by the advocates of modern, Western-style literature. However, the *gesaku*-style narrator who does occasionally intrude clearly offers a woman's perspective on social mores. This is where the text differs most markedly from those of Inabune's male peers and is what marks it as modern. While the characters in "The Temple of Godai" seem somewhat formulaic, there is a sharp eye in the background that focuses the reader's attention on the many double standards and obstacles confronting women in Meiji society.

Itoko may embrace the sweet, innocent personality and tragic fate of many of her literary predecessors without complaint, but she is not unequivocally admired for it. In fact, the narrator makes us conscious of her naïveté by criticizing her for being so easily taken in by Imamiya's smarminess. She is unquestionably one of the "daughters in boxes" of which Kishida Toshiko spoke so eloquently (see the text in this volume). Pampered by her parents and denied any real education, she gets lost in daydreams, only to find out that reality does not bear them out, in much the same manner that Shimizu Shikin warns her audience in the essay included in this volume, "How Determined Are Today's Women Students?" Nevertheless, Itoko is clearly unsatisfied with the idea of arranged marriage, as are the female characters in Nogami Yaeko's "Persimmon Sweets" and Shimizu Shikin's "The Broken Ring" (both in this volume). When she meets Imamiya and falls in love, she suddenly becomes a rebel, willing to sacrifice her family and any social respectability in order to be with him. In the dénouement, she is unafraid and committed to her love match, no matter how imperfect a man he may be. The severity of her choice, though, is revealed by the fact that she would rather die than confront her parents with her newly acquired shame.

If the female characters are subject to scrutiny, their male counterparts are more so. The irony of Itoko's drastic fate is found in the parallel plot involving the deflowering of her brother, the impressionable Fusao, which has also been engineered by Imamiya. Near the close of the story, we learn from Fusao's mother that he has run off to a hot springs resort with a second-rate geisha. However, his predicament will likely result only in embarrassment, not in suicide. This becomes obvious when his mother blames his father, who has regularly been keeping a mistress in his own household, for setting a bad example—an interesting reversal of the usual direction of such criticism.[13] We get a sense of the father's hypocrisy when he questions the moral fiber of writers like Imamiya without reflecting on his own lack of judgment. He is completely hoodwinked by O-Tsuyu, who aids Imamiya in his infiltration of the family, and is constantly corrected by his wife, who is neither shocked nor surprised by his continued foolish behavior.

The narrator reserves the most severe criticism for Imamiya, who heartlessly discards O-Tsuyu once she has fulfilled her purpose, gleefully leads Fusao down the path to debauchery, and flirts with Itoko in the hope of eventual material gain. Ultimately, however, the blame for the lovers' fate is placed not on Imamiya but on society itself. While the ending may seem too contrived for some readers, Itoko's goodness does convince Imamiya to rethink his cynical attitude toward the world; it is the condemnation of a Tokyo newspaper's gossip column that crushes his newly found optimism.

The importance of the mass media to the main character and to the final direction of the narrative is perhaps what is most Meiji about "The Temple of Godai." Newspapers (where most Meiji-period literary works originally appeared) were not only the main source of income for writers but also functioned as society's watchdog. They were clearly instrumental in determining the course of an author's career, and not only as venues for publication. As the story reveals, the gossip columns that flourished in all newspapers of this period had no small effect on the social status of their victims. "The Temple of Godai" thus updates the standard literary conflict between duty and emotion through its negative portrayal of the mass media. Imamiya's realization that his career is finished because of one slanderous article is perhaps not so extreme. Yamada Bimyō's career was destroyed in large part because the criticisms of his behavior that appeared in the press after Inabune's death, which was widely reported as a suicide. Even while Inabune was alive, her fame had at least as much to do with the buzz surrounding her affair with Bimyō as it did her own talent; her short life had even been the subject of a melodramatic piece in the *Yomiuri* newspaper, entitled *Inabune monogatari* (The Inabune story).[14] After her death, interestingly, a more sympathetic fictionalized biography, by Hasegawa Shigure, was serialized in the *Tokyo Asahi* newspaper as one of a seven-part series on notable women entitled *Shuntaiki—Meiji Taishō josei shō* (A springtime account—Portraits of women of Meiji and Taishō).[15]

The power of the Meiji mass media continues to pursue Inabune: in Donald Keene's comprehensive and canonical history of modern Japanese literature, *Dawn to the West*, Inabune appears once, mistakenly described as a "suicide," just as she was in the newspapers immediately after her death. Inabune, referred to simply as Yamada Bimyō's wife and a victim of his "allegedly callous treatment," is cited only as one reason for the failure of Bimyō's career.[16] Unlike her heroine, Itoko, however, Inabune did not offer her life to a man: she offered it instead to the opportunity for self-expression, using her writing to criticize society's resistance to change. It was because she kept writing while already ill, perhaps even on the manuscript for "The Temple of Godai," that this courageous young author was silenced so soon. We include her story here in the hope that it can be reread in a new context.

THE TEMPLE OF GODAI

Translated by Melek Ortabasi

1

This world abounds in pleasures, but not for the many husbands and wives who were unable to refuse a partner chosen by their parents.[17] Now, what if one were to hear of that betrothed's death, just before the wedding? There could be no greater joy! We are speaking here of Viscount Aoyagi's only daughter, Itoko, who had spent many a dark hour mourning her impending marriage to a man for whom she felt nothing. Recently, however, having heard that her fiancé had passed away because of a serious illness, happiness had brought the color back to her face, lending it an even greater beauty than before. Her grieving heart rose up, and, with her maidservants to join her, she again became absorbed in pleasant activities. On one of these occasions, her elder brother, Fusao, entered the room.

"Well now, Itoko, are you making flowers? My, O-Teru and O-Hatsu have become rather accomplished, too."[18]

The two maidservants were somewhat abashed. "Why, thank you, but we can't make them nearly so well as the young miss."

"Oh, come now. You're quite good."

Itoko smiled. "Brother, shall we make a flower basket for you, too?"

"Well then . . . peonies would be nice, I should think."

Itoko brushed wax onto a cherry leaf. "Oh, no, I'm bad at those."

"That doesn't matter."

"By tomorrow, then."

"Oh, by the way . . . I'm off to school for a bit. That Yoboro will probably drop by while I'm out. When he does, Itoko, would you keep him entertained for a while? I should return soon. He's no stranger, so you don't mind, do you?"

For some reason, Itoko's face flushed somewhat. "I don't know that I'll have anything interesting to say, but since O-Teru and O-Hatsu are both here, I'm sure we'll be able to detain him." She glanced over at the maidservants.

O-Teru chuckled. "I surely don't know how *we* would keep him. But since it'll be the young miss entertaining him, Mr. Imamiya will certainly pay no mind to time, no matter how busy he may be, right, O-Hatsu?" She peeked over at Itoko.

O-Hatsu laughed, too. "That's quite right, isn't it, young master, it's just as O-Hatsu says. Don't you worry; go ahead and leave."

****

Speak of the devil! Sure enough, Imamiya arrived shortly thereafter. He was of quite splendid appearance. Those lacking in judgment, overcome by his charm, would completely lose their heads. Those with common sense, however, regarded him as something of a dandy. He wore a dashing black *haori* jacket over three layers of *komon* silk. At his elegant *obi* from Hakata, there glinted a gold watch chain, and the subtle fragrance that wafted from his collar attested to his cologne's expense. O-Hatsu and O-Teru both gazed at him, mute with admiration for a moment. Watching them as they went out, saying that that they would bring some teacakes, Imamiya then turned to the rather embarrassed Itoko.

"Not here, is he? Rude of me dropping in while your brother's out."

Finally, Itoko managed to reply, shyly. "It's quite all right; my brother will be back before long. I'm sorry to make you wait, but won't you stay for a while?"

"Pleased to, I'm sure. Don't bother yourself about me."

Itoko brought out the photograph album at her side. "It's no bother at all. . . . Mr. Imamiya, have you seen our album?"

Taking it in his hand, Imamiya replied, "No, I haven't had the privilege. . . . My, this is you, is it not? Quite splendid!"

"Now, please don't tease me."

"Not at all! I mean it," he insisted, as he admired the photograph a while.

Changing his mood, he opened the next page. "This is Miss Hanazono, isn't it?[19] Do you know her well?"

"Yes, I do. She comes to call quite often."

"She's quite the talk of the town."

"Really? Well, actually . . ."

"They do say the worst things about her, but surely society's to blame for the way she turned out," Imamiya reflected.

"Apparently, her life has been rather troubled ever since she was a child."

"Is that right? . . . These women writers are certainly pitiful creatures. Whenever they allow themselves to describe even a little of their own thoughts, they are immediately derided as hussies. Fearing just this sort of reaction, they avoid writing what they really want to, both hoping to be praised as feminine and lacking the courage to go against public opinion. But Miss Hanazono certainly doesn't seem the timid type."[20]

"No, quite the contrary," Itoko responded. "Her manner and speech are overly vigorous, just like a man's. Actually, she's refreshing; she never cries, or simpers, or babbles on about things."

"Indeed? . . . So I suppose a passive, effeminate man like me wouldn't be to your taste," Imamiya chuckled.

Itoko suddenly looked uncomfortable, her face reddening. "Oh, I'm not saying that I like her."

Imamiya laughed. "Well, I'm not saying it's wrong of you to like her."

"Well, I don't. Actually, it's probably *you* who dislikes gloomy types such as me."

"I have no preference for brazen women."

"Oh, surely you jest . . . but I . . . I've given up, anyway."

Imamiya looked at Itoko, rather mystified. "What is it you've given up on?"

"Oh, it's nothing."

2

Accompanied by his maidservant O-Kyō and his beloved dog, Pochi, the master of the house stepped out into the garden, about to take his exercise under the shade of the new green leaves. But five minutes had scarcely passed when he suddenly reappeared in the parlor.

"What could he need me for so urgently?" thought the steward as he hurried up to his master and bowed.

With an unusually bad-tempered expression, the master began: "See here, Sugita, who is that talking with Fusao in the annex? I don't remember ever hearing the voice before."

"Hmm. What an odd thing for the master to ask," thought Sugita. He answered, "Ah . . . the guest is a writer the young master recently became acquainted with; his name is Hōtō Sanjin."

The master frowned. "Hm. A writer? Hōtō Sanjin . . . a rather pious-sounding sobriquet, no?"

"It's as you say, sir, a rather impressive one that recalls the bodhisat-tva of dance."[21]

The master smirked. "Be that as it may, you must know how it is that my son became associated with a popular writer!"

"Is he asking me how the young master came to know a writer?" wondered Sugita. Aloud her said "Ah, well, I'm not certain, but it would seem that the young master met him while on exam holiday in Kamakura and Enoshima, at the Ebisu Inn or some such place."

"Hm. Indeed. So who was with him then?"

"Well, actually, there wasn't really anyone accompanying him, only some other young gentlemen from school."

"Ah, so he went on his own . . . then it wasn't your mistake."

The steward jumped at hearing "mistake" and peered furtively at his master. The viscount added, "Now, an old man like me has no idea about the abilities of today's 'novelists' or about their behavior, but, in my day, those who called themselves popular writers were different from regular, decent people. That is, they didn't really have a profession or any real training. Perhaps a smattering of Chinese learning that they applied willy-nilly. They were of a character that would shock laypeople, always behaving vulgarly; in other words, most of them lived poor and miserable lives, trying to fool the world with what little talent they were born with. I'm not saying that today's 'novelists' are the same, but, because Fusao has a weak character, I'd like to make sure his companions are soldiers or the like. I'd rather he didn't associate with such literary types. . . . I'll have to think of something to keep him away from these unsavory people."

Now understanding what the master had meant by "mistake," the steward finally relaxed. "Certainly, sir. To my eye, Hōtō Sanjin seems to be a fine gentleman, but now that I've heard the master explain, I've become rather concerned for the young sir as well. I'll try to find out the worthiness of this gentleman; if I discover something objectionable, I'll do my best to let the young master know your opinion without angering him."

"It has little to do with the quality of the person. The word 'novelist' alone puts me in a foul mood. No, I insist that he be kept away from here."

Just then, the master's favorite, O-Tsuyu, came in quietly. She shot the steward a dirty look, then wheeled swiftly; the eyes she turned on her master were exceedingly gentle. Simpering flirtatiously, she stammered, "Excuse me, sir . . . I couldn't help overhearing from the next room?"

The master replied with a warning tone in his voice. "Is there something you want, O-Tsuyu?"

"Yes," she replied tearfully and turned to the steward. "Well . . . Mr. Sugita, I wonder if you could be so kind as to ask Sir if he'd let me take my leave as of today."

Completely taken aback, the master replied, "Why, O-Tsuyu, do you mean to say that you find employment in this house dissatisfying?"

With an even more tearful voice, O-Tsuyu stammered, "Oh, goodness, no . . . no, nothing like that . . ."

"Well, what is it then?"

"Yes . . . well, master, since that Hōtō Sanjin you dislike so much happens to be my older brother, Yoboro Imamiya, I don't feel I can stay . . ."

Hearing this, the viscount was quite thrown off. "I didn't realize he was your brother." Awkwardly, he turned to Sugita. "See here, Sugita, in that case, I don't mind. Why don't you offer him something good to eat?"

Frustrated with his master's whims, Sugita muttered out loud in spite of himself. "Whatever you say, sir."

3

Meanwhile, in the annex, Hōtō Sanjin had not an inkling of O-Tsuyu's intervention on his behalf. Did he owe the fair, smooth complexion of his handsome face, almost unlike that of a Japanese, to some medicinal tonic? Flashing his almost appallingly charming dimples, he exclaimed rather suddenly, "Upon my word!"

Fusao started. "Ah, what's the matter?"

"Your study."

"What about it?"

"Well, the first time I called, the books were neatly put away on the shelves, but lately, every time I visit, there are newspapers and magazines scattered all around. It looks rather like my own study. Why have you suddenly become so slovenly? It's a bit shocking."

"Ah, well, since I've met you, law has become so tiresome. It's too stiff and logical. Since I've always wanted to, I've started writing something, half in jest. I was hoping you might take a look at it. Ever since I've been at my writing, my study has naturally fallen into this state." The young master replied awkwardly, offering a weak excuse to cover up the fact that, in imitation of Imamiya, he had put his study in disarray on purpose.

Hōtō Sanjin pretended to listen, all the while thinking that no one was likely to be fooled by an impostor pretending to be the real thing. "So, the fine young gentleman doesn't know what to do with all his leisure time and thinks he can pass off his unconscious babblings as literature now that he doesn't like law anymore," he thought to himself. "What a laugh!" Secretly, he sneered at the young man's pretensions. Revealing none of this, however, he replied with apparent interest:

"Aha! Is that so? How splendid. Might I be so bold as to peruse what you've written so far?" He grabbed rudely at the scribbled sheets that lay scattered over the fine desk inlaid with mother-of-pearl.

Fusao, agitated, snatched the papers from Sanjin's hand. "Oh, you can't look at those yet!" Cruelly crumpling his carefully written sheets into a ball, he stuffed them into his sleeve.

Sanjin, laughing, didn't resist. "Oh, dear, it was rude of me to look at them when they weren't ready. Incidentally, what style are you writing in?"

Fusao, thinking that Sanjin may have caught a glimpse, blushed. "Style? ... Well, I'm not capable of anything really good; it's just a rehash of an old-fashioned love story."

"Ah, a love story? Why, there's nothing more difficult. It's rather presumptuous of me to say, but I very much admire that you're writing about a subject in which you probably have little experience, being so young."

Fusao, completely oblivious of Sanjin's implicit criticism, replied blithely, "Yes, it's quite a bother that I have no experience. Since I'm just a student, I can't really come up with anything interesting."

"Yes, you'd best leave it alone," thought Sanjin, countering instead: "Oh, that's not at all the case. As the proverb says, the true poet can know the famous places of antiquity without ever having visited even a one. I'm sure a person of your talent need not rely on experience."

Fusao scratched his head. "Well, that may be true for you, but it's very hard for someone like me to write purely from the imagination. The lack of experience really is a problem."

Sanjin chuckled. "Oh, not at all. The world is usually much as one imagines it."

Suddenly, as though remembering something, he looked at his watch. He chortled, "Well, if I can't be of any help here, shall we repair to a more proper place for conducting research on love?"

The same idea had also occurred to Fusao; it was as though Sanjin had read the young man's mind. He was secretly overjoyed at Sanjin's suggestion. "Oh, yes, why don't we? What time is it?"

"It's seven-thirty; just right."

"Well, if you'll pardon me while I change . . ." Fusao nodded to Sanjin and disappeared into the back room.

Sanjin chuckled gleefully to himself, surveying a meal tray littered with mostly empty side dishes that had gone a bit rancid. Upturning a carafe, he was disappointed when not a drop came out. He smoked some tobacco, but the young sir was taking his time getting changed and still hadn't reappeared. Becoming bored by the long wait, Sanjin stood abruptly and donned some wooden garden *geta*. Letting the breeze caress his handsomely ruddy face, he wandered aimlessly around the pond behind the ornamental mound. Like the writer he was, he went along softly murmuring a classical poem under his breath. He was standing absently when something grazed his sleeve. When he looked, he saw that a missive tied to a bejeweled hairpin had fallen at his feet, seemingly waiting for him to pick it up. Did the moon already know this was a sign of first love? It became lost behind a wandering cloud . . . the light waned, giving the night a romantic cast.

4

He had called in a geisha once or twice, but this was Fusao's first time in a place such as this. Observing the young man's apparent discomfort, Hōtō Sanjin was inwardly somewhat disappointed that Fusao didn't seem to be enjoying himself. As he was trying to make Fusao feel at ease, the mistress of the place came in bearing the tea equipment. She smiled with her usual affability. "Where will it be tonight, sir?"

Sanjin scratched his head and glanced at Fusao's face. "Hm . . . where shall we take you, then?"

Fusao became increasingly embarrassed. "Where? Anywhere is fine."

The mistress chuckled. "Why don't you go to the usual place, then? You haven't called at all lately; yesterday, there was even a message from the *oiran*, the top courtesan of the house. 'Mr. Imamiya is so cold, isn't he?' " Exposed by the mistress's flattery as though a mask had been ripped from his face, Sanjin was greatly annoyed, but now there wasn't much to be done. Deeply regretting that he had thoughtlessly followed his feet to a familiar teahouse, he laughed, discomfited.

"Oh, come now. Why would I have a favorite girl? . . . All the same, where shall we go?"

"Well . . . whether you have a favorite girl or not I can't say, but stop saying such fickle things and just go to the Ohiko, as you always do."

"All right then . . . are you agreed?" He addressed Fusao.

Fusao, unfamiliar with the game, did not find it all that interesting, but now that he had come he couldn't very well back out. "Anywhere is fine with me," he replied, haplessly. Tactfully, the mistress called the chambermaid.

"Ah—O-Matsu, won't you go over to the Ohiko and check whether there's a room available?"

"Yes, of course." The woman brought her hands together and, raising her head a little, caught sight of Imamiya. "My, whom should I see but you, sir! Lately, we'd all but given up on you."

The mistress laughed, "O-Matsu, the gentleman has simply found a new place to frequent. Make sure you let the *oiran* know!"

Laughing, O-Matsu left but not before saying, "Oh, how mean! I'll make sure she doesn't hear the end of it."

Imamiya ordered some food and *sake*, and the three of them engaged in all manner of silly conversation. Presently, O-Matsu returned.

"Gentlemen, they're ready for you."

5

Pulling off the silken bedclothes, Itoko's mother asked, "Dear, how are you today? Are you not feeling quite well?"

Itoko was grateful for her mother's solicitude, but she had been asleep, having a most pleasant dream. She answered rather thickly, "I'm well, thank you," and heaved a small sigh. Resting on both hands, she let her forehead sink to the pillow. She lay facedown, dejectedly.

The mother, worriedly stroking her daughter's slender back, muttered, "Oh dear, I knew something was wrong . . . what ails you?"

Itoko mumbled, rather glumly, "I can't really say . . . I just feel out of sorts."

"Here, dear, are you worried about something? Or is something bothering you? Don't hesitate to tell me if there's anything the matter."

"Oh, it's not like that, but . . ."

"Well then, it must be something in your chest. Doctor Hayama is coming later; we'll have him take a good look at you."

"It's just a trifle; I'll feel better presently."

"That's all well and good, but if you keep lying there like that, you'll get a headache, too."

Mrs. Aoyagi took out the book she had brought in. "See here, this is Fusao's first attempt at a novel. That Hōtō Sanjin touched it up."

Itoko lifted her head and glanced at the cover. "*Wandering Clouds*? . . . Why, that's not Brother's calligraphy."

"No, that's Mr. Imamiya . . . in the Saga style, and rather good at that."

"Mother, have you read it already?"

"Yes, I did; quite interesting . . . but, anyway, that's not what concerns me."

Itoko looked at her questioningly. "Oh?"

"Whenever that Mr. Imamiya comes, O-Tsuyu is all aflutter. . . . Of course, he's an eminent person, so that makes sense, but the other maidservants are saying all sorts of things about those two. Now lately Father has taken to chatting with Mr. Imamiya, so I can't upbraid O-Tsuyu for serving them tea or the like. I'm sure Imamiya is a fine fellow, but why is it that, ever since Fusao took up with him, he's out all the time? I'm sure it's not the case, but sometimes I think to myself, what if this fellow is actually a wolf in sheep's clothing? My dear, what are your thoughts?"

Itoko blushed involuntarily, thinking that perhaps her mother had glimpsed her real feelings. Feigning indifference, she replied, "But, Mother, O-Tsuyu is basically a low-class woman. . . . She always has photographs of the popular Kabuki actors and such . . . you know the type. She's probably just smitten with Mr. Imamiya's good looks and works herself up into a state. I'm sure he has nothing to do with it . . . and, as for Brother, he probably gets held up because their discussions about literature are so interesting."

Her mother listened carefully. "That's probably so, but . . ."

"Of course it's true . . . but, Mother, shouldn't you find a way to dismiss O-Tsuyu and engage another woman?"

"Ah, yes . . . another thing I've thought peculiar lately is that, although your father hasn't told me anything, O-Teru and O-Kyō claim that he said Mr. Imamiya is O-Tsuyu's older brother. Isn't that odd? Given how your father is, I think it likely that O-Tsuyu is pulling the wool over his eyes."

Itoko narrowed her eyes suspiciously—or was it angrily? "That's for certain. That's why you should get rid of O-Tsuyu, quickly!"

"Yes, I'll do something. And you, too, dear—I don't want you visiting with your brother when that person is here, either."

Itoko started. "Why, I've nothing . . ."

"No buts . . . you're in a vulnerable state right now, seeing as you're not yet married."

"Oh, Mother!"

"Now, don't act so surprised!"

6

Running into her elder brother's room holding a doll in one hand, Hanako called out in a sweet voice. "Brother, that pretty lady is here again."

Yoboro put down the Western novel he had been about to read. Frowning, he said, "Tell her to come in here. . . . So where has Mother gone?"

"To Uncle's, in Akasaka."

"Oh? Well then, Hana-*chan*, you can go out and play."

"Hooray!" She ran out happily.

The woman who came in after a moment was none other than Viscount Aoyagi's mistress, O-Tsuyu. She sat down next to Yoboro and cozied up to him. "How fortunate that everyone should happen to be out today."

Gloomily, Yoboro replied, "Yes, but Mother will return presently . . . why are you here? Is there something you want?"

She glared at him reproachfully. "So why is it that you haven't come to call at my master's house recently?"

Irritated, he responded, "I simply can't tolerate the old man's wearisome talk."

"You lie!" O-Tsuyu burst out, tearfully.

Yoboro grimaced. "Oh, you're imagining things again."

Angrily, O-Tsuyu retorted, "I am not. . . . You've tired of me, haven't you?"

"Don't be silly—it's all thanks to you that I've had free entry [to the Aoyagi household] until now."

"So you haven't forgotten, have you?"

"Now, would I?"

"But you . . ."

"What's the matter, then?"

"Oh, nothing. . . . By the way, the young miss is pining away for you."

"Don't be ridiculous. When I visited last, wasn't she cheerful, a picture of health?"

"That's right, she's quite well now . . . but since her illness has been cured, you've no longer come to visit. It looks suspicious." O-Tsuyu hung her coiffured head.

Inwardly, Imamiya's heart jumped but feigning indifference, he said angrily, "Oh, you do go on. . . . My business is with Fusao; I haven't reason to drop in on the old man so often. It's becoming tedious, your constantly nagging me like this."

O-Tsuyu burst into tears. "Yes, I suppose it would be, since I'm not as beautiful as the young miss!"

Imamiya was now quite put out. "So are you saying then that there's something between myself and Miss Itoko?"

"Yes . . . that's why I'm so envious!" O-Tsuyu sobbed.

"This is too annoying; I've got to get rid of her somehow," thought Imamiya quickly.

"Well, there isn't anything going on, but why don't you make something up and quit, so we can get married right away? Unless you want nothing to do with a pauper like me?" He guffawed disarmingly.

Won over by these words, O-Tsuyu's anger disappeared. Her tears drying, she said happily, "Do you really mean it?"

"Would I lie about such a thing?"

"I'm so relieved!" So saying, she glanced at the wall clock. "My goodness, it's already four, you cruel clock. Well, it can't be helped. I must return before I'm found out."

"Yes, indeed. That would be best." Inwardly, Yoboro hoped that O-Tsuyu would be discovered soon. "I hope they find her out and get rid of her—but without involving me," he thought.

7

The lady of the house straightened her back and turned to her husband with a set expression. "Now, dear, you shouldn't become so angry. It's because you're still confused that you say such things. How could he possibly be her brother? There's definitely something peculiar going on with O-Tsuyu and Imamiya."

Her husband looked terribly offended and said confidently, "And what real evidence have you of that?"

His wife said smugly, "I have indubitable proof. I sent Sugita to the ward office; when he examined Tsuyu's family register, he found that she has not a single male sibling!"

The master paused at this. With bitter resignation, he responded, "Really? Well, you still could have consulted me."

"Oh, you have some lingering attachment? Well, my dear, I can't imagine why. At your age, you would do well to limit yourself! Be that as it may, thanks to that Imamiya, things have come to a pretty pass."

"Well, I didn't like that Imamiya from the start, either, but he really is an outrageous fellow. And O-Tsuyu on top of all that, too . . . but what do you mean, 'a pretty pass?'"

"Only the unfortunate fact that, invited by Imamiya, our Fusao has apparently been doing nothing but visiting the Yoshiwara licensed quarters. Not only has he done an excellent job of failing in school, but he hasn't even come home for two days. When I had someone ask around as to his whereabouts—listen to this!—I heard that he's gone to Atami in the company of a woman he knows quite well from the Ohiko, named Kodaifu or some such."

The master, too, could not have been more shocked. "Our Fusao?"

His wife was in tears. "Yes, our Fusao—the same Fusao who is heir to the Aoyagi estate. . . . And though it's mainly Imamiya's fault, your conduct is also partly to blame. One could say that Fusao is following your selfish example, too!"

Sheepishly, the master replied, "Well, now, stop henpecking me like this! In any case, we can't leave things this way. Call in Sugita or someone immediately."

"Well, that goes without saying!"

Just then, O-Kyō came in agitatedly and touched her palms to the floor in greeting. "Milady, where has the young miss gone? I can't find her."

8

Imamiya sat by the brazier with one knee pulled up, the newspaper in one hand and a pipe in the other. Puffing diligently at his tobacco, he fixed his eyes on his mother, who was absorbed in her work. "Mother, where's O-Tsuyu gone to?"

In a tired, shriveled-up voice, she replied, "She went to the public bath."

"She's been gone rather long."

"So?"

"So isn't it about time that you started pushing her around and making her cry?"

"My, you say the cruelest things. When it was you who dragged her into it!"

"You don't understand, do you, Mother? When I first met the viscount, the old fellow didn't much take to me, and I was almost thrown out. Then O-Tsuyu, the old man's mistress, took a liking to me and told him that I was her older brother. Grandpa fell for it right away, end of story. Thanks to that, I was able to cheat that idiot Fusao out of his money and settle most of our debts. . . . But the lady of the house is none too dim and found out the truth about O-Tsuyu and me, so finally both of us were thrown out. . . . I felt somewhat responsible, so there was nothing for it but to take her in quietly. Because of that, though, my precious reputation as an author has been ruined. . . . She's quite outlived her usefulness. If we continue to keep her here, she'll only become a burden. So, Mother, make yourself heard and start doing some scolding."

His mother listened carefully to the horribly cruel words that spouted so casually from her son's beautifully formed lips. "Now that you've explained it, it makes sense. But, son, what's really worrisome is that you haven't been getting any work lately. . . . The *Tōzai shinbun* cut you off as soon as O-Tsuyu was dismissed. . . . We've taken care of our large debts, but I'm constantly being hounded about the smaller ones that are still left. What do you plan to do now?"

"Not to worry; I've still got my ways."

"Really? Would that it were true!" So saying, she looked closely at her son. "Honestly, with your looks, it's no surprise that the women make a fuss."

"Don't be ridiculous . . . it's better that you start doing a good job of laying into O-Tsuyu!"

"All right, I understand."

Just then, the lattice door opened with a clatter, showing the return of a freshly scrubbed O-Tsuyu. Putting on a fierce look, the mother winked stealthily at her son, as though to say "Watch me at work!"

"Well, it's about time! How can you be lazing around when we've so much to do? You waste precious time every day with your elaborate makeup, as though you were a prostitute! It's shameful, the way you let the train of your kimono slither along . . . !"

O-Tsuyu was accustomed to this kind of treatment, but this was too much. She cowered, shrinking into herself. "Please forgive me, Mother," she said timidly, "it's just that I ran into Mii-*chan* over there, and we got to talking."

Sharply, the older woman replied, "No doubt gossiping away about some actor or such. How stupid! . . . My, my, aren't you powdered up beautifully today? You look just like a thief in a flour mill!" She chortled. "Oh dear, she's going to cry . . . what's so sad, I wonder? Oh, it's the limit—here she is, stuck with this shiftless, lazy husband, and can't even go out and have a bit of fun. What's more, she has to take care of a wizened old crone like me. Yes, indeed, that *must* be wretched." She turned to Imamiya. "Now, son, since O-Tsuyu hates being here so much it makes her cry, be a man and let her go!"

Hōtō Sanjin had not so much as glanced at O-Tsuyu this entire time and had continued reading the newspaper. Now, he finally turned to face her. "Well, if you don't like it here, you're free to leave anytime. Even if you still have feelings for me, I don't have any in the slightest for you. Don't hesitate on my account—I won't have any trouble finding someone else." He glanced at his watch. "Mother, I must go out and meet someone today; lay out my kimono, won't you?"

"All right."

"Quickly; it won't do to be late."

Getting laboriously to her feet, his mother replied, "Be sure you come back soon."

"I won't be able to."

"Why then?"

"Never you mind; I'll explain later. Now, no matter how late I am, even if I'm gone for two or three days, don't worry yourself about it. And make the kimono the striped silk crepe one."

"All right." So saying, his mother went into the back room.

O-Tsuyu, who had been prostrate on the floor, weeping, sprang up in a trice. Suddenly clinging to Imamiya, she cried, "Is what you said just now true?"

Mercilessly shaking off her hands, he kicked her away. "Silence! Yes, it's too bad for you, but it's true."

9

There, by the edge of Shitaya Pond, is a small inn, The Lovers' Robes, with a name that matches its amorous nature. In a second-floor room, in which the blinds are pulled despite the terrible heat, a man and a woman take refuge from the public eye. They are clearly in the throes of love. The woman helps the man remove his summer *haori* jacket, smiling joyfully as she folds it.

The man, too, grins foolishly. "You did well in getting away today, didn't you?"

"Well, that's because I'm absolutely set on you," she replies affectionately.

He puffs on his pipe. "It must have been quite difficult, no?"

"Yes, it took some doing."

"My mother was rather suspicious as well."

"Why? Is she angry with you about something?"

"Oh, no, she wasn't angry . . . now that we're here, all is well."

"I do hope you're right . . . but what if someone followed us here?"

"There's no need to worry; even if they did, there's no chance that the innkeeper would let slip that the two of us were here."

"I suppose so."

"Of course it's so. . . . In any case, are you sure about leaving behind your family? That's what worries me the most, since your mother, particularly, profoundly dislikes me."

She drooped, sadly. "Why is Mother so unsympathetic, I wonder? . . . But don't worry, we're set for now." She removed a small silk-wrapped bundle from her bodice. "See, I've even brought two hundred yen with me."

Hearing the amount, the man became quite enthusiastic. "Is that right? Well, that's splendid! . . . Isn't it strange to think of what has happened since this spring, when you first gave me that letter in the garden? It seems like a dream that I am with you like this." He took her hand, with its faintly polished nails, and pulled her to him.

Bashfully, the woman moved closer and leaned against his knees. Tenderly, she looked up into the man's face. "Yes, darling," she said quietly, "why were you so cold to me then?"

Stroking her back, he replied: "Oh, no, I had no intention of being cold to you, but that was when your fiancé, young Lord Haruyama, had just recently passed away . . . and then I thought that this love had very little chance of a future. It was pointless to see you only at odd hours and then have only regrets later. In fact, I harbored the most torturous love for you in my heart."

"Oh, you liar, as though Haruyama were of any consequence. . . . I'm sure it was just because you would have preferred a vivacious woman like O-Tsuyu over a homely girl like me."

"I don't know how she feels about it. As for me, I hate that sort of cheap, immodest woman, much as I hesitate to insult a servant of your father's."

Gleefully, she said, "Hm, I wonder!"

"Still you wonder? If I'm lying, what shall you do then?"

She pinched him. "This is what I'll do!"

"Ouch! My, your fingers are strong. Quite out of keeping with those delicate, white hands!"

"Oh, stop your teasing!"

"Oh, are you angry?" He chuckled. "Anyway, are you truly willing to come away with me?"

"Why would I lie? You must of course take me with you, now that I've left my home in this way. I feel that I can withstand any difficulties as long as I can be by your side. What's more, you can't know how happy it makes me that you'll take me to places I've never seen before."

"Truly? Well, then, let's go as far as Ōmiya tonight."

She started. "Right now?"

"Well, there's still enough time. . . . If we do, we'll be able to travel more leisurely from there. And getting on the train at Ueno will be best during the afternoon, when few people are around."

"If I'm with you, it doesn't matter to me, but what will you do about your mother?"

"Oh, it's better that I send her a letter once we get there. . . . I'll tell her that I won't come back unless she accepts you as my wife, won't I?"

"Really? Oh, I'd be so happy!"

"Yes, really!" he laughed and pressed his ruddy cheek to her silken smooth one. "I'm telling you no lies; it's all the truth. I've never felt like this about a woman before. How is it that I've fallen in love so badly? Why, it's still a mystery to me."

Overjoyed, the woman responded, "Even if they are lies, I'll never forget those words."

"You'll know the truth of it before long . . . your brother has probably arrived at Atami by now. I'm envious!"

"We're leaving together now; there's no need to be envious of my brother, unless you've still got a soft spot for Hanakoshi or some other girl at the Ohiko!"

"Now don't be ridiculous. . . . Enough of the silly talk, you'd better get ready!"

10

The day on which they were to be wed properly found them all alone at the Moon-Viewing Pavilion Inn in Matsushima.[22] Standing near the edge of the third-story balcony, Itoko surveyed the view in all directions.

"What a lovely scene. Indeed, there can be no better view in all Japan."

Imamiya, who had been lying down, got up and came over. Placing his hand on her shoulder, he replied: "Quite! It's just like a painting, isn't it?"

"The island you can see over there, what is it called?"

"That? That's Ojima."

"And that one?"

"Daikokujima."

"And the one next to it?"

"Hoteijima."

"Why . . . they're named for the Seven Lucky Gods! Goodness, there are so many boats out today."

"Those are all fishing boats."

"Oh? It looks so pleasant."

"Well, if it were your family business, I doubt you'd feel it to be so pleasant. . . . Even the pleasurable business of being a writer has its share of troubles."

"You've had trouble?"

"Of course, I have."

"What sort?"

"What sort? Well, no particular thing, but let's just say that it's not as easy as it looks from the outside."

"I suppose you do have a point."

He looked thoughtful for a moment. "Anyway . . . judging by my mother's letter, it looks as though your family has put quite a bit of pressure on her."

"Yes," Itoko replied, looking worried.

Sighing deeply, Imamiya added: "So, my mother and younger sister are all alone and in a terrible spot. The letter both scolds and begs me to come back. Mother will definitely forgive us, but I'm still uncertain of your parents."

Itoko drooped. "If my parents don't forgive us, let that be as it may. I don't care what people say; if I can be by your side, then it matters not.

So, if you'd rather not return, why don't you just have your mother and little Hanako meet us here?"

"I have nothing against that, but, in my business, if I'm not in Tokyo, I can't work."

"Oh, that's right, isn't it."

"What's more, because of our stops in Nikkō and Iisaka, we don't have much money left. We're in rather a fix."

"Oh, dear. What'll we do?"

Just then one of the inn's maids tapped her hand on the outside of the *shōji* screen. Having been fooled in no small part by generous tips and Imamiya's well-groomed appearance, she treated this man, who normally rented a cheap tenement house in Tokyo, as the most noble of aristocrats. "Sir, the newspaper has just arrived . . . do you require anything else?"

"No, nothing," Imamiya replied gloomily.

"As you wish. . . . By the way, we're quite fortunate to have no wind today. Won't you consider a small visit to the temple?"[23]

"Oh, I've seen it before . . . it is rather grand, though, isn't it?"

"So they say," the maid giggled, "I haven't actually been even once yet!"

"So, miss, not from around here then?"

"Oh, no, I'm from Ōji. I've just come here to work."

"Is that right? Well, you must be quite homesick. If you have some time during the evening, do drop in for a visit."

"Why, thank you," she bowed and left the room.

Imamiya sprawled again on the floor and pulled the tobacco tray toward his pillow. He started reading the *Tōkyō shinbun* the maid had brought. A few moments later, his face suddenly went pale. He sprang up abruptly and turned to Itoko, who seemed to be lost in thought. "Itoko, it's all over . . . take a look at this."

She took the newspaper in her hands. "What is it?"

"This . . . look at this!" She looked down at where his finger pointed.

She gasped with surprise at the heartless headline, which announced the great disgrace of a writer. Her heart pounding all the while, she read to the end. Then the newspaper slipped, unnoticed, from her fingers.

****

Deceiving the public and the world with his talent, he had somehow been able to live a happy-go-lucky life until this day. But after he took

O-Tsuyu as his wife, his reputation had plummeted; kept at a distance by publishers, discarded by his acquaintances, and disowned by his relatives, he had lost the trust of society. In addition, he had to endure daily harassment by his creditors. Itoko's love for him had at first simply provided the opportunity to hide himself here. As they whiled away the days, their billfold had become thinner, but his cruel and feckless heart had truly been captured by Itoko's incomparable beauty and innocence. Though he had thought of her as a short-lived affair at the beginning, she had suddenly become so dear to him that he scarcely recognized himself. Now, his love was such that he would have followed her to the ends of the earth. There had to be a way for the two of them to become man and wife officially.

Such were the thoughts that turned in Imamiya's head. But when he looked back on his own actions, he saw there was no reason for Itoko's parents to give him their blessing willingly. And yet they could not remain here indefinitely, either. There was nothing for it but to return quickly to Tokyo before their funds ran out completely; then he'd have to come up with a plan. But just when he had finally come to a decision, he thought again of how his affair with Itoko had been reported in the newspaper; there was no returning now. No matter how thick-skinned he was, he couldn't stand facing the public eye again. What could he do? The more he thought it over, the more the world became distasteful. This dismal, cruel place, which knew not the true differences between good and bad, right and wrong—it would never change. If he could only leave this world behind and escape to the next, how then would his heart be at peace!

Like one possessed, he fled, letting his legs take him wherever they would carry him, but the cold wind blowing through the pine trees soon brought him back to his senses. Looking around, he saw waves washing the foot of a cliff; the sound was much like a woman's crying. His sleeves were moist. Was it dew from the pine trees, mist, rain . . . or his own tears? The lonely fires of the fishermen gleamed faintly in the offing; the moon shone dimly from behind the clouds, as though foretelling his end. He felt terribly empty when he thought of never returning and regretted the crimes he had committed.

Just then, from somewhere nearby, there came the scent of incense.[24] That's rather suspicious, he thought, there's someone lying in wait for me! While he was wondering who it could possibly be, out came the person he least expected: Itoko. He looked at her speechlessly for a moment, wondering how she had followed him, certain that she couldn't have known where he had gone.

She spoke, her voice quavering. "You . . . what an unfeeling person you must be, to leave me lying there and come to a place like this in the middle of the night . . . ! Have you realized at all where you are?"

Brought back to his senses by her question, Imamiya surveyed his surroundings once again. He had not seen until now that he stood near a very aged temple. In the moonlight, he could faintly make out the characters "Go," "dai," "dō." "That's right," he thought, "I vaguely recall the unearthly feeling of crossing the arched bridge that leads to the temple. I'll have to come up with some excuse."

"Oh, it's just the Temple of Godai," he responded. "The moon was so lovely, I just had to come out and admire it.[25] Of course, I didn't abandon you. There now, don't cry like that, all right? Don't cry."

Itoko only sobbed louder. "You . . . you lie! When you even left a suicide note. I already know what's in your heart! If what the newspaper wrote about you is all true, then your motives are understandable. That's why I won't stop you . . . instead, I want to go, too . . . won't you let me die with you?" She clutched him, imploring.

At this, Imamiya was rather at a loss but quickly pulled himself together. "I will never forget your devotion. But, Itoko, did you look at my will?"

"Of course, I did."

"In that case, be reasonable, and please let me die alone."

Itoko's voice shook. "If you still insist on such a thing, then it must be because you despise me. Think well. After being disgraced in the newspaper like that, even were I to live, I could never face my parents again . . . so, if you still say that you won't die with me, then I'll die alone, too." So saying, she got up abruptly and ran toward the precipice.

Frantically, Imamiya pulled her back. So be it, he thought. "Very well! Let us die together."

"Truly?"

"Yes."

"How happy I am!"

Such a bittersweet moment could scarcely even be imagined in a dream. Though the world might condemn the vanity of their blind passion, one can only imagine the joy that Imamiya, a loser in life but a winner in love, must have felt. Just then, the salty breeze strengthened, clearing the clouds. The moon shone down on everything once again. The lovers clasped hands and gazed for a while into each other's eyes, as if to say, "Is this our last glimpse of the world?" Wordlessly, they clung together, casting their bodies into the sea. Even the waves beating against the cliffs of Fukuura Island seemed to lament the passing of the two lovers.

****

Several days later, on the third page of the local newspaper, the *Sendai Tōhoku shinbun*, one could find a rather lengthy column about a writer who had committed a most unusual love suicide.

NOTES

1. The name means "a boat carrying rice sheaves" and has classical poetic associations. Her name is sometimes romanized as "Inafune." I have chosen Inabune because this is generally how she is cataloged in libraries.

2. Yukiko Tanaka claims that Bimyō "would not have married Kin had not his financial decline made marriage to her, the daughter of a wealthy family, seem the wise thing to do" (*Women Writers of Meiji and Taishō Japan: Their Lives, Works, and Critical Reception*, 1868–1926 [Jefferson, N.C.: MacFarland, 2000], p. 85). Shioda Ryōhei, on the other hand, suggests that, despite the negative gossip in some contemporary newspapers, the marriage was the natural "result of a long love affair" (*Shintei Meiji joryū sakka ron* [Tokyo: Bunsendō shuppan, 1983], p. 183). Itō Seiko probably has the most measured perspective: "Among all the women [Bimyō] knew, he found Inabune the most suitable to associate with publicly" (*Hono'o no joryū sakka Tazawa Inabune* [Tokyo: Tōyō shoin, 1979], p. 175).

3. Tanaka, *Writers of Meiji and Taishō Japan*, p. 84.

4. Cited in Shioda, *Shintei Meiji joryū sakka ron*, p. 186.

5. Ibid., p. 182.

6. For a detailed description of this first special issue (December 10, 1895) and the debate that surrounded it, see Rebecca Copeland, *Lost Leaves: Women Writers of Meiji Japan* (Honolulu: University of Hawai'i Press, 2000), pp. 215–225.

7. Cited in and translated by Copeland, *Lost Leaves*, p. 223.

8. Cited in Wada Shigejirō, *Meiji zenki joryū sakka ron: Higuchi Ichiyō to sono zengo* (Tokyo: Ōfūsha, 1989), p. 523.

9. Ibid., p. 527.

10. Tanaka, *Writers of Meiji and Taishō Japan*, p. 85.

11. Wada, *Meiji zenki joryū sakka ron*, p. 527.

12. Donald Keene, *World Within Walls: Japanese Literature of the Pre-Modern Era, 1600–1897* (New York: Holt, Rinehart, and Winston, 1976), p. 397.

13. O-Tsuyu is a *mekake*, translated here as "mistress," a word that has its origins in the sixteenth century. Originally, it meant a second wife or concubine, formally a part of the family system, who lived under the same roof. O-Tsuyu does not have this status; she is simply a maidservant. The *mekake* tradition went through something of a renaissance during the Meiji era, when upperclass men such as the viscount, Itoko and Fusao's father, adopted the practice as a tacit demonstration of their wealth. See Tanaka, *Writers of Meiji and Taishō Japan*, p. 54.

14. Ibid., p. 85.

15. Hasegawa's series ran from March to June of 1937 and clearly meant to recast these women's lives in a more positive manner than they had been previously. See "Tazawa Inabune," in Hasegawa Shigure, *Hasegawa Shigure zenshū*, 5 vols. (Tokyo: Fuji shuppan, 1993), 2:22–84.

16. Donald Keene, *Dawn to the West: Japanese Literature in the Modern Era*, vol. 1, *Fiction* (New York: Holt, Rinehart, and Winston, 1984), p. 126. Incidentally, Hasegawa Shigure, too, describes Inabune's death as a suicide ("Tazawa Inabune," p. 83).

17. The source text used for this translation is from Takada Chinami, Nakagawa Shigemi, and Nakayama Kazuko, eds., *Josei sakka shū*, Shin Nihon koten bungaku taikei, no. 23 (Tokyo: Iwanami shoten, 2002), pp. 239–272. This annotated text retains most of the formatting of the original, which often does not indicate clearly who is speaking. I have used modern conventions for styling dialogue to improve readability.

18. In the original, the women appear as both "Teru" and "Hatsu" and "O-Teru" and "O-Hatsu" (i.e., with the honorific "O" prefix that was common in women's names during the Edo period but increasingly out of fashion in the Meiji era). This is true of Tsuyu (O-Tsuyu, the viscount's mistress) as well. I have rendered the names with the "O" in every case to decrease confusion.

19. Hanazono's name (also pronounceable as "Ka'en") suggests that Itoko and Imamiya are actually talking about Miyake Kaho, since the first characters in both names are identical (花). Inabune has disguised this reference slightly by using a different second character (園) that nevertheless resembles the one in Kaho's name (圃).

20. A portion of this dialogue is taken from Rebecca Copeland's translation in *Lost Leaves*, p. 45. There is also some confusion in the source text as to who is actually speaking in this exchange about Miss Hanazono (Takada, Nakagawa, and Nakayama, *Josei sakka shū*, p. 243). After a consultation with Nakagawa Shigemi, one of the editors, I made a minor adjustment that seems to reflect more accurately who is speaking.

21. Imamiya's pen name (放蕩山人) is actually quite irreverent: "Hōtō," in this case, means "debauchery," so the image is of a dissipated mountain "sage." The steward lets the viscount assume it is Hōtō Sanjin (宝塔山人, "sage of the jeweled pagoda," i.e., temple), instead, a much more respectable moniker, to protect both himself and the young master.

22. Matsushima is on the northeast coast of Honshū Island and has been featured as a famous place in poetry since the Heian period. Known for its many islands, it is one of the so-called three most beautiful places in Japan (三景). By the Edo period, it had become a popular tourist destination.

23. The maid is most likely referring to Zuiganji Temple, a large complex reputed to have been founded in 828. The titular temple is much less imposing (see n. 25, below).

24. Editor Nakagawa Shigemi's note in the source text suggests that the scent is coming from Itoko's clothing, which, as was common practice at the time, would have been aired out with incense. It was a particular kind of incense and so would indicate to Imamiya the presence of a person.

25. The small wooden temple that lends its name to the story, first built in 807, is one of the main sights in Matsushima. Located on a small islet connected to the mainland by a picturesque bridge, it is a perfect locale for the final suicide scene because of the metaphorical association between bridges and death. When the lovers have their last conversation in front of the temple, the fact that they have crossed the bridge suggests that they have already entered the next world even before they actually die.

KITADA USURAI
(1876–1900)

Melek Ortabasi

KITADA USURAI, though largely forgotten today, was considered "on a par with [Higuchi] Ichiyō" while she was alive.[1] In 1894, after her story "Sannin yamome" (Three alone) appeared in the journal *Tōkyō bungaku* (Tokyo literature), a reporter dubbed the seventeen-year-old "the Murasaki of the Meiji Period."[2] While this was intended as the highest compliment that could be paid a female author, the comparison with eleventh-century author and aristocrat Murasaki Shikibu had more to do with Usurai's retiring nature and her cloistered life than her writing style. The promising young writer certainly had more in common with her Meiji peers than with the women writers of the Heian court. Her association with a male member of the literary coterie is responsible for her initial fame, since she had apprenticed herself to one of the greatest figures of Meiji literature, Ken'yūsha leader, Ozaki Kōyō (1867–1903).[3] This was apparently another opportunity for analogy, since this relationship earned her the alternate title of "the female Ozaki Kōyō."[4] But while these labels may tell us how others perceived Usurai, they give us very little sense of who she was as a writer.

Like nearly all the Meiji women writers, Kitada Takako was the privileged daughter of a well-to-do family; her life was governed by the decisions of the men around her. Her rather conservative education consisted of a degree from the Joshi bungei gakusha (Women's arts

FIGURE 6.1 Kitada Usurai (1871–1900)

school) in Kōjimachi Ward, Tokyo, which emphasized domestic rather than academic skills.[5] Her father, however, was supportive of her writing and arranged the apprenticeship to Kōyō through a mutual acquaintance, the owner of the Shunyōdō publishing house. It was her literary mentor who gave Takako her pseudonym, Usurai;[6] it was also he who arranged the match with artist Kajita Hanko (1870–1917).[7] The two were married in 1898, and she bore a son, Hiroe, the following year. Her body was considerably weakened by childbirth, and she died of intestinal tuberculosis just over a year later, at age twenty-four. Like so many other women writers of this period, her career ended before it really began.

Usurai was not an activist; her works do not advocate overtly for women's rights or education, as do those of Miyake Kaho, Kishida Toshiko, and Shimizu Shikin. Nor, as can be seen above, was she notorious for her private life, as were Tazawa Inabune or Tamura Toshiko; she played without complaint the roles of daughter, wife, and mother much in the way that Meiji-period government slogans prescribed. It is worth noting that her behavior, perceived as appropriately feminine and respectable, is probably one of the main reasons her male colleagues generally looked favorably on her work. She is well described as one of the women writers who accepted the contemporary "vision of female gentleness and purity."[8] It would seem that her obedience was not without its emotional price, though, since her writings are dominated by a sense of resignation.

Yukiko Tanaka, in her discussion of Meiji women writers, groups Usurai together with Higuchi Ichiyō and Tazawa Inabune because of the thematic similarities in their writings. She suggests that, given the increasingly austere political climate, these women writers felt they could do little but "[lament] over insoluble problems."[9] This elegiac tone certainly pervades Usurai's major works, in which good women are consistently mistreated by immoral, feckless, and unfeeling men. One could argue that this focus on women's hardships in love and marriage, while perhaps not satisfying to a feminist today, does express discontent with the existing patriarchal order in a way that was acceptable in the current political and literary environment.

Considering that her career lasted a scant five years, Usurai was unusually prolific. Clearly, her position as Ozaki Kōyō's first female pupil allowed her to publish work in the top journals.[10] After "Sanmin ya mome," which was edited by her mentor, Usurai published a number of pieces in the important journal *Bungei kurabu* (Literary arts club). Most famous among these is "Kuromegane" (Dark glasses), which appeared in the first special *keishū* (lady writers) issue in December 1895. In this story, a young woman is bilked out of her possessions and hard-won property by her husband, the debauched son of her mother's former employer. While the storyline is on the melodramatic side, one can also read it as a subtle protest against class and gender prejudice, since the young man marries the heroine only so that he can add her wealth to his own family's coffers. As his wife, she has no choice but to yield her property to him.

"Uba" (Wet nurse) is another tale of female disappointment; more important, it continues to underline the parallel threads of conservatism and innovation in Usurai's developing style. Kitada biographer Todoroki Eiko selects this story, which appeared in *Bungei kurabu* in 1896, as representative of "a clear improvement" in Usurai's writing.[11] About a wet nurse who undergoes considerable self-sacrifice to protect her orphaned ward, the story ends with a scene that suggests the older woman will eventually succumb to madness. Contemporary critics praised the piece for its characterization of the wet nurse, who was "traced particularly well."[12] While the theme of the story centers on traditional feudal values of duty and obligation, the psychological trauma resulting from adherence to those values is convincingly depicted. It is significant that this particular critic described the exploration of internality with a term now associated with image transfer: "trace" (*utsusu*, also "copy"; and the homophone "to photograph"). His terminology suggests that he perceived this aspect of the story as thoroughly modern, since related terms, "sketching" (*shasei*) and "realism" (*shajitsu*), became commonly used to describe the more lifelike psychological style of the naturalist writers a few years later.[13] In any case, it is perhaps in "Uba" where we first see Usurai's style turn "from plot development to psychological delineation."[14]

The first selection translated here, considered a later work, incorporates both the depiction of a woman subjected to the pitiless rules of society and a detailed psychological depiction of each character's motivations. "Shiragazome" (Hiding the Gray) appeared in the second, and last, "lady writer" issue of *Bungei kurabu* in January 1897; it encapsulates some of Usurai's most overt criticism of society's treatment of women. Of course, readers would be hard-pressed to sympathize with Jihei, the unattractive protagonist, at any point in the story; his neglect of his first wife and his unreasonable jealousy over the second make him a profoundly unlikable figure. At first, the title seems to indicate that the author is simply poking fun at the aging protagonist's vanity; Jihei's ridiculous attempts to look younger impart little sense that he may represent societal values concerning love and marriage. But the narrator's implicit criticism of Jihei ultimately reveals a scathing commentary on the social status quo, which punishes even women who behave the way society says they ought to.

Oito, Jihei's young and beautiful wife, is perhaps almost frustratingly virtuous to a contemporary reader, but it is important to a subversive reading that her character be unimpeachable. For example, while she longs to marry a handsome young man she has already promised herself to, her belief in a love marriage is quickly crushed when her suitor is easily bought off by the older, wealthier Jihei. Rather than being resentful of Jihei's physical unattractiveness, however, she decides to be a model wife; she is solicitous, devoted, and supportive of Jihei's business plans. In fact, it is her utter lack of awareness of her own feminine wiles that causes her failure to realize that the store's success is due to her sexual attractiveness to customers. Furthermore, the customers' admiration of her unaffected beauty is what finally whips Jihei into a jealous frenzy. As the story progresses, however, we become concerned less with Jihei's growing paranoia (although this is very convincingly portrayed) and more in tune with Oito's struggle to defend her own beliefs in the face of her husband's increasingly erratic behavior.

Oito's perfection, according to Meiji standards, is emphasized even further with the arrival of Jihei's first wife and son.[15] This episode, in which Oito takes pity on her rival in spite of the fact that her own position is threatened, is melodramatic to the extreme. Certainly, it is such plot twists that make Usurai's work resemble the sometimes overblown style of her mentor. But here, too, there is a possibility to read Oito as a subversive female character. Ozaki Kōyō, like many of his peers, took pleasure in depicting women who compete with each other over the affections of a man: his *Sanninzuma* (Three wives, 1892), in which a wealthy man's wife and two mistresses fight tooth and nail for his attention, reveals this "harem mentality."[16] "Hiding the Gray," on the other hand, reveals a world in which women, even those who conform to traditional roles, can relate to each other in a different way. Instead of joining Jihei in driving out Omine, Oito takes her in against his wishes. Clearly, her feeling of empathy toward Omine outweighs the sense that she should obey Jihei's orders. It is plain that both women depend on Jihei more for his money than for his love; they develop "sisterly bonds of affection" that uphold what they perceive as the sanctity of marriage.[17] The conclusion, however, reveals that womanly comradeship alone will save neither Omine nor Oito.

The last two paragraphs of the story indicate how little power Oito has within both her marriage and society in general. Jihei, who as the husband is the only one with the right to initiate and carry out a divorce, is convinced of its necessity only by Oito's lies. She has been unable to appeal to his sense of duty and so must confess that she no longer desires Jihei. Unwillingly assuming the role of the faithless woman, she leaves her husband's house with nothing but the clothes on her back. When she is murdered by an enraged Jihei that night, the third-person perspective is extended to the townsfolk, who assume that Jihei's anger is motivated by his wife's infidelity. Her soul must be left to wander the earth restlessly, since it seems there is no one to speak in her defense. In fact, it is the story itself that disavows her guilt: the reader has been privy to Oito's private thoughts and so knows the injustice of her fate.

The other piece included here, entitled "Asamashi no sugata" (Wretched Sights, 1895), also appeared in *Bungei kurabu*. The mixed impressions of the pleasure quarters found in Higuchi Ichiyō's most famous stories, such as "Nigorie" (Troubled Waters, 1895) and "Take-kurabe" (Child's Play, 1895–1896), are found here as well, though in slightly different form.[18] Ichiyō carefully paints bittersweet portraits of individual women in both stories; her protagonists have significant psychological depth and are easy for any reader to identify with.[19] Usurai, in her eyewitness account, observes the denizens of the pleasure quarters from a more aloof perspective.[20]

The essay is a brief account of a visit to the licensed quarters at Yoshiwara to observe a festival.[21] While the district had suffered financially during Meiji, there was still some of the pageantry for which it had been so well known during the Edo period. Edward Seidensticker describes the Niwaka festival as it was celebrated during Meiji:

> In late summer and early autumn the quarter set out lanterns in memory of an eighteenth-century courtesan of great popularity and sensitivity and high attainments, while dances known as Niwaka were performed on wheeled stages that moved up and down the main central street. They were sometimes humorous and sometimes solemnly dramatic, and the performers were the geisha, male and female, of the quarter.[22]

Usurai does admit that the scene is so "beguiling" that she lets herself "be pulled along by the crowd," only to have a rude awakening when she finds herself directly in front of a brothel, confronted with the reality of prostitution. Unlike the characters in Ichiyō's stories, the women in Usurai's account are undifferentiated, pathetic figures, all equally oppressed. But while Usurai does not identify closely with these women, she sympathizes with their fate and recalls an incident in her childhood that suggests she, too, could easily have ended as one of the women behind the latticed windows.

While contemporary readers will likely consider Usurai's view on prostitution fairly conventional for a middle-class woman, this short piece attracted a considerable amount of ire, much in the same way some of the other authors in this volume were attacked when they chose to discuss or depict female sexuality on their own terms. In the following issue of *Bungei kurabu*, an anonymous critic wrote a scathing review of the essay, in which Usurai is censured for her holier-than-thou attitude.

Strangely, the writer, most likely a man, adopted the persona of a gei-sha to make his argument. After proudly enumerating "her" hard-won skills as a geisha and accusing Usurai of snobbery, the narrator perhaps unwittingly betrays a male perspective: "Don't overstep your bounds as a woman. If you have the leisure to criticize us with that fancy writ-ing brush of yours, then your time would be better served sewing dust cloths."[23] While the "geisha" assumes that Usurai's commentary is an attack on the women of the licensed quarters, this vicious statement re-veals that it is instead the patriarchal system supporting the Yoshiwara that feels challenged by her words. The fact that Usurai's relatively mild repudiation of prostitution earned her such a rebuke reveals how wom-en's writing was regarded with benevolence only if it did not comment on issues of political and social importance. Despite their apparent con-servatism, Usurai's writings did just that. by focusing on the limitations and perils of the roles forced on women during this period, she added her voice to the building discussion on women's rights.

HIDING THE GRAY

Translated by Melek Ortabasi
and Yukiko Tanaka

1

There was a new drugstore on Nihonbashi Avenue.[24] Hanging along the five-*ken*-wide storefront was a brand new *noren* curtain with "Sumiya," the shop's name, dyed in vivid white against dark blue.[25] A large lantern dangled proudly from a long pole jutting out from the eaves, and many smaller red ones, also hanging high in the air, looked like fireworks from a distance. Among them fluttered the Japanese flag, adding an air of respectability to the occasion.

The store was turned out with style today. A flame-red woolen rug was spread out at the center of the store, and on it sat a large, sturdy charcoal burner. The customers seemed awed at these arrangements but struggled to appear nonchalant. With inviting smiles on their faces, the young shop attendants moved busily through the throngs, sometimes (it seemed) deliberately running into each other. Since it was opening day, everything was half price, and, on top of that, an advertisement announced that there would be a grand giveaway. People, whose greedy hearts are always on the lookout for a bargain, descended on the store, forming quite a crowd. Lured by the loud cries of "come in, come in" and "thank you so much," even old folk who had just been passing by came in, leaning on their canes, to buy stomach worm medicine for their grandchildren. Customers had to smile when a young woman asked for a perfume made of Chinese musk. Outside, in front of the store, a few hired hawkers handed out advertisement flyers scented with perfumes and powders. The passersby scrambled to pick them up, making a terrific racket in the process. When night fell, a band began to play, parading through the streets to the store, disrupting the evening calm. Any and all who came by stopped and gathered in close, either curious about the music, unusual in that neighborhood, or to take a peek at what was going on in the store.

The owner of the store, a man in his forties, sat at the counter trying to appear prudent. With thinning hair, a forehead broadened by a receding hairline, a stubby nose, and protruding lips, he was ugly indeed, one had to admit. The woman sitting next to the man, who was busying herself with the accounts, was another matter entirely. Although she must have been twenty-two or -three, she looked too young for her high *Shimada*-style bun.[26] Her lovely round face with its fair complexion spread cheerfulness all around her; her eyes and nose were perfectly aligned; her powdered face and freshly rouged lips looked glamorous even under the gaslight illuminating all corners of the store. The elegance that filled the entire place when she walked, rustling the hem of her double-layered silk kimono, made male customers forget the band music entirely. The way in which this woman attended to the customers with the loveliness of a true flower, as well as the sensitivity and care she exuded were, one must say, beyond verbal description; it truly showed that the world couldn't do without women. Who was this beautiful woman? Was she a daughter of the house, a relative? What about the man? Was he her father? A brother? People wondered, determined to find out. Those with an amorous nature were particularly eager and exchanged opinions among themselves.

The ugly man sitting next to the beauty looked pleased with himself when he saw the commotion made by the curious bunch of onlookers, but the customers found the way he glanced at the woman, with a prideful smirk, offensive.

"Who is that fellow? What an offensive slug! It's really too vulgar!" One of the customers, a student perhaps, gave voice to his envy of the man.

"Don't you all know?" A woman who lived in a nearby tenement house answered knowingly, pushing herself to the front of the crowd.

She sneered, "She's the wife of that ugly shop owner. She's his precious, little wife, whom he puts above his own life. Can't you see how besotted he is?" And she was right. But how queer it all seemed. What kind of fate could have possibly brought these two together? With brows creased in wonder, the curious gathered round to learn more. The story went something like this:

His name was Jihei; he was said to be a reputable silk merchant from the north. A year ago, he left his wife and child behind to do business in the city. Once in the flowery capital of Tokyo, he became so dazzled that he did not want to return to his home in the backward provinces, and so he simply stayed on at an inn in Nihonbashi. There, he saw the innkeeper's daughter, who had the reputation for being the most beautiful girl in the neighborhood—and that was the beginning of his infatuation. Now, the daughter, called Oito, was not only beautiful but very good at handling the inn's guests; witty and clever, she could pacify the most irate customer with a single word. As Jihei became more attracted to Oito, his feelings toward his wife back home, older than he and without a touch of elegance, began to sour. Why live with such a woman? he asked himself, resenting the memory of his wife and loathing the photographs she had sent along with her letters. In a fit of pique, he threw away everything, along with the amulet his wife had sewn for him, the one he had kept next to his skin. He replaced it with one of Oito's hand towels. What a wretched man! One wonders what dreams his wife might be having back home on cold winter nights.

When human beings become obsessed, they tend to forget the importance of duty and compassion—just as Jihei did. Paying no attention to the fact that his wife and child might starve without him, he gave his immediate desires free rein. He wanted to leave behind his past, let come what may. He wanted to do what he wanted to do. Ours is a floating world, after all, where nothing lasts forever—so why not indulge oneself? Unable to forget Oito and knowing that his wealth covered his other flaws, he approached her parents and requested their daughter's hand. Persuaded by the power of money, what could they do but accede? But there was another obstacle: Oito wouldn't agree, insisting that there was another man to whom she had plighted her troth. She wouldn't marry someone like Jihei under any circumstances, she declared. It was hardly an encouraging answer, but Jihei took her words as a sort of challenge and went about finding out the identity of the man for whom this beautiful woman yearned. Oddly enough, the man, named Sōjirō, turned out to be the second son of Sōroku, a friend from Jihei's village, for whom he had done many favors. Sōjirō, streetwise and clever by nature, had come to Tokyo as an apprentice some time ago and now worked for a Chinese import goods store across from Oito's house. Sōjirō had turned into a handsome man who wore a finely woven cotton kimono; Jihei was envious of Oito's trim, neat-looking young lover. Yet Sōjirō was penniless, and Jihei had plenty of money. Using its power unsparingly and relying on the sense of past obligations, Jihei persuaded Sōjirō to give up Oito. Perhaps a bit heartless to start with, Sōjirō became greedy and conceded. Thereafter, whenever he met Oito, he hinted that he was no longer interested. Finally, he broke with her.

As for Oito, she had really been in love. Thinking that Sōjirō felt the same way, she had set her maidenly heart on him. Since she had secretly hoped to be his wife, Oito was devastated at Sōjirō's sudden change of heart and resentful of his claim that there was another woman, a flower more beautiful. One could not describe the mortification she felt when she realized that Sōjirō must have seen her only as a pleasant pastime. As she spent her days in tears, feeling wretched, Jihei approached her, feigning genuine sincerity but secretly congratulating himself on the success of his scheme. Oito appreciated Jihei's attention at the height of her unhappiness and felt bad for having treated him so dismissively before. Perhaps as retaliation against Sōjirō and as a natural response to kind words, she was able to overlook Jihei's ugliness and agreed to marry him though he was almost old enough to be her father. She didn't realize Jihei was heartless, even more so than Sōjirō. Surely, theirs was a marriage destined by some past life.

That had been the spring of the previous year. The couple had set up house in Koishikawa, and, since Jihei's interest income supported them nicely, they wanted for nothing. But though he was able to enjoy Oito's beauty to his heart's content day in and day out, Jihei soon felt dissatisfied. It didn't seem right to be keeping the perfect jewel in his possession hidden in their quiet residential quarter, not exposing her even to the neighbors' eyes. He wanted to put Oito in a busier section of town so people could envy his success in love; he wanted to show the world how happy they looked together. Once the idea had occurred to him, he felt compelled to put it into practice. Fortunately, he had a license to deal with medicines; thus, after he had discussed it with Oito, he opened a drugstore. Jihei's store came to be known simply as "the love wife's drugstore"; no one in the neighborhood ever used its proper name.

2

The day after opening, the store was considerably quieter, and customers fewer, though shelves still brimmed with an inventory of all and sundry. The customers who did enter were little more than tourists, there to see for themselves the beautiful woman who worked alongside the clerks, serving the customers with smiling, friendly tact. Within a month, Sumiya became well known in the area, rivaling other more established stores. No doubt, this was all thanks to Oito.

Jihei was overjoyed; he had been right in thinking that inspiring curiosity was a good way to stimulate business. Certainly, no one could call him a fool. Acquiring a beautiful wife, he became convinced, was the best thing a man could do. Sitting at the counter and toying with his abacus, Jihei thought only of Oito. His eyes followed her as she moved around the store; though he was together with her every night and day, he never tired of looking at her and appreciating her charm. He was reluctant to leave her side for even a moment. All one heard was Oito this and Oito that; the way he fawned over her so obsessively was a bit much. Oito, however, moved by his apparent kindness, continued to treat the ugly Jihei with affection, and so the marriage was as harmonious as possible.

As she helped at the store, Oito naturally became familiar with some customers; she treated everyone well, even those who came in for just one medicinal plaster. Although her genuine smile and welcoming "Come and sit, why don't you?" or "A nice day, isn't it?" were bestowed equally on all customers, the men, of course, seemed particularly appreciative. Conceit probably made them think her words and smiles were for them only. Some smug fellows took this as an invitation to sit down and chat, taking a pipe out of their pockets and puffing away. Seizing on Oito's propensity to be friendly, they would say something funny and laugh out loud, not caring what people might say, all the while gazing at Oito's face as if they couldn't get enough of it. Others, more sly, claimed they had minor cold symptoms and, even though the directions were obvious, would ask Oito for instructions on how to take the medicine. As she explained, they would sneak sidelong looks at her. Since so many customers came only to see Oito, like flower viewers eager to witness even the most minute changes in the color of a cherished bloom, one may imagine how busy she was; Jihei and his employees, on the other hand, were left to twiddle their thumbs.

Jihei was quite contented in the beginning; he was proud of himself, believing that everybody was jealous of him for having such a fine wife. He did everything joyfully and laughed often and openly. But suddenly he changed. Now, a sour expression on his face, he looked depressed all day long; his appetite decreased as well. Oito could not understand what might be bothering him.

"What's the matter? If you don't feel well, why don't you have the doctor take a look at you?"

Jihei shook his head. "Nothing's wrong. I feel fine, there's no need for you to be concerned." But his voice betrayed him, and as time went by he grew crabbier and crabbier. As he sat in the store, constantly sullen and curt with the customers, people started to talk.

"How mean the owner is," they whispered. "What a difference from his wife!"

Jihei became so unpopular that some customers turned away when they saw him sitting in the store alone.

"I'm not going in if it's only that scary husband who's in the store," they would say.

One day, when Oito was at her parents' house on an errand and Jihei sat forlornly at the store counter with his usual sour face, a tall, good-looking man breezed in. It was Kisaku, the young man from the nearby fancy goods store that bought its face powder from Sumiya. "Hello there," he said, sitting on a chair and looking around as though trying to find someone. Not seeing Oito anywhere, he turned his puzzled face to an employee, ignoring Jihei.

"Where's the Mrs.?" he asked with a certain urgency.

"She's not in right now," said Matsukichi, who was a bit of a joker. Laughing, he added: "She's gone to the theater with her lover."

"Stop fooling around. Where has she really gone? I have something to tell her," Kisaku insisted. His earnest manner would have invited a smile from others, but not Jihei. Listening to the exchange from behind the counter, he glared at Kisaku. He scolded his young employee rather loudly. "Matsukichi! What sort of nonsense are you spouting?!"

Reprimanded, the boy looked down at the floor meekly, hunching his shoulders a bit. Kisaku, too, felt uncomfortable and stood up without a word. He was about to leave when Jihei addressed him.

"I gather you need something, Kisaku. Oito is at her parents' and won't return till evening, but if there's anything you want of her, you can tell me. I'm her husband, after all. You can be sure I'll let her know."

"Well, it's not that important. I don't live far from here, so I'll just come back later." Kisaku, who liked neither the innuendo in Jihei's words nor his smug attitude, responded with a sneer and turned his back. "Sorry to have bothered you," he tossed over his shoulder as he dashed out. Jihei, frustrated, watched Kisaku until he disappeared. For whatever reason, he looked worried and depressed.

That afternoon, Kisaku was back, acting as if he could hardly wait for Oito to return. He paced up and down in front of the store, peering inside now and then. Jihei watched him, consumed with jealous indignation. What does Kisaku want from Oito? he asked himself. Why is he waiting around for her, a married woman, as though he had the right? If he needed something from the store, he should've asked me this morning, since I know more about it. What nerve! Is he infatuated with my wife's beauty and just hanging around even though he has no real business here? So he cooked up a good line to tell Matsukichi just because he wants to see her? That still doesn't explain why he's walking back and forth in front of the store, though. How vexing! It just makes me sick to my stomach. There's not a soul in town who doesn't make a fuss over Oito, but Kisaku, he's a handsome fellow; I ought to be on my guard with him. What if Oito is sick of me because I'm old and is secretly carrying on with him?

A thick cloud of doubt was spreading throughout his chest, weighing him down. He couldn't stand to be in the store, where he could see Kisaku's comings and goings, so he went to the living quarters to lie down. Jihei was so distressed that he was unable to think straight now, and although he usually yearned for Oito's swift return, he now wished her to come home late so that Kisaku wouldn't be able to see her.

3

"Well, I'm sorry, I should've come back sooner, but here I am," Oito said with her usual cheerfulness when she returned that evening, stepping into the store and looking around. "Where's the master?" she asked, with a puzzled look; the clerks said he had gone to lie down because he wasn't feeling well.

"That's not good! I wonder what's wrong. When I left this morning, he was fine . . ." Oito knit her brow, looking concerned. Told that it was nothing serious, only a bit of a headache, she seemed relieved. She took out a large packet wrapped in bamboo bark, which she handed to the boys: "This is for all of you, go ahead and eat." The clerks gazed after her retreating figure, thinking that Oito had somehow gained the look of a respectable matron even though she still wore the *Shimada* hairdo favored by younger women. What a nice woman, they agreed: it is a pity she ended up with a husband like Jihei.

Because of what had happened earlier in the day, Oito's return did not make Jihei happy. He was lying with his back to her, pretending to be asleep. She tiptoed up to him and peered at his face worriedly.

"I'm back. Sorry I'm so late. I hear you don't feel well. What's wrong?" She spoke gently as always. Although her words somewhat eased his consternation about Kisaku, Jihei didn't want to respond right away. He didn't move his body and continued to feign sleep.

"Oh, he's sleeping. I wonder how he's feeling?" said Oito to herself, placing her hand on his forehead. "He doesn't have a fever, but perhaps I should give him some cold medicine." Since her words conveyed the genuine concern of a wife with nothing but her husband's welfare on her mind, Jihei's fear left him; he was now ashamed of himself for imagining her infidelity. He stopped Oito as she was about to go back into the store.

"There's no need to worry, Oito. I had a bad headache a while ago, so I took medicine just in case I was coming down with a cold. But I feel much better now that I've had a good nap," he told her, sitting up. Hearing this, Oito seemed relieved.

"Thank goodness. I was quite worried it might be serious!" Her furrowed brow disappeared, replaced by a bright smile. "Have you eaten, dear? Shall I make some gruel for you?"

Jihei responded to this offer with sudden lightheartedness: "No gruel, but I'll have a drink with my meal as usual; I need to feel my best." One might find Jihei's behavior silly, but Oito, who knew nothing about what had happened, was simply grateful that her husband felt better; she called a maid in a cheery voice and ordered her to prepare his dinner right away.

When the meal was ready and brought to him, Jihei sat down to it with his *haori* jacket draped over his shoulders.

"Oh, a treat! It's my favorite, *tempura*. It must be from Renkin."

"You've guessed it! The boys like sweets, so I brought them the usual *mochi* rice cakes. But for you, I thought I'd get something different, something you really like, so I sent someone specially to the store in Kyōbashi," Oito smiled. She joined her husband in a drink. As the two filled each other's cups, they certainly looked as though they were enjoying themselves.

But just then Matsukichi poked his head in and announced, "Madam, Mr. Kisaku is waiting out in the store. He's already stopped by several times since this morning, and he says he really wants to see Madam if she's back." Hearing this, Jihei's mind returned to its earlier turmoil. That rascal! So he's hanging around again, he thought, gnashing his teeth but maintaining a cool facade.

"Oh, that's right, I'd forgotten. Whatever it is, he says it has to be you. He's been waiting for you all day. Why don't you go and see what he wants," Jihei said nonchalantly, watching Oito's face carefully. Ignorant of her husband's true feelings, Oito stood up, beaming.

"Oh, he's here, is he? Wonderful! I wonder if my comb is ready," she said to herself, and hurried out of the room, looking pleased. Left alone, Jihei looked down, lost in thought. Presently, he stood up and, after making sure no one was around, tiptoed over and stood behind the curtain dividing the store and the living quarters. No doubt about it—he was planning to eavesdrop on Oito and Kisaku's conversation.

Not realizing he was being spied on, Kisaku looked as though he were ready to take advantage of Jihei's unusual absence to complain about the bitter tongue-lashing he had received that morning. When he saw Oito, though, he smiled.

"Oh, Madam, you're back at last. As you weren't in this morning when I came, I got a terrible scolding from your husband. It was terrible—terrible, I tell you." Oito burst into laughter at Kisaku's serious expression.

"Poor dear! But that's what you get for saying bad things about me. I'd say the fault is yours!" Oito teased, thinking that Kisaku was joking. He was a bit put out that she wasn't taking him seriously.

Placing two thumbs above his ears like horns, he said mockingly, "No, no, you're wrong, the truth is he's got a couple of these growing," suggesting that Jihei was jealous.

"Oh, don't be silly. But what is it that you wanted from me? My comb is ready, is it? I'm anxious to see how it's turned out. Do let me see," Oito urged Kisaku.

"I haven't got your comb. It'll take another four or five days, since the craftsman is busy with something else," Kisaku answered, unperturbed. "I need face powder, the same amount as usual . . . although it's not really that urgent," he grinned. "Actually, I just had the sudden urge to see your lovely face. You don't know how many times I came by! That's real devotion, wouldn't you say?" It was just typical flirting, and Oito responded to it with her usual lighthearted banter; she knew how to treat men like him.

"Oh, that's too much! Who wouldn't fall for flattery like that? You're wicked because you don't really mean what you say, but I guess that just means you're a real man," she shot back. Kisaku stroked his chin with his fingers, pleased with himself.

"Oh, I don't know about that, but I don't mind saying that there might be a woman or two who's crazy about me. But, you know, lately it seems I'm losing weight. My cheeks are a bit drawn, don't you think? Maybe I should take some medicine. You see, looks are important to me. Do you think a health tonic will work?"

"Now the truth's out! Yes, a health tonic would do you good." Oito tried to keep a straight face. "They are just the thing for men like you. I'll give you some. If you take it tonight, you'll feel quite spry tomorrow morning." Oito bantered. "But, you know, even if you watch your health, you're still in trouble, since the girls won't leave you alone. The tonic can't help you there!" Kisaku was overjoyed at Oito's responses but deliberately maintained a serious expression as he stole a look at her.

"Madam, you sure have a sharp tongue, teasing me like that. But remember what you just said! I'll get you back for it someday. . . ." Reluctantly, he finally left the store—without buying anything.

4

Some might raise their eyebrows at Oito's behavior and the way she talked and sparred with male customers like this; her lightheartedness could be considered inappropriate for a married woman. But she was outgoing by nature and raised to believe that pretty words were a useful tool; she tended to speak openly and freely. She did not believe, even now that she was married, that there was anything wrong with speaking her mind if she had nothing to hide. Particularly now that her husband had opened the store, it was her womanly nature to strive for success that would inspire the envy of the other neighborhood shopkeepers. Such is the mystery of being in trade! Even if the price is the same, the fact is that customers will be offended if they are attended by someone with a stubborn, sour face who greets them half-heartedly, and they won't come again. They would rather go to the merchant who is cheerful, one who serves them tea even after they've overstayed their welcome; they'll naturally decide that it's the only place to shop. In any case, Oito certainly knew that flattery was the secret of success in business. Jihei, on the other hand, was rigid and very jealous by nature, and he was not good at controlling his temper. Now, listening to Oito and Kisaku, he could hardly keep silent. Every time he heard something questionable, he had to restrain himself from jumping out from behind the curtain in rage. He was disgusted with the way Kisaku was acting; Oito's chatter also made him jealous. But he was unable to find anything specific to object to.

Though Jihei tried to pretend nothing was the matter, he continued to dwell on the problem; it was easy to see that there was something on his mind. Surely, it was the worries that consumed him, but he was shocked when he looked in the mirror and saw how terribly he had aged. He was not a good-looking man; there was not a feature he could be proud of. But even though his complexion was dark, his face had looked healthy, his cheeks full and in good color. What had happened in such a short time? Indeed, he looked old, in fact three or four years older than he really was. His face was a greenish gray, like that of a dead man, and his cheeks were bony, further emphasizing his ugliness. His forehead had become covered with tiny lines, and he seemed to have more gray hair. How must he look to his young, beautiful wife? Surely she would lose interest in him, he thought. He was mortified and uneasy. He had to do something; he could not sit around looking so gaunt, he said to himself. Gripped by panic, he secretly began to apply an egg and bran mix to his skin and put special toilet water on his face; he wore cologne and hid the gray in his hair with dye. But because he carefully hid these efforts, Oito had no idea what was going on.

While Jihei carried on in this way, Oito, who noticed not a thing, was her usual self, attending to her husband's needs with care and kindness.

He appreciated her attention, but her flattery of the customers, which continued and even increased, caused him great consternation and robbed him of sleep. He wanted to tell her to stop, but he realized it was good for business. Besides, what would people say if he gave Oito such an order? He certainly did not want them to think he was jealous and shallow. What he was most afraid of, however, was Oito's leaving him because she found him despicable. Since he couldn't tell anyone what was bothering him, he went on suffering, his feelings bottled up inside.

Meanwhile, Kisaku of the fancy goods store, a poisonous serpent in Jihei's eyes, continued his daily visits. Impudently cozying up to Oito to chat with her, he exercised no restraint even in Jihei's presence. Hating him even more, Jihei suspected Kisaku was trying to get back at him for what he had said a few days ago. How can a wife of mine treat this man with such familiarity when I hate him so? She should be a bit more modest, Jihei silently reproached the unknowing Oito. It sure *looks* fishy, he thought, and so doubt crept into his mind: there was something going on between them. Everything about the way Oito interacted with Kisaku seemed to confirm his suspicions. He just couldn't stop thinking about it.

One evening, Jihei, feeling merry because of the sake he had had with dinner, invited Oito to go out to see the Jizō Festival in Nishigashi. Oito, who was unfortunately suffering from a headache, told Jihei she felt too listless to walk and asked him to go by himself. Just after Jihei left, a gloomy look on his face, Kisaku came in. As usual, he chatted with Oito. Though she didn't quite feel up to it, he was a good customer, so she was friendly as always. Meanwhile, Jihei came rushing back in, apparently having changed his mind. Without a word, he sat by Oito, and stared straight at Kisaku. Embarrassed, Kisaku stopped talking and turned away, leaving Oito caught between the two men and rather at a loss. She was ashamed of Jihei's odd behavior but also felt bad for him.

"Hello, dear. You're back early. You didn't go to the festival, did you?" She smiled, trying to ease the tension.

"Well, I thought Kisaku might come around, so I decided to come back so that I didn't miss any interesting stories. Do tell me, too, Kisaku, not just my wife." Jihei spoke through clenched teeth, his voice full of hatred. Kisaku feigned indifference. Oito looked on worriedly, realizing that because Kisaku had taken advantage of her husband's absence to visit, Jihei must mistakenly suspect she was having an affair. She also wondered whether Kisaku had read her husband's mind and now took him for an idiot. Jihei, oblivious to her wifely concern, was angry at her, too, thinking that she was trying to trying to cover for Kisaku.

"So, let's hear it," Jihei prodded Kisaku, angrily. What a turn of events!

"Why, you needn't be so serious, dear! The story has just started. So, Kisaku, you said it was terribly funny, but what did the old man do next?" Oito went on, smiling weakly. She was distressed at her husband's shocking behavior, but she did not know what else to do. Guessing that Oito wanted to avoid a scene and keep the conversation light, Kisaku responded cheerfully.

"Well, as I was saying, he's gotten himself this young mistress, even though he's near seventy with a hunched back. He got self-conscious about the way he looks, I guess. He dyed his hair, you see, and with his black and shiny hair, he came to my store, looking for cosmetics that would make the lines on his face disappear. I couldn't believe it! He's got one foot almost in the grave and probably hasn't got that long to live. What could possibly have possessed him to do such a thing?" Kisaku laughed loudly. Realizing that he could be the old man of the story, Jihei felt faint. He thought Kisaku was telling the story to be spiteful.

"Oh, how repulsive," laughed Oito, who had no idea what her husband was thinking. "What an affected fellow. Hiding the gray when you're still young is one thing, but why in the world would you dye hair that has turned gray naturally with age? No matter how he tries to hide it, people will find out sooner or later, you see. If anything, it will likely make his mistress reject him! I hate that type myself. It's best for old folks to be tidy and modest." Oito went on, glancing at her husband. Jihei looked extremely uncomfortable, his face bright red. He suddenly stood up and left the room without a word. Kisaku grinned with satisfaction; Oito looked puzzled. Then Kisaku hit on something:

"Oh, I get it! Your husband's doing it, too," he said and started laughing.

5

That night, Oito felt terrible. She'd had no idea her husband was keeping a secret until Kisaku mentioned it; now she began to realize what he'd been up to. But for Kisaku to say such things in front of her husband, who was already angry, was really uncalled-for. She blamed herself, realizing that Jihei could have taken it as a scheme to shame him in front of others. Unable to succeed in putting her husband in a good humor as she usually did, Oito quit her husband's side and retired early, saying she still had a headache. She was unable to sleep, however; her mind raced with all kinds of worries. Her headache was real the next morning, and she felt physically weak as well. Staying in bed past the usual hour, Oito did not appear at the breakfast table.

Jihei, who misunderstood the whole thing, stewed in his chagrin and self-pity; his chest felt like it would explode under the pressure. Although he had long suspected that something was going on between Oito and Kisaku, the way the two were behaving last night gave him proof. Oito, who had never done so before, declined his invitation, complaining of a headache. But she had looked quite cheerful in his absence, chit-chatting with Kisaku! They clammed up as soon as they saw me, he told himself, and then the way they looked at me while Kisaku was telling that story made it seem like they were talking about *me*. He couldn't understand why they had abused him so. Oito had even declared that she found it disgusting when old men dyed their hair. Did she already know that I do it, he wondered, and was Kisaku helping her devise a way to let me know indirectly that she no longer wanted me? That must be it, because otherwise she would've been more compassionate; she would have comforted me in my distress. She seemed preoccupied afterward and wouldn't talk much; she went to bed early, too. Not getting up for breakfast must have been an excuse so she wouldn't have to see my face. . . .

The doubts Jihei had planted himself had grown to tremendous proportions, causing him excruciating pain. His case was weak, though; he could not openly accuse Oito. If he did, or even hinted at his doubt, she might use it as an opportunity to leave him once and for all. Lost in a quagmire of doubts and suspicion, Jihei now felt too awkward to carry on even a casual conversation with Oito. Thus the couple became separated by a sturdy wall, one that anyone would find difficult to break through.

How strange are human emotions! For whatever reason, once discord grows between a couple who had earlier talked and confided in each other, they find it hard even to sit together, awkward to exchange words, and soon their affection dissipates. Jihei's mind was now like a fire in a gusting wind: at one moment, on the verge of extinction but burning even more strongly the next. Initially, Oito seemed to fear him, but, as the days went by, there was no sign that she disliked him. He yearned above all to make up with his sweet and lovely wife. Oito, who noticed none of this, went on, maintaining a generally restrained attitude about everything. She was quieter now, as if something heavy sat in her heart, and Jihei felt there was nothing he could say. So the two passed their days, each hiding their unhappiness.

Then one day a woman came to the store. She wore dirty clothes and looked like a beggar. With her was a boy of twelve or thirteen. Without asking permission, she barged into the living quarters. "Please, I need to see Jihei. Tell him Omine, his wife, is here."

Jihei had gone to Yokohama on business; for Oito, this was a bolt from the blue. Utterly shocked, she had no idea what to do. Although poverty had taken its toll on her looks, the woman, in her early forties perhaps, did not seem a bad sort. Her hair, tied in a simple knot, had not entirely lost its original sheen, and, though the dye was now chipping off, her teeth had at one time been properly blackened. In other words, she looked like she could have been the wife of a respectable merchant. Glancing at the boy, Oito saw at once that there was a clear resemblance to Jihei around his eyes, nose, and mouth; the ties of blood were evident. Realizing that these two were without a doubt Jihei's wife and son, Oito felt like she was having a nightmare. Not once in their many nightly tête-à-têtes had Jihei even hinted at a previous marriage. He had repeatedly said how lucky he was to have married such a beautiful woman as herself, especially as he was no longer young and thought he had missed his chance to marry; he would be a proud man when he returned to his native village. He sounded indeed as though he'd never married before. Oito had found his gratitude endearing. Taking it to heart, she had resolved to be good to Jihei and to make their marriage a long and happy one. Now, learning that he had another wife and a son, whom he had deserted, she realized she had known nothing about Jihei. How shameless, how heartless he was! She'd been deceived all along!

But Oito was a warm-hearted woman and, forgetting her own wretched situation for a moment, took pity on the woman and the boy who had suddenly appeared in front of her. She showed them into the living quarters, settled them down, and urged the woman to tell her more. Perhaps feeling ashamed in the face of such kind treatment, the woman seemed puzzled and could only blush. However, when she realized that Oito was entirely innocent and that her kindness was genuine, she seemed relieved and started to relate what had happened to her, sobbing all the while. Her story was a sad one indeed.

The woman, Omine, had been married to Jihei for over ten years, and until the very day he left for Tokyo on business, she and her child had led a life free from want. But he did not appear on the day he was to return, and no letter came. Omine spent many days sadly wondering whether something had happened to him. Worriedly, she asked some people to find him, but Tokyo was so far away and so big that it was impossible without knowing his address. Eventually, it became all too clear that the fate of mother and child would be starvation. Yes, she was able to earn a bit by running errands and doing laundry, so keeping the two of them alive. Spending her time thus, she tried to invoke the mercy of the gods and Buddha. Having placed what offerings she could in front of the tablet that bore the date he left, she prayed every day for her husband's safe return. She hoped that this was a bad dream from which she would soon wake, but a year quickly passed without any news from him. It seemed her prayers would go unanswered. Omine knew not what to do. It was particularly hard when she had to take her son out of school; she had wanted her only child to receive the education necessary to become a fine young man. If Jihei were here, she told her son, they wouldn't have to live such a miserable life. Not a day went by that mother and child did not bemoan their wretched fate.

Then one day Omine heard a rumor: Jihei was well, his new drugstore was flourishing, and he was married to a lovely woman much younger than he. She could hardly believe this rumor at first; how could that be her husband? Still, there was supposedly a person who had seen Jihei in the flesh. One can imagine how hurt and resentful Omine was, having her self-respect trampled on this way. She had heard, however, that Tokyo was a dangerous place where even the shrewdest could be taken in. Perhaps the wealthy Jihei had been deceived by a disreputable woman? Unless he was careful, Omine thought, he could lose everything he had. In her mind's eye, she saw a pitiful man, discarded and penniless. Wanting also to let Jihei know of the sad state in which she and his son found themselves, she decided to go to Tokyo to find her husband. In her agitated state, Omine didn't think much about the details. Bringing her son as her only support in this wretched quest, she traveled for many days.

Worried that the new wife was a villain and would refuse her and her son entry, she hesitated for a moment on reaching Jihei's store. But taking heart from her love for her son, she had resolved to kill herself in such a case.

"That was why I acted so shamelessly. But please do not think that I am a bad person," she begged Oito.

<h1 style="text-align:center">6</h1>

Omine's story was so wretched that Oito could not pretend it had nothing to do with her own affairs. Quite distressed, she could find no words with which to console Omine. Jihei's role in this, about which she heard now for the first time, was unforgivable. Guessing how Omine and her son must feel, Oito's heart was torn in two. She could not help recalling how she suffered when Sōjirō rejected her; the tears she shed now in sympathy could well have been for the sad fate she herself might have had to accept. Meanwhile, eagerly waiting for Jihei's return, Omine drew a picture of how he would regret what he had done when he saw them in person. Since even Oito, her rival in love, had shown such compassion, Jihei would take pity on them, too, would he not?

When he finally returned that evening, he blanched, shocked to see them. Although his color soon returned, his face remained twisted with concern, worried, no doubt, over what Oito now intended to do. But soon, having struck upon a plan of his own, he declared that he would have nothing to do with the two.

"We can't have total strangers in the house," Jihei insisted, looking as fierce as though he might strike mother and son with his own hand. Omine started wailing at this heartless treatment, overwhelmed with sadness.

"Those are cruel words. You may no longer have any affection for me, but how can you treat your wife of ten years like this, a woman who has given you a son? Look how he has grown. You may have let the devil get in you, but that's no excuse for leaving us totally helpless while you have a good time. . . . How can you be so immoral, with not a thought of the consequence?" Omine raged, challenging Jihei.

"Ask Oito if you think I'm wrong to accuse you!" Omine did not let go. "You can imagine how hard it was for us to come all the way to

Tokyo. Just look at us! Even if we're strangers now, we still shared the sacred bond of marriage until a year ago. Didn't we live together under one roof and share our meals from one pot? Didn't we share the pain in difficult times? Given our past, how can you treat me like this, without a single kind word? If it was my shortcomings that made you leave me, I won't blame you; I know such cases are all too common in this world. But think of our son! He's not getting the education he should, and, no matter how I try, I often can't manage to feed him three square meals a day. He's already suffering now. If he doesn't learn a trade, isn't he doomed to a lifetime of suffering? That's what makes me the saddest of all. I don't care what happens to me, but I was hoping you'd at least take responsibility for your son's future. What a cruel man you are, pretending not to know us and trying to throw us out! Don't you have any affection even for your own son?" Omine was sobbing uncontrollably now. Spoken in dialect, her imploring words sounded even more pitiful, but Jihei was undaunted, eager to prove himself before Oito.

"You crazy woman, how dare you say you're my wife, as filthy as you are," Jihei raised his voice menacingly. "I can't have strange people in my house like this. Who knows what trouble it'll cause? Get out! Oh, you won't get out, will you? I'll show you!" He got up abruptly and tried to drag Omine out of the room by her hair.

Oito clutched Jihei's arm to intervene. "Jihei, please, don't do that. You'll hurt her. Don't you see how concerned I am?" she wailed, finally managing to pull her husband away from Omine. Tears welling in her lovely eyes, she looked Jihei unwaveringly in the face.

"How can you tell such terrible lies? I have eyes, and this boy is the spitting image of you!" said Oito, her eyes firmly on Jihei's. "Hiding all this from me was already inexcusable, but now, pretending innocence in the face of unquestionable proof? I'm so sad and disappointed I hardly know what to say. Why won't you be honest? Do you think I'll be jealous? I'm not that kind of person. Now that I know I came between you two, I won't have a moment's peace. If you had told me the truth and asked me what you should do, I wouldn't feel so bad now. But treating this woman so roughly when in fact she seems to be a fine person is simply wrong. Are you listening to me? Do you think I could keep my mouth shut and let it be? Well, I can't be so heartless!" Breathing hard, she pressed her point. Jihei, knowing he was wrong, did not pursue the issue.

"What a stubborn woman!" he spit out, glaring at Omine hatefully, and left the room.

Already lost and defenseless, Omine now felt utterly defeated at Jihei's harsh treatment of her. Holding her child tightly in her arms, she cried desperately, having forgotten Oito was there. Her lusterless, tangled hair now hung loose over her shoulders, which were covered by her worn, patched kimono. Seeing that Omine was without even a half coat in this cold weather, Oito's heart ached. She mused over the fact that Jihei might have gone back home to his wife if he hadn't met her. Even he, unreasonable as he was, would probably not have stayed on in Tokyo, neglecting his wife and his son's education. He and his family would have lived happily together as they had before. Oito was ashamed of her fine kimono of handwoven Okinawan silk and her nice warm half coat; she felt as though she had committed a terrible crime. She was so uncomfortable she simply wanted to disappear.

7

Oito tried to console Omine and her son the best way she knew how: by serving them carefully prepared meals and giving them new clothes she had sewn herself. Omine shed tears of gratitude at Oito's kindness, which did not diminish as the days went by. However, because she could not understand Jihei's continued cruelty to her, she remained distraught. Concerned, Oito kept after her husband to tell her what was on his mind.

"Why do you go on looking so grim? Can't you say something nice to her? What are you thinking?" She challenged Jihei whenever she had a chance, but he continued avoiding the issue.

"Well, if you are really such a heartless man, I'll have to think of a solution myself," she said irritably, hoping to make an impact on her husband.

Jihei was taken by surprise and responded agitatedly.

"I am sorry I made you worry, Oito, but I'm a man, you see. I don't want to take Omine back, and I don't want to let you go. I'm now tied to you by my marriage vow, and I intend to stay with you as your husband. Because you're treating Omine so nicely, I can't really force her to leave, but having her around is a nuisance I can hardly tolerate. I've had it! If you went back to your parents now, you'd lose face because it would look like Omine threw you out. I think we ought to disregard feelings of duty and such for now and work on getting rid of those two. What do you say?" Jihei looked eager, as though he had come up with a most ingenious plan.

"What? I don't want to hear it. I didn't talk to you with such terrible thoughts in mind." She glared at Jihei in disgust. "I feel so bad for Omine, seeing her suffer like that; she's a good person and means no harm. I want to help you open your heart, so that the two of you can get along the way you did before. That's what I'm asking you. How can you suggest that I throw her out of the house? I would rather you divorce me. I won't care a bit what people will say about me! My fondest wish is that you and Omine get back together and share a long, happy marriage, so please divorce me right this minute. There is the paper and ink; shall I bring the inkstone?"

After Oito harangued him in this way, Jihei sighed deeply and sank deep into thought. Suddenly, he looked up and glared at Oito. "Well, I see you don't want me anymore. Is that right?" he said, reproachfully.

Oito, shocked at Jihei's pronouncement, responded, "Why, what do you mean by that? What do you suspect me of?"

Interrupting her, Jihei went on, now in a harsher voice than ever before. "It's not just a suspicion; I'm sure it's the truth. It must be! Despite what you say, you must be very smug at how things are turning out. Ever since we moved from the quiet suburbs to open the drugstore, you've become a different person. You're always aflutter now—and you know very well why! It's that Kisaku, isn't it? I can't stand that fellow. I feel like an idiot for letting myself be deceived all this time!"

Oito was horrified at Jihei's unreasonable accusation. Tears flowed freely down her cheeks. But realizing she should not let it go, she forced herself to inch forward on trembling knees. Steeling herself, she replied in a shaky voice, "What are you saying? I'm thinking only of you. I'd split my heart open to prove it! I am innocent. Why would you think me so fickle? You say I'm having an illicit affair with Kisaku. When did I do such a thing? You tell me!" Oito demanded, gnashing her teeth in anguish; her sincerity revealed itself in her voice.

Heedless to this, Jihei still looked angry. "Don't make excuses, Oito, I'm not making it up. I'm not blind or deaf, you know! Even the store clerks will say you've spent lots of time chatting away with Kisaku while I was out. Anyone would be suspicious, seeing the way you two behave," Jihei declared high-handedly. "So, if you still have something to say, let's hear it."

"Are you accusing me? But there's no truth to what you say. I don't understand you!" Oito, not knowing what else to say, repeated herself; bitter tears streamed down her face.

"To tell the truth, I hadn't thought so much about it before," Jihei announced, looking smug, "but I'm convinced now that you've asked for a divorce, you see. You want to leave me and get together with Kisaku, and you're just patronizing me. A married woman would never ask for a divorce, no matter how difficult a husband she might have. Am I wrong in saying this?" Jihei felt he had really hit on something.

Oito was at her wits' end. What an unreasonable, suspicious man! Why would she entertain such thoughts about Kisaku, for whom she cherished not the faintest desire? He was just a good customer, she thought; it was simply her nature to treat him well. How else should she have treated him? But Jihei had seen everything in a suspicious light and come to his own conclusion. Then she remembered Kisaku's story about the old man. She didn't know Jihei's secret at the time, and she felt sorry for what she had said. Anyone would have been angry. What a mistake! Now she regretted it day and night. Why did Kisaku have to tell the story in front of Jihei on purpose like that? she thought angrily. Ever since Kisaku's vindictiveness that day, she had thought him a shallow, hateful person and had avoided interacting with him. But apparently Jihei had taken it differently: he had assumed she was being deliberately aloof to distract him from her guilt. What could she do now to persuade him of her innocence?

Since the situation had developed in this way, Oito could not mention divorce again. All she could do was tell Jihei repeatedly that she was innocent. But this didn't solve the problem of Omine and her son. How long might she be able to stay in this house in a world where one man cannot have two wives? Oito couldn't stop worrying. She felt as if her heart would break.

8

For Jihei, on the other hand, it was as though the dam had broken. He felt better now that he had finally confronted Oito about Kisaku. The doubts that had weighed so heavily on his mind for months were dispelled when she denied having an affair. Once it seemed he had dissuaded her from contemplating divorce, he felt as if an afternoon shower had cleared the air. Now that the wall separating them had been removed, he felt completely relaxed. If only Omine weren't around, he and Oito could stay married and live happily ever after. He had no compassion for Omine, who seemed even uglier when compared with Oito; he even thought her impudent. He gave not a thought to the sad situation in which mother and child found themselves. All he could think of was that, unless Omine left, Oito might still want a divorce. Since Omine had nowhere else to go and showed no sign of leaving on her own, he must force her out, he decided. Jihei abused her verbally every chance he had, and his general mistreatment of her increased as the days went by. Omine's feeling of helplessness deepened, and she wept into her pillow every night. Oito couldn't bear to see this, so she, too, lost sleep. Tearfully, she pondered throughout the night about what could be done.

It's me who's in the way, Oito finally concluded. If I weren't around, things would work themselves out. I would rather let Jihei suspect me of doing wrong than continue suffering this way, she thought. She went over the plan in her mind many times, and finally, one day, she asked Jihei for a divorce again. He was furious.

"If you hate me that much, go ahead and do whatever you want!"

Oito sensed Jihei was trying to make her change her mind again and felt guilty. She wanted to give in but maintained tight control over her feelings and said,

"Yes, I am tired of you, so please give me a divorce."

"Are you serious? Gotten tired of me, you say?" Jihei's voice quavered, his eyes fixed on Oito.

Oito did not want to say what was not true, even if it was for Jihei's sake, but she went on, determined. "Why would I lie? Of course, I am serious. I'm tired of being with you in this house day in and day out. I would rather be home with my parents!" She would rather not have to part with hard feelings, but trying to reason with him was impossible, so it seemed there was no other way for her to leave him.

"The sooner I can leave, the better," Oito announced, turning her face away so that Jihei wouldn't see the tears streaming down her cheeks.

Jihei was floored. "Oito, I can't believe what you're saying. I've shown you no small measure of kindness, you know; I've outdone myself, I would say. And now you say it's meant nothing to you? Instead of being grateful, you tell me you don't want to be with me anymore. You are shameless, and I'm sorry I've wasted my time on such a rotten woman. Fickleness is your nature, I now know. I suppose you're going to get together with Kisaku. Fine! If that's what you want, I'll write you a divorce!"

The three-and-a-half-line divorce decree Jihei scribbled at the height of his anger was smudged, blurry; it seemed to tell the destiny of two whose bond in this lifetime had been tenuous at best. Knowing she could not confide in Jihei and let him know what she really felt or even apologize to him, Oito swallowed her grief and left the house right then and there. She thought of how Jihei must feel and felt her heart lurch. As she slowly made her way toward her parents' house, she heaved a deep sigh. Looking up, she was disappointed to see no sign of the moon in the dark, cloudy sky.

****

Late that night, people heard a terrible commotion at Oito's parents' house; they learned that it was Jihei who emerged, trussed up and surrounded by policemen. Many said that Jihei deserved pity and ought to be spared the death penalty. It was her own fault that the adulterous Oito was killed. It was a fitting end for a fickle woman, they agreed.

Who then will take pity on poor Oito, murdered by such a stupid man? Her soul must wander, bitter and restless, in the shadowy grounds of the Yanaka graveyard.

WRETCHED SIGHTS

Translated by Rebecca L. Copeland

FOR YEARS, I had heard of the lively Niwaka Festival in the plea-sure quarters.[27] But as a woman I had felt uncomfortable entering such a disreputable place and so until this year had never seen it. This summer, I visited a friend who lived near the quarters. An easygoing sort, he of-fered to escort me through the district, encouraging me to take advan-tage of the timing of my visit to finally view the festival. Refusing to listen to my objections, he led me off with a knowing look.

The minute we stepped through what must have been the main gate, the scene that spread before me was livelier than anything I could have imagined. How different and how incredible it all appeared. The Niwaka celebrations seemed to be at their height. Lilting voices sang ballads, *tokiwazu*, and love songs, accompanied by the twang of the shamisen and the thump of the drum. Music poured forth in every direction, and I felt my spirits quicken in response. I'd seen geisha and their young apprentices rushing along the streets to and from parties or practice, so seeing them now was not particularly remarkable. But I had never before seen women playing the drum, and glimpsing them here decked out as drummers and jesters was quite a beguiling sight. Among the costumes was that of Momotarō, the Peach Boy, on his voyage to Devil Island. The costume is much in vogue these days, appearing in celebrations of our recent war victory. Carried away by the festivities, I allowed myself to be pulled along by the crowd until I found myself in front of the establishments for prostitutes. The touts in the quarter were not allowed to venture beyond their own establishments and so would clutch at the sleeves of passersby, behaving scandalously in an effort to detain them. The way they called after the men, urging them to step inside, was odious and detestable. In front of one of the establishments—I cannot remember the name of the house now—a gang of touts was swarming around a large man in his forties who looked to be a shopkeeper of sorts. They seemed to be doing their utmost to drag him inside. The scene had nothing to do with me, of course, but still I felt anxious for the man, and I stopped briefly to watch what would happen. The man did not seem particularly weak-willed, and he looked to be desperately trying to shake himself free. But still, even when they tugged at him, he did not lose his temper. In fact, he smiled at them and, looking somewhat baffled, seemed to be offering his apologies when, just at that moment, the glass *shōji* door slid open and a prostitute in a long outer robe stepped out. She whispered what must have been words of encouragement in the man's ear for quite some time and, refusing to take no for an answer, led him inside. Surely, he has a wife and child awaiting him at home. If they hear of what has taken place here, how they will weep.

Prostitution is just a trade like any other, I have heard it said. But another with such horrible consequences is hard to imagine. And the odiousness of the trade is not limited to scenes like this. The prostitutes sit alongside one another until one drags herself to the lattice and, murmuring words of encouragement, thrusts a tobacco-filled pipe out to the hordes of men sauntering by. These women even compete with one another to sell their favors to men who are no better than beggars. I have heard it said that there are three thousand women involved here in this despicable trade.

Born pure, these women sink deeper and deeper into the muddy depths of prostitution. Like the caged bird unable to soar into the sky, how pitiful they are. Laughing, they put on a brave face, but deep in their hearts their sorrow knows no end. Unbeknownst to others, how they must resent the bitterness of this floating world. Since they have chosen of their own volition to live unchaste lives, it is by the natural laws of fate that they end up adrift in the world as prostitutes. And yet there are among them as well those who—being filial daughters—sold themselves into the trade out of a deep love for their parents. When I think of these women, I cannot hold back my tears.

Seeing these sights today reminded me of a time when I was just a little girl. My elder sister and I were playing house in an empty lot near our home when a seedy-looking man, his head wrapped in a scarf, strode straight up to where we were. Beckoning to us with friendly gestures, he coaxed, "I've got something good to give you. Come along and see." He spoke as if he knew us and offered to take us with him somewhere to look for the treat he promised. Our childish hearts filled instinctively with fear, and we began to wail at the top of our lungs. Our maid heard us and, glad to discover our whereabouts, came running. Seeing her, the man took to his heels, leaving behind his sandals in his hurry to take flight. He fled toward the main street and disappeared. Later, when I put two and two together, I realized that the man who had appeared that day was likely a kidnapper. Had he led me away then, I, too, might have ended up a wretched sight in a quarter such as this. The thought gave me such a fright that I felt a chill seep through my thin kimono, though it was a summer night. Tugging the sleeve of my escort, who was still engrossed in the festivities, I urged him to leave, and we hastened home.

NOTES

1. Marianne Mariko Harrison, *The Rise of the Woman Novelist in Meiji Japan* (Ann Arbor: University of Michigan Dissertation Services, 1994), p. 92.

2. Cited in Todoroki Eiko, *Kitada Usurai kenkyū* (Tokyo: Sōbunsha, 1984), p. 38. Rebecca Copeland partially translates the quotation; see *Lost Leaves: Women Writers of Meiji Japan* (Honolulu: University of Hawai'i Press, 2000), p. 36.

3. The other members of the Ken'yūsha, or Friends of the Inkstone, included Yamada Bimyō (1868–1910), onetime husband of Tazawa Inabune; Kawakami Bizan (1869–1908); Hirotsu Ryūrō (1861–1928); and Iwaya Sazanami (1870–1933). As a group, this powerful literary society was known for "its emphasis on the craftsmanship and entertainment value of the novel" (Copeland, *Lost Leaves*, p. 134). Though they were diverse in style, Donald Keene maintains that "the rediscovery of the Genroku [1688–1704] classics, especially the works of Saikaku [1642–1693], exercised a far more conspicuous influence on the Ken'yūsha writers than did any theories borrowed from the West" (*Dawn to the West: Japanese Literature in the Modern Era*, vol. 1, *Fiction* (New York: Holt, Rinehart, and Winston, 1984), p. 121.

4. Copeland, *Lost Leaves*, p. 4.

5. Todoroki, *Kitada Usurai kenkyū*, p. 11.

6. The name literally means "thin ice," though the reading of the characters is unusual. It suggests the thin, crystalline layer that forms over a stream or lake when it is not cold enough to freeze over entirely. In classical poetry, the word is associated with early spring. An alternative reading for this name is Usurahi.

7. Kajita had done the illustrations for the writer's most famous serialized novel, *Konjiki yasha* (The golden demon, 1897).

8. Copeland, *Lost Leaves*, p. 37.

9. Yukiko Tanaka, *Women Writers of Meiji and Taishō Japan: Their Lives, Works, and Critical Reception*, 1868–1926 (Jefferson, N.C.: MacFarland, 2000), p. 56.

10. Another area of Usurai's work that deserves attention is her numerous children's stories, published mostly in the journal *Shōnen sekai* (Children's world). Todoroki devotes a section of her book to the works that appeared there (*Kitada Usurai kenkyū*, pp. 157–160). Harrison comments briefly on the involvement of the literati in children's literature and more specifically on Usurai's stories for young girls (*The Rise of the Woman Novelist in Meiji Japan*, pp. 160–161).

11. Todoroki, *Kitada Usurai kenkyū*, p. 44.

12. Cited in ibid., p. 45. The unnamed critic wrote for the journal *Seinenbun* (Youth writing).

13. Like any literary movement, naturalism is hard to define or to delimit. In Western literature, it is associated with authors such as Émile Zola (1840–1902) and Henrik Ibsen (1828–1906), who were part of the "systematization of a literary aesthetic that sought to reconcile the aims of art and science by subordinating creative individualism to the laws of causality" (Alex Preminger and T. V. F. Brogan, eds. *The New Princeton Encyclopedia of Poetry and Poetics* [Princeton, N.J.: Princeton University Press, 1993], p. 818). While this is somewhat true of so-called naturalism (*shizen shugi*) in Japan as well, contemporary writers, struck more by these authors' frank and uncompromising views of human nature, tried to create a sort of realism that was unadorned in style and "mercilessly candid" in content (Keene, *Dawn to the West*, p. 223). For more on the Japanese naturalists and how they variously interpreted and redefined naturalism for themselves, see ibid., pp. 220–304.

14. Tanaka, *Women Writers of Meiji and Taishō Japan*, p. 59. Todoroki makes the same argument, albeit about works including and after "Kuromegane" (Dark glasses) (*Kitada Usurai kenkyū*, p. 55).

15. Incidentally, the actual occurrence of men leaving wives behind in the country was not at all unusual. We see it happening in Shimizu Shikin's "The Broken Ring" (reprinted in this volume). In fact, Ōi Kentarō, Shikin's lover, left his own wife behind.

16. Tanaka, *Women Writers of Meiji and Taishō Japan*, p. 55.

17. Harrison, *The Rise of the Woman Novelist in Meiji Japan*, pp. 173–174. Harrison further notes that this "empathy for rivals" is a feature of Meiji women's writings in general (p. 174).

18. "Troubled Waters" is an interesting companion piece to "Hiding the Gray," since there is a murder at its conclusion as well. Despite the fact that the female protagonist has selflessly rejected the man she loves so that he will go back to his wife, he kills her in a fit of jealousy. The townspeople, like those in "Hiding the Gray," assume the woman has been justly killed for faithlessness.

19. Todoroki also comments on similarities between the two authors (*Kitada Usurai kenkyū*, pp. 39, 116–136).

20. Usurai does have one short story, "Aki no sora" (Autumn sky, 1896), in which the protagonist becomes a geisha to raise money for herself and her husband. True to Usurai's sensibilities, however, it is the woman's virtue and love for her husband that motivates her decision, not a moral failing. Her husband, now rich from selling his wife, discards her for another. A translation of the story appears in Harrison, *The Rise of the Woman Novelist in Meiji Japan*, pp. 181–190.

21. Prostitution was legal in Japan until 1958. While the height of licensed prostitution, especially in the famous Yoshiwara district where Usurai attended the festival, was during the Edo period, it was still a lively business and the focus of much political debate. For more information, see Vera Mackie, *Feminism in Modern Japan* (Cambridge: Cambridge University Press, 2003). See also Tanaka, *Women Writers of Meiji and Taishō Japan*, pp. 54–56.

22. Edward Seidensticker, *Low City, High City* (Cambridge: Harvard University Press, 1991), p. 173.

23. Cited and translated in Copeland, *Lost Leaves*, p. 40.

24. The source for this translation is *Bungei kurabu* (Literary arts club) 3 (January 1897): 102–126.

25. One *ken* is approximately 1.818 meters.

26. This was the hairstyle adopted by a young woman when she married.

27. The source for this translation is *Bungei kurabu* (Literary arts club) 4 (March 1895): 230–233.

SHIMIZU SHIKIN
(1868–1933)

Rebecca Jennison

SHIMIZU SHIKIN,[1] like many of her contemporaries, was actively engaged in the political, social, and cultural milieu of her day. By the time she reached the age of twenty, she had been married and divorced, was making speeches at rallies for the Jiyū minken undō (Freedom and popular rights movement), and, at the request of well-known activist Ueki Emori (1857–1892), had contributed a preface to his work *Tōyō no Fujo* (Women of the Orient, 1888), proclaiming the vital importance of "the woman question." In 1889 Shikin moved to Tokyo to become an editor for *Jogaku zasshi* (Woman's education journal), where she worked under the direction of Iwamoto Yoshiharu (1863–1942) and interacted with other influential Meiji thinkers who were promoting new roles for women of her class in the modern family and state.

Shimizu Toyo was born in Okayama Prefecture, the fifth child of Shimizu Sadamoto. Sadamoto was from a relatively wealthy and powerful family and had received a distinguished education for someone who was originally of peasant stock. The family moved to Kyoto when he was asked to oversee the government bureau responsible for the modernization of the old capital. Toyo advanced to the Kyoto Municipal Women's Teacher Training School and graduated at the young age of fourteen, having completed a high level of education for a woman of her era. She also had access to her father's library, where she probably continued to study on her own after leaving school. Nevertheless, it is likely that her desire to proceed with her studies came into conflict with her father's wish to see her suitably married.

At this time, Shikin's family was living in an area of Kyoto where activists held lectures and meetings to help spread the views of the Jiyū minken undō. Kishida Toshiko was invited to lecture at a nearby theater a number of times, and, while it is not certain that Shikin actually heard her speak, she may well have been aware of these activities.[2] At the age of eighteen, she married a young lawyer who was also somewhat connected to the movement. It is thought that, through him, Shikin met Ueki Emori, Kageyama (Fukuda) Hideko (1865–1927), and others who were actively giving speeches and rallying support in Kyoto and Osaka. Early in 1899, her marriage to the lawyer ended in divorce; after this, she became more involved with the movement.[3]

During that year, Shikin herself began to make speeches advocating women's rights. Such speeches most likely formed the basis for her early essays, one of which, "Tōkon jogakusei no kakugo wa ikan" (How Determined Are Today's Women Students? 1890), is translated here. Later the same year, Shikin met Nakae Chōmin (1847–1901), an outspoken proponent of heiminshugi (commoners' rights) who argued for improvements in the status and living conditions of the outcast group known as burakumin.[4] Shikin, now twenty-two, accompanied Buddhist priests and other Jiyū minken undō activists to Yanagihara-chō, Zeniza Village, a buraku neighborhood in south Kyoto, where she spoke before a large audience, possibly on the importance of women's rights. Almost a decade later, she would draw on her impressions of this visit in one of her last works of fiction, "Imin gakuen" (School for Émigrés, 1899), also translated here.

Shikin was twenty-three when she moved to Tokyo to work for Jogaku zasshi. She arrived in the capital at a time when important legal reforms were under debate. The Imperial Constitution had been promulgated in 1889, but on July 25, 1890, an act was passed prohibiting women from participating in political assemblies. Shikin responded by writing several polemically charged essays in which she argued strongly for a woman's right to equal participation in politics. In the first of these, "Nani yue ni joshi wa seidan shukai ni sanchō suru to yurusarezuka?" (Why have women been prohibited from participating in political assemblies?), published in August of that year, Shikin protested the barriers prevent-

FIGURE 7.1 Shimizu Shikin (1868–1933)

ing women from attending political hearings and debates. Several weeks later, she wrote "Naite aisuru shimai ni tsugu" (To my beloved sisters in tears), in which she again argued strongly against the exclusion of women from the listener's gallery of the Diet. Shikin, with a rhetorical skill remarkable in so young a writer, argued that these prohibitions were "tantamount to one half of society controlling the other."

On November 15, 1890, Shikin published another important work, "Tōkon jogakusei no kakugo wa ikan" (How Determined Are Today's Women Students?). Here, Shikin lobbies for practical reforms in "the home as well as in relations between the millions of young men and women of marriageable age." She calls on students at women's schools to become principal actors in bringing about such reforms but warns that they will most likely face opposition from husbands or parents-in-law who do not understand them.

Not long after this, Shikin wrote "Koware yubiwa" (The Broken Ring), published under the name "Tsuyuko" in the January 1891 issue of *Jogaku zasshi*. This much-noted work addresses in fictional form some of the social problems Shikin had discussed in "How Determined Are Today's Women Students?" Employing a lively and direct first-person narrative, the story explores the personal dilemma of a graduate of a women's school. Copies of the issue in which the story appeared quickly sold out, indicating that readers found the work timely and convincing.

Contemporary reviews of the story described it as "realistic," like a "photograph of a fine, young maiden's heart that reveals her innermost feelings." Mori Ōgai (1862–1922) noted the author's use of "an unusually natural voice," and Miyake Kaho complimented the effect created by the direct voice of the narrator.[5] As many scholars of Meiji literature have noted, this was a period of experimentation with new forms of literary style, marking a shift from neoclassical language to *genbun itchi* (unity of speech and writing), which is more closely associated with spoken language. Indeed, readers of this story, both then and now, have been struck by the immediacy of the first-person narrative, which addresses the themes of women's education, marriage, and the formation of a new community of young women readers.

The work is structured around the narrator's explanation to the reader—assumed to be the graduate of a women's school—of her reasons for wearing an unsightly "broken ring." As the narrative unfolds, the reader learns of the protagonist's struggle to express herself to her unsympathetic father and, later, to her inattentive husband. At first she resists the pressure to give up her studies and marry, but she is repeatedly silenced by her father and finally submits to his demands, entering into a marriage that soon proves to be unhappy. After many attempts at reconciliation with her husband and the death of her mother, she resolves to end her marriage. The last lines of the story, however, suggest lingering regret over the failure of her marriage. This shift suggests that the protagonist's choice may have been difficult for Shikin's audience to accept. One scholar has interpreted the ending as an attempt to soften the "threatening implications of the story's feminist message."[6]

In the spring following the publication of "The Broken Ring," Shikin's own life took a dramatic turn. She was called back to Kyoto to care for her father, who had fallen ill. One month later, she applied for a leave of absence from her work as editor at *Jogaku zasshi*, and, in late November of that year, she gave birth out of wedlock to the child of former Jiyū minken undō activist Ōi Kentarō (1843–1922). Shikin arranged for the child to be adopted and raised by her brother's family. She then returned to Tokyo early in 1892. But the stress caused by these events in her personal life led to her hospitalization twice that spring. It was not until September that she was able to resume her work at *Jogaku zasshi*.

The journal had undergone major changes during her absence. In response to pressure from Kitamura Tōkoku (1868–1894), Shimazaki

Tōson (1872–1943), and others of the journal's regular contributors who disagreed with his views on the function of literature, Iwamoto divided the journal into two different editions: "White" and "Red." The change took place from June 1892. Of this shift in editorial policy, Iwamoto wrote, "White is for young men, who like the Genji are virile and brave. Red is for young women, who like the Heike adorn themselves and know deep sentiment."[7] The "White Cover" edition, which was soon to evolve into *Bungakukai* (Literary world), a separate literary journal altogether, was directed toward a readership interested in contemporary issues and literature, while the "Red Cover" edition aimed at a readership of young married women and contained more practical advice about household matters. Upon her return to work at the journal, Shikin was asked to write for the "Red Cover" edition.

Through her brother, Shikin met Kozai Yoshinao (1864–1934), a promising young scholar on the faculty of the Tokyo School of Agriculture. Soon, Kozai began corresponding with her. As a divorced woman, Shikin assumed that when he found out about her past, he would give up the idea of marrying her. But Kozai continued to court her, and they were married in 1892. Their first son was born in September of the following year. In 1895 Kozai accepted a grant from the Ministry of Education and traveled to Germany to study. Shikin went to live with her mother-in-law in the Hanazono district of Kyoto while he was abroad. There, she continued to write essays for *Jogaku zasshi* and other periodicals. It was during this time that she began more consistently to use the pseudonym "Shikin," comprised of the characters for *murasaki* (*shi*: purple, the name of the famous author of *The tale of Genji*) and *koto* (*kin*: harp and a homophone for "now," "today"), making the name of both classical and modern literary women.[8]

The third and most difficult work by Shikin introduced in translation here, "Imin gakuen" (School for Émigrés), was published in *Bungei kurabu* (Literary arts club) in May 1899, near the end of Shikin's stay in Kyoto. The neoclassical style of this work makes it much more challenging for both reader and translator. Themes from earlier works—such as women's education and marriage—appear in the story but are interwoven with the subject central to the narrative: the discrimination against *burakumin*. As mentioned above, the work was likely inspired by Shikin's 1889 visit to Zeniza village, a *buraku* neighborhood in south Kyoto. During the Tokugawa period (1603–1867), discrimination against *burakumin* had been severe. When the new Meiji government was formed, their status was debated, and numerous proposals were put forth, including that they be given the status of *shin heimin* (new commoners) and sent to Hokkaido to help develop what was then the new frontier.[9] On August 28, 1871, the Emancipation Edict abolished the derogatory terms "*eta*" and "*hinin*" ("much filth" and "nonhuman"). But in spite of new legal measures, the *burakumin* living in segregated communities throughout the country continued to suffer severe discrimination. In 1922 the Suiheisha (Levelers' association) was founded to combat this injustice, and, in the postwar era, the Kaihō dōmei (Buraku liberation league) continues to work for the rights of *burakumin*, but marriage and job discrimination still persist to this day.

Perhaps the most well-known work of literature treating the subject of the *burakumin* is Shimazaki Tōson's *Hakai* (The broken commandment), published in 1906. Tōson's work has been hailed as one of the first modern novels in Japanese and was a pivotal work in establishing Tōson as a naturalist writer. Recent studies of this work have shown the link between the confessional narrative structure of the novel and the formation of modern literature as well as the relationship between social discrimination and the formation of the nation-state.[10] But neither Shikin nor Tōson were the first to write literary works on the subject of *burakumin*. As Rebecca Copeland has noted, other works on the subject had been published earlier, though their treatment of the issue tended to be more stereotypical.[11]

Like Tōson's *Hakai*, "School for Émigrés" is structured around the protagonist's gradual revelation that she herself is a "new commoner." In contrast to Tōson's much longer and more fully developed work, however, Shikin's story is written in a stilted style reminiscent of earlier literary and dramatic forms. Consisting of four sections narrated from multiple perspectives, the story unfolds with the kind of dramatic devices frequently found on the Kabuki stage. Characters' identities are revealed to be multifaceted, the exterior belying a significantly different interior. For example, the first section of the story begins with a monologue by the protagonist, whose name, we later learn, is Kiyoko (Okiyo) Imao. Immediately, the reader's attention is drawn to the uncomfortable tension between her inner, melancholy state and the view that others hold of her as a selfish social climber. This device of contrasting external appearances with internal reflection appears throughout the text.

Other narrative strategies include the use of the well-timed letter and unexpected scene shifts. In the second section of the story, for example, just after Kiyoko recalls a letter from her father commanding her never to seek his whereabouts, she is met by the unexpected delivery of another missive in an unfamiliar hand. This one informs her that her father is seriously ill. This news in turn signals startling change of scene.

Like the theatrical productions of the day, this story, too, is not without its humorous moments, here represented by the inappropriately catty society matrons who appear at the end of the first section. It is they who help underscore the vulnerability of Kiyoko's social situation. Interestingly, many of the predictions they make about her duplicity, while essentially true, are undercut by the story's triumphant, if not somewhat escapist conclusion, which has been compared by many to that of Shimazaki Tōson's *Hakai*.

Shortly after writing "School for Émigrés," Shikin's husband returned from Europe, and she rejoined him in Tokyo. After that, Shikin produced only a few more works, the last of which, "Natsuko no mono omoi" (Natsuko remembers), was published in 1901. The concluding lines of this personal reflection convey a sense of frustration and sorrow at being unable to continue to write. Just why Shikin stopped writing has been the subject of much conjecture. Rebecca Copeland cites the dilemma of the Meiji-era woman writer who attempts to continue writing after marriage.[12] In Shikin's case, this was compounded by child rearing and the pressures of being the wife of a rising scholar who was to become the president of Tokyo Imperial University of Agriculture. As the proper wife of such a public figure, Shikin herself, like Kiyoko, could not afford to be too visible. Feminist scholar and critic Komashaku Kimi has argued that Shikin is important because she advocated women's human rights and that only when her feminism is recognized and understood "will we be able to understand the weight of her silence."[13] The works reproduced below reflect Shikin's rich complexity. It is hoped that perusing them will help readers come to a fuller appreciation of the complicated challenges that confronted intelligent and ambitious women like Shikin.

HOW DETERMINED ARE
TODAY'S WOMEN STUDENTS?

Translated by Rebecca Jennison

HOW MANY YOUNG WOMEN STUDENTS are there in our country today?[14] And how many of you are ready to take it upon yourselves to become reformers or leaders someday? I am not asking that every single one of you become such a reformer or leader. I am simply asking whether you have this kind of determination because I believe it is absolutely vital to our country today.

No doubt, most young women hope to accomplish many things in addition to their studies and work. After graduating from a women's school, you will surely want to find a good husband and create a happy home, aspirations that are both worthy and true to your nature. But I wonder, will it be that easy to find such a man or make a happy home? Where are the men with noble and truly loving hearts who will bring you happiness when you start out in life with a flourish, so full of hope and joy? And where are the progressively minded parents-in-law who will welcome and praise you when you put into practice the methods of child rearing and household management you have dreamt of since learning them in school?

If we approach the question in this way, it becomes clear that today's women students must be determined to become leaders and reformers. And if you can find neither a husband who suits you nor a family where there is hope of reform, you may even decide not to marry at all. To do either of these things, you will have to endure many long years of suffering. I know you are still innocent and inexperienced and have not yet considered these matters. No doubt you believe that husbands treat their wives in the kindly manner that foreign missionaries do. You may imagine that your future husband's family will treat you as your friends at school have: generously and without discrimination. You may think of married life as something to be embarked on without apprehension or anxiety, something that promises hope and happiness, joy, and peace. I cannot help feeling deeply concerned each time I see this. It is as if Eve were singing to herself while walking unknowingly toward the coiling snake or a sheep were being sent into a den of tigers, wolves, or other wild beasts. In order to avoid being devoured by beasts, the young woman must give up her sheeplike gentleness.

You probably have not experienced the heartlessness and coldness of the world. You may mistakenly confuse the harsh school regulations, or the dormitory mother's warning about eating too much or staying out too late, with such coldness and heartlessness. Falling ill at school and lying in your dormitory bed with no one to care for you as your mother would or doing poorly on an exam may be the worst hardship you have experienced. But once you graduate and marry, you will have to spend all your days and nights with people whose habits and sentiments are completely different from your own. They will watch everything you do. This is when your real trials and difficulties will begin.

Your sorrow may deepen when the husband on whom you once relied begins to show little sympathy for you. With time, his affection may dwindle, and he may begin to go out to flower and moon viewing parties, enjoying himself without giving even a thought to household affairs. Your parents-in-law may say you have served him poorly, blaming you, the new wife, rather than scolding their son. And when you can no longer endure this and start to make the slightest objection, they will interrupt, saying, "You see, that's why we didn't fancy a bride who's been to women's school." If you ask them to explain, they answer that such girls are too argumentative. If you go on to reply that you do not want to start an argument, they silence you again, saying your queries prove your insolence. Then, realizing that it is utterly impossible to express the truth before those who insist on brandishing their authority, you may decide to give up trying to speak to them and seal your lips. But, just then, they demand that you apologize. Wondering just when the wrong

was committed and what sort of wrong it was, you nevertheless decide
to smooth things over and apologize in form only, while shedding bitter
tears in the depths of your heart.

To relieve your troubled heart, you may decide to tell your own family about these unhappy circumstances, only to hear example after example from your mother and older sister of the trials they have undergone.
They tell of the hardships your grandmother endured, saying that you
are much better off than they are. Ah, but isn't it useless to think it a
woman's fate to live in sorrow, never knowing any joy or good fortune?
Your mind full of thoughts like these, you may feel surrounded by enemies on all sides, with no one to comfort you. Moreover, the dreams
you cherished as a schoolgirl, dreams of life with an ideal husband in a
warm and happy home, haunt you, thus adding to your sorrows.

All graduates of women's schools will experience such difficulties
to some degree. Because they cherish lofty and somewhat extravagant
dreams, they suffer more than young women with old-fashioned views.
Only those of you with great patience and understanding can endure
this suffering. If you persist, after many years of effort, you may at last
come to influence your husband and parents-in-law and reach a state
of harmony with them. But someone who is short-tempered or weak-
willed will probably lose herself along the way; abandoning her high
hopes, she will become a mere slave of habit and end her days mechani-
cally fulfilling her duties.

There are still other reasons why a graduate of a women's school who
marries may feel dissatisfied. The affairs of the world are more complex than you can imagine, and households and individuals differ widely.
Thus problems that arise in such situations are not easily resolved. Especially in today's world, it is not enough to think only of oneself and
one's family; it is necessary to bear responsibilities on behalf of our fellow citizens and our nation as well, adding yet other layers of complexity to our lives.

Nevertheless, there are many young women who have only a limited
understanding of the world. Having never experienced real misfortune
or really suffered, some young women look forward to marrying as
soon as they graduate from school, believing that marriage will be joyful. Some of you may even become engaged while you are still students.
I cannot imagine what makes you want to do this. In some cases, the
pressures of household circumstances or family make it impossible for

a young woman to avoid getting married. Then, you should enter into marriage with the conscious determination to become a leader and reformer, never thinking that it is simply a way to settle down. You should not marry with false expectations and a sense of relief like that of the young man who mistakenly imagines that all his troubles are over when he receives his first paycheck. Your new home will not, in reality, be a paradise or a haven; at times, it may well be a "paradise lost," a den of suffering. Only through your patience and effort can this hell be transformed into a haven and your husband transformed into the man of your dreams.

Two or three of my acquaintances have recently decided to marry and are anxious to have their weddings soon. Even though they have not completed their studies and in fact have the means to continue them for two or three more years, they recklessly hope to enter the difficult circumstances of married life without serious consideration. When I told one of them that I thought her attitude was mistaken and advised her against marrying so soon, she replied that, because she was weak and sickly, she hadn't the strength to study anymore and so had begun making plans to settle down. I was very surprised when I heard this. How can someone who doesn't have the strength to go on with her schooling possibly endure the difficulties that come after marriage? How does she expect to take on the responsibility of being a wife and mother if she is so physically weak? In the end, she didn't listen to a word I said. This is either because she still believes in an ideal that does not exist or because she has allowed her judgment to become clouded by one or two exceptional cases. As a result, she still clings to the mistaken notion that marriage will always be happy. The number of young women students today who hold this view is by no means small. It is for these reasons that I wanted to share my thoughts with you.

The road before young women today is indeed as long as the situation in our nation is complex. There are innumerable things that must be reformed in the home as well as in the relations between the millions of young men and women of marriageable age. Who else but the young women students of today are in a position to make these reforms and bring about these changes? I am asking you to consider seriously whether you are firmly resolved to bear this responsibility precisely because I have high hopes that you yourselves will begin to recognize this responsibility and shoulder it with confidence.

THE BROKEN RING

Translated by Rebecca Jennison

I KNOW YOU ARE bothered by this ring of mine with no stone.[15] A broken ring like this is not, as you say, very becoming. Perhaps you think I should put in a new stone—anything would do. But this broken ring is a kind of remembrance for me, and I cannot possibly change it. The months have passed quickly since that day two years ago when I broke it. And now you are asking why I still wear a ring so strange. I have my reasons, and, because it is you who ask, I will explain.

Each time I look at this ring, I recall the heart-wrenching pain I have suffered. Even so, I cannot bear to take it off, even for a moment, because it has also been my benefactor. You ask why? Somehow, thanks to the suffering it has caused me, I've been able to become a more mature person. It has given me strength and encouragement. I know it appears unsightly to others, but to me it is a jewel, a treasure. It suits me so well that I would not exchange it, even for millions. So let me tell you my story. My life resembles this broken ring. Like the ring, I have been criticized by many. But I had my reasons and knew from the start that I could expect such treatment, so I did not let this trouble me. True, there are times when I find myself thinking, "Ah, dear ring, how pitiful we are," and cannot help shedding a few tears. Then, I take comfort in the notion that God is merciful and knows what is in my heart. Ah, will it take a hundred years before even a few will come to understand the precious value of this ring?

As I begin to tell my story to you, I again feel as though my heart will burst. It was on that unforgettable day five years ago, in the spring of my eighteenth year, that I came to wear this ring. That was the day I married, the day my husband gave it to me. Although he did not think of it as a wedding ring, I suppose you could call it that. In those days, the seeds of women's education were at last being sown in our country, but I myself did not have even halfway modern views. Although this was a mere five years ago, I was living in the provinces at the time, and things were very different from Tokyo there. I couldn't possibly have imagined the sort of relationships Western women have with their husbands. I knew only of the old customs and thought of them as natural. I had no idea about new kinds of marriage. At the women's school I attended, they gave us moral instruction in the Chinese manner, and we read such books as Liu Xiang's *Stories of Chaste Women*.[16] Without even being aware, I was greatly influenced by the ideas in these books. We were taught that if a young girl's hand were promised to a boy whom she had not even met and that boy were to die young, she was bound to cut off her nose or an ear to prove she would never be of two hearts. We also learned that if a cruel mother-in-law tried to drive a young bride to hang herself, even that would not be sufficient reason for her to leave her husband. To endure such things was considered an insurpassable virtue in women. A woman could never be sure what sort of husband she might end up with. Like drawing a fortune stick, there was no telling whether she would have good luck or bad. The choice was left up to fate, and all she could do was accept it.

My mother was a woman who took pride in modeling herself after the ideal of womanhood found in the *Greater Learning for Women*.[17] When she spoke to my father, she would kneel respectfully in the doorway. She always treated him like an honored guest, so I was astonished when I saw other fathers who seemed to get along well with their children. I was greatly influenced by my mother's subservient and reserved behavior toward my father and couldn't help thinking a woman's fate was pitiful and unfortunate. But I knew I had misgivings about this notion, too. When I thought about my plight, I began to wonder if there might even be some way to spend my life peacefully, without marrying at all.

When I was fifteen or sixteen, my parents began to urge me to look for a suitable partner. This happened more than once or twice, and, though I objected each time, they went on recommending different men saying,

"How do you like this one?" "Now what about that one?" Each time I thought to myself, oh no, not again, and each time I somehow managed to refuse. At first, my mother spoke up on my behalf saying, "She's still young; perhaps we should think it over . . ." But when I turned eighteen, she was no longer able to fend off my father's demands. He was short-tempered and scolded my mother sharply, saying, "The girl is just selfish! It's your fault for bringing her up so badly."

One day, my father called me into his room. I knew immediately from the look on his face that he was very impatient. Before I could sit down, he commanded me to accept a new marriage offer. I was shocked! Recalling it now, I almost break into a cold sweat. Knowing this might happen, I had planned answers to the arguments I guessed he would make; it had not occurred to me that he would confront me with such utter, uncompromising authority. Completely overwhelmed, I could do nothing but look up meekly at his stern face, which seemed to demand, "If you dare to say no, say it now!" I waited for a moment, believing that my mother would say something to help me, but she was silent. I could not tell whether she feared my father's authority or had in fact discussed the matter with him beforehand. She only looked at me with a worried expression, as if begging me, "Say yes, and do it quickly!"

With one parent glaring at me sternly and the other pleading with her gaze, I was at a loss for words. I felt embarrassed and uneasy in front of my father, but I bit my trembling lips and, with great effort, whispered, "Please allow me a little more time to finish my studies. . . ." Before I was through, he flashed a sharp look at me and said, "What unfinished studies? Don't be a fool! I've seen to it that you've been given a good education, so what do you mean? Why are you complaining, you selfish girl?"

My mother shot another glance at me that said, "You shouldn't make your father so angry." I wanted to explain myself further but again could not find the words. Finally, gathering my courage, I spoke, "But please, I would like to go to the Teacher's Training School in Tokyo . . ."

Again, I was cut off by my father's sharp words.

"What?! Teacher's School? Absurd! Just how do you think you would survive as a schoolteacher? It's no easy thing for a girl to go through life alone. I'll hear no more of this nonsense. You must do as I say. In any case, it's too late to change the arrangement. I've told your mother all the details, so listen carefully." With that, he stood up quickly and stormed out of the room.

My mother then tried to console me, pleading in a soft, tearful voice. "Whenever your father speaks like that he isn't likely to change his mind . . . especially since this time he seems to like the young man in question. The go-between is Mr. Matsumura, who is surely acting on your behalf. You know it's not easy to find someone who is so accomplished and learned. And it's better for a young woman to marry at the right age because otherwise she will lose all her chances."

If this had happened today, I would never have said yes. But, then, I was truly innocent of the world. I had resigned myself to the fact that I would have to marry someone, sometime, so I weak-heartedly agreed even though I had only been half-convinced by my mother's words. But when I look back on it now, I can't help thinking it odd that I did not refuse more forcefully. My mother began to tell me about the meeting with the go-between they were planning. It would be in two days, so she told me to start arranging my hair and to select a suitable kimono with matching accessories. There was nothing I could say. Later, when I went back to my room and thought it over, I realized that my father had already made a final decision about the matter. Even if I were to protest at our first meeting with the groom, there would be no reason to expect them to listen, and I would only suffer great embarrassment. Just the thought that I would be seen by the young man was truly unpleasant. So, with singular resolve, I told my mother that I would not attend. But again it was no use.

Looking back, I have sometimes wondered whether this was just another foolish failure of strategy on my part. But now I've come to realize there was nothing I could have done. As a child, I rarely had the chance to meet people other than relatives and school friends. Whenever my father had visitors, my mother would rush me to the back room, telling me to stay out of sight. And so I have never been a good judge of people. I understood little of what was said at the meeting to discuss the arrangements. Although I knew the marriage would be difficult, I resigned myself to thinking that at least the formal meeting would be something to remember and managed to enjoy a few moments of pleasant anticipation, wondering what sort of person he might be.

The ceremony was held in March of that year, just when the cherries were beginning to bloom. After two or three months of marriage, I still could not grow used to living with my husband and began to doubt seriously whether I could stay in that house for the rest of my life. I couldn't tell whether my husband cared for me or not. Sometimes he would take me to a museum or some other place and would offer to buy me things. But I never felt comfortable accepting gifts from him. I felt uneasy, as if I were not a member of the household. When we did go out, I never enjoyed it in the least. On such outings, I would constantly think of my home and wish that my mother and sister could be there, too.

Then one day, a girl of fifteen or sixteen came to the house with a letter. Our maid took it and started to bring it to me, but my husband thrust out his hand and glared as if to say, "Bring that here!" I didn't have the slightest notion of what the letter might contain and only remember thinking what a short-tempered person my husband was for getting angry over such a trifling thing. He read the letter, awkwardly rolled it up and tucked it into the sleeve of his kimono. He told the girl to convey a message that he would send a reply soon and then sent her away.

That very night, he went out, saying he would take a short walk in the neighborhood. But by ten o'clock he had not returned, nor by eleven, or even twelve. Naturally thinking I should wait up for him, I didn't ask to have the bedding laid out. As I sat writing letters to school friends, the night grew later and later, so I told the house girls to go to bed before me. One of them came and sat beside me, saying she thought I must be lonely. As she watched me writing letters, she carelessly remarked, "How nice your brushwork is. . . . The former mistress didn't have such a . . ."

I had just caught the words "former mistress" and, without really intending to, asked, "Oh, was there someone here before me?" The girl had been working in my husband's house for some time and felt obliged to answer my question. I watched her face closely as she half murmured to herself, "How could I have been so careless?" Then she turned to me and said, "I know it will make the master angry, but I must tell you. Until five or six days before you arrived, there was another woman here. Most certainly she is the daughter of the family where he had lodgings during his student days."

I thought to myself—that messenger who came today!—and I wondered whether . . . but I dared not show my feelings in front of the house girl. I tried to appear calm, as though I had taken no notice of what I had heard, and simply replied, "Oh, is that so?" But from that moment on, my spirits began to sink, and I began to wonder how my husband could do such a thing. If there were another woman in his life, he should never have married me in the first place. But now that we were married, he should certainly have ended the involvement. Of course, it was unthinkable for me to speak of these things to anyone, so I kept them hidden deep within my heart for many joyless weeks and months.

From that evening on, my husband's outings became more frequent, from March to April, from April to May, and finally he would go out and not return home at all for three or four days at a time. In the beginning, I stayed awake for two or three nights in a row waiting for him, but on the next night, unable to keep my eyes open any longer, I finally dozed off. It was my misfortune that he came home that very night. I was suddenly awakened by the sound of pounding at the door, and, when I rushed to open it, there was my husband, the smell of sake heavy on his breath. He glared at me sharply and said, "What's this? I was pounding hard enough to break down the door, wasn't I? Why didn't you open it? If the neighbors heard me, that will cause a stir, won't it! What a fine wife I have, who makes her husband stand outside while she sleeps soundly."

How I suffered on hearing his harsh words. I listened in silence, hoping the house girls would not be wakened by that loud, angry voice in the middle of the night and mistakenly think that I was arguing with my husband for coming home so late. I knew that if I tried to speak, he would only complain more loudly. I handled him as gently as a piece of damp paper; placating him with apologies, I helped him into bed without further mishap.

Each time something like this happened, I would recall my days at school with a deep sense of longing. I'd heard that among my best friends there was one still unmarried and another who had become a schoolteacher. I wondered if it was only I who had been weak and married, only to undergo this suffering. At times, in spite of myself, I would break down in tears.

Just at this time, my father was away, so I went home occasionally to visit my mother. She naturally sensed that I was troubled and would say, "Your face is pale, and you've lost weight. You're worried about something, aren't you? If your father were here, there might be some way to talk things over with him. But since he is away, I can do nothing. Please do take better care of yourself and don't worry so much . . ."

How sad I felt on hearing her words! I tried so hard not to cry. But being with a husband whose heart I could not know and hiding my feelings from the maids had become such a strain that my mother's sympathy touched me deeply. While uttering fine phrases like, "Oh, there's really nothing at all to worry about," a flood of tears more honest than my words confessed the truth to her. From behind my handkerchief, I could see that her eyes, too, were already red from weeping.

This continued until Mother, who had always been weak, suddenly took to her bed in a constant state of worry about me. Then, in the autumn of my nineteenth year, she passed away like the morning dew. Was I not the real cause of her death? I was heartbroken when I realized that the very marriage to which I had so reluctantly agreed in the hope that my mother might be relieved had actually resulted in the premature end of her precious life. I thought my heart would be crushed under the weight of this sorrow. Knowing that this misfortune was a result of my own lack of foresight and understanding, my unhappiness multiplied, and I spent all my days for the next two years deep in sorrow.

I am sure you can imagine how discouraged I felt. Yet, during the two or three years following my marriage, a strong sense of indignation on behalf of young women had also begun to stir in me. New ideas about women's rights were being debated, and the notion that sorrow and tragedy are not necessarily woman's fate was gradually spreading. As a matter of habit, I always kept new publications near at hand and glanced at them between tasks around the house. What I read about Western views on women's rights impressed me deeply, and I began to understand that Japanese women also had the right to seek the fulfillment and happiness that are their due.

To console myself and to help alleviate other women's unhappiness, I began to write occasionally on these difficult subjects. In doing so, my own way of thinking changed. Once I had believed in the Chinese moral code, which teaches that it is virtuous for a woman to endure all kinds of suffering, sacrificing her own happiness for the sake of her husband. But I had ceased to be satisfied with this passive view and came to hold more progressive ideas. I decided to try and guide my husband so that he might change his ways and become a fine man of whom I need not feel ashamed. I made the sincerest of efforts to persuade him. But he was several years older than I and much more experienced in worldly affairs, and so he would not listen to me. Before long, whenever I tried to speak about these things, he would stop me, dismissing all my words in one breath.

"Not that again . . . aren't you acting just a little too clever . . . letting all that learning go to your head?" Sadly, my efforts were to no avail. I lacked the strength of someone like the virtuous Monica and only wished I were worthy of commanding a little more respect from my husband.[18] But just as the torn cloth cannot easily be mended and the broken stone cannot be restored to its original form, here, too, it had become impossible to make amends. Though loath to do so, I decided to leave him, knowing that if I stayed, it would be worse for him as well.

Since then, I have decided to work solely for the betterment of society. As a reminder of that vow, I myself struck the stone from the ring I am wearing. Although I cannot say I have endured as much as Gou Jian, I gaze at my ring morning and night, reminding myself of what it represents.[19] And though my humble gestures cannot compare to lying on a pyre of firewood or tasting bittermeats,[20] I most certainly have vowed to ensure a better future for the many lovely young women of today, in the hope that they will not follow the same mistaken path as I have.

Nowadays, with reforms in marriage customs, we see many fine couples living together happily. As I gaze at my broken ring, I cannot help wondering why I failed to earn the love of my husband and why I myself was unable to love him.

By good fortune, my father is still in good health and now has come to have great sympathy for my long years of suffering. He often writes thoughtful letters filled with regret that the foolish interference of an old man resulted in the breaking of a fresh, young branch. Now, he praises my aspirations and offers encouragement; this has given me the greatest pleasure amid days and months of sorrow. My only remaining hope is that this broken ring may somehow be restored to its perfect form by the hand that gave it to me. But I know, of course, that such a thing is not yet. . . .

SCHOOL FOR ÉMIGRÉS

Translated by Rebecca Jamison

I AM NOT of the class of women who wear rich brocades and reside deep in the chambers of jeweled palaces.[21] Yet when people hear my husband's name, they nod in recognition. We eat polished rice morning and night and are of such status that we could afford to wash a whole year's worth down the drain and never notice. Callers come uninvited to ask favors of my husband, and though I myself would prefer to shun all social intercourse, when the wives congregate, I am always offered the seat of honor. All applaud me as the wife of Mr. Imao. Such is my misfortune.

When the cherries bloom in spring and the autumn moon is full, my husband, though extremely busy with worldly affairs, takes me with him on outings to Ueno or Sumida, where the blossoms and moon are best enjoyed. When the cherry tree in our garden is in bloom, he cannot enjoy it unless I am beside him. He turns away from the moonlight glittering through the window if I am not with him. He asks me to dry his tears and share his joys. Kind to all, he always seeks to please me. How then might my life be called unhappy? And how was it that I, who admired him from afar for his great learning, generosity, chivalry, and skill as a statesman, had the good fortune to become his bride? Now we call each other husband and wife. If I were to call this misfortune, then what, pray tell, would happiness be?

Only God can know absolute perfection. For worldly beings, there can be no perfect happiness free of sorrow, no misery untouched by joy. Those who try and make heaven and earth their own without enlightenment will never find satisfaction. But those who are enlightened instantly enter a world where happiness and sorrow no longer exist and can be content, even if homeless in the three realms.[22] Yet it is those whose lives are tainted with a mixture of joy and suffering who are the most interesting.

I, too, am among those unable to step outside the realm of worldly distinctions.[23] I hide my excesses of joy and sorrow beneath a robe of false contentment and drown in a pool of tears unseen by others. How I envy those naive enough to covet the glory of others. Do they not realize that tears fall not only on the sleeves of worn and tattered kimonos? The jewels that spill, glittering, onto my brocade are the very water of my life, but they are mistaken for mere ornament. Although no one notices, my heart is shattered into a thousand pieces. Perhaps only when these pieces fall and return to their origin in the realm where sentient beings wander will people take pity on me. But, now, they still think of me as one who rides in a jeweled palanquin, so who will listen to my sorrows? The heavens reach infinite heights, but we never hear them boast; the earth has boundless depth, but we never hear it complaining. Why is it that only humans waste the brief moments of their lives disputing trivial distinctions? Even knowing as I do of this pitiable state, it is difficult to break the ties of love and duty between young and old, man and woman, that still bind me to this world. Meanwhile, those who know nothing of my sorrows are starting to spread rumors.

1

"I must say, I really dislike social climbers like that Mrs. Imao, who does just as she pleases! Maybe she's always looking glum because she's afraid we'll find out where she's really from if she looks too happy with herself. And that husband of hers, saying this and that to humor her . . . really, isn't she a disgrace . . . ?"

"How true! And here it is all I can do to keep the household running year round. I can't even remember when I last got dressed up and went to see a play. And even though I handle my husband like a tender sore, he complains about all sorts of trivial things. I suppose if he told me to leave, I could still go home to my mother and father. They say my brother's business is going well and that he's got three or four people helping out. If I left, it's my husband who'd have a hard time. I'm sure my mother wouldn't tell me I was being selfish, and I'd never have to worry about pleasing my sister-in-law. But, you know, I suppose it's a woman's duty to put up with this sort of thing and try to make her husband happy. Maybe I shouldn't say this, but my husband treated me decently for only a month or two after our marriage. Then he started insulting me, calling me clumsy and ugly, as if this nose of mine that I've had from the start had suddenly gone flat. If I ignore him, I can get by all right. Now he even leaves it to my brother to be the guarantor for the house. You know, I can't even buy lining for an *obi* sash with the spending money my mother gives me. Oh no, so much for the *obi*. Again and again that money has to go to running the household, a little for this and a little for that. If I could buy an *obi* with it, that *obi* would be as long as the giant centipede wound seven times round Mount Mikami.[24] But do you think he's grateful? Oh no. He's out after other women. No, I'm not joking! If, as they say, being born a woman means you get less than your share, then I ought to just give up. But hearing about Imao's wife, well, I think, she's a woman, too; why is she so lucky? I tell you, I despise my parents for even having had me—they're the ones who gave me this ugly face. . . ."

"Yes, I feel the same way you do, but look at it this way. Your nose may be a bit pudgy, but you're not so bad off if you have time to worry about it. And you're breathing through both nostrils, which proves you haven't cursed anyone.[25] Now that high-bridged nose of Mrs. Imao's may look like someone was paid to make it, but, with that pointed tip, it looks too haughty and will invite the scorn of others. So you see, beauty is a woman's worst enemy. Just look at her. She's beautiful. She's educated, too. She's this and she's that, and the men, especially the bachelors, are head over heels for her, wishing they could have her as a wife. My husband, too. If he were talking to himself, it would be one thing, but he goes on about her fine qualities right in front of me, as if I weren't even there. But you know, my dears, excessive praise is the seed of censure. Now, someone who was bothered by all this fuss asked around and found out everything about her past. Everyone sees the beautiful flower blooming high on the branch . . . but what of the roots? Isn't it odd how people slander what's out of their reach. When I heard my husband making nasty remarks about her, I thought, that's funny, he's certainly changed his tune . . . so I purposely said some nice things about her. When the next round of harsh words poured from the mouth that had praised her, I thought, this is good punishment for a man who cheats on his wife."

"Oh, aren't you wicked for saying such things! Well, let me tell you what I know. She may say she's from the Akita family, but they're only posing as her parents for the sake of appearances. Her real father was a moneylender who started out with a little capital that he loaned at high rates. And either because he was too eccentric or too pressed for money, he hired no maid but raised his daughter on his own, cooking with one hand and managing his business with the other. Gradually, his profits grew—which he spent all on you-know-who, sending her away to a women's school, where she stayed till her graduation. Then she taught at the very same school. She might have been a modern girl, but she was a pampered daughter all the same. Protected in her glass box, her beauty was luminous. With her long hair wound in coils around her head and her graceful figure, she soon caught the eye of Mr. Imao, who no doubt thought her too precious to be wasted in a place like that. I don't know who arranged for the introductions, but he married Miss Akita. The wedding was a grand affair, as you can imagine. She wore fine silks made just for the occasion and dazzled everyone with her beauty. All's well that ends well, but then her father up and disappeared. Rumors went round that he'd moved away, just vanished like a mirage. Some say he went bankrupt because of a bad loan. Others, that Mr. Imao is hiding him somewhere. There are all sorts of rumors, but one thing's certain: he's hiding away somewhere or other. Even the ward office can't find him and said he can't be traced. She's got real nerve, ignoring her position when she's got a father like that. She's living in such luxury that she can just throw away the peel of her rice cake—or maybe the peel is stuck to that face of hers. Even the maids are saying they can't understand what lies beneath the thousand layers of her shameless, melancholy face. But I really hate it when my husband says he can't believe all the rumors, as if he has some lingering affection for her. . . ."

"Ha ha ha, I dare say you're simply a bit jealous. You're all right. You're still young, like a *tatami* mat of fresh straw. But me, I'm being beaten like a bare wooden floor, stomped all over by a man with his shoes on. I don't even have a chance to get jealous, and, if I'm not careful, I'll be splintered into little bits of wood for the fire. Each time I think about it, my anger turns to seeds of envy. But now that we've heard about that woman's past, there's nothing to get envious about. And no matter how high her husband rises, she's the sort to keep showing an unhappy face to the world, hoping he'll rise even higher while hiding her secret satisfaction. It's not a sign of refinement, no indeed. Those are the true colors of a social climber. Now that I think about it, a woman who puts up with a husband who scolds her and manages in a household of limited economic means can still make a virtue of the fact that she doesn't stand out too much. Yes, I prefer to endure my hardships . . ."

"Ho ho ho, however much you say you're 'enduring hardship,' there are those who envy you. Even if your husband has faults, we hear that he works very hard to keep you satisfied."

"Oh my, how wicked you are. If that's how you see it, then let's leave it at that. But I don't just sit back and make him do all the work. I put in twice as much effort, you know."

"Maybe so, but didn't you give him a little special service the day after his salary went up to two thousand a year?"

"All right, all right, that's enough. There's no point in setting the sparks flying between us by arguing over this and that—things an out-sider can't understand anyway. If you were in my position, you'd see that even if my husband's salary does go up, none of it comes my way. It may flow quickly downtown to Shinbashi or Yanagibashi, but mean-while the shrine of the mountain god is in ruins.[26] If there were just enough to send a little more upstream, then I'd be running a fine house-hold on eight hundred a year."

"You know, come to think of it, it's really Mr. Imao who's the unfor-tunate one. He owns so much property that he doesn't even need a salary, but he's never even once had a mistress. He just devotes himself com-pletely to that wife of his as if she's as fragile as a butterfly or a flower and never leaves her side. But where does she think she's flying? Perhaps she thinks that the higher he rises, the prouder she'll be. And he keeps trailing after her, trying to please her. It doesn't suit a man who is due to become a minister in the Second Cabinet. Oh, what a business it all is."

The young wives went on and on in a manner most improper for women of their rank. But their retribution will come. For these fine ladies in flowered kimonos who chatter on and on do not even realize that they are no different from the workers' wives who live in row houses.

2

Harue Imao was quite tired. He had been busy enough with party affairs, but after being asked to join the new cabinet, visitors had started coming at all times of the day or night so that he never had a moment's rest. It might have been different if they had important matters to discuss, but this evening, anticipating new arrivals from the provinces coming to seek appointments, he asked the maid to tell all visitors that he was out. For the first time in a long while, he retired to his study, hoping to relax. Now Harue Imao sat quietly on the edge of the veranda, stroking his moustache.

He had the thick brows of a man not yet forty. The light in his eyes was sharp and penetrating, and yet there was an air of gentle refinement about him as well.

"You must be very tired," said his wife, who was kneeling a few feet away. She smiled as she waved her fan to send a cool breeze toward him. So this was the woman who was the object of rumors. Who could have imagined that this elegant young woman, with her softly glistening hair done up in a neat chignon and summer kimono draping in soft lines over her shoulders, had once been a schoolteacher?

A smile spread over her face as she said, "Look at the water dripping from the leaves. Sanzō has worked so hard watering the garden. It's as if we've just had an evening shower. See how the water glitters like fireflies among the garden hillocks. Shall we compose poems on the theme, 'moon over the government mansion'?"

She asked Hana to bring the hot water and with a few graceful movements began to make tea. Who could possibly say that this young woman's refined face was less pure than the fine drops of green tea? Ordinarily, she would wait until she had time alone to think over her troubles, not wanting to bother her husband with them. But today she could not hold back her tears; they fell together with the white powder from her face into her palm. She also used rouge to conceal her melancholy from her husband. Only her eyelids, the color of cherry blossoms fragrant in the mists of far mountains, remained untinted, reddened instead from weeping. She had hoped that after days and months of wearing this disguise, she would be able to forget. She thought to herself, "With my husband's remarkable successes, everyone is watching and asking about my past. Yes, I wish I could hear just one word from my father, even in a dream, telling me where he is now, however far away it may be. Then I would surely feel some consolation, even as I continue to honor his command never to seek him out. I still recall his letter . . .

"'Owing to unavoidable circumstances I have been forced to go into hiding. You must think of me as someone who no longer exists in this world and devote all your attention to your husband. I have always been a stubborn man and disliked the company of others. Nevertheless, I exposed myself to the cold winds of the great metropolis. For whom have I thus sacrificed? It has all been for you. I was a proper father to you until I saw that you were married to the very best of men. Now you are Harue Imao's wife and are no longer my daughter. From now on, my life will be an odd but happy one spent gazing at the moon from my humble abode, surrounded by wild grasses. Should you ever forget, please accept that it is your fate to be separated from your father, your only living relative. Don't waste on me the affection you must now devote to your husband. And should you be struck with the desire to seek me out, turn that desire into even greater affection for your husband. Through long years of devotion earn your place beside him and join the Imao family in their grave. Return to the earth as a member of the Imao family, and, one day, our souls will surely meet in the other world. Only then will I be able to tell you my reasons. Until then, please comfort yourself in knowing that I have done nothing to be ashamed of before heaven. Still there is shame in this world of ours, and so I must hide with this secret in a place far from the eyes of society, while you take pleasure in the long life with which you have been blessed. To search for me out of a half-hearted sense of fidelity would be to hurt me and expose my shame to the world. This would be an unfilial act and the most disloyal thing you could do to your husband. So respect my words, and never, in your entire life, try to open the secret box of my whereabouts.'

"After receiving this strange and troubling letter, I heard nothing for months and months and thus not only suffered greatly but also had to hide my tear-dampened sleeves from my husband. This letter is a living remembrance, but when I ponder the secret I may never know, I once again grow anxious about him. All alone, I worry for him when it rains or snows. Unable to confide in my husband, who is such an open-hearted man, this suffering has grown into a barrier between us. I tell myself I must keep this secret and thus remain loyal to my father, but then I feel I am deceiving my husband. Each time I hear his kind, gentle words, I feel pain more intense than if I were being cut in two and can only endure in silence. To go alone in search of my father would be to betray his words, so there is no point. With nothing to console me, I weep to myself and continue smiling before others. How could I have allowed my tears to spill through a crack and thus provoke their scorn? If there were a country where kings and nobles never show their tears, perhaps I should go there to be ridiculed. Or perhaps it's better to endure the shallow suppositions of those who see my tears and ask why a woman who has everything would weep than to have them know the real reasons. No, there is nothing I can do but continue to put on a smile in the face of dark rumors."

Harue had also been concerned about his father-in-law's whereabouts and had tried to console his wife at the time of the wedding. But since he had become so busy with his work and knew his wife to be capable of handling household matters, he had more or less forgotten the issue. Her hollowed cheeks, however, were beginning to make him wonder whether she was still anxious about her father. Eyeing his wife's willowy wrist as she fingered her fan, Harue spoke.

"Kiyoko, is something the matter? You're looking so pale these days. I wonder if you might be ill? You must take good care of yourself, especially in summer. Why don't you see a doctor?"

Trying to look as lively as she could, Kiyoko replied, "Ah, you aren't worried because I look thin, are you? I've been like this in summer all my life. This year, I'm keeping my weight up better than usual by drinking milk, so there's no need for me to see a doctor. By autumn, I will have gained quite a bit. Soon, you'll be laughing at me for being too heavy. On the contrary, you are the one we should worry about. You seem busier than ever."

"What? Worry about me? I'm not that weak. You might say this work I do is a kind of pleasant pastime. If work one enjoys doing were such a tiring business, then I'd surely be dead by now. We are only at the beginning of a very long path, and if I were too weak to go on now, I should never have gotten mixed up in politics in the first place. At last, they've formed the new party cabinet, but it's still in its infancy. The first began well but then petered out and fell quickly into clan favoritism. They're all new to the job and don't understand the issues well, so debate is intense. Regrettably, we haven't yet reached our goal of promoting the national interest and the well-being of the people. Having suffered such a setback, the most pressing issue now is to recover faith in the administration. That's why I reluctantly agreed to take the stage. I wonder if this is what has caused your low spirits?"

Harue's sudden query caught Kiyoko off guard. She suddenly felt wary that he was trying to uncover the real cause of her melancholy. Uncertain of what he was thinking, she made an effort to sound especially vibrant when she spoke.

"What difficult matters you speak of! Why, if I were able to understand such things, I would be better equipped to share your burden. But I only look at your busy life from a distance, from the comfortable position of one who knows nothing of what the cabinet is really like and just sits back, waiting for news. And now that you receive so many messages of congratulation, even I, unworthy as I am, have been blessed with honors too numerous to count. Yet I wonder whether I, who am so ill-suited, should . . ."

Harue was startled by her faltering words but pretended not to notice as he quickly said, "Why, what strange things I hear! Ill-suited? What do you mean, ill-suited? In terms of age, I am ten years your senior, but that has always been so. Do you mean that this bearded face is not fit to be seen beside such beauty as yours? Well, there's no point in saying that now. Oh, I see. You have the mistaken idea that an ambition for higher rank led me to join the new cabinet and no doubt are thinking a man like this is not fit to be your husband. So Harue Imao has come to be doubted, even by his wife." He placed one hand on his brow as he spoke, pretending not to look at Kiyoko but hoping to probe her thoughts more deeply.

Each word her husband uttered made her feel as though her heart might shatter. She decided to reveal some of her true feelings rather than seem dishonest.

"You tease me again, saying ridiculous things, so let me tell you the truth. I meant simply that an unworthy person like myself is ill-suited to an honorable person like you. It would be different if I were a well-educated merchant's daughter. Then people would keep quiet. But in times like these when it's fashionable for men to have wives of higher status than their own, I tell you, people are spreading rumors that I am not really the Akitas' daughter. Of course, it is bothersome, but when I am reminded of my many faults, I worry that I might damage your reputation. I am so very sorry . . ." Her voice trailed off as Harue quickly countered.

"How foolish! Knowing you as I do, I thought your concerns might be a little more grounded in reason. But you don't seem to be yourself these days. What has suddenly caused you to change your beliefs? This may sound odd, but come now! If you were a country person ignorant of the sort of wives the first Meiji leaders had and how well-accepted they were in society, I would understand.[27] But for someone raised in the city, who was a teacher, and who knows the difference between titles bestowed by heaven and by man, aren't you overreacting? Though I may be foolish, gaining wealth and fame is not my main aspiration in life. I admit that I agreed to join the cabinet now, but only to help the new government. That may be a sign of success in the eyes of the world, but I don't see it as such. Even without rank or office, Harue is still Harue. I plan to devote myself to my people's rights, and if one day I'm handed the honor of cabinet minister, or even prime minister, you will still be my wife. There is no reason for our relationship to change. As Harue Imao's wife, you can go out into the world with confidence, adhering to your principles and resisting society's pressures. Can't you just banish thoughts of those men who rely on the status of their wives to climb higher? And of those women who use their dowries to buy their way into marriage as well? Ah, but I can't pressure you, who, like the willow, can't bear too heavy a burden. At least, I hope you will stop allowing yourself to be bothered with such trivial things and have more confidence in yourself." The clear and forceful tone of Harue's words left Kiyoko at a loss for a reply. Her hot tears began to fall just as the moonlight poured down on them from between the clouds. It seemed that the strong affection between them would shine forever.

Glad to have relieved his wife's worries, Harue said, "Now that I know you understand, it's all right. Perhaps it's because you are feeling weak that this is troubling you. I still think you should see a doctor, but I cannot force you. You know, at first I was unwilling to pretend that you were a member of the Akita family. But your father insisted, saying he wouldn't allow us to go ahead with the marriage until you had been adopted, so we had no choice but to go along with his request. It's true, we've heard nothing from him since then, and I've been wondering whether we might hear news of him sometime soon. It's not as if this has never bothered me. It's just that I've found it difficult to keep track of both domestic and outside affairs. I have left household matters to you, but I admit that I was a bit surprised when you didn't seem more concerned."

Spoken as an afterthought, Harue's words sounded an alarm in Kiyoko's heart. The knot in her throat that had melted with gratitude a moment ago now rose in her throat once more. She tried to sound composed as she told him, "Please don't let it worry you. As I have said, he is an odd old man who shuns all social contact. Though it was always just the two of us, from childhood he kept telling me that just having me around was a bother to him. That's why he sent me to boarding school. He had me stay at school rather than come home on Sundays so as to avoid his bad temper. So I learned to endure the loneliness. There was rarely a day when I did not receive something from him, but he would visit only occasionally. So you see, he was so eccentric that he wouldn't allow even me, his loving daughter, to be near him. Although he lived in Tokyo for twenty years, he trusted no one, shunned all social contact as insincere, and was proud of the fact that he had not a single friend. As soon as we were married and settled, he left. I'm sure he is hiding away in some secluded place but still hope he will remember my affection for him and visit us someday. There is no need to worry. But I have dwelled on my sorrows too long and no doubt have added to your burdens. Let me serve you some beer to help relieve your fatigue."

With a light, quick move of her right arm, she picked up the bell to ring for the maid, Hana. But just as she had grasped it, her husband's assistant appeared in the doorway. He kneeled and bowed deeply, handing her a letter. It was addressed to her, but in a hand she had not seen before. And her father's name was on the envelope. Trying to conceal the trembling in her hands, she stood up and said, "When you go, will you ask Hana to come here? Oh no, it's all right. I'll go call her myself." Then, straining to sound as if she were pleasantly amused, she added in the feigned but lilting tones of a noblewoman, "Please wait for a moment, will you, dear?" Regaining her composure, she left the room, knowing that she should avoid her husband's glances as she sought the privacy to read what would doubtless be a disturbing letter.

3

Though less crowded than Shinbashi in Tokyo or Umeda in Osaka, throughout the four seasons countless travelers pass through Shichijō Station on their way to see the sights in Kyoto. They come from all over to enjoy the blossoms in spring and the turning of the leaves in autumn. In summer, they come to cool themselves along the banks of the Kamo River, a drop of whose waters is worth a fortune, much more than a patch of earth in the Eastern Capital. Even when there is no need to rush, they come by express. And now a drove of new arrivals flooded through the ticket gate; there was no distinction between high and low, noble and common. Amid the bright colors, a woman with her hair done up in an elegant chignon moved slowly, drawing curious glances. Hoping to nab a good customer, the rickshaw drivers eyed her and cried out in the lilting tones of the Kyoto dialect, "Ma'am, please hop in . . . I'll take you right to your doorstep. . . ."

The woman sat down on a stool in front of a tea stall, but the lady shopkeeper insisted she move to the back room for special guests. Slightly annoyed, she replied, "I'm fine here, and I'm in a hurry. Please have someone pick up my luggage and call for a rickshaw." The shopkeeper asked where she was going.

"To Yanagibara, Zeniza Village."

"Did you say Yanagibara? Ma'am, there must be some mistake," she replied with a doubtful look on her face.

Kyoto drivers are famous for being slow, and this one was no exception. They finally arrived at Zeniza Village, the place she had been so anxious to reach. Leather straps used to make wooden clogs were hanging out to dry on the eaves of small houses on either side of the muddy road. Dirty, barefoot children with sores on their shaven heads were playing all around. They rushed up to the rickshaw to have a look at the unusual visitor and then followed along behind. After two or three blocks, the foul smells that engulfed her made Kiyoko feel extremely uncomfortable. Dead rats and the discarded stems of green onions were piled on long-abandoned garbage in the gutters. Even the occasional house that looked clean had freshly flayed hides hanging out to dry both inside and out. Disturbed by what she saw, she asked the driver where they were.

"It's a village for outcasts," he said.

"Couldn't there be another village called Zeniza in Kyoto?" she asked, suddenly feeling she had no business being in a place like this. The driver, too, couldn't help wondering.

"Yes, Ma'am, you may well ask, but this is the only village by that name," he replied.

Kiyoko thought that if this were true, she would have to go ahead and ask the next question.

"Then could you find out whether a person named Taiichi Kawai lives here?"

"Certainly, Ma'am." He called out in front of one house. A woman in a white apron came running out and said, "If you're looking for Taiichi, turn left at that corner . . . it's the third house on your left. He's a friend of mine, so I'll show you the way." Throwing on a summer vest, she came along with them and in a friendly manner started telling all her neighbors about this rare, important-looking guest. She called out to everyone they passed. But the woman in the rickshaw began to get gooseflesh; a chill crept over her even though it was midsummer.

"Father, how do you feel? I tried to get here as quickly as I could, but the journey took fifteen hours, and I've only just arrived. I'm so sorry to have kept you waiting." Kiyoko spoke to the old man who lay, facing the wall, on a paper-thin mat spread on a worn *tatami* floor. As she sat down, she felt as though she were dreaming and could not keep her knees from shaking. The evening sun grew stronger, so she closed the sliding doors, also hoping to keep away prying eyes.

"Well, where shall I begin? You left Tokyo so suddenly, and I spent sleepless nights longing to see you. I kept reminding myself of your command to me but still wept, both day and night. I was so happy to receive the unexpected letter but worried when I learned of your illness. I don't know who wrote telling me to come urgently, but I beg you not to be angry. How much happier I would be if I could pay this visit without concern for your health. I quickly got my husband's permission to come and take care of you, so, please, rest at ease. Surely it has been difficult to endure this illness alone, but now I am here. It will be as if you were in a hospital. If you just leave everything to me, I'm sure you'll be well in no time. You look better than I had imagined, so I'm quite certain you'll recover soon. But first, relax. That's the most important thing. And the best medicine."

Looking at his gaunt silhouette, she could tell that his cheeks must be hollow and the angle of his brow sharp. This shocked and saddened her. She pretended his condition was less grave than it appeared and moved closer. Thinking that a gesture of filial affection would be the best way to start, she began to stroke his back. But he brushed her hand away sharply and began to speak.

"Nonsense! I have no idea who this woman is, but she speaks to me as if I were her father. This is absolutely absurd! Judging from her fine appearance and character, she could not be the daughter of a new commoner. How then, did she ... did you manage to come to the wrong place? This will ruin your reputation, so please leave at once. . . . Ah yes, this old man does have vague memories of a daughter, but she should have received his letter informing her that, because of certain circumstances, all ties between them had been severed. He would no longer be her father, she no longer his child. Don't be foolish! It was a grave mistake to come to a place like this looking for your father. You say you received a letter about my illness. Ridiculous. Someone must be playing a bad trick on you. But why would anyone send such a letter to someone like you unless it was a prank? Ah . . . the harder one tries to hide something, the more quickly it is revealed. It will be a real disaster if anyone finds out that you're here. Even if there were something here for you, no one would unveil such a secret willingly. If you go now, you can still say that you were mistaken and came to the wrong house. Before the whole world gets wind of this, please leave quickly! Go home! Though all bonds between my daughter and me have been severed, I still know what it is to be a father. You are not my own, but I am concerned for you. If you are mistaken for the child of a new commoner, both you and your husband will deeply regret it. These are the true words of a father speaking. Even though it's the wrong house, this old man you've called on will recover his health. He won't die. So stop worrying and go home now. . . . What's this? You're still sitting here? You haven't left yet? What a dull young woman! Well, if that's the case, then this feeble old man will just have to show you that even he can throw you out!" Wobbling precariously, he attempted to stand but soon fell to the floor. No longer able to hide her anguish, Kiyoko began to weep. Only the old man's voice was firm as he said over and over, "Go home!" His eyes filled with the tears of their shared sorrows.

Just then, the door opened, and a man rushed in. The *haori* jacket he wore did not look like that of a man of dubious means. His eyes were reddened from his labors, and he held a leather tobacco pouch in one hand. He sat down, crossed his legs, and began to speak.

"Taiichi, please don't be so angry. I'm the one who should apologize. And do calm yourself there, Miss. You've come all this way, so please listen a moment. Taiichi's been ill for a while now with a high fever. Well, you see, I just thought he wasn't going to pull through. Around here, we take care of each other like we're one big family, much more than other folks do. And we were really worried about him. Taiichi taught me all that I know; I feel I owe him a lot for his kindness. He came back here last spring, after twenty-five years. We've been like brothers, so I was doubly worried. I remembered the bouncing baby girl he had with him when he went away. He never told me where she was, but I figured, if worse comes to worst and she's still alive, I should let her know. If I didn't, I thought, she'd feel wretched. But however many times I told him, he wouldn't listen. He said he gave her away when he ran into trouble on the road. I had no idea if she was dead or alive. He'd say things like, 'Forget it! I never want to see her again,' to try and shut me up. But when his fever went up, he started talking. Over and over he'd say things like 'Okiyo, Okiyo . . . I hear Harue has become a minister! Congratulations . . . you must be so happy. How sad, Okiyo, that we can never meet again, but it's your father's fate.' My ears pricked up when I heard him say the name Okiyo, and 'Harue has become a minister.' Hey, I said to myself, surely he had his reasons, but, come to think of it, one of those new, young ministers who's making a name for himself these days is called Harue Imao. And I was sure Taiichi had been in Tokyo. Even if he never said so, there was no mistaking his Tokyo accent. You often hear of fellows selling off their daughters in the pleasure quarters. Then they get hooked up with someone, so I thought she must be with this man Harue.

"Now, please, don't get angry. My wild guess just happened to be right. If you missed her that badly, I thought I'd be doing you a favor if I could arrange for her to come. So two or three days ago, when that doctor fellow shook his head as if the end was near, I thought, well, it might be wrong, but it's not something I'll go to jail for. Knowing my chances were slim, I went ahead and dashed off a letter asking her to come as fast as she could. But I didn't even know where to send it, so all I wrote was

'Okiyo in the household of Minister Harue.' The gamble paid off, and your daughter has come. I was hoping to get credit for bringing you two together, I thought I was doing something pretty clever by sending that letter without telling Taiichi. A few minutes ago, my wife told me a fine-looking lady had come here. Thanks to the gods, I thought. I was right! So, expecting to come here and find your jolly faces, I dressed up like this in my best *haori* jacket. When I stood outside and heard Taiichi saying things like 'it's all a mistake, you're wrong, go home!' oh, I felt just awful. The poor young woman, I thought. I know you're angry 'cause you love her, but it's really all my fault for meddling too much. Please, Taiichi, listen to me. I know you don't want people to know she's the daughter of a new commoner, but now that she's here, there's nothing we can do. It won't matter if you talk with her today. I won't tell a soul the man's name, so even if the neighbors find out she's your daughter, they'll never know who she's with. I'm not just trying to talk my way out of a corner. Please, Taiichi, I swear before the gods that neither my wife nor I will say a word about this till the day we die. Please relax and talk with her. Isn't that so, Okiyo? You won't remember me at all, but I'm Kahei, the drummaker. I'm over forty now, but I really had my hand in it back when I was twenty. I even played to celebrate the day you were born. I can still see your little face and never dreamed you would grow up to be such a fine young woman. Oh dear, I must sound rude talking to you like this. Here in this village we don't bother being formal . . ." Hoping that no one would overhear, Kahei spoke in a whisper, nervously leaping up and then sitting down again, which only made the situation worse. There was an air of sadness about Taiichi as he watched.

"Kahei, sit down! What's the use now? Stop acting like a fool. Do you think that just by closing the door you can keep people from knowing? You idiot. What will become of us now?" There was anger in his voice as he spoke. Exhausted, he lay grasping his pillow and let out a deep sigh of anguish.

"You must be suffering terribly. Please allow me to rub your back," said Kiyoko, who, no less distraught than her father, timidly moved closer to him and began stroking his back. She let her thoughts wander.

"So it's true. I am one of them. If people are already spreading rumors about me, I dread to think what they will say now. No, I cannot go back to my husband. I'll live here as a new commoner. I prefer to be here with my father than to be lauded as a lady of high position and be far away. I will stay here and take care of him, as anyone would do. New commoners are just like everyone else. But why, then, are commoners designated 'new' or 'old' if we are all human beings? They claim there is no discrimination and that they use the word 'new' simply because people take pleasure in it. But isn't this misleading? When placed before the word 'commoner,' doesn't it come to mean all that is impure or defiled?

"Even I, who have followed my husband in believing that nothing can surpass the ideal of people's rights, am wavering. On hearing that I myself am a new commoner, I have the sense that I, too, must be impure or defiled, a feeling that I never expected and that comes from outside the realm of reason. If even I feel this way, imagine what those who hope to climb to the heights of respectability must think? And what of those lowly folks who, even though they have to sell their daughters and wives to keep clothes on their backs and food in their stomachs, still think of themselves as a notch above new commoners? Those who think only *eta* are defiled should know that it is their own hearts that are full of filth. Yes, I will stay here for the rest of my life and care for my father with all my heart. After I nurse him back to health, we will devote ourselves to those whose names have been tainted in the same way. Yes, that will bring us happiness, and there will be no need for regret.

"Wait a moment. This all makes good sense, but what am I to do for my husband, whose name will be ruined when the news gets round tomorrow that his wife is the daughter of a new commoner? I knew nothing of this when we married, but, now that I do, should I tell him the truth and leave him with good grace? Would that save him from the shame that will be poured upon him? Had I known all this much sooner, I would never have married my beloved husband. But in my ignorance, we married so carelessly, not knowing that our love could not continue for life: if we part, waves of painful longing will wash over me, day in and day out, like the ebb and flow of the tides. Where did I ever learn that a faithful wife who is a burden to her husband should leave him? Oh, my poor father. If you had only told me earlier, I would never have married a man so well known. My only other complaint is to those who treat new commoners with such coldness."

Kiyoko quietly wept, holding back the desire to speak these thoughts aloud. Seeing her dampened cheeks, Taiichi lifted himself up and spoke.

"Don't cry, Okiyo, I want to tell you something now, so please listen. And Kahei, you're mixed up in this as well, so stay and listen, too. And get me some water in that old cup, will you?"

He took the cup from Kahei and quietly took a few sips, moistening his parched throat.

4

"Ah, how wretched I, Taiichi, son of a well-known doctor from the heart of Kyoto, have become. I was raised by my stepmother and grew to have a twisted character. Even the maids and servants spoke ill of me, saying I wasn't good like my younger half-brother. Now I can see it was probably part of her plan. It was all quite unpleasant for me. I liked to read, but whenever they found me with a book, my half-brother and stepmother would annoy me with their scornful taunts. So I started going out to get away from them. I began to mix with bad company and, before long, found myself sitting over morning drinks in teahouses. That way of life became a habit, and I started spending money set aside for odds and ends, as well as fees my father's patients had paid for medicines. When he found out that I was even taking money from his purse, he fell into a rage and disowned me on the spot.

"At the time, I really didn't think I'd done anything wrong; now I see this was part of my stepmother's scheme to have her son inherit the family property. How I resented my father, who showed no compassion toward me! Now that I know what it is to be a father, I realize he must have been weeping bitter tears while putting up a stern front when he disowned me. If I had gone to a relative and asked for help in making amends, that might have settled the matter. But when he told me to get out, I left knowing that I wanted nothing to do with a father who had decided to leave everything to my half-brother just because I'd used a little of his money. So at eighteen I left home, telling him not to expect me back. I was sure that a young man like myself would be worth a lot, even though I had nothing, and that I would find someplace to go. Unable to stop the downward spiral of my misfortunes, I soon found that the world is a frightening place. Perhaps one can buy kindness anywhere, but if you're looking for a bit of it in Kyoto for free, you'll find 'sold out' signs everywhere. The light of parental love may shine bright, but he who leaves it behind is blocked in all directions. There were some who gave me food or clothing from time to time, but, not wanting to offend my parents, they never did more to help me rebuild a bridge to society. It was then that I understood for the first time the true value of parental protection. Occasionally, I thought of going to relatives, but I was too proud to do that, knowing what my stepmother must have said about me. So I ended up living the wretched life of a wanderer.

"I never reached the point of thinking I would take my own life, but one night I found myself near the Katsura River, too disheartened to go another step. Luckily, it was late at night, and there was no one in sight, so I decided to stop there and think things over. I was leaning against the rails of the bridge, listening to the sound of the water, when a man walking by noticed me. Without a moment's hesitation, he insisted on seeing me home, perhaps because he thought I was about to jump. He treated me as his own, as if he already knew he would become my father-in-law. When I told him I had been disowned and had no place to go, he grew even more determined to keep an eye on me. As my luck had run out, when he said I could stay as long as I liked, I decided to follow him through the moonless night to this place. I had no idea that I would find myself in a village like this. When morning came, I could see that I was in a shop, and, judging from the decor and my host's demeanor, I thought they were running some sort of small business. They were far friendlier than my own parents. As they had closed the shop to keep away prying eyes, I couldn't tell what sort of business it was. I'd planned to rest here for a day or two but soon began to think I might stay longer, especially when the sound of their daughter's *koto* harp began pulling at my heart. I thought I would stay until they asked me to move on, but that was my mistake. I didn't see that I had fallen into a trap. The chill cast upon me by my stepmother's cruelty was warmed by the rare kindness of these people. I lost track of the passing days and months, and when I finally realized where I was, it was too late. Moreover, I was already intimate with their daughter. When I think of it now, this place was a haven from worldly distinctions. I realized it would be better to live where, although they might be called *eta*, people have hearts that bloom like flowers. Better to live here than in a place where outer appearances conceal the hearts of demons. Those who know nothing of the beautiful spirit of these people are the ones who are truly defiled.

"I began to feel I had done the right thing, and, as time went by, what had first looked dreadful, no longer seemed so. Offensive smells bothered me no more. I stayed in the village and married your mother, and then you came along. Seeing you now, I cannot help recalling my own father, who would never have imagined this. However errant I was in my youth, he would never have disowned me if he had known I would end up here for the rest of my life.

"There I was, a useless good-for-nothing, a man who had brought shame to his family and would bring ruin to his own daughter. There was no hope for me, but I didn't want my daughter to suffer the same fate. For a child born in an era when *eta* were now called new commoners, there was no reason to feel bound to raise her in this village. To redeem myself, I wanted to find a way for you to grow up in the outside world. Your mother understood this. As she lay ill and dying, about to leave behind the babe still nursing at her breast, she said, 'Please try and cleanse the impure blood of this child. The Kawai family name matters nothing; all the treasures of this household will be hers. If the child is made pure through your commoner's blood, there is no reason for the ancestors to object. And I can see the smiling faces of her grandmother and grandfather, so I will be able to die contented.' Her smile had a dignified quality unexpected in someone of her birth.

"After her death, I decided to sell the family treasures and move to Tokyo. I told no one where I had come from, changed the family register, and bought a house. As I led a life of virtue, no one suspected I was from a village like this. Fortunately, I was able to send you to school. I had begun work as a moneylender and kept the business small. I steered clear of other people as I didn't want them to learn of my past through some unintended slip of the tongue; nor did I want to waste a penny. So I took every precaution and kept to myself.

"When it was time for you to marry, there was nothing I could do about the indelible stain, but I did my best to make sure you learned skills proper for a young woman and provided you with the kimonos and household goods you would need to ensure your happiness. I lived the life of an odd recluse, devoid of all pleasures, for many years. All alone, I had severed connections from friends and relatives and didn't even have you near me. I had decided that, once you married, I would cease to call myself your father; that is why I was so cold toward you. I thought it would be best to keep my distance from the beginning and promised myself not to show even the slightest affection that a normal parent would. Living this way for a few years might be one thing; twenty years later, I've become a truly eccentric fellow. You must have doubted whether I cared for you at all. Although I never saw your tears or knew of your resentment, I, too, have been weeping all these years. When I knew I could give you away to a man of good reputation whose fine countenance and character were striking beyond anything I might have hoped for, I realized that my task was done. I made arrangements with your adoptive parents and took care to erase the Kawai name, thereby fulfilling my role as father to you. Feeling that I would be a hindrance if I lived near you, I came back to this place, beyond reach of the eyes and ears of the world, where I have a special sense of attachment.

"Odd though it seems, once a beggar, always a beggar. I went to Tokyo and suffered because of it, having chosen not to raise you here, but now I want to live out my days in this village. My plan was to live the rest of my life in seclusion; my head was well hidden, but my tail was not. It was my carelessness that led me to fail. How can I make it up to you! If I had revealed the truth to you earlier, you would have known never to come here. There were moments when I wanted to tell you but held back, thinking I would spare you the burden you would then carry the rest of your life. But my lingering affection has become the seed of the error that I now sorely regret. There's nothing I can do. Even if Kahei had said nothing, I was wrong to think I might conceal everything.

"When word of this spreads and your husband hears the truth, he'll be even more upset. He'll not only resent me but will also imagine that, as kindred spirits, we have both been deceiving him. If he accuses you, who have done no wrong, I fear that you will be deeply hurt. So go to him now and ask for a divorce. Perhaps, to save face, he will refuse. Or if he says it doesn't matter to him that his wife is a new commoner, that would certainly be a miracle. Whatever you do, please think of me as never having existed and try a hundred or a thousand times harder to become a model of virtue, one who is ten thousand times more virtuous than ordinary women. If people seem to think that new commoners are 'impure,' show them that they are wrong. This is all I can think of just now. If we wait even a moment longer, more rumors will spread. Kahei, carry her things and help her find a rickshaw." Taiichi spoke in the firm but compassionate tones of an elder, apparently unhindered by his serious illness.

After a pause, Kiyoko replied. "Now knowing of your deep concern for me all this time, I can see how undeserving I have been! How could I have felt resentment? Please forgive me! I understand your reasoning, but under such serious circumstances, if leaving you to go back to my husband is the duty of a faithful wife, how am I to fulfill my duty to you? My husband is not worried about my social status, and even if he were to object when I inform him of my decision to stay and care for you, that would be a breach of his earlier promise. I'm sure he would never do such a thing. When I showed him Kahei's letter, he said he wanted badly to come himself but couldn't; he asked me to convey his regards and take doubly good care of you for him. He even told me to take one or two servants along. But, remembering your admonishments, I didn't, thinking it better to be cautious and keep this secret until I learned more. So the truth of my origins won't spread so very quickly. In any case, I will stay for four or five more days until your condition has improved. I will not be delayed long and will be able to leave feeling relieved that you are better."

Kiyoko tried to appear calm as she continued thinking to herself.

"Harue and I are not like other couples, who, even after one or two years of marriage, do not know each other. The gods of Izumo brought us together as husband and wife, but we were not forced to marry.[28] Strangers at first, we considered one another carefully before deciding to wed. Even if we could be together for only a day or an hour, we are different from those who, although they may live side by side for life like the dolls on festival day, don't know each other in the slightest. Our happiness exceeds that of those who have been together for tens of thousands of years. In all this, I never dreamed that I could have come from such a place. How can I possibly tell him that I didn't know and ask his forgiveness? No, I can't possibly go to him and tell him something that would cause us to part. If this were something I could speak to him about so easily, then there would be no need to divorce. But, as I cannot face him, I had better stay here in this village and care for my father. Yes, I will spend the rest of my life here and send a letter to Harue explaining my reasons. And though my father may lament the fact that I will never see my husband again and think me foolish for choosing to live in a place like this, he must realize that if, out of such compassion for me, he sacrificed twenty years to raise me as an ordinary person, then I, too, as his child, have feelings of loyalty to him that run deeper than the sea and higher than mountains. If I were to abandon him now and go back to my husband, and if he were to say that my history doesn't matter at all, then I would not feel it necessary to divorce. But wouldn't that also mean being unfaithful? As always, it is my father's nature to wish only for my happiness. He would again say we are no longer parent and child and sever all correspondence, and there would be no way to show my loyalty to him. How could I wish for such a thing!" These irrepressible thoughts weighed upon her and left her feeling distraught.

Taiichi suddenly glanced sharply at Kiyoko and said, "How foolish you are! Why are you still sitting here? Are you worried about my illness? Do you mistakenly think I might live a day longer if nursed by my daughter? First, go home and talk things over. Until then, you are not my daughter. Do you think I would touch even a cup of water if you asked me to drink it? Even if you try, I will refuse. There is no point in staying here. Kahei and everyone else in this village is kind to me. That's why I came back here. You should go home now. Can't you see that the few moments you spend here will make the twenty years I've suffered for your sake go to waste? Are you such a fool that you can't understand what I have just explained to you so clearly? I have nothing else to say to you. Do what you please!" He picked up a pillow and tried to throw it, but he was much too weak.

Kahei cried out in surprise. "Please don't get so angry, you'll make yourself worse! I'm the one to blame for this. Let me explain . . . I'll tell your daughter, so just listen, Taiichi. Wait, Miss, I'll explain." He sighed, now realizing the seriousness of his mistake.

"Please forgive me. I did have my reasons and sure felt obliged to help Taiichi, but it's really my fault for doing something I shouldn't have. Now I can see it won't be easy to make it up to you. I'm the one who did wrong, and I know this isn't something you can patch up with a simple apology. But please, Miss Kiyo, please listen. I beg you, Miss Kiyo, as long as you stay, Taiichi will be angry, and it will mean tears for you. I can understand both sides, but I can't bear hearing you cry. Let me try and get us out of this mess. Please, for my sake, too, please leave now. If you do as I ask, I'll repay you by taking good care of Taiichi. I'll nurse him in your place. Right, Taiichi? Your daughter is just trying to show her filial duty, so you shouldn't get so angry. You told her to leave, and now I'm asking her, too. So, Miss Kiyo, it's better if you leave as soon as you can. That's the best way to show your loyalty." Kahei stood up and began preparing for her to leave. Though pretending not to notice, Taiichi could not help watching; when Kiyoko glanced back, their eyes met for an instant. As she walked, her tears fell, leaving a trail in the earth that then turned to mud.

Within days, news of Harue Imao's resignation—and along with it, word that his wife was a new commoner—shocked the world. As a minister in the cabinet, he had been honored by an invitation to visit His Majesty, the emperor, but now, he knew it would be viewed as disgraceful for him to attend. Fearing the opposition would childishly use this against the ruling party, Harue felt he had no choice but to step down. When he heard this, the prime minister laughed and told him not to worry so much. Nevertheless, Harue decided to resign. Rather than waste his life battling with those whose barbaric hearts could not be concealed behind feigned aspirations for civilization, he would devote himself to education, biding his time until things improved. He and Kiyoko would take everything they owned and move to Hokkaido, gathering children from all over the country who had grown up in unfortunate circumstances. Together, they would start a school for émigrés and raise a new generation of citizens, as fresh as the land of Hokkaido was new. To those who asked, he would say with a smile, "We will redeem ourselves by helping the children of new commoners, I as their father, Kiyoko as their mother."

It is said that only a few warm-hearted souls went to see them off at Ueno station when they left, taking a band of those children with them.

NOTES

1. Like many authors of her day, Shikin used a number of pseudonyms during her career. Her works also appear under the names of Tsuyuko, Toyo, and Fumiko. She did not begin using the name "Shikin" until 1896. As this is the name cited in most critical and biographical works, I have chosen to use it here.

2. Yamaguchi Reiko, *Naite aisuru shimai ni tsugu—Kozai Shikin no shōgai* (Tokyo: Sōdo bunka, 1977), pp. 56–58.

3. See ibid. and Rebecca Copeland, *Lost Leaves: Women Writers of Meiji Japan* (Honolulu: University of Hawai'i Press, 2000) for more detailed analysis of this phase of Shikin's life.

4. *Burakumin* (*buraku*, community or village, and *min*, people) refers to a minority group that has suffered severe discrimination in Japan. In the Tokugawa period, they occupied the lowest level in the social hierarchy and were forced to live in communities separate from the rest of society. Historically, they were associated with butchering, leather tanning, and other occupations thought to be unclean or polluted. Though the highly derogatory terms *eta* (much filth) and *hinin* (nonhuman) were abolished in the Meiji period, the term *burakumin* is still used to refer to this minority group, whose members, because of their common heritage, are victims of prejudice and discrimination. For a thorough explanation of this history, please refer to George De Vos and Hiroshi Wagamatsu, *The Invisible Race* (Berkeley: University of California Press, 1967), and I. Roger Yoshino and Sueo Murakoshi, *The Invisible Visible Minority* (Osaka: Buraku kaihō kenkyūsho, 1977).

5. Cited in Yamaguchi, *Naite aisuru shimai ni tsugu*, pp. 136–137.

6. Copeland, *Lost Leaves*, p. 182.

7. Rebecca Jennison, "Equality and Difference: The Shifting Terms of Discourse in Selected Essays by Shimizu Shikin," *Journal of Kyoto Seika University*, no. 8 (1995): 97, cited in Yamaguchi, *Naite aisuru shimai ni tsugu*, p. 233.

8. Copeland, *Lost Leaves*, p. 191.

9. Yoshino and Murakoshi, *The Invisible Visible Minority*, p. 46.

10. Watanabe Naomi, *Nihon kindai bungaku to "sabetsu"* (Tokyo: Ōta shuppan, 1994); Michael Bourdaughs, *The Dawn that Never Comes* (New York: Columbia University Press, 2003).

11. Copeland, *Lost Leaves*, p. 196. For example, the well-known socialist Kōtoku Shūsui (1871–1911) wrote "Okoso zukin" (Woman in the Okoso scarf), a work that poses serious ethical questions about social hierarchies. In 1896 Tokuda Shūsei (1871–1943) published "Yabu kōji" (Spearflower), and Oguri Fūyō (1875–1926) published *Neoshiroi* (Bedtime makeup).

12. Copeland, *Lost Leaves*, p. 213–214.

13. Komashaku Kimi, "Shikin shōron—Joseigakuteki na apurōchi," in *Shikin zenshū*, ed. Kozai Yoshishige (Tokyo: Sōdo bunka, 1983), p. 609.

14. This and the other two translations included here are based on versions of the original texts that appear in Shikin's complete works, *Shikin zenshū*, ed. Kozai Yoshishige (Tokyo: Sōdo bunka, 1983). I am very grateful to the publisher and to the family of Kozai Yoshishige for permission to publish these translations here. I am also greatly indebted to Professors Brett de Bary, Victor Koschmann, Naoki Sakai, Asai Kiyoshi, Kurisu Akiko, and Inui Chizuko for their support, encouragement, and invaluable help at various stages of the translations. Additionally, the Resource Librarian at the Kyoto Institute for the Study of Buraku Issues provided great assistance in finding materials about "School for Émigrés."

15. An earlier version of this translation appeared in my "Narrative Strategies in Shimizu Shikin's 'The Broken Ring,' " *Journal of Kyoto Seika University*, no. 3 (1992): 18–36.

16. Liu Xiang's (79–8 BCE) Han dynasty text *Lie nüzhuan* (Stories of chaste women) is referred to in Japanese as *Ryūkyō retsujoden*. This Han dynasty text was used in the moral instruction of young women of high social status.

17. *Onna daigaku* (Greater learning for women, 1716) was a manual of ethics and proper behavior for women of the samurai class. It is attributed to Kaibara Ekiken (1630–1714) and was used widely in the late Tokugawa period.

18. This is most likely a reference to Monica (331–387 CE), mother of Augustine. Monica is much lauded in the history of Christianity for her strong determination to educate her son in the teachings of Christianity.

19. Gou Jian (Kōsen in Japanese) was king of the ancient Chinese kingdom of Yue (or Etsu in Japanese), which was at war with the kingdom of Wu (Go).

20. "Lying on a pyre of firewood and tasting bittermeats" is a reference to the phrase *gashin shōtan*, which in turn draws on accounts of the king of Wu, who lay on firewood to prepare himself physically and mentally before battle with Gou Jian to avenge the death of his father. Guo Jian, in turn, is said to have tasted bittermeats when preparing for battle. In colloquial use, the phrase *gashin shōtan* means to endure severe hardship for the sake of future success.

21. In a note on the version of this story used for this translation, the editors of the *Shikin zenshū* explain that they have revised some *kana* readings in a manner more consistent with contemporary practice. To corroborate, I have also used a version that was published under the name "Shikin Joshi" in *Buraku mondai bungei sakuhin kaidai*, vol. 10 of *Buraku mondai shiryō bunken sōsho*, ed. Kitagawa Tetsuo (Tokyo: Sekai bunko, 1972).

22. A reference to the Buddhist notion of the "three realms" that make up the world of sentient beings: the realm of *yoku* (worldly desires), that of *shiki* (attachment), and that of *mushiki* (nonattachment). This also resonates with the commonly heard phrase "A woman has no home in the three realms."

23. The original text uses the word *sabetsu*, which may also be translated as "discrimination."

24. Two puns seem to be in play here. The Chinese character for *obi*, the wide cloth sash used to secure a kimono, is also used in the compound for "household." The money she would like to spend on a new lining for her *obi* must be used for household expenses. These are in turn compared to the giant centipede that was said to have wound itself seven times around Mount Mikami in Shiga Prefecture.

25. Here we see another complex play on words involving a proverb stating that, if you curse someone else, you yourself will fall into a hole and die. There is also wordplay involving the mythical Tengu, known for his long nose, and

with the notion that flat noses are ugly, while high, pointed noses may be thought beautiful but indicate haughtiness.

26. All the money goes to the pleasure quarters, and nothing goes to the "shrine of the mountain god," meaning the wife.
27. Many were former geisha.
28. It is the deity of Izumo Shrine who presides over matchmaking.

HASEGAWA SHIGURE
(1879–1941)

Carole Cavanaugh

WHEN HASEGAWA SHIGURE wrote her first play, for a Tokyo newspaper contest in 1905, Japanese theater included a standard repertoire of established dramas, new melodramas (*shimpa*), and modern plays (*shingeki*), as well as productions of Shakespeare, Ibsen, and Chekhov.[1] Kabuki nonetheless dominated. Its memorable plots, lush costumes, stunning makeup, extravagant style, and loyal audience were a formidable obstacle to competition from newer kinds of drama. Intellectual writers famous for their prose, who were amateurs in the world of Japanese theater, attempted fresh Kabuki dramas that reflected their interest in the realism of Western theater. To encourage experimentation in *shin kabuki*, or new Kabuki, the literary critic Tsubouchi Shōyō (1859–1935) launched the *Yomiuri* newspaper contest and, as its judge, immediately recognized the importance of Hasegawa's entry. Despite its flaws, *Kaichō'on* (The sound of the sea) expressed for the first time within the conventions of the Kabuki theater the emotional conflicts of women.

Middle-class merchants in downtown Tokyo, like the Hasegawa family, were the heart of the Kabuki audience. They preferred flamboyant tales of bombastic courage, deadly swordplay, and doomed love to the subtler psychological conflicts of realistic characters in everyday settings found in modern drama. Hasegawa's father, a solicitor and small-time

FIGURE 8.1 Hasegawa Shigure (1879–1941)

politician, was an avid Kabuki fan; he regularly gathered at his home a group of aficionados who discussed plays, new productions, and the nuances of their favorite actors' performances. Born in 1879, Yasuko, who would take the pen name Shigure in 1902,[2] grew up in an atmosphere of enthusiasm for the Japanese stage. When she was very young, her father regularly took her to the theater. Whether or not she understood the convoluted plots and historical references, she delighted in the spectacle of Kabuki. Actors moved through the audience on the *hanamichi* (flower path), the raised passageway to the stage, appeared and disappeared on trap lifts, and effected sudden changes in mood or character through outer costumes that fell away with the pull of a few threads. Even the stage itself revolved to show a change of place or time, and in some theaters a second inner stage could revolve again in the opposite direction.

Theatergoing was an all-day event, and when Yasuko grew tired, she was left to amuse herself in the theater tearoom, where she leafed through the periodical *Kabuki shinpō* (Kabuki news), a magazine she would remember as having had more influence on her interest in drama than the performances themselves. First published in 1879, *Kabuki shinpō* included theater gossip as well as critical essays and translations of European plays. Too young to read, Yasuko colored in the woodblock pictures of her favorite actors, enlivening the black-on-white prints in a way that anticipated the tinge of personal sensibility she would later bring to Kabuki's traditional outlines.

As the oldest of seven children, Yasuko soon had little free time to pore over magazines or indulge her growing passion for reading fiction. She would bitterly recall the time her mother found her reading a paperback novel, ripped the book from her hands, tore it to pieces, and burned it in the garden. Despite her mother's disapproval, Yasuko and a group of friends produced a little magazine of their stories and poems. Her schooling ended with graduation from the sixth grade, but during her adolescence a university student who boarded with her family opened to her a new world of literary possibility. Usawa Akira, editor of a student magazine, often brought his friends to the Hasegawa home, where their enthusiastic exchanges on Japanese classics and Western novels were her first introduction to writing with more intellectual depth than the popular fiction and traditional tales she had loved as a child. Yasuko reclaimed some of the education her circumstances denied her by devouring the notes Usawa brought home from his university lectures.

In 1894, when she was fifteen, she became a literary apprentice to the poet and scholar Sasaki Nobutsuna (1873–1963). This tutorial arrangement was not unusual for young women with literary talent, but for Hasegawa it was short-lived. Her mother, believing that preparation for marriage was more important than training for a literary vocation, found a live-in domestic position for her with a wealthy family named Ikeda. She stipulated that her daughter be given nothing to read, but Hasegawa managed to peek at the old newspapers wrapping the milk cans delivered to the Ikeda home each day. She found an advertisement for a "Women's Correspondence Course" and with her first monthly wage sent away for the lectures, studying them secretly at night.

In December 1897, her parents arranged her marriage. She was nineteen. The Mizuhashi family was prosperous, but her young husband, a carouser and womanizer, had little interest in her. Hasegawa was ironically more free as a married woman than she had ever been. She had money to buy books and the leisure to read them, at least until her husband's parents, weary of his dissolute ways, cut him off financially. Trapped in a loveless, nearly penniless marriage, Hasegawa began to write. Her first slim work, "Uzumibi" (Embers), was published in *Jogaku sekai* (Women's education world) in 1901. The story articulated a theme she would return to again and again in her fiction and plays: female endurance under the crushing force of the patriarchal family.

Hasegawa eventually divorced and tried to make a life for herself outside the economic and social conventions of the traditional family, as did other women writers of the time, such as Tamura Toshiko, who either lived with female companions or with men not chosen by their parents. Their essays, poems, and short stories earned them only a meager living but rewarded them with intellectual independence. In coteries of poets and novelists, dominated by university-educated men, they joined the debates on the purposes of literature and argued the comparative merits of Western and Japanese modes of expression. Hasegawa associated with a group that included Uno Kōji (1891–1961), one of the most prominent writers in the I-novel genre. Within that circle, she also met and eventually fell in love with Mikami Otokichi, a struggling writer who had just graduated from Waseda University. The practice of women taking younger lovers was not uncommon among urban bohemians, who referred to the men in such arrangements as *wakaki tsubame*, "young swallows." In 1915, when they married, Hasegawa was thirty-six, and Mikami twenty-five.

Before she met Mikami, in the years between 1905 and 1914, Hasegawa devoted herself to her first love, the theater. In 1908 her play *Hanomaru* was staged at the Kabuki-za Theater in Tokyo by an important troupe of actors. It was the first play written by a Japanese woman ever produced in Japan. It opened to enormous fanfare, and Hasegawa became famous overnight. She wrote several more plays, winning a measure of acclaim, but critical success came with *Sakura fubuki* (Blizzard of blossoms), a monumental drama in five acts, produced in 1911. Set in medieval times, the play deals with revenge, a typical Kabuki theme, but the avengers are women rather than men. Though some casts of Hasegawa's plays included actresses, *Sakura fubuki* was performed in conventional Kabuki style. *Onnagata*, male actors who specialize in female roles, took the leading parts of a dead man's wife and his mistress, former rivals who join forces against his enemies.

In 1911 she saw a production of *A Doll House*, and it was not long afterward that she began to write *Chōji midare* (*Wavering Traces*, 1911, translated here). The importance of Ibsen's play to Japanese feminism is evident in the decision by the editors of *Seitō* (Bluestocking) to devote an entire issue of the magazine to responses to the production.[3] In his review, the critic Ihara Seiseien used the phrase "new woman" (*atarashii onna*) to describe a "Japanese Nora" he noticed in the audience, who had been brought to tears by the drama. That woman was Hasegawa

Shigure. The phrase "new woman" was first coined in Europe to describe Ibsen's heroines, and Tsubouchi Shōyō (1859–1935) used the term in his 1907 lectures on the dramatist. The meanings of "new woman" would divide the *Seitō* writers in their debate over whether feminism for Japanese women should be a demand for legal equality, special protection, or liberation through socialism.[4] For Hasegawa, at least at this phase in her career, the immediate problem was how to translate the sensibility of the "new woman" she felt so deeply into a character suited to the Japanese theater.

Wavering Traces was first staged in 1913 at Tokyo's top theater, the Ichimura-za, to full houses during its run. Onoe Kikugorō VI, the greatest star of his day, played the lead. Kikugorō (1885–1949) was a pioneer in the development of modern Kabuki. Incorporating ideas from Western theater, he excited audiences with his special sensitivity for the characters in new dramas.[5]

Hasegawa's drama falls into a subgenre called *jidai-sewamono*, plays that dramatize domestic conflict in a period setting. *Wavering Traces* is different from its traditional forebears in that its emotional focus is on the woman and not her husband. Hasegawa set the play in the past to defamiliarize a modern issue: a striving husband's inability to recognize his wife's self-sacrifice. The feminist emotionalism of *Wavering Traces* evoked wild appreciation from its audience. On the last day of its run, the stage was covered with flowers thrown as a tribute to the author and the star. It was an affectionate gesture and by all accounts unprecedented in the memory of the Kabuki theater.

Four of the seven dramas Hasegawa wrote during these years were staged. She also formed her own performance company and published a short-lived theater magazine with a group of colleagues. By the 1920s, however, her beloved Kabuki had returned to its classical roots and resisted experimentation. She left drama after her marriage to Mikami for the more dependable market of popular romantic fiction. She remained an energetic and active writer of essays and fiction until almost the day she died, of leukemia, on August 22, 1941.[6] Today, she is less remembered as a playwright than as the founder of the important feminist magazine *Nyonin geijutsu* (Women and the arts), which ran from 1928 to 1932 and was devoted to writing "of women, for women, by women."[7]

Because *Wavering Traces* is dependent on the theatrics of Kabuki, its text is more easily read with some prior sense of the plot. Set in ancient times, the play takes place in two scenes on a single night. Hatsushimo and her husband, Masakuni, live in a remote wood with their two small children. Masakuni, a maker of swords, is obsessed with his ambition to craft a masterpiece. He works incessantly, neglecting his family emotionally. A monk delivers a sword Masakuni has made from the sword finisher in town, whose job it was to polish and add the fittings to the blade. Hatsushimo recognizes in the finished sword the craftsmanship of a masterpiece. She reveals that this is the final night of a hundred nights she has secretly vowed to pray for her husband at a nearby temple. We learn later that Masakuni is aware of her nocturnal departures but not the reason for them. He apparently suspects her of infidelity. The monk believes the blade bears an evil omen. Because of his warning, Hatsushimo hides the sword from Masakuni, inadvertently setting in motion the tragic ending of the play.

The many references to frost, such as in the name Hatsushimo (first frost), are associated with the cold water used in sword tempering but also with aging beauty and vanishing love. *Wavering Traces* looks at the disappointments of a faded romance when lovers are supposed to have lived happily ever after. Hasegawa chooses sword making as the husband's craft to give their marriage an inherent conflict. The title refers to the unique temper patterns hammered into swords and identifiably associated, along with file marks on the tang, with any of two hundred sword-making schools. In the period when the story is set, a swordsmith and his apprentice would have lived an ascetic, almost monastic life, following the austerities of their school. The unspoken problem in the play is that, having acted on selfish desire by breaking with his familial line and marrying for love, Masakuni is now spiritually prevented from achieving the perfection of his art. Hatsushimo tries to repair his internal conflict through her selfless devotion. The feminist ideal of the play is the belief that female love is as powerful as the traditions that ennoble sword making, a craft epitomizing patriarchal dominance.

Kabuki is famous for its tricks. Red coloring, inserted in the sword ridge, flows like blood when a character is struck. Hasegawa used conventions like these, as well as the *mawaributai*, the revolving stage that shifts the scene from exterior to interior. She also incorporated newer elements, like innovative lighting and offstage sounds. Kabuki lighting is flat and is not reduced for night scenes. Hasegawa's attention to the effect of cross-lighting on the fallen leaves and to the setting sun, rising moon, and gradually darkening night in her stage directions indicates a modern use of atmospheric effects closer to those of the representational theater of the West. Her use of sound also breaks the boundaries of Kabuki, where only the observable limits of the stage have theatrical significance.[8] When offstage sound effects are used in Kabuki, they correspond to onstage action. A thematic element in Hasegawa's play, however, is the recurring offstage cry of the fox kitten, an animal associated in Japan with the supernatural. The orphaned fox also reminds us of the vulnerability of the children caught in their parents' discord. Hasegawa grasped the theatrical potential of sound to penetrate unseen space and expand the dramatic dimensions of the stage in her use of the fox cry, the ring of the hammer, the trickle of water, and the voices of characters before entry.

Otherworldly beings are frequent in Kabuki, but Hasegawa treats the supernatural with subtlety. In a scene that seems to have nothing to do with the rest of the play, Masakuni notices a young man and woman outside his window. They are eloping, just as he and his wife did years before. Although the couple is "real," they also figure as a ghostly visitation from Masakuni's past and as a dramatization of happier times. Whether actual or imagined, these secondary characters give a psychological dimension to Kabuki's traditional treatment of unexplainable apparitions and odd coincidences.

Wavering Traces is a melodrama, a term with an unfavorable reputation and almost synonymous with soap opera. Peter Brooks has suggested that the designation can be more effectively applied as a neutral description of a style with certain features and characteristics rather than as a pejorative dismissal of plays with high emotion. In melodrama "characters assume primary psychic roles, father, mother, child and express basic psychic conditions."[9] Melodrama often gives prominence to the experiences, emotions, and activities of women, and so the genre has special potential to expose patriarchal ideology.[10] The wistful tenderness in the dialogue between Masakuni and Hatsushimo when they recall the time they were most in love is unusual in Japanese literature. Typically, characters do not express their affection directly to each other, and love is often presented in terms of isolated male suffering. Hasegawa's play is modern because it is honor that stands in the way of love rather than the other way around, as in traditional drama. When recognized unapologetically for its value as melodrama, *Wavering Traces* becomes an exceptionally fruitful exploration of women's emotional lives.[11]

WAVERING TRACES

Translated by Carole Cavanaugh

Characters

RAI MASAKUNI, a swordsmith
HATSUSHIMO, his wife
ICHIWAKA, their eight-year-old son
SOMEGO, their one-year-old daughter
MASAKI MORITO, a masterless samurai
A MONK
KOROKUTA, a swordsmith's apprentice
A YOUNG MAN AND WOMAN

The play takes place on a single night in late autumn sometime during the Kamakura period (1185–1333) in the province of Musashi. Scene one is outside a swordsmith's workshop and in his family's living quarters; scene two is near a temple in the forest.

Scene 1

At stage left is an old, bare ginkgo tree. Just beyond it is a swordsmith's workshop. A large window wraps around the smithy. From the eaves, covered with vines, are suspended sacred Shinto straw festoons. Attached to the workshop on the right is the swordsmith's home. A tattered shōji is the door to the kitchen. Bamboo grows on both sides of the house. Near the kitchen entrance is the well sweep. The fading sunlight glances off piles of fallen leaves. In the middle of this scene, the sun sets; in the next scene, the moon comes out, and a misty night falls. When the curtain rises, Hatsushimo is taking down laundry. When she is finished, she goes back into the kitchen. From the darkness of the forest comes Ichiwaka's voice singing a lullaby.

ICHIWAKA: (*Singing offstage*) The fox kitten born last night is softer than the inside of a flower, warmer than dried grass; mother holds me to her breast and whispers, "Go to sleep."

Coming out, Hatsushimo listens and then draws some water from the well.

ICHIWAKA: (*Singing offstage*) The fox kitten sang last night, crying, though it has not even opened its eyes; mother who asked, "Do you want some milk?" was captured in a trap and carried away by the hunter . . .

Ichiwaka, singing and carrying Somego on his back, enters, guiding a Buddhist monk.

ICHIWAKA: (*To the monk*) My mother is right there.
HATSUSHIMO: Waka, you're home. Was Somego fussy?
ICHIWAKA: Somego was fine. I took her into the grove, Mother, and we fed the fox kittens our rice balls. Then we gathered some acorns.
HATSUSHIMO: Well then, you're both good children. Will you take good care of her for me tomorrow, too? She was safe and sound today. And look, now . . . aren't you clever! You made Somego a pinwheel from maple leaves! (*To Somego*) See the pinwheel spin? See?
ICHIWAKA: (*Pointing to the monk*) Mother, there's a monk waiting for you over there. He says he's come to see you about something.
MONK: I beg your pardon. When you hear the sound of that hammer, you don't have to ask if this is the house of the swordsmith who lives in these woods.
HATSUSHIMO: (*Untying the cords that hold up her sleeves*) Oh my, how rude of me, please forgive me. What can I do for you? Has my naughty son played some prank?

MONK: No, no, nothing of the kind. I was entrusted with this delivery for you from the sword finisher in town.

HATSUSHIMO: A delivery? Oh, the sword!

MONK: He said he has sharpened and polished it. See for yourself.

HATSUSHIMO: He has finished it!

MONK: Here it is.

She takes it from him and, closing her eyes, carefully removes the scabbard. She opens her eyes and looks at the sword.

HATSUSHIMO: Aah, here it is—a misty aura seems to arise from it—the patina of the polish, its aroma! Look!

MONK: Can you see all that in the blade?

HATSUSHIMO: I can't help appreciating the fine work my husband forges! Even if I were blind, if someone brandished one of his swords before me, I would surely know it was his work.

MONK: The sword finisher said it was a rare piece of craftsmanship.

HATSUSHIMO: The sword finisher said so, too? Oh! But now listen to me—sounding so proud of my own husband! I shouldn't go on like this.

The sound of hammering against metal comes from the smithy.

MONK: But your husband does not seem satisfied with himself. Even my poor monk's ears are not deaf to the passion in his hammer. Who is he trying to please with such single-minded concentration?

HATSUSHIMO: (*Dispirited*) It's not that he's trying to please anyone. He won't even let his darling children near him. He washes with the frost in the morning, and, at night, if he sleeps at all, the hammer is his pillow. Day and night, he hammers away. But no matter what, the swords he makes are not good enough for him. He exhausts himself fretting over the temperature of the water he uses for tempering. He has grown terribly thin.

ICHIWAKA: Late at night, Mother goes off alone, Reverend, and hides from Father.

MONK: Where?

ICHIWAKA: To the lonely forest.

MONK: Why does she go there?

ICHIWAKA: To pray. She is praying each night for one hundred nights.

HATSUSHIMO: Tonight is the last night. I vowed to perform this secret penance because I wanted *this* sword to be a masterpiece. I thought it would console my husband's tormented heart.

MONK: And tonight you will fulfill your vow?

HATSUSHIMO: My hundred-night pilgrimage to the temple in the woods will pass tonight like a dream.

MONK: I am a monk of meager virtue, but since it was I who carried the sword wrapped in my shabby sleeves, I must tell you. This splendid masterpiece you have been praying for is cursed by an evil spirit.

HATSUSHIMO: This sword? Cursed?

MONK: I came here as an unworthy messenger, poor and humble as I am, to warn you of its wickedness. When I passed in front of the sword finisher's workshop, I heard him say, as he gazed on that sword, that it was a work of art, a masterpiece! Then, suddenly, I noticed that it brimmed with murderous intent.

HATSUSHIMO: What?

MONK: I was not going to tell you what I suspected, but now, hearing of your devotion to your husband, I think to withhold from you what I've seen will be far more dangerous. Look, the misty aura, as you call it, arising from that sword is an ominous cloud hovering over it.

HATSUSHIMO: This cannot be . . .

MONK: Do not let him see it. The swordsmith, being the man that he is, should not be tempted to stray. Without this sword, this harbinger of evil, he will continue his single-minded fervor with no misgivings.

ICHIWAKA: (*Tossing acorns, in a sing-song voice*) One is for Somego, and one is her age. Somego is a girl. I'm her big brother, and I'm a boy. One is for Mother; one is for Father; one is for the Reverend Monk; one is for the fox kitten. The acorns I gathered one by one—one by one I toss them.

As Ichiwaka tosses the acorns, the monk draws the boy's palm toward him, counts the acorns, looks troubled by what he sees, and closes his eyes.

MONK: (*Woefully*) What an omen, what a strange sign has appeared! Take it to heart that I say you must never show that sword to anyone. Especially since your husband is so full of passion, never show that sword to him.

HATSUSHIMO: I am grateful for the warning you have given me.

MONK: Tomorrow, perhaps a true masterpiece will arrive, and when you compare the two, you will agree with me. Until then I will pray for your health and well-being.

ICHIWAKA: Reverend, are you leaving now?

MONK: Farewell, my child.

Saying his beads, the monk leaves. Hatsushimo puts her hand on Ichiwaka's shoulder and watches intently after the departing monk. Night begins to fall.

HATSUSHIMO: I was so sure of myself. I was so convinced of my husband's fine workmanship. The reverend is a holy sight. These words have not been wasted on me. I will remember them—aah, now I have even more worries!

ICHIWAKA: It's already dark. Let's go in, Mother, and you can feed Somego.

HATSUSHIMO: Oh dear, I forgot! Her crying will disturb your father. Yes, let's go.

ICHIWAKA: Mother, don't cry. If you cry, the demons will come and take you away.

They go into the house together. Silhouetted on the paper window of the smithy is the shadow of the swordsmith working his hammer. At stage left, a young man and woman, in sedge hats and travel clothes, emerge cautiously from the shadowy grove.

MAN: No one will see us in this place. It's already dark. Why don't we rest here?

WOMAN: But it's getting late.

MAN: (*Gently*) Are you afraid? Didn't you say you were ready and eager to travel along the dark roads at night?

WOMAN: I'm not afraid; it just feels so eerie here.

MAN: I need just a little rest—your delicate legs have made *me* tired. We haven't even had a sip of water since we left the inn today. Aren't you thirsty, Somoji?

WOMAN: (*Rubbing her feet*) I *am* thirsty.

MAN: This is a sword maker's place, isn't it? I heard the sound of his hammer echoing back in the woods. Let's just ask—I'm sure it's not much more than a couple of miles from here. (*Going up to the window*) Hello! (*The hammering inside stops.*) Sorry to bother you, but how far is it to Azabu from here?

From inside the window comes the voice of Korokuta, the young apprentice.

KOROKUTA: Uhh, let's see . . . less than two miles. If you go very quickly, you'll get there this evening.

MAN: Much obliged. Sorry to have interrupted your work. (*Moving away from the window, he says to himself*) I guess we won't make it before late tonight. (*Aloud*) Ahh, a crescent moon has come out. (*Going over to the young woman*) It's only a little way now, so let's go just a little faster.

WOMAN: I said I was thirsty.

MAN: Now that the end is in sight, you're relaxed enough to give me just a little trouble, eh?

WOMAN: Uhh . . .

MAN: All right then. There's a well over there. Let's go have some water. Come on.

The man draws some water. In her cupped hands, the woman scoops it and drinks. Scooping some more, she offers it to the man. He drinks thirstily. In the dim light coming from the papered window of the back door, they take each other's hands and depart. Just then, the window of the workshop opens a bit; Masakuni, a look of exhaustion on his face, looks out and spies the pair. The stage revolves to reveal the inside of the house. At stage right is the smithy at ground level. One step up is the living quarters with rustic kitchen, stage left. There is a hearth between the kitchen and the living area. A sliding paper screen separates the living quarters from the smithy.

ICHIWAKA: (*Playing with a shadow puppet in the lamplight*) Mother, when I put the shadow puppet up close to the lamp, even though it is only a little devil, its shadow looks dark and fierce. When I go like this, it's big but blurry and not so scary. Why?

HATSUSHIMO: (*Holding Somego and stoking the hearth fire*) I'll tell you, but first go see what Father is doing.

ICHIWAKA: Father scares me even from far away. I hate it when he scolds me.

HATSUSHIMO: Call Korokuta then.

ICHIWAKA: Korokuta won't come, either. He's afraid of Father, too. If he puts down his hammer, Father gives him a nasty look.

HATSUSHIMO: All right then.

Hatsushimo stands up and puts Somego down to sleep behind a folding screen. ICHIWAKA tiptoes to the smithy and peeks in.

ICHIWAKA: Mother! Father is standing near the window, and he looks worried about something. Korokuta is cleaning up and putting out the fire.

The forge fire is out in the smithy; only a votive candle is burning on a shelf before a small shrine.

ICHIWAKA: Korokuta, if you're finished work, come on in here.

KOROKUTA: (*Entering the living quarters*) I have to go on an errand, Ichiwaka.

ICHIWAKA: Where are you going?

KOROKUTA: To buy metal, from that devil who sells it.

ICHIWAKA: Can't you play with me? I'm lonesome.

HATSUSHIMO: You must be tired, Korokuta. It's still early, so even if you rest a bit, you won't be leaving very late. You must be hungry. You'd better eat some dinner before you go.

KOROKUTA: No, if I eat dinner, I'll get too full and too sleepy to walk a step.

HATSUSHIMO: You're just the same as he is—you never put down your hammer, night and day. You must be exhausted. I'll go on the errand for you. You eat and get some sleep.

KOROKUTA: No, please, let me go. I haven't seen my mother for a long time, and I would like to call on her. I don't know when I'll be able to go that way again.

HATSUSHIMO: Well, then of course you may go. But what will your mother think when she sees how thin and worn out you look? Apologize to her for me for not doing well enough by you.

KOROKUTA: Don't worry. I'll just tell her that I ran over in the middle of a very busy time.

HATSUSHIMO: How is your mother?

KOROKUTA: She's old and forever coughing.

HATSUSHIMO: I'd like to send her something—you so rarely have a chance to visit her. Ichiwaka, are there any chestnuts in that basket?

ICHIWAKA: These are all the chestnuts I have. (*He shows her the basket.*) We have hardly any millet either.

HATSUSHIMO: Haven't I told you not to tell what you have not been asked?

KOROKUTA: (*Calling to Masakuni, who stands by the window*) Will that be the only errand?

Masakuni nods.

KOROKUTA: (*To Hatsushimo*) Well, then, I'm on my way.

Korokuta bows and exits. Masakuni leaves the window of the smithy and comes into the house.

ICHIWAKA: (*Happily*) Father, are you done for the day?

Masakuni nods.

MASAKUNI: (*To Hatsushimo*) Give me some water.

HATSUSHIMO: Yes, of course.

She hurries to the back. Masakuni follows. Ichiwaka puts chestnuts on the hearth fire. Somego begins to cry. Ichiwaka goes to her, pats her, and calls Hatsushimo.

ICHIWAKA: Mother, Mother!

HATSUSHIMO: (*Entering*) Oh, did she wake up?

She takes Ichiwaka's place and comforts the baby. Masakuni sits down. Ichiwaka tentatively offers Masakuni some roasted chestnuts. Masakuni gently pulls Ichiwaka toward him and hugs him.

MASAKUNI: Has Somego fallen asleep?

HATSUSHIMO: (*Cheerfully*) She was a good girl all day. Ichiwaka carried her on his back, and she slept a good while, but now she's restless. She's wakeful and fussy just the way she usually is at bedtime.

MASAKUNI: Why does she wake up crying every night?

HATSUSHIMO: What?

MASAKUNI: You're right there next to her, aren't you? I'd think you'd nurse her to settle her down.

HATSUSHIMO: Uh . . . does her crying disturb you?

MASAKUNI: It disturbs me that she cries for you night after night. It torments me.

HATSUSHIMO: Does she cry that much?

MASAKUNI: She cries as though you're not here. Didn't you know?

HATSUSHIMO: Oh, I never dreamed. . . . I had no idea she slept so fitfully. I'll be more attentive, starting tonight.

MASAKUNI: Sometimes she cries at midnight, sometimes at dawn. My muscles are tired from hammering night and day. When I doze off, I can hear the sound of someone's sandals, someone running away, stepping on my chest. I have painful nightmares. And at the same time every night, Somego cries.

HATSUSHIMO: (*Lightly*) Worrying about your work all the time is giving you nightmares. Well now, Ichiwaka can have dinner with his father tonight—he hasn't done that in a long time.

MASAKUNI: Hatsushimo, is there any wine?

HATSUSHIMO: Just the sacred wine for offering.

MASAKUNI: I'll drink that.

ICHIWAKA: (*As though suddenly remembering something*) Papa, please let me see you smile a little!

MASAKUNI: Why? What's troubling you?

ICHIWAKA: Your scary face. I hate the way Mother always looks so sad, and I hate the way you work at the forge all the time and look so angry. I forget how your face looks when you smile.

MASAKUNI: (*Taking the wine from Hatsushimo, smiling sadly*) Once you grow up, you can't be laughing all the time. When you were born, Mother and I smiled all the time for no reason at all and passed the days just gazing at each other.

HATSUSHIMO: (*With a faraway look*) Father was tender in those days . . .

MASAKUNI: Your mother still wore a long-sleeved kimono then, her teeth were not yet blackened . . . she was an innocent bride devoted to her husband.

HATSUSHIMO: We eloped, and you took me away from Kamakura. As we ran away along the road at night, I was happy and afraid. I was so frightened by the howling wind, I clung to you. I cried when I couldn't see you. Then we laughed at ourselves together.

MASAKUNI: Happy or sad, our hearts were one. That was a long time ago. Now autumn has fallen in our hearts. What's worse, our little Ichiwaka feels sad.

ICHIWAKA: No, I'm not sad at all. Tonight I'm so happy!

He lays his head on Masakuni's knee.

HATSUSHIMO: No, not sad at all. And certainly not sad about being poor. I could have sold my mirror, I suppose, but I've kept it because I want to put on a better face for you than this one worn by daily cares.

MASAKUNI: (*Sardonically*) A woman would paint her lips on her deathbed.

HATSUSHIMO: But those are the tender feelings of a wife for her husband, you know.

MASAKUNI: Would you like to return to the dream of those bygone days?

HATSUSHIMO: Yes, I would. Even if, to do it, my life had to be taken with the cold blade of a sword. I would return. If you would take me warmly in your arms, just once more, then I would die happily without a single regret.

MASAKUNI: Really, now. You don't say.

HATSUSHIMO: You've never spoken that way to me before! Or looked at me with those cold eyes!

MASAKUNI: Are you blaming me for that? Look into your own heart. When the red flowers bloom in one place, they fade and fall in another. Melted in a different crucible, old metal doesn't take on a new sheen. Until her mirror fails to compliment her, a woman can live in a dream world. I have no time for that.

HATSUSHIMO: I know that well.

MASAKUNI: I want to leave this world a masterpiece made by me, Rai Masakuni. I was a victor in love, oh yes, and look what I've become because of it! But even if you step on my face with your muddy clogs in the night when you go away—even if I am utterly disgraced—my arms, tempered by resentment, will rise again. Is my desire to make a masterpiece not also passionate love?

He holds Ichiwaka and lies down heavily.

HATSUSHIMO: You're angry at me because I am the only one you have to let out these frustrations on. And it is because of me that you are what you are now.

She clears away the wine bottle and cup, takes out their bedding, and covers them both. Masakuni and Ichiwaka fall asleep.

HATSUSHIMO: You're exhausted, aren't you? When you've finished your work and feel completely satisfied, I know I'll see your smiling face again. I want to be comforted by your face, happy the way it used to be, just once more. Ahh now, Ichiwaka's face, smiling in his sleep! There, there. Hold on to your father, and don't let him go.

The faint sound of the bells marking the hour echoes from afar.

HATSUSHIMO: (*To herself*) Tonight is my last night of prayer, but somehow I don't want to go. Maybe I should reveal everything to him before I leave. But no, no, the reverend monk said I should not show the sword to him. (*She looks at the sword.*) How happy he would be to see this work that he has made. I'll show him tomorrow. (*Whispering to the sleeping Masakuni*) Please, please . . . it is just this one last night—let me go for just a little while.

As Hatsushimo goes out, Somego begins to cry. She pauses. Somego quiets down. She leaves, closing the door.

MASAKUNI: (*Opening his eyes*) Hatsushimo, Hatsushimo, Somego is crying.

He gets up and looks all around as though he suspects something. He suddenly notices the sword. Just as he is about to touch it, he hears the sound of footsteps stealing through the fallen leaves piled outside. Listening, he

glares in the direction of the door, turns up the lamp wick, takes the sword
from the scabbard, and stares at it.

MASAKUNI: These wavering traces! My marks on the blade are translucent as the morning frost. They rise like the mist and gather into
clouds. This seems to be my work but . . . no, no, it cannot be mine.
The patina, the tempering! This is not the kind of sword I forge with
these dull arms of mine. Though I may be an unknown swordsmith,
my vision is not clouded. Slipped from its scabbard, the edges of this
work of art flow like a double stream of water in autumn. How hateful! Whose work has she placed here? Has passion killed my senses?
I am a thirty-year-old man! Has love for a woman extinguished my
spirit? Hatsushimo! Hatsushimo! Where have you gone? Who has
done this, this act that speaks contempt for me, this act meant to hu
miliate me? I want to know!

Carrying the sword, Masakuni goes out the door.

MASAKUNI: (*In the shadows*) Where have you run to? Hatsushimo!
Hatsushimo!

Ichiwaka wakes up and weeps softly.
Curtain

Scene 2

In the forest. The sound of a light wind blows through a stand of cedars.
In the center of the stage is a huge oak reaching toward the sky. Within
the wood is a weathered, rundown temple dedicated to Kannon. There is
no moon and the woods are gloomy. Under the tree, Masaki Morito, a
masterless samurai, is raking a fire of fallen leaves. Beside him stands
the monk.

MONK: I wasn't startled. Such things have happened to me before.
MORITO: I can see the good results of your ascetic training. Now, as for
me, I'm far from being a monk.
MONK: I am like a leaf blown by the wind. Apart from loneliness, I have
nothing to fear. Encounters such as these make people believe they've

seen a ghost, but I suppose, after all, I was snoring rather loudly, though I was only dozing.

MORITO: Ha, ha, ha. In all my many travels, I thought I had disciplined myself, but I'm no monk like you. To tell the truth, a little while ago I heard a baby's cry in the woods and was taken aback. I thought it must mean something, so I stopped here and made a fire. The child's wail sounded through the firelight.

MONK: Hmm, maybe it was a fox.

MORITO: If it was a fox kitten, its eyes are not even open yet.

MONK: The swordsmith's boy was saying there was a fox kitten whose mother was captured by a hunter.

MORITO: A swordsmith in the woods back there?

MONK: You know of him?

MORITO: I *have* made a mistake then! Let me tell you why I'm camping here tonight. The truth is, last night I lost my way and came upon the forest path. From somewhere came the sound of hammering clear as frost. It was intense, I tell you. I didn't know who it was, but the sound was something splendid. He may not be a famous swordsmith, but my heart quickened at the thought that he will create a masterpiece! The strange thing was, though, all of a sudden the hammer missed a beat. I wondered why, when, before I knew it, a black shadow slipped by me without a sound and disappeared into the darkness.

The monk nods knowingly.

MORITO: You seem to know what it was.

MONK: First, tell me more.

MORITO: Well, I couldn't go any further since I didn't know my way on the dark road. I was still curious, but I never found out what it was. Going about my business today, I walked around this area and realized that this grove must have been the place where I lost sight of that shadow. I was concerned about the swordsmith, so I decided to spend the night here. When I saw you stir under the eaves of the temple just a little while ago, I thought *you* were the one I had seen last night, and, I'm terribly sorry, I came up on you and startled you.

MONK: That shadow was the swordsmith's wife.

MORITO: What? His wife?

MONK: She said tonight is the last night of her one hundred nights of prayer in the temple. I am a monk, but, even so, I don't want to be any hindrance to her prayers. I was just about to leave the temple when you came along and surprised me.

MORITO: Why is she praying?

MONK: So that her husband will accomplish his great work.

MORITO: (*Hitting his arm*) Last night, I had my hand on the very hilt of my sword, as usual not thinking a thing of it, and just now I was ready to draw it. I'm stupid and reckless and so eager to show my courage. Reverend, if I had not met you, I might have thought that virtuous wife was a ghost haunting the swordsmith tonight, and I would've surely killed her!

MONK: (*Sadly*) She does have about her the sign of death by the sword.

MORITO: Really?

MONK: And, what's worse, the sword her husband made was filled with a murderous air.

MORITO: Did you warn her of it?

MONK: I who am so poor in virtue can only preach about the next world. I lack the power to rescue anyone from the sufferings of the present.

There is the sound of someone performing ablutions in the temple. From within the forest comes the faint sound of a woman's voice.

HATSUSHIMO: Lord Buddha, please wrap him in the sleeve of your benevolence. Let him make a true work of art.

The monk and Morito look surprised.

MORITO: (*Whispering*) Don't you worry. Tomorrow I will go and have a good look at that sword for myself. Throughout this night, I vow to protect the virtuous wife who has fallen under an omen of death.

MONK: (*Opening his palms*) Merit beyond measure be yours. It is in *your* power indeed to rescue her from her fate in the present.

MORITO: I humbly accept this task.

MONK: I will trust you to accomplish it. Now I feel the clouds of my apprehension clearing. I will leave you to take care of matters here while I go to the swordsmith's.

MORITO: Farewell.

The monk tips his hat and disappears into the woods.

HATSUSHIMO: (*Praying*) Please let my husband know the joy of the answer to my prayers. Hail, Kannon, in the morning and in the evening!

Her husband, Masakuni, enters, running, with the sword in his hand. Morito sees him, follows him, and then hides behind the tree. Without noticing Morito, Masakuni looks around, goes to the fire, and gazes at the sword.

MASAKUNI: (*Loudly*) Aha! This *is* my work after all, and it is splendid! There is no name on this sword, but there can be no doubt the wavering traces of my hammer are the signature of the line of sword makers from which I myself descend! Where is Hatsushimo? Hatsushimo! Look at this! Hatsushimo!

He looks admiringly at the sword in the light of the fire. Hatsushimo, hearing her husband, emerges and approaches Masakuni. She silently looks at his face and at the sword, but Masakuni does not notice her. With a smile of triumph on his face, he suddenly swings the sword.

HATSUSHIMO: Aaa!

Struck unaware, she falls, bleeding, to the ground. Masakuni sees the blood on the sword. Shocked, he drops it.

HATSUSHIMO: My husband!

Masakuni, surprised to hear her voice, embraces her and trembles.

MASAKUNI: Who . . . who are you?
HATSUSHIMO: My husband!
MASAKUNI: Oh, no! Hatsushimo! Where is the wound? Where?
HATSUSHIMO: (*With difficulty*) My husband . . . the sword?
MASAKUNI: (*Without answering, he looks for the wound.*) Where is the wound?
HATSUSHIMO: The sword finisher said it was a true masterpiece.

MASAKUNI: (*Hurriedly*) You can tell me about the sword later. Where are you cut? You must tell me! Don't die!

HATSUSHIMO: (*Clinging to him*) Are your doubts gone, my husband? (*Pointing to the temple*) Tonight is the last of my one hundred nights of prayer.

MASAKUNI: Do you think I struck you with the sword because I doubted you? No! It was an accident!

HATSUSHIMO: I wonder if the sacrificial blood cleansed by these one hundred days has purified the evil from the sword.

MASAKUNI: What do you mean by sacrificial? I never wanted, never dreamed, of winning honor by sacrificing you!

HATSUSHIMO: I had not known that I would be the one to test the sharpness of the very blade that has bound our hearts.

MASAKUNI: It was not a test. Do not say such a scornful thing! How heartless!

HATSUSHIMO: (*Getting weaker*) Heartless are the things men do for the sake of their honor. Honor! I despise the word!

MASAKUNI: Aah, my heart became the home of an evil demon. I did not realize what a fool I was. All I worried about was producing a masterpiece. Now I am about to lose my beloved wife. There is no honor in my work if I've killed you. (*Drawing the sword close to him*) Our names sung together in love will be our legacy.

Hatsushimo clings to his arm, looks up at him, and smiles. A fox kitten cries in the distance.

HATSUSHIMO: Aah, my son, Ichiwaka . . . my baby, Somego . . .

Masakuni, losing heart, gazes at Hatsushimo.

HATSUSHIMO: Where is Somego? And Ichiwaka?

She slumps. Masakuni immediately embraces her more tightly.

MASAKUNI: Hatsushimo!
HATSUSHIMO: My . . .

She dies.

MASAKUNI: Is this my cruel punishment? Even the fire has gone out! Let me see you one more time, even if it is just in a vision! Please say something! Hatsushimo, Hatsushimo! How will I tell our children?

Taking the sword, he is about to kill himself when Morito comes out and grabs his hand.

MASAKUNI: Who are you? How cruel not to let me die when I have every good reason.

MORITO: I understand your torment, but didn't your wife say your children's names just now with her dying breath? If you die, you will escape your own suffering, but how long will your children suffer? She would not want that.

Morito pulls the sword away, and Masakuni falls onto Hatsushimo.

MASAKUNI: (*Holding her body*) Forgive me!

Masakuni sobs quietly. Morito wipes the blood from the blade and peers at the sword in the dark. A fox kitten cries in the distance.
Curtain

NOTES

1. An earlier version of this introduction and translation appeared in Katherine E. Kelly, ed., *Modern Drama by Women, 1880s–1930s: An International Anthology* (London: Routledge), 1996.

2. *Shigure* means "a passing rain shower" and has poetic associations with winter.

3. Sharon Sievers, *Flowers in Salt: The Beginnings of Feminist Consciousness in Modern Japan* (Stanford: Stanford University Press, 1983), p. 170. See also Ayako Kano, *Acting Like a Woman in Modern Japan: Theater, Gender, and Nationalism* (New York: Palgrave, 2001), pp. 19–21.

4. Laurel Rasplica Rodd, "Yosano Akiko and the Taishō Debate over the 'New Woman,' " in *Recreating Japanese Women, 1600–1945*, ed. Gail Lee Bernstein (Berkeley: University of California Press, 1991), p. 176.

5. Samuel L. Leiter, ed., *Kabuki Encyclopedia: An English-Language Adaptation of Kabuki Jiten* (Westport, Conn.: Greenwood, 1979), p. 295.

6. For her complete works, see Hasegawa Shigure, *Hasegawa Shigure zenshū*, 5 vols. (Tokyo: Fuji shuppan, 1993).

7. For more on *Nyonin geijutsu*, see Joan E. Ericson, *Be A Woman: Hayashi Fumiko and Modern Japanese Women's Literature* (Honolulu: University of Hawai'i Press, 1997).

8. Earle Ernst, *The Kabuki Theater* (Honolulu: University of Hawai'i Press, 1974), p. 65.

9. Peter Brooks, *The Melodramatic Imagination: Balzac, Henry James, Melodrama, and the Mode of Excess* (New Haven: Yale University Press, 1976), p. 4.

10. Wimal Dissanayake, introduction to *Melodrama and Asian Cinema*, ed. Wimal Dissanayake (Cambridge: Cambridge University Press, 1993), p. 2.

11. The source text used for this translation is Hasegawa, *Hasegawa Shigure zenshū*, 2:77–106.

NOGAMI YAEKO
(1885–1985)

Eleanor J. Hogan

THAT A WRITER WHO lived just shy of one hundred years would have been prolific should come as no surprise. What is notable, however, is the variety of genres in which Nogami Yaeko published. Her complete works—totaling fifty-seven volumes—include short stories, lengthy novels, plays, essays, children's stories, diaries, travel narratives, and translations. Moreover, the spectrum of subjects covered within her oeuvre ranges from marriage, cannibalism, politics, and war to the lives of historical figures and personal reminiscences.

Nogami Yaeko was born as Kotegawa Yae on May 6, 1885, in Usuki, a small town in Oita Prefecture on the southern island of Kyūshū. She was the eldest daughter of Kakusaburō, who owned a sake brewing business still in existence today, and his wife, Masa. The family business was prosperous, and her father's brother Toyojirō was sent to the United States to be educated, obtaining a Ph.D. in economics from the University of Michigan. Yae was also to benefit from her family's wealth and open-mindedness, receiving the best education money could buy. She had every opportunity to read and study, both in school and with a private tutor. At a time when most girls did not complete lower elementary school, Yae finished both lower and upper elementary schools, graduating in 1899.[1] In 1900, with her uncle Toyojirō as her guardian, Yae was permitted to leave her home in the countryside and travel to Tokyo, where she enrolled in Meiji Women's School. She selected this school because she wanted an atmosphere where she would "truly be able to study."[2] The choice proved to be an important one.

Meiji Women's School was closely linked to *Jogaku zasshi* (Woman's education journal), edited by Iwamoto Yoshiharu (1863–1943), who was also the school's headmaster. Iwamoto's goal was to "improve women's condition by combining the Western ideals of the emancipated woman with the native ideas of feminine grace—thereby 'creating a perfect woman.'"[3] Meiji Women's School was quite different from more nationalistic institutions as it did not require its students to recite the Imperial Rescript on Education,[4] sing the national anthem, or listen to traditional lessons on Confucian morals.

Kotegawa Yae graduated from Meiji Women's School in 1906 and married Nogami Toyoichirō shortly thereafter. The reason for her marriage was pragmatic. As a married woman, she could remain in Tokyo. After her marriage, an editor mistakenly added the "ko" to her name (a common suffix for women's names), and thus Kotegawa Yae became known as Nogami Yaeko. Although Nogami insists that she did not expect to become a writer,[5] the marriage proved beneficial to her literary career. Toyoichirō attended author Natsume Sōseki's (1867–1916) Thursday night meetings [Mokuyōkai] and brought her manuscripts to Sōseki for his comments.[6] Editorial decisions about what would be included in the journal *Hototogisu* (The cuckoo) were often made at these meetings, where manuscripts sent to its new editor, Takahama Kyoshi (1874–1959), were read aloud and discussed. Nogami's first published work, "Enishi" (Ties that bind, 1907) was vetted at one of these meetings and appeared in the January issue with an introduction by Sōseki.[7] Without this mentorship, Nogami's entrance to the literary scene would have been considerably more difficult.

From her debut in January 1907 to her death on March 30, 1985, Nogami Yaeko published in a variety of journals including *Kaizō* (Reconstruction), *Chūō kōron* (Central forum), and *Seitō* (Bluestocking). Her works were also published in book form in both hardcover and paperback and are still being reprinted today. Nogami is most remembered for her novels: *Hideyoshi to Rikyū* (Hideyoshi and Rikyū, 1962–1964), a sweeping novel about the lives of two important cultural figures, and *Mori* (The forest, 1972–1985), her semiautobiographical novel about her experiences at the Meiji Women's School.

FIGURE 9.1 Nogami Yaeko (1885–1985)

Several of Nogami Yaeko's earlier works focused on marriage and were published in *Hototogisu*. "Kakiyōkan" (Persimmon sweets, 1908), translated here, appeared in the January 1908 issue. Since the members of Sōseki's Thursday night meetings, including Takahama Kyoshi, were interested in sketches from life (*shasei*), Nogami was careful to include details of daily life and vivid description in her work. As she was to explain in a later essay, "While I was reading one of those short works in *Hototogisu*, half in fun, I thought to myself, 'I'll try my hand at this kind of writing.' And with that, I started writing."[8]

Since *Hototogisu* was known for its light pieces, its audience would not expect a story with dark undertones. Nogami's narrative, with its many layers, simultaneously creates charm and mystery and mixes humor with gravity. The first layer of "Persimmon Sweets," the frame story, is cheerful, with Tokiko, her sister-in-law, and her brother talking about and interacting with Yoshida, the narrator of the second story. Yet the second layer, or the story-within-the-story about Yoshida's marriage, is initially dark and replete with metaphors of death. Nevertheless, when the context of Yoshida's marriage is understood, the darkness dissipates, and the story of Osetsu becomes one of triumph and not tragedy.

Yoshida claims to have a wife, while his friends think that he could not possibly be married. They mock him about his lies, and he promises to tell them the real story. When he finally recounts the circumstances of his marriage, his tale leaves both his listeners and the readers perplexed. Uncertain whether he is telling them a true story or merely teasing, Tokiko and her sister-in-law find they are left with more questions than answers. But one thing is certain: Mr. Yoshida is a very odd man.

The viewpoint of the internal audience is important. Both women— Tokiko, as an unmarried woman, and her sister-in-law, as a married woman—have certain ideas about what the word "marriage" signifies. During the Meiji period, married women legally became part of their husband's family. Upon marriage, a woman's name was removed from her own family registry and entered into that of her husband's, with some exceptions. Tokiko and her sister-in-law would expect that spouses would live together and that a married woman would live with her husband and his family, just as Tokiko's sister-in-law does. Yet Yoshida lives with an elderly woman, who is his maid. His constant assertions that he is married are deliberately confusing.

The expressions used in Japanese to describe marriage are difficult to translate succinctly into English. When Osetsu speaks of her marriage, she never actually uses the word "marriage" but rather the phrase "oyome ni ittan desu," or "to have gone as a bride." The term thus connotes the change of family from her own to her husband's. Osetsu's subsequent description of leaving the marriage or, in effect, divorcing her husband is explained by "modotte kita," literally, "I returned." The context makes it obvious that she left her husband's family and returned to her own. At the time, it was uncommon for a woman of her rank to divorce; this act is a clear break with convention. On the one hand, her actions could be interpreted as indicative of strength and an unwillingness to be sacrificed; conversely, they could also be seen as simply foolish or, worse, overly willful. Living alone at some distance from her family's mansion, Osetsu inhabits a marginal space in society, a fact that Yoshida's unkind words force her to realize.

During the Meiji period, arranged marriages were not uncommon, and neither was it unusual for daughters to be married against their will. Society expected young women to submit to their fathers and, later on, their husbands. Several Japanese women writers have focused on the sacrificing of daughters within the marriage system.[9] Shimizu Shikin's "Koware yubiwa" (The Broken Ring, 1891) and Higuchi Ichiyō's "Jūsanya" (The thirteenth night, 1895), as well as Nogami's short story "Shion" (The aster, 1908, published the same month as "Persimmon Sweets" in the journal *Shinshōsetsu* [The new novel]), depict the trials women faced in bad marriages.[10] Shikin's heroine escapes from hers, whereas the female protagonists in Nogami's "Shion," and Ichiyō's "Jūsanya" are forced to remain in unhappy unions. In essence, it was better for the woman's family, both financially and socially, if the daughter stayed with her husband—even if he were abusive.

While neither the readers of "Persimmon Sweets" nor its internal audience are privy to the details, Osetsu's marital situation was distasteful enough for her to prefer the consequences of leaving rather than staying married. Osetsu describes how she had intended to handle her unwanted marriage with the words "shinda tsumori ni natte ittan desu," which literally means "it had been my intention to die." Here, she is not stating that she planned to kill herself but rather that she would live on as if dead. In other words, Osetsu would live her married life in an emotionless state, having effectively killed off her own feelings and hopes. Yet, unable to do this, she explains, "I could not completely kill my old self off no matter how much I tried."

Equating marriage with death can be traced back to earlier eras.[11] The Shingaku movement in the 1770s, for example, taught women that as brides they "must become like a dead person"[12] and join themselves to their husbands. Only by doing so could they become good wives. In order to become a successful wife, a woman must relinquish her identity as a member of her natal family and must be willing to be reborn, so to speak, into the traditions and expectations of her husband. The concept of "good wife, wise mother," which would become prevalent in the Meiji period, had its roots in these Confucian-based ideals[13] and was also entangled in Victorian notions of domesticity, as is noted in the introduction to this volume.

Mr. Yoshida's response to Osetsu incorporates the same dark metaphor: "If marrying were really that horrible, then rather than pretending to be dead while married, wouldn't it have been best simply to die? That would have been much more sensible." These words make Osetsu cry, and Yoshida's callousness causes Tokiko and her sister-in-law to sympathize with her.

While Osetsu's tears are certainly understandable, what Yoshida relates as having occurred ten days later is surprising and propels his story in a new direction. Yoshida receives a letter from Osetsu's father asking him to accept a package with Osetsu's hair arranged carefully inside.

The letter further explains that Osetsu had wanted to marry Yoshida before she died. The critical word, of course, is "died." The death referred to here was not physical death but the now familiar metaphor for a woman's loss of self in marriage. Yoshida had told Osetsu that she ought to have died before she married (rather than pretending to be dead once married), and Osetsu declared that she would do so next time. Yoshida relays the above information about the letter and the box and then ironically states, "Well, I imagine the identity of my wife has become clear now." But it is not yet clear; turning to the symbolic value of hair allows for more understanding.

In Japan, women's hair has been a sign of beauty and femininity from ancient times.[14] During the Meiji period, as in the earlier story by Miyake Kaho, a woman might cut her elaborate coiffure if her husband died. Doing so signaled that she would not marry again. By cutting her hair, Osetsu shows that she is severing her ties to the world. She is, in essence, illustrating to Yoshida that she is capable of "dying." Osetsu's action is shocking to Tokiko and her sister-in-law. Since a woman's cutting her hair may symbolize entry into religious life, Osetsu's action illustrates that she is relinquishing her ties to the world and the marriage/family system, resulting in "total self annihilation."[15] With this symbolic death, there are two possible ways to interpret Yoshida's tale: the story is true, and Mr. Yoshida has been teasing his listeners about his marital status, or the story is pure fabrication, and Yoshida has just captured his listeners' attention with his superb storytelling capability. In the first scenario, the twist, of course, is that Yoshida's "wife" is actually a nun, a fact that he has been able to hide until the end of the tale. Yoshida's inability to produce the chignon as evidence does nothing to dispel the mystery and serves only to baffle his audience and the readers further. Yoshida's offering of persimmon sweets—a well-known product from Gifu—in lieu of the severed chignon is an amusing substitute that proves he went to Gifu but offers no closure to his listeners.

Yoshida's aptitude for keeping facts hidden allows him to create a better story. For example, it seems that Yoshida and Osetsu had a stronger relationship than he initially indicates in his story. While the details of their friendship are not given, Yoshida's impulsive decision to visit Osetsu without prior invitation, hoping for dinner and an overnight stay, suggests an intimate bond. Concealing his "wife's" identity until the last moment also builds suspense. His word choice as well reflects his uncanny ability to craft his narrative. Referring to his wife as "*okusama*," a word used for someone else's wife and not a term indicative of one's own, such as "*nyōbō*," "*tsuma*," or "*kanai*," Yoshida deliberately confuses readers and listeners alike. Additionally, Yoshida places "*san*" after Osetsu's name, indicating that she does not belong to his in-group and further illustrating that they would likely not be husband and wife. Moreover, the combination of Yoshida's use of "*okusama*" and "Osetsu-*san*" to refer to the same person, who is discovered actually to be his absent "wife," is highly unusual.

Yoshida chooses his words carefully so that his audience would not expect him to have married Osetsu. And, indeed, he did not marry her, as her religious affiliation would preclude such a relationship. In an ironic twist, readers and listeners alike learn that he is married only to Osetsu's hair, not the woman herself! Early in the narrative, Yoshida gives an important clue when he explains that someone is looking after his wife; the words he uses make it seem that she is an object and not a person. Yet ultimately his word choice makes perfect sense. The priest was looking after Osetsu's hair, or Yoshida's "wife." The use of honorifics in reference to his "wife" indicates Yoshida's respect for Osetsu. Whereas it is difficult to assert with conviction that Yoshida "learned his lesson," the fact that he remains unmarried, leads a seemingly monastic life, and pays regular summer visits to Mount Kokei suggest at least a form of penance. Perhaps he has been enlightened to the cruelty of his behavior and the burden society places on women in marriage. Additionally, his habitual references to his "wife" also make clear that he does not want to be considered a potential mate for Tokiko; he is, in all respects, unavailable.

In "Persimmon Sweets," Nogami Yaeko rewrites the Meiji equation— marriage equals death—to be life affirming. For Osetsu, her decision to cut her hair and become a nun allows her to live a life without men and the burdens of family life. This toppling of the early Meiji image of the suffering wife who sacrifices herself (or is sacrificed by others) in an unhappy marriage and who vows to live on in death suggests an important paradigm shift. Osetsu saves herself twice. The first time, she leaves a bad marriage; the second time, she opts to become a nun. While Yoshida appears to control the narrative, when the tale is over, we see that Osetsu has been the active agent in their story. It is Osetsu who operates within the limited confines of Meiji society to turn her misfortune around. Fact or fiction, Yoshida's marriage anecdote in "Persimmon Sweets" is really

Osetsu's positive story of triumph against marital odds. Unlike some of her literary counterparts, Nogami Yaeko's ability to present serious issues regarding the marriage system under the guise of a comical story told by an odd man with an unconventional life illustrates that she was aware of the power of humor. Written toward the end of the Meiji period, "Persimmon Sweets" leads Meiji women's literature into the next era, where female protagonists and women themselves more actively engage in debates on women's roles in society.

PERSIMMON SWEETS

Translated by Eleanor J. Hogan
and Midori Yonezawa Morris

Part 1

"Mr. Yoshida is certainly an odd person, isn't he?"[16]

To this, Tokiko's sister-in-law responded, "Well, he's interesting, no doubt about it!"

"What? He's distinguished, if you ask me!" Tokiko's elder brother retorted. "If there were two or three more men like him in the world, it would be better for all of us!"

Tokiko thought that her brother was rather odd himself and wondered exactly what about a man like Mr. Yoshida was so distinguished. Mr. Yoshida and Tokiko's brother had been classmates from higher school through college. Now, Mr. Yoshida was a German teacher. Well over thirty years old, he had neither wife nor family. He lived in the woods of Sugamo with an elderly maid who was hard of hearing. Tokiko thought that the dark quiet of Sugamo seemed an appropriate place for an insane asylum. What a suitable place for the likes of Mr. Yoshida. She had heard that his monthly salary from the school was a respectable eighty yen. Yet he went through all of it each month, spending half on living expenses and half at the Maruzen Bookstore. Despite all his book purchases, he did not appear to study much at all. Rather, he wandered idly about here and there regardless of the time and would often stop in to visit at Tokiko's house. Sometimes, he might even stop by twice! On Sundays, he planted himself in their house all day long, scarcely budging an inch until nearly midnight. Tokiko's brother would keep him company without ever seeming to tire of him. Tokiko often wondered what her brother found so interesting. Why didn't he ever grow weary of his companion?

"It's late, won't you please spend the night?" they all would ask. Yet, despite being urged to remain, Mr. Yoshida inevitably responded,

"No, I must return home to the missus. She's waiting for me." Then he would trudge home in the dark, walking about two and a half miles to the far side of Sugamo.

"What a joker! He has no wife!" exclaimed Tokiko as she and her sister-in-law looked at one another and laughed.

Each year when summer arrived and vacation began, Mr. Yoshida invariably stopped his wandering and went to Mount Kokei in Mino Province.

"You don't have to go as far away as Mount Kokei, do you?" Tokiko asked. "Couldn't you practice your Zen meditation at a temple in Kamakura?"

"I don't go there to sit and meditate; I go there to take naps!" replied Mr. Yoshida. "It's too loud to sleep in Kamakura."

"You mean that you go all the way to Mount Kokei just to take naps?"

"Yes, I do. It's quiet there, and I feel quite comfortable," he responded with a straight face.

Tokiko wondered how much of this was intended simply to tease her.

Whenever Mr. Yoshida wanted a kimono altered, he always brought it to Tokiko. It would have been best if he had brought advance payment, too, but he never did. Some days, he would even come and say, "I need it today," or "I need it tomorrow."

"That's ridiculous! There's no possible way I can finish it so quickly!" Tokiko would snap.

"Just stop talking and start sewing!" Then he would take the opportunity to jump in and begin lecturing her, "It's terrible if a woman can't do this sort of thing!"

Tokiko would hurriedly finish the sewing only to hear, "Well, Toki, you can sew better than I had expected. So, you'll be just fine when you marry. I'll take care of finding a good match for you."

Was this praise or simply more teasing? Tokiko was uncertain. Yet one thing was clear: Mr. Yoshida never thanked her for the alterations she made on his kimonos.

"You don't have to worry about me! But you should find yourself a wife, so you don't have to rely on me for such things. Don't you agree?" Tokiko asked her sister-in-law.

"Really, Mr. Yoshida, why is it that you don't have a wife?" Tokiko's sister-in-law asked in all seriousness.

"You may think I don't have a wife, but I do," replied Mr. Yoshida.

"Well then, where is she?"

"I've got someone looking after her."

"You're making fun of us," said Tokiko as she burst into laughter.

"What? Well, it's true."

"So when did you marry?"

"Well, it was a long time ago; when I was in college."

"That's a lie."

"Do I look like someone who would lie? Just because something isn't true, doesn't mean it is a lie."

Tokiko's sister-in-law giggled in spite of herself.

Mr. Yoshida added, "I have a lot of interesting stories about that, so another day I'll let you hear all about it."

"Yes, please do," Tokiko's sister-in-law replied, laughing.

"Why not tell us now?" inquired Tokiko.

"Hmmm. Let me see," he paused. "If I don't think about it ahead of time, I'll forget the details and get into trouble. So, anyway, I'll tell you next time," he replied casually and then left.

Part 2

The late autumn garden was alive with the pale red sasanqua, now in bloom. Tokiko and her sister-in-law were sitting in the family room taking in the view when Mr. Yoshida abruptly appeared and asked for Tokiko's brother. "Is he out?" he inquired.

"Come in," replied Tokiko's sister-in-law. "He went to Ushigome this afternoon. Please have a seat," she said, offering him a cushion.

"I'll just sit over here," he said, bringing the cushion out to the veranda.

Mr. Yoshida sat with his back to the two women, basking in the sun as he idly gazed at the garden. Since they knew him so well, there was no need for formal greetings, and so Tokiko's sister-in-law continued to sit and sew.

A sparrow flew down from the eaves, perched on the sasanqua, and then spread its wings while the fragile petals scattered. Mr. Yoshida's keen eyes followed the blossoms as they fell from the branch to the ground. The petals softly came to rest on the deep, green moss.

"How beautifully they scatter," Mr. Yoshida mused aloud.

"Why don't you finish the story you started the other day, Mr. Yoshida?" Tokiko urged from the family room.

"What? You mean about the missus?"

"Yes."

"Shall I tell you the story?" Turning toward them, he continued, "But, in return, you must promise to let me finish the whole story."

"We'll listen carefully, won't we?" Tokiko responded. Her sister-in-law simply smiled back at Tokiko as though she were suspicious about the kind of tale he was going to tell them.

"I . . . when was it? . . . It was the summer of my second year in college. As usual, I trekked into the mountains," he began.

"Mount Kokei, you mean, right?"

"Of course. I didn't have much money, so I decided to buy a ticket as far as Nagoya and then walk the rest of the way. When I passed through Gifu, I was broke. I was in trouble and very hungry, and I still had far to go. The hot sun was beating down on me. So, I sat on a rock in the shade at the side of the road pondering how I would continue my journey from there. When I thought about it all, I felt helpless and alone."

Tokiko, feeling that if this were just going to be an average travel story he need not bother to tell it, was about to complain. However, the story changed entirely as he continued:

"Just then, I happened to remember Miss Osetsu."

Immediately Tokiko asked, "Who is Miss Osetsu?"

"Well, you see, Miss Osetsu was the daughter of a wealthy farming family in Gifu. She was a relative of a family I knew and, because she used to come and stay with them for a while, I became acquainted with her. So then I was suddenly inspired and thought I would ask her if I could stay at her place for just one night. I asked people if they knew her and immediately found out where Miss Osetsu lived. I crossed a small stream and strolled up a hill. At the top, there was a stately house surrounded by white walls. Once inside, I noticed quite a few maids picking mulberry leaves and singing inside the enormous garden.

" 'Is Miss Osetsu here?' I blurted out unceremoniously. All the women turned toward me at once, white cotton cloths draped protectively over their heads, but no one answered me. Uncertain, I asked again, 'She isn't here?'

"An elderly looking woman came toward me and said, 'No, she is not at home now. May I ask who is inquiring?'

" 'Even if I gave my name, no one but Miss Osetsu would know me.'

"She stared at me with deep suspicion and asked, 'Are you from Tokyo?'

" 'Yes.'

" 'Oh, is that so? Well then, the young lady is down that way. If you follow the river to the east about half a mile, you'll soon come to a cluster of trees. She lives alone right there in a house with a new thatched roof. By all means, please go visit her. I am certain she will be pleased,' replied the woman.

"I thought it all very strange, but since the sunlight was fading, I could not very well hike up the mountain then, either. So I followed the woman's directions and, sure enough, I came upon the house by the trees with the newly thatched roof. Out front there was a short lattice fence and behind it a garden with many sunflowers in bloom.

" 'Miss Osetsu!' I shouted from outside the fence.

"I heard the sliding doors open with a swish, and she popped her head out the door. Since it was growing dark, she could not figure out who I was at first and peered into the darkness, asking 'Who is it?'

" 'It's me!' I yelled.

" 'Oh!' she exclaimed and ran out of the house. 'What brings you here?' she asked.

" 'We'll talk about this in detail later on, but could you fix me a little something to eat? I'm completely famished!' I explained.

"She ushered me inside and treated me to a large helping of grilled eggplant with miso paste, saying that it was all she had on hand. But, as you two are well aware, I am quite fond of grilled food, so I was very grateful. I ate it with gusto until I was completely full. When I saw the way her house looked, it appeared that she really did live alone. So I had to ask her why she would live in such a place all by herself with her family's magnificent mansion so close by.

" 'Well, there are various reasons,' she replied.

" 'Reasons? What might they be?' I probed.

"She was silent for quite some time and then said, 'I was married, you know.'

"I was shocked. 'You came here, to a house like this, as whose bride?' I asked.

" 'No. I used to be married. I cannot live with my family, and that is how I came to live here,' she answered.

" 'What foolishness! It isn't proper for a woman to marry and then simply walk away! So, you really did that? I never thought of you as that kind of woman,' I said, harshly reproaching her.

" 'The marriage was not my choice. I was forced into it by family obligations, and so I convinced myself to submit to the arrangement, thinking of it as a form of self-sacrifice. I would pretend that the person I knew as myself was gone forever—dead. Yet, despite my resolution, I could not live like that. I could not completely kill my old self off no matter how much I tried. So, I left the marriage,' she explained.

" 'That's preposterous! I had no idea there were women who could be married one minute and then just get up and leave the next. If marrying were really that horrible, then rather than pretending to be dead while married, wouldn't it have been best simply to die? That would have been much more sensible,' I remarked.

"I remember that my words made her cry. I, too, was distraught and, even though I had intended to stay the night, I thought it best to leave. After all, I was full, the moon was beautiful, and getting on my way seemed better than lingering there to be eaten alive by mosquitoes.

" 'Well, good-bye,' I said, thanking her for dinner. She walked me to the gate.

" 'The next time I marry, I will certainly die,' she declared.

"And that . . . that's what turned into such a serious matter," said Mr. Yoshida, pausing to take a deep breath after his long speech.

"You said 'serious.' What happened?" Tokiko asked earnestly.

Tokiko's sister-in-law, who also sympathized with Miss Osetsu, added, "You speak so harshly that I feel sorry for her."

"I became so carried away telling my story that I've become very thirsty. I'm just getting to the main part of my story, so please bring me something to drink," directed Mr. Yoshida.

Tokiko went into the living room and came back with coffee.

"So, then . . . ?" she urged him to continue.

"You are quite enthusiastic!" chuckled Mr. Yoshida, in no rush to finish his coffee.

"And then . . ." said Mr. Yoshida as he continued his story.

"Yes?" replied Tokiko. She set aside her sewing and slid forward on her knees, inching closer to him.

"I'm going to skip the whole part about climbing the mountain. So, anyway, let's imagine that I arrived safely at the temple on Mount Kokei. Then, after I had been there exactly ten days, I received a strange package and a letter. And who do you think it came from?"

"It must have been from Miss Osetsu, of course!" Tokiko replied immediately.

"No. The letter was from Miss Osetsu's father. Despite the obvious difficulties, he wanted me to accept the package because she had said that she wanted to marry me at all costs before she died."

"Oh!" exclaimed Tokiko and her sister-in-law as they both held their breath for a split second.

"Inside the package was Miss Osetsu's chignon, which had once been beautifully arranged, but now it had been cut at the base and placed inside a box. Well, I imagine the identity of my wife has become clear now," said Yoshida as he drank down his coffee.

The two women felt both tricked and bewildered. They could not determine whether he was telling the truth or lying.

"Is this a true story?" asked Tokiko.

"If you think it isn't, I imagine you'll be persuaded when I show you the chignon as evidence. It has been stored properly," Mr. Yoshida answered.

"Well then, don't forget to bring it with you tomorrow."

"Being impatient will not help matters any. I gave the chignon to a priest at Mount Kokei and asked him to hold on to it for me. So you'll have to wait until I bring it back next year," replied Mr. Yoshida casually. As he spoke, he turned toward the garden again to bask in the sun.

Two petals fell from the sasanqua, one after the other.

When Tokiko's brother returned, Tokiko and her sister-in-law repeated Mr. Yoshida's story.

"Ha, ha, ha," laughed Tokiko's brother. "That's amusing."

"Well, is it the truth? Or a lie?" Tokiko's sister-in-law asked her husband.

"Well, we just won't know until next summer, when we see if this evidence of his really exists or not."

Part 3

Six months later, Mr. Yoshida went to Mount Kokei for his summer vacation.

Upon his return, Tokiko's family asked him if he had brought the chignon back with him.

"Well," he said, "Something troubling happened. The priest with whom I entrusted the chignon is elderly; he's over eighty years old. It seems that he has liberated himself from the affairs of this world and on top of that is just plain forgetful. When I asked him if he would please retrieve the item quickly for me, he explained the situation, 'Without a doubt I was keeping it for you,' he said, 'but since I thought it was a very important thing, I put it away in a very safe place. I put it away too well, I fear, for now I have forgotten where it is.'

"The priest was beside himself, saying that this was very serious. He looked everywhere for it. He searched all over the temple and even inside the boxes of Buddhist scriptures. But he couldn't find it. Certainly next year we will find it, and I'll bring it here. I've brought you these, instead. So please be patient this year," he said, handing them two packages of persimmon sweets—a specialty from Mount Kokei.

NOTES

I would like to thank Ogikubo Yasuyuki, professor emeritus of Kokugakuin University, for his insight and assistance with my study of Nogami Yaeko, and Mr. Nobukatsu Shimoyama, director of Kokugakuin University's International Exchange Center, for providing me with access to affordable housing and a wonderful library. Finally, I gratefully acknowledge the assistance from Gettysburg College's Research and Professional Development Grant for my work on Nogami Yaeko while in Tokyo and Kyūshū.

1. Watanabe Sumiko, *Nogami Yaeko kenkyū* (Tokyo: Yagi shoten, 1969), p. 45. See also Eleanor J. Hogan's "Marriage and Women as Intertext in the Works of Nogami Yaeko and Jane Austen," (Ph.D. diss., Washington University, 2001).

2. "Tsuma to haha to sakka no tōitsu ni ikita jinsei" (Life as a wife, mother, and writer), interview by Takenishi Hiroko, in Nogami Yaeko, *Nogami Yaeko ʒenshū,* supp. 2 (Tokyo: Iwanami shoten, 1982), p. 122; and Watanabe, *Nogami Yaeko kenkyū,* p. 52.

3. Rebecca Copeland, *Lost Leaves: Women Writers of Meiji Japan* (Honolulu: University of Hawai'i Press, 2000), p. 13. See also Michael Brownstein, "*Jogaku Zasshi* and the Founding of *Bungakukai,*" *Monumenta Nipponica* 35, no. 3 (1980): pp. 319–336.

4. Promulgated in 1890, The Imperial Rescript on Education was memorized by students and read by principals at official school events. Intended to solidify a nation-state, the rescript "celebrated the family-state and its correlative, the patriarch family system, emphasizing filial piety in the classroom and family life as the source of national virtue" (Barbara Rose, *Tsuda Umeko and Women's Education in Japan* [New Haven: Yale University Press, 1992], p. 99; see also p. 100). Education gave women a role outside the family and therefore the rescript itself was rather paradoxical in regard to women—a good reason for students at Meiji Women's School not to recite it.

5. She was to state: "I did not think that I would write; however, I wanted to continue looking for knowledge and growing as a human being" (Nogami, "Tsuma to haha to sakka no tōitsu ni ikita jinsei," p. 129).

6. These informal gatherings about literature were held weekly at Sōseki's home and were attended by Sōseki's friends and fellow writers, as well as his students/disciples. See Angela Yiu, *Chaos and Order in the World of Natsume Sōseki* (Honolulu: University of Hawai'i Press, 1998), p. 216.

7. Nogami Yaeko, "Sōseki Sensei no omoide," *Nogami Yaeko ʒenshū* (Tokyo: Iwanami shoten, 1982), 22:389.

8. Nogami Yaeko, "Natsume Sōseki," in *Nogami Yaeko ʒenshū* (Tokyo: Iwanami shoten, 1982), 23:272.

9. For more on this topic, see chapter 4 of Copeland's *Lost Leaves.*

10. See Rebecca Copeland's "Shimizu Shikin's 'The Broken Ring': A Narrative of Female Awakening," *Review of Japanese Culture and Society* 6 (December 1994): 38–47; and chapter 4, on Shimizu Shikin, in her *Lost Leaves.* On Higuchi Ichiyō, see Robert Danly's translation of "Thirteenth Night" in *In the Shade of Spring Leaves: The Life and Writings of Higuchi Ichiyō, A Woman of Letters in Meiji Japan* (New Haven: Yale University Press, 1981), pp. 241–253.

11. Jennifer Robertson, "The Shingaku Woman: Straight from the Heart," in *Recreating Japanese Women, 1600–1945,* ed. Gail Lee Bernstein (Berkeley: University of California Press, 1991), p. 97.

12. Ibid., p. 95.

13. Oseki in Higuchi Ichiyō's "Thirteenth Night" uses similar terminology when she says, "Watashi sae shinda ki ni naraba," which roughly translates as, "If

I could just feel as if I were dead," when she returns to her abusive husband after telling her parents she wanted a divorce. See Higuchi Ichiyō, "Jūsanya," in *"Jūsanya," "Warekara" hoka sanpen* (Tokyo: Iwanami bunko, 1938), p. 19. Danly translates this as "I will consider myself dead," p. 249.

14. Cutting hair was the subject of debate and regulation early in the Meiji period. In 1872 a law was passed prohibiting women from cutting their hair because it would destroy "the essence of a woman's beauty" (Nishikawa Sō, *Zatsu-gaku—Kayō Shōwa shi* [Tokyo: Mainichi shinbunsha, 1980], p. 33, quoted in Barbara Sato, *The New Japanese Woman: Modernity, Media, and Women in Interwar Japan* [Durham, N.C.: Duke University Press, 2003], p. 53).

15. Ivan Morris, *The World of the Shining Prince: Life in Ancient Japan* (New York: Kodansha International, 1994), p. 120.

16. The source text for this translation is Nogami, *Nogami Yaeko zenshū*, 1:65–79.

MIZUNO SENKO
(1888–1919)

Barbara Hartley

"SHIJŪYONICHI" ("For More Than Forty Days," 1910) is a remarkable text written by Mizuno Senko, a young woman writer active in
the closing years of the Meiji period and the first half of the Taishō era.[1]
The text is a narrative account of the inscription, literal and figurative,
of women's bodies. It also relates the aspiration of one young woman
in provincial Japan to subvert the dominant social practices that exact
this inscription. The principal sociopolitical element underpinning the
narrative is that of *ryōsai kenbo* (good wife, wise mother). This was the
all-encompassing policy imposed with increasing vigilance throughout
the Meiji period as the sole normative experience for women in the new
nation of Japan. Senko's text provides concrete insights into the manner
in which the demand to be a wise wife led to an existence of exhaustion
and drudgery for the women charged with the onerous duty of keeping
physical order in a household. This it does through the representations
of the narrator and her work-worn mother. In addition, the account
provided of a young woman hovering near death following the loss of
her infant at birth clearly depicts the life-threatening physical effort demanded of women who would assume the mantle of good mother.

Poet Imai Kuniko (1890–1948), a contemporary and friend of Senko,
has written that the issue of pregnancy and its impact on women was
of vital concern to the author,[2] and it is this topic that is the focus of

"For More Than Forty Days" (hereafter "Forty Days"). The text tells of events in the Yamazaki household following the prolonged labor, and loss of a child at birth for the second time in a year, of twenty-nine-year-old O-Katsu, the eldest of three daughters in a family of moderately successful merchants. In the absence of household help and with the mother fully occupied tending to the needs of her seriously ill daughter, responsibility for the day-to-day conduct of domestic matters falls to the youngest daughter, O-Yoshi. The narration is given from the perspective of O-Yoshi, twenty years old by *kazoedoshi*, the Japanese count of ages that designates the individual as one year old at birth and then one year older on the first day of January in each successive year. The girl might thus be up to two years younger by the Western count.

Mizuno Senko, whose real name was Hattori Tei, sometimes given as Teiko or Sadako, was herself the third of three daughters in a family of merchants. She was born in 1888 in Sukagawa City, Fukushima Prefecture, where she received the newly introduced elementary education, now advocated for girls as well as boys.[3] A number of commentators, including Maeda Ai,[4] have noted the impact of the introduction of compulsory education for girls on patterns of Meiji readership and text production. Not content merely to read the texts now being written specifically for these educated girls, Senko, like the narrator of "Forty Days," began to send contributions to literary journals while still in her teens. She was first published in 1905 in *Joshi bundan* (Women's literary world, 1905–1913).

Shioda Ryōhei has noted a "firm style, free from superfluous adornment" in certain of Senko's works,[5] an element that undoubtedly ensured her success as a contributor to *Joshi bundan*. Her work appeared in other publications, including *Bunshō sekai* (Writing world, 1906–1920), edited by Tayama Katai (1871–1930), whose *Futon* (The quilt, 1907) had earlier caused a literary furor. It was Katai's ecstatic review of Senko's "Torō" (Vain efforts, 1909) that saw her entry to the literary world. The support of the editor-writer would become instrumental in both a literary and more quotidian sense, with Senko boarding briefly at the Katai household when she left Fukushima for Tokyo in 1909. Her growing stature as a writer resulted in publication of her work in journals of the caliber of *Chūō kōron* (Central forum) in 1910 and the new woman's journal *Seitō* (Bluestocking) in 1911.

FIGURE 10.1 Mizuno Senko (1888–1919) on the cover of *Joshi bundan* (April 1908)

In 1911 Senko married writer Kawanami Michizō, a union that appears to have been of little comfort to the young woman. Yukiko Tanaka cites Igarashi Rantei's suggestion that Kawanami, whose health was poor, was envious of Senko's popularity and success.[6] A number of Meiji women, including Higuchi Ichiyō and Tazawa Inabune, literally wrote themselves into the grave. Senko, too, perhaps with what Katai referred to as her "provincial shop-keeper's" sensibilities,[7] assumed huge responsibilities for supporting herself and her ailing husband. This she did through a combination of fiction writing, journalism, and editorial work. The pressure eventually proved overwhelming, and in 1916 she was diagnosed with tubercular pleurisy. Senko died in May 1919 at the age of thirty-one. She continued writing until the final year of her life, with many of her later works having a hospital setting.

"Forty Days" marks Senko's maturity as a writer of narrative. Shioda cites it as the first of her texts to demonstrate structural coherence.[8] Katai noted that the young woman's production of the work within a month of arriving at his home in Tokyo was a testament to both her exceptional talent and personal qualities.[9] The text offers a stark representation of the inscription of dominant social discourses on the body of the unmarried girl protagonist and the associated imperative of becoming a work-worn wife and mother. As the story progresses, however, this starkness is balanced by a subversive tone that resonates throughout the narrative,

the result of O-Yoshi's attempts to resist and evade the domestic responsibilities that befall her. This she does by seeking out, quite understand-
ably, the company of friends and engaging in acts of reading and writing. She also contemplates flight from the provinces to the capital, where
friends she has never met recognize her writing talents.

Critical reception of Senko's texts, however, was not always completely positive. Shioda himself found her early writing rather "frag-
mentary,"[10] while Arishima Takeo commented on an ambivalence in
Senko's work that he attributed to "self-intoxication arising from emo-
tive demands."[11] It can be argued, however, that some textual fragmen-
tation and ambivalence are only to be expected in "Forty Days." The girl
protagonist has a strong desire to distance herself from the domestic milieu and the narrowly defined roles performed by the older women in her
family. But she also simultaneously identifies with her mother and sister,
that is, with the women who assume these roles. In response to charges
of inconsistency in the writing of women in early modernity, Rebecca
Copeland has pointed to the use of ambivalence as one of a number of
"strategic subliminal devices" deployed by these writers.[12] Citing Moira
Monteith, Copeland notes that the representation of multiple subjectivi-
ties evident in their texts reflects "the writer[s'] own conflicted ambivalence and subconscious outrage—or at least confusion—at the contra-
dictory and complex demands placed upon women."[13]

"Forty Days" features little overt outrage. As the text progresses,
however, a growing sense of resistance is apparent. O-Yoshi might initially demonstrate compliance with the social norms intended to prepare
young women to be the good wives and wise mothers of the policies
promoted by the authorities. Nevertheless, she is simultaneously gripped
with the desire to avoid being sentenced to a life similar to that of her
sister or mother.

Although the protagonist of "Forty Days" is an unmarried girl, the
narrative graphically foregrounds the childbirth and postpartum experiences of this girl's married sister. It also relates the damaging, even mu-
tilating effect this has on the latter's body. As O-Yoshi notes, the "bitter
whirlpool" of marriage, that is, sexual activity followed by childbirth, is
the fate imposed on all women of the era.[14] In a discussion on *ninshin
shōsetsu*, pregnancy novels, Saitō Minako notes that pregnancy is of interest to prominent male writers only if it involves scandal or illicit liai-
son.[15] Pregnancy in the respectability of marriage, she claims, perhaps

ironically, is a call for celebration and therefore lacks the tension required for the creation of a literary space.[16] Vera Mackie's discussion of early-twentieth-century women writers' representations of the maternal body, featured in her book *Feminism in Modern Japan*, offers an alternate reading, highlighting instead the difficulties of pregnancy and birthing for women of the time.[17] Certainly, the protagonist of "Forty Days" finds nothing celebratory in her sister's experiences of "respectable" pregnancy or childbirth. On the contrary, she dreads the fact that there is no option but the specter of repeated and possibly unsuccessful childbirth, resulting even in death, for this sister, herself, or any other woman who would choose, or be required, to have sexual relations with a man.

Birth control was not unknown in Japan at the outset of the Meiji period and before.[18] By the close of the era, however, following the entrenchment of "good wife, wise mother" attitudes, giving birth had assumed a strong political imperative. The mother was now a national commodity whose role was to ensure a steady supply of young men to provide the labor and might necessary for the program of *fukoku kyōhei* (enrich the country, strengthen the military). In its quest for self-definition, the emerging nation of Japan marshaled a range of increasingly detailed regulations around the act of birthing itself. These regulations were embodied in the person of the so-called modern midwife, trained in newly introduced Western paramedical practices. A compassionate version of this new entity appears in the "Forty Days" text in the character of Sawada-san, whose modern training permits her to tend to O-Katsu's medical needs following the birth. Arguing in favor of the introduction of midwifery reforms, prominent obstetricians noted the need to nurture "new young men (*shin seinen*) for a new Japan."[19] Little consideration was given to the mother in policy deliberation. More important, the new style of midwife was expected to be cognizant of her "tremendous responsibility" to contribute to "not only the fate of families, but of the nation."[20] While midwives of the old school had also been purveyors of abortifacients and other methods of birth control, modern midwives were regularly cautioned that any aiding or abetting of these procedures was a crime.[21]

The impact of these new policies was distilled onto the birthing body, presented concretely in this text in the person of the narrator's sister. As sites of political and physical constraint, women's bodies became the object of a double bind of powerlessness. For the restraint of the birthing body was not totally the construction of patriarchal authorities performing the nationalist script of the time, according to which the only viable role for women in the emerging nation was childbirth and motherhood. Even for women who engaged in these activities purely by choice, pregnancy and childbirth could result in dramatic changes to, and sometimes the incapacitation of, the body. While "Forty Days" was written in the context of increasingly harsh demands on women, there is a textual urgency that also foregrounds the purely physical imperatives to which the bodies of women were subject. In other words, the text emphasizes physical constraints as much as cultural and political constraints. These constraints are foregrounded throughout the narrative by dramatically juxtaposing the pitifully sexualized body of the incapacitated O-Katsu against the freedom of the body of the unmarried O-Yoshi. While O-Katsu lies maimed and unwell, the embodiment of sessility, O-Yoshi is highly mobile, moving energetically in and out of the family house and around the town.[22]

A pivotal strategy employed by Senko is the contrapuntal placement of the longing for flight and pleasure on the part of the young unmarried girl against the rigidly constricted physical experiences of her older sister. This counterpoint generates a narrative territory in which corporeal experiences can be transmitted between women in a family community. Thus O-Yoshi understands her sister's ordeal as if it has been "brutally gouged out before her." This territory of transmission, however, also has a strong potential for resistance. The protagonist's observations of her sister's condition, while sympathetic, are also subversively egotistical. Elizabeth Grosz argues that women's awakening sexual identities are "dramatically overcoded with resonances of motherhood."[23] In other words, many young women have a tendency to regard motherhood as an inevitable element in the expression of their adult sexual identity. For O-Yoshi, however, intimate knowledge of her sister's maternal ordeal only activates a longing for flight and freedom and a desire to resist the demands of both domesticity and maternity.

In the closing scene, the exhausted mother expresses her frustration at being asked once more for assistance by the convalescing O-Katsu. Observing the fatigued exasperation of the older woman, whose unruly graying hair she finds "unclean," O-Yoshi is overwhelmed by the oppressive atmosphere of the sickroom, here a metonym for the "good wife, wise mother" discourse itself. Thus the dusty leaves of the alcove cuttings, the shadow of which is presented in tandem with the threateningly oversized shadow of the work-worn mother, confirm the impossibility of the project of sociopolitically defined domesticity. It is difficult to condemn O-Yoshi for self-indulgently desiring the joy of seasonal card festivities, the company of her friends, or the thrillingly seductive lure of the metropolitan literary community when the alternative is the confining and cheerless desolation of her family. For this young provincial woman, flight to Tokyo and the community of artists who recognize her prodigy offers the only possible release from the claustrophobic circumstances of family life, her mother's shadow, and the harrowing experience of childbirth to which her sister has been subject.

Ultimately, however, "Forty Days" is an account of life and vitality. For, in spite of the dire nature of the fundamental core of the narrative, there is a vigor and energy to the text that defy the oppressive discourses being visited on the girl protagonist. Both the card game and the joy of social exchange are offered repeatedly as alternatives to the drudgery of domestic confinement. The text closes with O-Yoshi finally able to indulge the former option, a triumph of play over the oppressive demands of national duty. "Forty Days" also features the pleasure of the text and the reading subject as a subversive agent, resisting the notion of woman as commodified object. It might be noted that New Year card games in Japan also involve the act of reading. The card face is inscribed with either classic texts or more pedestrian proverbs that players must read aloud and match.

A further sophisticated strategy used by Senko to inject a sense of dynamism into the narrative is to position the work, marginal provincial setting notwithstanding, firmly within the central literary community of the day. This she does by selected references to the commercial texts of highly regarded contemporary writers. Five texts are mentioned, namely Murai Gensai's *Chi no namida* (Tears of blood) and *Koneko* (The kitten),[24] *Ichiyō zenshū* (The collected works of Ichiyō),[25] Futabatei Shimei's *Sono omokage* (*An adopted husband*),[26] and Natsume Sōseki's *Wagahai wa neko de aru* (*I am a cat*).[27] While Futabatei's star may have subsequently dimmed in the literary firmament, and Murai's has been almost extinguished, both were immensely popular at the time. It is also interesting that a twenty-two-year-old provincial woman would have the perspicacity to affiliate in this way with two writers, Natsume Sōseki and Higuchi Ichiyō, who would both later be recognized as undisputed stellar performers in the field of Japanese literature. Thus, in the final analysis, "Forty Days" subverts the dominant narrative of women as commodified wives and mothers. This it does by profiling the conviviality of friends, the justifiable self-indulgence of festive gatherings at which both women and men can sustain themselves in the face of social constraints, and the liberating power of the text.

FOR MORE THAN FORTY DAYS

Translated by Barbara Hartley
and Tomoko Aoyama

1

O - Y O S H I   S A T at the heater, asleep, her head resting on her arms.[28]
Waking suddenly, she realized that sunlight was streaming through the
window high on the wall above her. She leaped to her feet with a start
and looked around the room. The street outside was already filled with
the clatter of passing traffic and the noisy voices of children. Everyone
in the shop, though, was still sleeping soundly. "Seiji, Seiji, wake up!" she
called to the shop's errand boy as she loosened the obi that was coming
undone and tidied the front of her kimono. It had been just dawn when
the two doctors, lanterns in hand, had left the front entrance of Yamasa
to make their ways in opposite directions, north and south, along the
street outside. Even so, it had taken almost an hour for the family to
settle down and catch some sleep. The midwife had stayed to tend the
patient after the birth. Finally, undoing the kimono sleeves she had tied
back for work, she made ready to take her leave. Neither O-Yoshi nor
her mother wanted her to go. But the woman was exhausted. She had
been at the bedside for a night, a day, and then another night and could
stay no longer. Instead, at the urging of the girl and her mother, the midwife agreed to return later that day after resting. O-Yoshi, wandering
aimlessly through the house, had peeked into the formal room where her

sister lay. Seeing the restless girl, Mother had sent her to get some sleep. Then the older woman covered herself with a quilt and took watch over her eldest daughter, who had just given birth.

As O-Yoshi recalled the dreadful turmoil of two or three hours before, her sister's cries resounded once more in her ears. Last night, she had made a light meal of boiled eggs for the people gathered in the house. Several were tending the patient; others were just waiting for the birth. O-Yoshi had been the only one there to look after the guests, and the shells still lay where the eggs had been peeled on a plate in the kitchen. A bottle stood in a corner with a few remaining servings of yellow Masamune. This was the sake O-Yoshi had fetched from the shop and served her guests instead of tea.

Mother was fearful her eldest daughter would not recover. It was always hard when a newborn died, and this had been a very difficult birth. It was not unexpected, though. Barely a year before, the young woman had suffered a similar ordeal and been bedridden for two months or so. Seiji was sent to fetch Senzō, an old worker from the Echigo region who was often seen in the shop. While the patient slept, a box of white wood was placed gently down on the verandah, fastened with rope, and then hoisted onto the old worker's back. Mother wrapped a kimono lined with red around the little coffin, and Senzō covered this with a straw cape to hide it from view. Dressed in a loose coat and with a handful of red incense sticks in the sleeve pocket of his kimono, Sōzaburō, O-Katsu's husband and the father of the dead child, finally set out with the older man following.

The midwife returned in the early afternoon to tend the patient and check her temperature. "How is she? It's not too high, is it?" asked the young woman's mother, supporting herself with her pipe as she made her way across the floor on her knees toward the midwife. "It's not so good," came the answer. "I'd expect a small rise, but it's about thirty-eight point five," said the midwife, holding her head to one side and looking concerned.

The next day, the patient complained of swollen breasts. Though the young woman's nipples were still quite small, Mother took them between her fingers and sucked at them like a child, spitting the fluid she drew into a teacup. At first, all that appeared was a pale, watery liquid. However, Mother tried to make time to suckle her daughter's breasts now and again, and the liquid gradually became thick and white. Filled with sadness at the thought of emptying the girl's milk into the privy, Mother diluted it with water and poured it into the kitchen sink.

In the lamplight of early evening, the patient's face was clearly flushed. So Mother and O-Yoshi found the thermometer stored in the chest of drawers. O-Yoshi sat knitting beside the brazier in the living room when Mother called her to check the temperature. The girl was alarmed to see the reading of the thin stream of mercury in the thermometer the older woman placed before her.

"What does it say?" asked Mother.

"Thirty-nine point two," replied O-Yoshi.

"Thirty-nine point two?" echoed Mother.

"Thirty-nine point two?" chimed in O-Yoshi's elderly father, listening from his seat beside the heater.

During the past two years, father's sight had gradually dimmed, as if layers of silk had fallen, one by one, across his eyes. As a young man, he had often read medical books and knew a little about health matters. He would also become alarmed at the first sign of illness. The girl's parents called Sōzaburō in from the manager's office, and the three gathered around the heater wondering whether to call a doctor. While they were talking, the patient's voice was heard behind the screen. "Mother, Mother," she called in a weak voice to the older woman.

2

The family decided to call Doctor Seto, who wore tinted glasses, and his rickshaw was often seen standing outside the house. The midwife had trained in modern nursing and also came each day to tend the patient. She looked concerned as, with her pencil, she methodically recorded the highs and lows of the young woman's temperature on a chart.

Later that night, while her mother rested, O-Yoshi sat watching the patient, whom she thought was asleep. Suddenly, her sister murmured something in a dull voice. "What is it? Is something wrong?" O-Yoshi cried. Laying her magazine on the little heater at which she was warming her hands, she looked down at her sister's face. The young woman's eyes gazed back blankly. Alarmed, O-Yoshi called to her mother. "Katsu, O-Katsu, are you in pain?" asked Mother, gently placing her hand on her daughter's forehead. "I knew something was wrong before when her face was so flushed," said the older woman to herself.

Sōzaburō was quickly summoned and immediately sent Seiji for the doctor. The patient's temperature had soared to just over forty-one degrees, and, with the expected crisis finally upon them, the family gathered restlessly around the sick bed. The doctor, who apparently hired a rickshaw only for day rounds, arrived in his house clothes lighting the way with a carriage lamp. Seiji, medical bag in hand, followed in the sleet behind the doctor's old-style umbrella. The doctor made a routine check of the patient's pulse and then her temperature, which had dropped a degree or so. But her breathing was still labored, and she complained of the heat of the quilt at her chin. When the doctor left, Seiji went off to get the prescribed medicine.

News soon spread, and various people came to inquire after the young woman's condition. One was the mistress of Kanōya, a condiment wholesaler Father had often helped out. She and her husband looked for every tiny profit and had made a worthwhile fortune with their penny-pinching ways. She came by regularly to offer advice, pointing out, for instance, that there was no need to make tea for every visitor. Much better, she said, for the family simply to send a thank-you gift later. She also told O-Yoshi how to make a simple but tasty dish of preserved vegetables.

O-Take came, too. She was a distant relative who ran a dry goods store in Shin-Yoshida and was disliked by the whole family. Most of her time was spent finding fault. Envious of success, she loved nothing better than to see others struggle and fail. O-Katsu hated the woman, saliva wedged in the corners of her mouth, and would feign sleep at the sound of O-Take's voice to keep her out of the sickroom.

There was also the wife of a friend of Father's, a man who had been O-Katsu's tea ceremony teacher when she was young. Lame since childhood, he now earned his living soothsaying and making herbal remedies. His wife was a good woman, although perhaps a little simple. She would stay in the sickroom, even when the doctor and nurse washed their hands and put on their white coats to tend the patient. She seemed to have no idea of the embarrassment this caused to the others in the room.

Some visitors looked in only now and again, including the women from the neighboring houses and the family opposite. "There's nothing to be done for the baby," each said as she left. "It's the mother you must care for now. She's young. She can always have another child." Gifts also came from businesses that dealt with the shop. Many sent eggs to build the patient's strength.

The patient's temperature was not constant at forty degrees. The nurse's graph was a series of ups and downs, and there were days when the reading was almost normal. The family, however, lost confidence in the doctor with the tinted glasses. It was no longer just a case of childbirth, and there was a feeling that someone with modern medical training was needed. Finally, the family decided to consult a young doctor, fresh from medical school, whose practice had opened just the previous week. People love novelty, and this doctor was so popular that appointments were only by special request. Luckily, the proprietor of Kanōya had the contacts needed and went after hours to the doctor's back door to plead the family's case.

That evening, the patient developed a terrible case of the tremors. Alarmed, neither O-Yoshi nor Mother was sure what to do, and they hurriedly called Sōzaburō. Tetsuo, one of the workers from the shop, went for the doctor but returned to say he was at the house of another patient. The tremors had by then subsided, but the patient's temperature now soared, and she threw off her quilt. The new doctor, a remarkably tall man, appeared the next day just as O-Katsu was struck by a second bout of the tremors. "I'm freezing, I'm freezing," she cried. Mother and O-Yoshi rushed to help. They covered the young woman with every flat quilted cushion at hand and pressed with all their might to warm her. Very soon, though, O-katsu complained of the heat. Keeping her covered, the new doctor gently took her pulse while calmly questioning Sōzaburō about the illness. The family no longer called the doctor with the tinted glasses. They paid him the bill owing for medicine and sent half a dozen bottles of beer as thanks for his service.

3

The shortest day of the year came and went. The weather was bitterly cold, and snow fell daily. O-Yoshi's diary often read:

25 degrees.

A freezing, freezing morning, and a cold, cold day. Offering rice froze in the bowls on the family altar.

Another morning she wrote:

Broke the ladle smashing the frozen surface of the water tank.

The pigeons' feet left maple leaf patterns across the white frost and snow covering the frozen ground in front of the storehouse. The bucket slipped and slid on the ice formed by water spilled around the edge of the well. The bucket rope was so cold it was painful to touch.

By now, O-Yoshi was in charge of both the upstairs and downstairs of the house. She would never have thought she could manage alone or that she ever would have had to. In the past, she helped her mother and eldest sister each morning and evening. But, like other girls her age, she also went to sewing school. She would leave the house when her chores were done and often did not return until nightfall. O-Yoshi felt no obligation to help out in the house. In fact, until now, she had managed to enjoy each day without too many worries at all.

O-Yoshi loved reading. Her obsession with books began in her early teens when she still wore her hair with bangs. It was then that she discovered stories, such as Murai Gensai's *Tears of Blood* and *The Kitten*, hidden beneath her middle sister's sewing. Japanese verse, modern poetry, novels: she read whatever she could. She knew nothing about the differences between women and men until she was seventeen. It was then that her body began to change, and she burst into tears when her mother first told her about being a woman. But neither her shock nor her amazement lasted. "I hope you'll all congratulate me. I'm nineteen now," she had cried last New Year as she visited her teachers and friends. They were often amused by the odd things she said. But she could scarcely believe she was so old. Even the sound of the word "nineteen" rang strangely in her ears.

"Good morning." Or, "Isn't it dreadful weather?" People would greet her politely, but O-Yoshi would barely reply. Then Mother would scold her and tell her to be more grown up. But O-Yoshi was proud to be called childish. With Mother now often at her sister's bedside, however, it was O-Yoshi who had to receive the guests when they came to ask after the patient. She gradually learned to be more polite, becoming less awkward and chatting confidently with adults. But as she sat beside the long open heater, offering tea and tobacco to guests, she began to understand that being a woman inevitably meant marrying and becoming a housewife.

She brought tea to the visitors, lit braziers to warm the doctor's carriage men, provided hot water to wash hands, made more tea, and checked for dust on the leaves of the sacred bamboo cuttings in the vase on the family altar. She even tidied the shoes left inside the entrance. Responsible now for the whole house, she realized just how much there was to do. Sometimes, she worked into the night. With only a hand towel over her head for cover against the bitter weather, she would wash the rice for the evening meal in a pail on a board across the frozen well. Flakes of snow whirled around her and melted softly into her kimono. Hearing the sound of the squeaking well pulley from the sickroom, her sister would murmur in a querulous voice, "Oh dear, poor Yoshi, out in the snow still working. . . ."

O-Katsu lay on her sickbed watching events around her. "When will I ever get well?" she thought anxiously to herself. "I'm twenty-nine and have been pregnant yet again. But I've nothing to show except sadness and pain. I did so resent the gods for leaving me childless. But I can't think forever like that. As I lie here, it's clear there's so much to do. Father is blind, and can Mother's hair really be turning gray? There are my sisters, as well. They need me, too. But it's Sōzaburō who needs me the most. He's rushing around trying to manage alone with the end of the year upon him. But there's so much to do. The shop staff are still wearing their outfits from autumn, even though we're well into winter. And when Seiji came in with my medicine just now, his big toe was sticking right out of his *tabi* sock. This is all too much! I can't bear being like this. I must try to get well."

The sounds in the cramped house echoed sharply in O-Katsu's ears. The voices of the delivery boys and clients doing business, the footsteps of staff rushing with goods to the storehouses out back: she heard it all as if it were right beside her. And she noticed all sorts of things around her. There was the missing glove she had searched everywhere for, now shabby and mouse-eaten, lying at the back of a cupboard, and the shaft jutting out from a broken cart yoke leaning against the fancy-goods shop next door.

4

"O-Yoshi, I know that you're busy, my dear. But Mother would like you to go to the Inari Shrine and pray for your sister. Make sure the god knows that if she recovers we'll make an offering to the shrine."

Although she was too young to scorn her father's ideas openly, as she changed her clothes, O-Yoshi dismissed his simple beliefs as nothing more than superstition. Even so, she, too, wanted to believe that an offering to the gods might somehow help her sister. A light snow had fallen earlier in the evening and was now melting, dripping down from the eaves between the houses. Snow covered the mud and lodged in the ridges of her street clogs, wetting her *tabi* socks.

"Mother is fretting," she thought to herself. "She thinks nothing can help O-Katsu. But can people really die so easily? Surely my sister won't die. How could she possibly die?" O-Yoshi had heard of people dying before but had never really been troubled about it. She had certainly never thought of death visiting her own family. "Will O-Katsu die? Please don't let her die!" The mere idea was unbearable. O-Yoshi shuddered as she thought of the effect her sister's death could have on the family.

"Sōzaburō is the Yamazaki family's adopted son," she reasoned. "But if O-Katsu dies, then his bond with our family will be broken, and my parents and he would part ways. And what if he married again—maybe someone from outside the family? My parents and he would drift even further apart. But sometimes they marry a younger sister to an adopted son when the older girl dies. Oh no! What if they married *me* to Sōzaburō?? How unbearable! I would hate it. The very thought terrifies me. If they made me do that, I would die. But dying is not for me. It might just be my chance to leave at last for Tokyo. . . ."

More than anything, O-Yoshi longed to be a writer. She had been writing for some time now and had already sent letters and stories to various magazines. But there was little hope. A woman could never do what she liked. "Dear Inari, if you really exist," she thought to herself, "take me and let my sister live." As her feelings welled up inside her, O-Yoshi became quite despondent. And although before long she was passing beneath the shrine entrance, she was too distracted to join her hands dutifully and deliver her mother's prayer.

5

The nurse who came each day from the doctor's to tend the patient often gossiped with the midwife. Her favorite stories were about the doctor's wife. One day, however, O-Yoshi overheard the pair together on the veranda.

"Sawada–san," said the midwife, "you know O-Sumi, the young woman from the Ishii family? Would you believe she's in hospital?"

"What? Again?"

"That's right. I heard she's had no period for three months, so . . ."

O-Yoshi's face reddened as she walked away. She was shocked to think that nurses and midwives talked about such things.

The woman from Kanōya offered to send a maid to help out. But O-Yoshi said she could manage alone. So she did all the household chores, even washing Sōzaburō's underwear. When she was younger, her own *tabi* socks would be quickly soiled by the muddy puddles of snow melting in the street. Returning home, she would take them off and throw them down, not bothering to look for a fresh pair when none were at hand. Mother would scold O-Yoshi at the sight of the girl's bare, chilblained feet. The older woman could often be found washing dirty *tabi* socks beneath the broken icicles that hung from the eaves at the back of the house. When O-Yoshi returned from school or, as she grew older, from sewing classes, Mother would be bent over the brazier, sewing. The girl recalled how, having chosen the whitest socks that needed the least darning, Mother would cut the thread as she finished her stitching. But only now was it clear to O-Yoshi that it was a woman's lot to wash and mend clothes, especially for the men in the family.

Although the house had a bath, O-Yoshi tried to make time to visit the local bathhouse. But the cold outside turned her lips blue, and she had gone without bathing for three or four days. Finally, however, she ventured outdoors, towel in hand. It was dark outside so she did not bother to change from the old quilted jacket she wore in the house. As she rounded the corner into the side street to the bathhouse, she met a friend from her school days lighting the way with a lantern.

"Goodness, is that you, O-Yoshi? Whatever are you wearing?" asked the friend, laughing.

"Well, I do have to work now, you know," replied O-Yoshi.

"Work? Are you really working?"

"Don't you believe me? Look here. Look at how hard I work," declared O-Yoshi, thrusting her clenched fists out before her friend. The backs of her hands were chafed, making them rough and scaly. "Oh, that's terrible," cried her friend, looking shocked. At school, O-Yoshi had been a lively and friendly girl. And being able to write had made her the teachers' favorite. It was clear her friend found it hard to believe she should now have to work in this way.

Seiji was a good-natured boy, and he soon made friends with the live-in apprentice at the pharmacy store he visited daily for O-Yoshi's sister's medicine. Sometimes, he would stay talking too long and be scolded by Sōzaburō. Even so, he was often thoughtful enough to bring remedies home for O-Yoshi's chafing and frostbite. One day, when he returned with ointment for her feet, he also gave O-Yoshi a letter.

"Yoshi, Yoshi, Kimishima sent this for you," he cried.

"Kimishima?" O-Yoshi asked.

"You know. The young man from the pharmacy store. The apprentice," Seiji explained in a hurry.

O-Yoshi opened the letter, read it and smiled, then threw it away. There were a couple of simple verses declaring the writer's love. O-Yoshi often received love letters from young men that, like this one, praised her writing talents.

The frostbite on O-Yoshi's feet was raw and bleeding and refusing to heal. "It's too much for one person. Why don't you let someone like Tami give you a hand?" suggested Sōzaburō's elder sister when she dropped by one day. "My goodness, my dear, you do work hard." O-Yoshi's labors always impressed the woman from Kanōya, whose second son would soon be taking a bride.

6

An assortment of gifts was exchanged at the end of the year. There were mandarins, fish roe, cotton padding for quilts, dried tofu, bags of sugar, and salted salmon, their tails tied with ceremonial string.

For some time now, there had been a hard swelling on the left side of O-Katsu's abdomen. Her temperature was no longer abnormally high. But, since it was still above normal, the doctor was keen to apply leeches. So, one day, O-Yoshi was sent to buy a supply from the house of a farmer behind the town. A few patches of snow remained in the hollows between the vegetable fields and at the foot of tree stumps around which wound spindly dead vines. In the gray dark of the twilight, the wind blew icily against O-Yoshi's cheeks. Stands of one or two thatched houses were dotted around the lonely outskirts of the town.

The old farmer, his face red from the glow of the fire, had nothing to sell. "You can offer as much as you like," he explained, "but I'm afraid I can't help you. It's winter. They curl up like little beans and hide away. You could offer a fortune for each leech, but there's not a one to be found. There's nothing I can do," he said from his seat by the fire. They finally bought the leeches through a contact in another town. Luckily, they were no longer needed by the time the small parcel arrived, and the leeches were just put to one side, moving around in the bottle.

"Why, hello there. Come on in," O-Yoshi cried. She missed her friends, and when one young woman came by after sewing class to drop something off and to ask after the patient, O-Yoshi urged her to stay.

"Who's still going to class these days?" she asked. "Has Taka-chan been there?"

"Taka-chan's been away for a while," came the reply. "It's the end of the year so everyone's busy. It's my last day, too. And O-Hide's been so ill with a cold she's hardly been seen at all."

"Really?"

Taking a break from her chores, O-Yoshi thought wistfully of her friends sitting in their sewing class circle. She recalled them bent over their work and how, now and again, they would stretch, exchange glances, and laugh noisily.

"How's your sister? Is she on the mend?" inquired the friend.

"She's getting better, but she's not really recovered yet. Her temperature is still up."

"You're so busy, doing everything yourself . . . and look at your hands." The friend grasped the hands that O-Yoshi was warming over the brazier and frowned.

"They're so rough," said O-Yoshi. "They don't even seem like my own hands . . . and look at this." Laughing, she pulled the torn opening of the sleeve of her red undergarment out from her kimono.

"Our teacher says hello," said her friend. "She's wanted to visit your sister, but she's been too busy with work. You remember. It's the betrothal of the boy from Iseya. Our teacher has made some beautiful things, especially the obi. It's just wonderful. Why don't you come and see for yourself when everything's finished? There's only the black kimono left to do. After that, the whole outfit will be ready."

"When's the wedding?"

"February the first."

"Fancy Bon-chan getting married." Hearing the nickname "Bon-chan," both girls burst into laughter.

"What are you sewing?" As her friend was about to leave, O-Yoshi peeped into the girl's sewing bag. "How lovely," she cried. "Is it for you?"

The friend laughed happily and nodded.

"Oh well," said O-Yoshi, "you won't be seeing me at any New Year card games this year." She gave a rather lonely laugh as she said good-bye.

That evening, O-Yoshi made up a parcel to send to her middle sister studying medicine in Tokyo. The girl had written a note to say she needed a new kimono. Mother had bought and dyed some cheap silk, and the finished kimono had been delivered earlier that day. O-Yoshi was struggling to wrap some sweet bean jelly and rice cakes with the outfit. Mother, anxious to have the goods sent, tried to intervene. "Leave me alone! I'm doing it, aren't I?" O-Yoshi retorted impatiently, red in the face, making an even greater mess of the parcel.

"Don't talk like that to your mother, you cheeky girl. There's no need to be so cross. I only said we needed to hurry up and send it off to Kimi. She's waiting down there in Tokyo with no idea of what's going on here. We don't want her worrying with exams drawing near."

"All right! I heard you!" O-Yoshi snapped crossly.

Aware she was behaving badly, O-Yoshi nevertheless longed for the freedom to do as she pleased. And, jealous of those who could do what they liked, she became angry and fell into a sulk. After a while, the thin sound of her sister's voice came from behind the screen. "Yoshi, Yoshi," the patient called. It was too much for O-Yoshi. Clenching her teeth in frustration, she could not help bursting into tears.

7

The seasonal rice cakes were made by Sōzaburō's sister's family. With their help, O-Yoshi and her parents eventually managed the usual New Year celebrations. Now that the old year had ended, O-Katsu also seemed to improve. There were even whole days when her temperature remained normal. But she was still very weak and found it hard to bear sounds like the endless voices of clients in the back rooms or the opening and closing of doors. Signs were put on the doors requesting quiet when entering or leaving a room. Thoughtless Seiji, however, was scolded two or three times a day for stamping noisily through the house and slamming the doors behind him.

Invitations came regularly to card games at friends' houses. O-Yoshi wrote back to decline. Feeling sorry for her, Mother and O-Katsu bought her a copy of *The Collected Works of Ichiyō*, which O-Yoshi longed to own. They also gave her a novel by Futabatei Shimei that people were reading, called *An Adopted Husband*.

One evening, O-Yoshi was on her way to buy the special New Year edition of a magazine. As she passed by the house of a friend, she decided on whim to drop in. "Well, if it isn't O-Yoshi," greeted the mother, calling her daughter. A group of four or five had gathered in the cheerful formal room for a game of cards. O-Yoshi longed to join in. "Hello," she said as she entered the room. Everyone turned, and she was suddenly embarrassed to realize she was wearing her ordinary work clothes. "Hey, look who it is. We haven't seen you for ages," cried the younger brother of one of the girls.

Because O-Katsu complained of the weight, the quilt had been hung from the ceiling with cord. But the young woman still found it painful to lie still for too long. Her leg would cramp, and she would jump and cry out in pain if it was touched. To turn her, someone would slip both hands under the quilt and roll her by grasping her waist. The patient had also been wrapped in cotton wadding to protect against bedsores. O-Yoshi kept watch until ten or eleven each evening, after which Mother or Sōzaburō took over. Snuggling beneath the small quilt that covered the heater, O-Yoshi would sit beside the steaming brazier reading magazines and listening to the ticking of the bedside clock. She also read Sōseki's *I Am a Cat* out loud as O-Katsu listened.

Now and again, O-Yoshi wrote letters to friends she had never met in Tokyo and other large towns. Many urged her to leave for the capital. She would explain that she was caring for her elderly parents and her family. But the reply always came that she needed to think of herself. Warming her frozen hands over the fire, she would write back to say that she just couldn't leave. The letters from men often had words crossed out that O-Yoshi was unable to read. Tilting her head bemused, she would smilingly hold the paper up to the light and try to make out what they had written at first.

One day, the midwife, Sawada-san, missed her daily appointment at the house. The nurse waited some time, but there was still no sign of the other woman. Since Seiji was out on an errand, O-Yoshi was sent to the midwife's room in the boardinghouse run by the Oki family. Many of the boarders were students at the local sewing school, and the merry laughter of a card party could be heard behind the wooden fence. O-Yoshi was told that Sawada-san had been called at dawn to the house of a woman about to give birth and had not yet returned. As the girl turned to leave, the sliding door of the party room opened with a clatter.

"Why, Yoshi-chan." A young woman's face appeared at the door.

"Oh my, what a surprise," said O-Yoshi.

The young woman was a friend of O-Yoshi's middle sister. As a child, O-Yoshi had been a favorite of the girl, who was now here for the card games. "They said your eldest sister's been unwell. How is she?"

"Not too bad, thanks."

"Well, I hope she takes care of herself."

The girl's family was wealthy, and her outfit neat and stylish.

Just at nightfall, Sawada-san appeared, flustered, at the back door of the shop. "I'm so sorry about today," she apologized. "Young Mrs. Okano went into labor. It was actually quite an easy birth for a first baby. They said she started having pain about two this morning. Her father-in-law made a great fuss, but in the end she produced a perfectly beautiful baby girl." She slapped her flushed cheeks with both hands. Remarking how hot she felt, the midwife explained that the Okano family had insisted she stay for a drink.

8

One day, Mother was sitting with Father by the brazier. "Have you noticed how inconsiderate Sōzaburō has been?" she asked. "You'd think he'd realize how everything must sound to someone who's so unwell. But he just keeps banging that pipe of his against the metal brazier. It's so loud, it even makes me feel on edge when he does it beside me."

"Mm, you're right," agreed Father. "He really should take more care. He's not a bad person, more like thoughtless. But it's a problem." The old man rested the arms he had been warming on the edge of the brazier.

"What can we do when he takes no notice?"

Just then, Sōzaburō came in busily from the shop and cast a glance at his in-laws.

"Have you finished in there? Would you like some tea?" asked Mother rather uncomfortably, picking up her pipe as if she had just remembered it.

"No, thanks," said Sōzaburō curtly, returning to the shop.

"We have to make sure Kimi passes her exams. We can't expect Sōzaburō to keep supporting her." As Mother and Father drank their tea, the conversation once again turned to their son-in-law. Finding them whispering as he came down the stairs, Sōzaburō went straight into the shop, looking annoyed.

Three days passed uneventfully. The next evening, Sōzaburō returned home with a cut of pork in bamboo wrapping tucked into the front of his kimono. O-Yoshi brought the portable burner to the table and set up the pot for cooking. As the white steam bubbled up beside the lamp, the unfamiliar aroma of pork fat wafted through the house.

"Father, the meat is cooked," said Sōzaburō, piling the food onto a plate himself and offering it to his father-in-law.

"What have you got there?" asked the old man. "Pork? I'm afraid I'm not eating today."

"Not eating?"

O-Yoshi stole a glance at Sōzaburō's face.

Certainly, since her father was blind, it was hard for him to realize what was going on. But her mother, too, seemed to have difficulty understanding Sōzaburō's feelings. Only O-Yoshi was concerned and uneasy. By now, both sides were on edge, so that even a small cough seemed suspicious. O-Yoshi wanted her mother to realize why Sōzaburō looked at them warily. When her parents whispered together, she would talk about other things to have them leave off conspiring. At mealtimes, she gave Sōzaburō the choicest morsels, even when serving plain broiled fish.

One day, Sōzaburō was away from the house all day. He would generally let his young wife know his plans. But this day he left saying nothing.

"I say, O-Sen, do you think Sōzaburō is fed up with our daughter and her illness?" The aging father had spent the day crouching over the heater. When night came without the sound of Sōzaburō's voice, he had worriedly called to his wife as he heard her footsteps pass by.

"Of course not. What a thing to say! Absolutely not!"

Mother herself seemed not so concerned. Sōzaburō eventually returned and casually told them that he had dropped in at his sister's on the way home from work and ended up staying for dinner. Everyone was relieved that there was no flush of alcohol on his face.

It was a rare sight to see Sōzaburō open a bottle of sake and place it on the tray before him. But this he did one evening after speaking to no one throughout the day. He settled himself beside the iron brazier, where, in between drinks, he would draw on his pipe, banging it loudly again and again against the metal heater. Since he almost never drank, his face quickly became bright red. He roundly chastised Seiji, who looked puzzled at the novel sight of his master drinking. Finally, without eating, Sōzaburō left the house. The old couple sent Seiji after him, and the boy reported that the master had gone drinking with a friend in Shin-Yoshida.

O-Katsu also noticed the tension between her husband and her parents.

"What's going on, Mother? Whatever have you done?" she asked worriedly.

"I don't know what the problem is. I've said nothing. He's just being hard to get along with."

At this point, O-Yoshi joined in. "I told you this would happen, Mother. You've actually said all sorts of things. . . ."

For some reason, we always complain about those for whom we care the most.

"What have I said?" asked Mother, looking shocked at her daughter's accusations.

"You mightn't have said anything today, but lately you've done nothing but whisper with father about Sōzaburō."

"But we haven't said anything bad about him, have we?"

"You shouldn't have said anything at all. And every time he comes in, you just stop. It would make anyone suspicious. Of course he'd think you were talking about him."

O-Yoshi attacked her mother, tears streaming down her face. All the worries in her heart seemed to well up in a tangle, making her words very sharp.

"Oh, I see. It's all my fault, is it?" cried Mother. "It's me who's the only bad one, is it? Well then, if that's how it is, perhaps the gods should take me away instead of O-Katsu. I could die having spent my whole life worrying about my children. . . ."

Mother was crying now, too. Quick though she had been to attack, O-Yoshi couldn't bear Mother striking back. She cried all the more and buried her face in her sleeve in distress.

"What shall I do? This is all because I'm sick. . . ." Tears also streamed down O-Katsu's face.

"Katsu, Katsu, please don't worry yourself," cried Mother, alarmed. "It's nothing. There's nothing to worry about. You'll end up making yourself unwell again."

Sōzaburō came in around ten, his face bright red. "Would you like me to grill some rice cakes for supper?" O-Yoshi asked. Sōzaburō noticed his sister-in-law's swollen eyes. "I don't need to eat," he replied gently. With that, he stretched out on his back at the heater and fell asleep.

9

O-Katsu was clearly improving day by day. However, she still needed help to turn over or change position in bed. Having seen his ill wife's tears, Sōzaburō mended his ways and made sure he spent time with the family each morning, especially his in-laws.

The nurse and Sawada-san, the midwife, continued to visit the house. After tending the patient, they gathered around the brazier to gossip. O-Yoshi would bring them tea and something to eat, such as a vegetable condiment she'd made. Occasionally, she grilled them a rice cake. As Sawada-san was leaving, O-Yoshi often wrapped up a small parcel of mandarins or dried persimmons for the midwife's children.

Dust had gathered on the necks of the bottles of wine and medicine that stood on the small, low table beside the patient's bed. Here and there, in amongst the writing on the screen that had been used to shield the sick bed all this time, O-Yoshi could see faint marks. They looked like splatters of blood. Staring at them closely, she was reminded of that terrible, terrible evening. To be a woman meant having children and giving birth to a new generation for the family. She had heard it said that adopting a husband into the family could be good for a daughter, but it could also cause deep pain. As she thought about this, it became clear to O-Yoshi what her sister had gone through, as if all the demands that consumed O-Katsu had been brutally gouged out before her. It was the fate of every woman, including herself, to be drawn into this bitter whirlpool. She thought of her friends who urged her to Tokyo.

"Mother, I'm sorry, but can you turn me over again?" pleaded O-Katsu in an apologetic voice.

Mother, who was nodding off to sleep under the quilt she had pulled over herself, sat up abruptly. "Again?" she said, dragging herself to her feet. "This is all such a bother. I just turned you over not so long ago."

"Sorry," replied O-Katsu pathetically, in a low voice.

The older woman's words sounded harsh to O-Yoshi. How could Mother say such a thing after having been so worried about O-Katsu? O-Yoshi suddenly recalled the other day when her sister had confided, "I think Mother is getting a bit tired of all this." At the time, O-Yoshi thought her sister ungrateful. Her mother's graying, fuzzy hair now appeared unclean. As the older woman lay slumped across the heater, stealing some sleep, her oversized shadow loomed above them on the wall. The vase that held the sacred bamboo cuttings was now dry, and the dusty leaves threw their own shadow across the scroll that hung on the alcove wall. O-Yoshi felt the air in the room become oppressively close.

"We're so relieved and thankful." O-Yoshi listened as her mother reminisced to the woman from Kanōya. "It's been forty days or more for all of us. O-Yoshi and I barely had time to change our clothes. We just took turns sleeping here beside the heater. It was dreadful. We were all beside ourselves with worry."

A few days before, O-Katsu suggested that, when she was well enough to get out of bed, O-Yoshi should invite all their friends, including the nurse and Sawada-san, for a card day. Finally, O-Yoshi had something to look forward to.

NOTES

1. Mizuno Senko, "Shijūyonichi," in *Meiji joryū bungaku shū*, vol. 2, ed. Shioda Ryōhei, vol. 82 of *Meiji bungaku zenshū* (Tokyo: Chikuma shobō, 1965), pp. 354–364.

2. Imai Kuniko, "Mizuno Senko-san no omoide," in *Meiji bungaku zenshū* 82 *(Meiji joryū bungaku shū* 2), ed. Shioda Ryōhei (Tokyo: Chikuma shobō, 1965), pp. 399–405. See p. 401.

3. For a more detailed account of Senko's life, see Fukuya Yukiko, "Nenpu," in *Meiji bungaku zenshū* 82 *(Meiji joryū bungaku shū* 2), ed. Shioda Ryōhei (Tokyo: Chikuma shobō, 1965), pp. 427–437.

4. Maeda Ai, *Kindai dokusha no seiritsu* (Tokyo: Iwanami shoten, 1993), p. 151. Here, Maeda discusses newly educated girls who read aloud to their families.

5. Shioda Ryōhei, *Meiji joryū sakka ron* (Tokyo: Nara shobō, 1965), p. 323.

6. Yukiko Tanaka, *Women Writers of Meiji and Taishō Japan: Their Lives, Works, and Critical Reception, 1868–1926* (Jefferson, N.C.; McFarland, 2000), p. 115. The citation given is Igarashi Rantei, "Hyōden Mizuno Senko," *Gakuen* 294 (June 1, 1964): 51–52.

7. Tayama Katai, "O-Tei-san no shū no mae ni," page.freett.com/Schuricht/oteisan.htm, accessed May 10 2004, p. 1.

8. Shioda, *Meiji joryū sakka ron*, p. 323.

9. Tayama, "O-Tei-san no shū no mae ni," p. 1.

10. Shioda, *Meiji joryū sakka ron*, p. 323.

11. Arishima Takeo, "Mizuno Senko-shi no sakuhin ni tsuite," www.aozora.gr.jp/cards/000025/card214.html, accessed May 10 2004, p. 2. Although Senko and Arishima never met, the latter became her literary mentor by correspondence in the closing years of her life.

12. Rebecca Copeland, *Lost Leaves: Women Writers of Meiji Japan* (Honolulu: University of Hawai'i Press, 2000), p. 84.

13. Ibid.

14. The impact of pregnancy and childbirth on women's lives is addressed in at least two other Senko texts: "Torō" and "Joi no hanashi" (Story of a woman doctor, 1912).

15. Saitō Minako, *Ninshin shōsetsu* (Tokyo: Chikuma shobō, 1997), pp. 10–11. Saitō's focus is largely writing in the postwar era.

16. Ibid., p. 11.

17. Vera Mackie discusses texts in which women record the distress associated with the birthing process, including the 1904 autobiography of *Heiminsha* member, Fukuda Hideko, Yosano Akiko's "Ubuya monogatari" (Tales of childbirth, 1909), and Nogami Yaeko's "Atarashiki seimei" (A new life, 1914). See Vera Mackie, *Feminism in Modern Japan* (Cambridge: Cambridge University Press, 2003), pp. 52–55.

18. Susan L. Burns, "Introduction: Pregnancy and Childbirth in the Context of Modernity," *U.S.-Japan Women's Journal* 24 (September 2003): 6, for example, cites Fujime Yuki's observations concerning the routine occurrence of abortion "sanctioned by the family and local communities" in Tokugawa and

early Meiji Japan. For further information on pre-Meiji attitudes to women's bodies and reproduction, see Sawayama Miyako, "The 'Birthing Body' and the Regulation of Conceptions and Childbirth in the Edo Period," in *U.S.-Japan Women's Journal* 24 (September 2003): 10–34.

19. Terazawa Yuki, "The State, Midwives, and Reproductive Surveillance in Late Nineteenth- and Early Twentieth-Century Japan," *U.S.-Japan Women's Journal* 24 (September 2003): 66, citing Nikawa Toshio.

20. Ibid., citing Ogata Masakiyo.

21. Ibid., p. 67.

22. This is in spite of Shioda's claim that the text is centered on one room (p. 425). See Shioda Ryōhei, "Kaidai," in *Meiji bungaku zenshū* 82 *(Meiji joryū bungaku shū* 2), ed. Shioda Ryōhei (Tokyo: Chikuma shobō, 1965), pp. 413–426.

23. Elizabeth Grosz, *Volatile Bodies: Towards a Corporeal Feminism* (St. Leonards, Sydney: Allen and Unwin, 1994), p. 205.

24. Murai Gensai (1863–1927) was a best-selling novelist of the Meiji and Taishō periods. While his fiction is now rarely read, he is still remembered for *Kuidōraku* (Gourmandism, 1903). *Koneko* (The kitten, serialized 1891–1892, published in book form 1897) is the success story of a fisherman's boy. *Chi no namida* (Tears of blood, serialized 1895, book 1896) deals with Japan's frustrations following the Sino-Japanese War.

25. Higuchi Ichiyō (1872–1896). Her most well-known works are "Takekurabe" (Comparing heights, 1895–1896), the coming-of-age tale of a girl destined to work in the pleasure quarters (see "Higuchi Ichiyō," n. 1), and "Nigorie" (Troubled waters, 1895), the story of a man's neglect of his wife and child because of his obsession with a prostitute. The first edition of *Ichiyō zenshū* was published in 1897, only two months after her death.

26. Futabatei Shimei (1864–1909) is the author of Japan's first modern novel, *Ukigumo* (Drifting clouds, 1887–1889). *Sono omokage (An adopted husband*, 1906) tells of the tension between a man and the women in his family.

27. *Wagahai wa neko de aru* (*I am a cat*, 1905–1906) is an early work of the doyen of early modern letters in Japan, Natsume Sōseki (1867–1916), in which a cat comments on modern society.

28. The source texts used for this translation are in Shioda, *Meiji joryū bungaku shū*, pp. 354–364, and on the Web at www.aozora.gr.jp/cards/000112/files/601. html, accessed May 10, 2004.

TAMURA TOSHIKO
(1884–1945)

Edward Fowler

TAMURA TOSHIKO, feminist author, recalcitrant wife, renegade lover, and long-time expatriate in North America and China, was a largely forgotten woman at the time of her death, yet she is a bright star in the firmament of modern Japanese women writers. A "consistent violator of norms" in the words of one critic,[1] she was perhaps the prototypical dangerous woman, being neither "good wife" nor "wise mother" (never becoming a mother at all, for that matter), in defiance of exhortations by Meiji officialdom. She was born both too late and too early: too late to be numbered among the literary pioneers of the modern era, some of whom appear in this volume and were active decades before her own career took off, and too early for her radical vision of female identity to take hold during her lifetime. Not yet the subject of a "complete works" (*zenshū*) nor the object of extensive criticism, she has, until quite recently, fallen through the cracks of literary history. It is perhaps emblematic of her standing in the literary world that the best-known work about her is not by a critic but by another author, Setouchi Harumi (Jakuchō, 1922–), herself a notorious violator of social norms, whose biography, originally published in 1961, was awarded the first Tamura Toshiko Prize.

Tamura's career spanned three imperial reigns—Meiji, Taishō, and Shōwa—beginning with her meteoric rise at the close of the first modern-period reign and ending with the Pacific War. Although recent research has focused on her later years, spent mostly abroad, it is for her earlier work, which garnered the immediate respect of her contemporaries, that she is still best known today.[2] Raised initially in the romantic tradition but subsequently schooled in gritty naturalism, Tamura, one of the first women to write in the vernacular, developed a grammar of sexuality that generated a new syntax of gender relations in early-twentieth-century Japan and made her the leading female author of her time. In the words of Setouchi Harumi, "Although blessed with neither the genius of Higuchi Ichiyō (1872–1896) nor the intellect of Miyamoto Yuriko (1899–1951), Tamura Toshiko's literature did possess a natural sensibility that, honed to perfection, gave expression to a distinctive and dazzlingly carnal world."[3]

A Tokyo native, Tamura Toshiko was born Satō Toshi, the elder of two daughters, to a rice merchant's family living in the Kuramae district of Asakusa Ward. Her father, after failing at the business, seems to have evaporated from family life; her mother took up with several other men and had little interest in the children. After completing six years of elementary school, compulsory for both sexes, Toshiko gained admission to a middle school for girls, where she cultivated her interest in literature. Like other girls her age, she was also trained in the various female accomplishments: music, poetry, dancing, and flower arranging. At the age of seventeen, she entered the literature faculty of Nihon Joshi Daigakkō (Japan Women's College, founded in 1901, now Japan Women's University). The long commute by foot, however, from her home east of Ueno to the campus in Mejirodai near Ikebukuro (a distance of at least eight miles round-trip), affected her health and forced her to withdraw after only a single term.

The following year, 1902, was an eventful one in Toshiko's life. No longer in a position to continue her formal education, she resolved to become a writer under the tutelage of Kōda Rohan (1867–1947), who, along with Ozaki Kōyō (1867–1903), was one of the most respected literary men of the day. She favored Rohan because of his reputedly lenient attitude toward the theater, in contrast to Kōyō's rather severe position. Rohan, known for his ornate style and deep familiarity with the premodern canon, immediately had her read the classics. This training led to several short stories written in the ornate idiom of Higuchi Ichiyō, including Toshiko's first publication, "Tsuyuwake-goromo" (The dew-drenched robe, 1903), which appeared in the well-known literary journal *Bungei kurabu* (Literary arts club). The year 1902 also saw the death from illness of her sister, who was only twelve, and the beginning of her relationship with her future husband, Tamura Shōgyo (1874–1948), himself an aspiring writer and Rohan disciple. Toshiko was just eighteen years old.

Promising to marry her when he returned, Tamura Shōgyo left for the United States in 1903 to become a student at, among other places, Indiana University. He did not return to Japan, however, until 1909. During his six-year absence, Toshiko continued to publish short stories while turning her attention to the theater. And although she took up residence at one point with her mother in the precincts of an out-of-the-way temple in Asakusa Ward, she apparently did not live like a nun. Under suspicion by the wife of the temple's head priest of having all too cordial relations with her husband, she was forced to vacate the premises.

In 1906, the year that Shimazaki Tōson (1872–1943), a romantic poet turned naturalist fiction writer, published *Hakai* (The broken commandment), Toshiko ended her association with Rohan. With the appearance of Tōson's pathbreaking work, the naturalist movement was clearly in ascendancy; Toshiko, dissatisfied with the direction of her own writing, which adhered to the classical idiom at a time when the vernacular had at last become standard, felt compelled to reexamine her attachment to the romantic school. Her interest in the theater gathered momentum, meanwhile, and in the same year she joined a troupe led by Okamoto Kidō (1872–1939), the renowned playwright who was instrumental in the revival of Kabuki. A year later, she performed her first role with another troupe and devoted most of her energies over the next couple of years to the stage.

During this period, Toshiko found inspiration in Shimamura Hōgetsu (1871–1918), the great critic and dramatist. In 1909 Hōgetsu had begun publishing a series of landmark essays, thought to have been an influence on her work, which, on the one hand, energetically engaged the naturalist movement and, on the other, encouraged the development of *shingeki* (new theater), modeled after the drama of European playwrights like Ibsen and Strindberg.[4] Toshiko was surely aware, moreover, of the meteoric rise of Matsui Sumako (1886–1919), who more than any other actress of the era embodied the role of the self-fulfilled "new woman" and starred in Hōgetsu's acclaimed production of Ibsen's *A Doll House* in 1911.

FIGURE 11.1 Tamura Toshiko (1884–1945), July 1911

The year 1909 also saw Tamura Shōgyo's return to Japan. Shōgyo and Toshiko were wed soon after (their marriage was not legally registered) and set up house together in the Yanaka district of Shitaya Ward. Incidentally, this area is the setting for the second half of "Seigon" ("The Vow," 1912), translated here, where the couple returns from their abortive excursion to Kōnodai. The Tamura marriage was not a happy one, as is easily discerned in much of Toshiko's written work (including "The Vow"), which addresses head-on the difficulty of conducting a spousal relationship in anything but the traditionally prescribed manner. Shōgyo did play a role, however, in lifting Toshiko's career as a writer to new heights. He encouraged her (albeit in a way that suggests coercion) to submit a manuscript in 1910 to the Osaka edition of the *Asahi*, a major newspaper, which was holding a literary contest. Her elegantly written submission, "Akirame" (Resignation), which uses the theater as a motif and grapples with such themes as the social status of women and same-sex love, won the top prize late that year and had the honor of appearing in serialized form in the newspaper's pages starting on New Year's Day, 1911. It also earned her an unusually lucrative award of one thousand yen. The story was published as a book later that year.

Flush with the success of "Akirame," Toshiko, who had just played the lead in a stage production by a major *shingeki* troupe only to see the troupe dissolve immediately after the production's end, abandoned her acting career to concentrate on her writing. In these last years of Meiji, she began publishing the stories, including those translated in this volume, that would seal her literary reputation. In 1913, when she was still not yet twenty-nine, her work was the subject of a special issue of *Shinchō* (New tide), an important literary journal with contributions by some of the best-known writers of the day. She was the subject of another special issue the following year in *Chūō kōron* (Central forum).

In the meantime, however, her marriage was crumbling. The precise reasons, albeit the subject of considerable speculation, are difficult to ascertain. The breakup very likely had to do in part with Shōgyo's intransigence, but it also had to do with the fact that the parameters of married life were simply not wide enough to corral Toshiko's notions of interpersonal relationships. She may have been bisexual. Some of her earlier fiction, including "Akirame" and "Onna sakusha" (A woman writer, 1913), as well as that written later on, hints at this. (She also left a diary detailing her infatuation with a female English instructor during her time in college.) In 1915 she became acquainted with Yuasa Yoshiko (1896–1990), a renowned translator of Russian literature best known for her relationship with Miyamoto Yuriko in the late Taishō period, and began sharing a house in Yanaka with her in 1916. (Shōgyo had left her by this time and opened an antique shop in a nearby neighborhood.) The following year, however, at a time when her writing career and financial security were ebbing, she fell in love with a married man, writer and labor activist Suzuki Etsu (1886–1933). They took up residence in several locations around the city, doing their best to avoid her acquaintances and his wife. In 1918 Suzuki sailed to Canada in hopes of bolstering his career as a journalist. Toshiko followed suit a few months later, after raising money for the journey through her writing and, increasingly, doll making, which had grown into a lucrative avocation for her since the early 1910s. She lived with Suzuki in Vancouver for nearly fifteen years. They were married in 1920, after Suzuki formally divorced his wife.[5]

The years in Canada and, later, the United States and China will be only briefly recounted here. Toshiko remained extremely active, albeit no longer as a writer of fiction. She worked closely with Suzuki, who wrote for one and later published another Japanese-language newspaper in Vancouver, home to Canada's largest Japanese immigrant community, and frequently contributed essays aimed at raising the consciousness of women recently settled from Japan. She also exploited her youthful training in haiku and served as poetry editor for yet another periodical.

Suzuki died unexpectedly after leaving Toshiko and returning to Japan in 1933. She moved to Los Angeles, where she lived and worked for more than two years. In 1936 she returned to Tokyo, where she attempted to revitalize her career, taking up with old literary acquaintances and making new ones, in particular such proletarian movement writers as Miyamoto Yuriko, Kubokawa Tsurujirō (1903–1974), and his wife, Sata Ineko (1904–1998). Once more inviting notoriety because of an affair with a married man—this time, Kubokawa—Toshiko again left Japan. Intending to stay for a month or two, she flew to China in 1938 as a special correspondent for *Chūō kōron*. Finding herself in the company of high-ranking military officers as well as several famous writers, many on assignment as war correspondents, she kept extending her stay.[6] In 1942, having settled in Shanghai, she founded a Chinese-language magazine, *Nü shēng* or *Josei* (A woman's voice), with backing from the Japanese Army. Just as she had done while in North America, Toshiko threw herself into her work, writing and fund-raising for the magazine as well as editing it. To what extent she was a pawn of the imperialists or a critic of the colonialist enterprise is still a matter of debate. Be that as it may, she devoted herself to her magazine right up to her death, in the spring of 1945, from a stroke, never having returned to Japan.

Tamura Toshiko's stories had appeared as early as 1903, as previously noted, but 1911, the last full year of the Meiji reign, was doubtless her breakout year. In addition to her prize-winning "Akirame," she also published "Ikichi" (Lifeblood)—also included in this volume—a compelling and seminal work that signaled a fresh direction in her writing, which had long taken a backseat to her stage career.

"Lifeblood," which describes a young woman's psychological reaction to the loss of her virginity, succeeds because it is the product of a narrative consciousness far more knowing than the woman herself. Critics suggest that the story is based on the author's own experience and that the callous male partner is modeled on none other than Tamura Shōgyo, with whom Toshiko had by this time become quite disenchanted.[7] Yet more than the story's possible autobiographical inspiration or even its richly evocative setting, which offers an appealing specificity of place, it is the universality of the woman's predicament that stirs the reader nearly a century after it was written.

Rather than depict the brute sexual act endured by Yūko, which, given the times, would have certainly failed to pass the censors' scrutiny, the author focuses instead on the trauma of memory as it plays out the day after Yūko's deflowering, as well as on a series of displacements: the inn garden at sunrise, rendered as an ominously *gendered* space (flowers colored only in red and white connote female-male in the symbolic imaginary and, perhaps more important, the binary of innocence and experience); the bloody penetration of a goldfish—inevitably one not yet initiated into a gendered field by the metaphorical act of naming (which Yūko has carried out through her use of nicknames, based on dyed fabrics common in women's garments, for the other fish); and, most spectacularly, the young foot juggler in a makeshift Asakusa theater who performs while lying vulnerably, seemingly spread-eagle, on her back, her long kimono sleeves spilling off the stand in suggestive disarray. The performer is inexorably linked, moreover, with the bizarre, menacing image of a bat, which first accosts Yūko in the theater balcony and later haunts her imagination as a blood-sucking vampire.

Other densely allusive imagery abounds, much of which eludes translation. One example is the rich array of clothing. The Japanese language has at its disposal a seemingly limitless vocabulary with which to denote the immense variety of traditional men's and women's wear that is all too frequently rendered into English by the serviceable but ultimately inadequate generic term "kimono." Not only the gender of the person wearing it but also his or her age and calling are all suggested with exactitude by the particular style or cut of a robe or undergarment or sash.

The story's setting, in and near Asakusa ("the park"), the plebeian heart of Tokyo and site of the city's most popular temple and busiest amusement quarter during the Meiji era, is equally symbolic. Yūko and her companion studiously avoid the temple's radiance and steal around the shadowy backwater of Okuyama, Asakusa's locus of seedy entertainments and the home of Hanayashiki Amusement Park and Gourd Pond. The narrative begins in an inn just north of the park, which fact the reader can establish from its proximity to Matsuchiyama Shōden, a cozy temple overlooking the Sumida River from atop the area's only hill. Unmentioned in the narrative but inferred ironically from the context are the associations, both pictorial and ritual, with conjugal bliss for which the temple is famous: the decorative painting, adorning the main hall, of two suggestively intertwined daikon; and the annual Daikon Festival, which confers prosperity and marital harmony to those partaking in a specially prepared dish served on the temple grounds. Finally, the narrative course comes full circle with the couple ending their walk where they had begun it: the Sumida River, Tokyo's most storied waterway and the backdrop against which Yūko ponders her fate.

"Lifeblood" is important not just for its startling content but also for the venue in which it appeared: the inaugural issue of *Seitō* (Bluestocking, 1911–1916), the journal of early-twentieth-century Japan's most celebrated feminist group, of which Toshiko was a supporting member. Even the story's place in the journal resonates with significance. It immediately precedes the celebrated manifesto by Hiratsuka Raichō (1886–1971), the group's founder, with its often-quoted title: "Genshi josei wa taiyō de atta" (In the beginning, woman was the sun), made in reference to the glory days of court women writing nearly a thousand years earlier in the Heian period and in the expectation of more glory days to come.

If "Lifeblood" voices the lament of a young woman coping with the indelible scars of her forced sexual awakening, "The Vow" is the bold manifesto of a woman who has gained confidence in both her physical and emotional identity. Once again, Toshiko endows the setting in the story's first part with a rich sense of specificity: a temple atop Mama Hill near Kōnodai, for centuries a destination for pilgrims.[8] The narrative contains some classical elements. For example, careful use of mostly floral imagery is made to indicate the season (late spring), and the rise and fall of the main character Seiko's affection for her mate very roughly follows the conventional poetic trajectory depicted in all the imperial anthologies, rendering a happy ending highly improbable. Tamura's take on this standard trajectory, however, is a more extreme version of the classical literary depiction of disenchantment. In addition, the narrative frame is utterly modern, for the plot's unstated but undeniable guiding force is economics, not the natural progression of the seasons.

The frame, moreover, turns Seiko's particular situation into a quandary that innumerable women have shared. The question inferred by the narrator at the story's end is not, "How will Seiko return to her proper place beside her husband?" but rather "How can she survive without the physical shelter and financial support a husband provides?" Thus the success of the story depends on readers recognizing at least the possibility of a woman leading her life independent of a mate. The author's other stories from this period attempt very tentatively to chart a path in this direction.

Tamura Toshiko herself aspired to the independent life, although she never rid herself of a deep ambivalence toward it, and her aspiration did not prevent her from squandering some opportunities to forge a new kind of relationship with men. None of that, however, detracts from her remarkable literary accomplishments. Indeed, if the stories featured in this anthology are any indication, her early, Meiji-period career is a fitting cap to what was already, despite suggestions to the contrary, a rich and important period in the history of women's literature in modern Japan.[9]

LIFEBLOOD

Translated by Edward Fowler

1

Without a word, Akiji left the room to wash his face.[10] Yūko stood alone on the veranda, still in a daze, the sound of his footsteps ringing in her ears. Her unlined kimono, made of silk crepe dyed a deep violet, enveloped her heels, its upturned hem spilling onto the floor.

In every corner of the garden, red and white flowers lolled their heavy eyelids beneath a dimly glowing sky that cloaked the inn, much as the gossamer had draped her reclining figure the previous night before being rudely stripped off.

Stealing up from the damp ground below, a silky breeze caressed the sole of Yūko's foot—the one dangling over the veranda's edge—and slipped softly away.

Yūko eyed the goldfish bowl at her feet. She knelt down next to it, a look of amusement spreading across her face.

"Crimson Dapple. . . . Scarlet Fawn. . . . Sunrise Glow. . . . Hailstone. . . ."

Pointing her finger at the goldfish, she named each one after a dye pattern. The bowl caught the dawn's white rays and sent them shimmering, like flakes of silver, over the water's surface. Scarlet Fawn darted tomboylike through the water.

Yūko plucked a lavender blossom off a dwarf chrysanthemum that had been placed next to the bowl and let it fall into the water. A bright red goldfish—one she had not yet named—brushed its tiny, puckered mouth against a petal only to shake its large tailfin skittishly and sink to the bottom of the bowl. Silvery flakes of light flickered in the water.

Resting her left arm on her raised knee and her right elbow on top of that, she braced her forehead with the palm of her hand. Her frail wrist was bent at an odd angle to support her head's weight. Her thumb pressed against the corner of her eye, skewing it upward. . . .

A woman bites down on the scarlet crepe border of a mosquito net. She is crying. Her companion gazes out the window at the street lamps, a breeze-blown Iyo blind rattling against his back.

"There's no use fretting about it now," the man says with a smirk. . . .

The raw smell of goldfish wafted across the room

Yūko breathed it in slowly, intently, unaware of its source. Again she breathed it in. And again.

"The smell of a man . . ."

The thought made her shudder. Whereupon she felt something pulse through her body and leave her trembling from fingertips to toes.

"No! Stop! Stop it!"

Ah, to grab a sharp object and lash out at something—anything! . . . How many times had the urge seized her since last evening?

Yūko stuck her hand in the goldfish bowl and grabbed one of the fish, as if it were the object of her wrath.

"Well, I shall string you out to dry!"

Scooping the goldfish out of the water, Yūko removed the gold pin that secured her kimono, which she wore over her bare skin, at the collar. The water in the glass bowl now roiled, distorting the streaks of light.

The goldfish's eye was no larger than a sesame seed. Taking careful aim, Yūko jabbed her pin into it. The fish's tail flapped violently against her wrist. Drops of raw-smelling water splashed onto her pale blue-gray sash. She thrust the pin all the way through the goldfish, piercing the tip of her forefinger. A rubylike drop of blood formed at the edge of her nail and swelled slowly.

The fish's scales took on a bluish glint. The red speckles went dull and dry, their sheen completely gone. The fish lay belly up in her hand, dead, its mouth agape. The tailfin, once stretched wide like a floral dancing fan, now drooped down, wilted.

Yūko held the fish up against the light for a time and then hurled it into the garden, where it landed on a stone step. The early morning sky, brightening with each passing moment, spread its light in all directions and enveloped the fish in a faint white glow.

Yūko stepped back from the veranda into her room. The light from an electric lamp, not yet turned off, made her forehead flush luminously. Settling herself on the floor in front of a large mirror below the window, she inserted her bleeding forefinger into her mouth. Tears welled up in both eyes and overflowed their lids.

Yūko pressed the sleeve of her kimono against her face and wept. No matter how much she cried, her sorrow would not abate. Yet a kind of sweet nostalgia flowed with the tears, shed in the manner of a woman pressing her cheek affectionately against the breast of a long-lost love.

"I can feel the warmth of my lips on my own finger when I suck it—why should that seem so very sad?" Yūko thought to herself in the midst of her sobs.

Surely her crying would never cease. Indeed, if the tears stopped flowing, wouldn't her breathing come to a halt as well? Yes, as long as she had breath left in her, she would go on crying indefinitely.

If only she could weep until the bitter end, shed all the tears that could be shed, and then breathe her last, strangled by the dew that clung to the lotus blossoms shrouding her in her final sleep—how happy she would be then! Oh, hot tears! Yet however much she was steeped in them— even to the point of their burning her skin away—her body would never return to its former state. Never again could she be her old self. . . .

Biting her lip, Yūko raised her head abruptly and gazed into the mirror. The glass reflected the form in front of it unerringly and unwaveringly. Her deep violet kimono was undone at the knee, revealing a redness underneath.

Staring intently at her kimono, Yūko pondered the fate of the body just beneath that single layer of crepe.

Once defiled, she would never, ever be able to rid herself of the taint, whether she pierced every pore in her skin with a needle or scraped away at every inch of her flesh. . . .

Akiji, who had gone out to wash his face, returned to the room, a muslin towel draped over his shoulder. Seeing Yūko, he stepped silently into the next room. A maid must have followed him in not long after that; Yūko could hear them chatting.

Presently, the maid entered Yūko's room and put away the bedding. She greeted Yūko with a smile, but Yūko did not so much as glance in her direction. Then, as if jolted into consciousness after an exhausting dream, she slumped to one side on the floor, unmindful of how she looked, and whimpered like a child, her head shaking all the while.

The clatter of opening and shutting glass doors echoed throughout the inn: morning cleanup had begun. Listening to the grate of a passing streetcar, Yūko recalled to her dismay that the inn faced a row of houses on the main street. How on earth to make her exit? Should she ask a maid to let her out the back way? Mulling over her options, she took a thin sheet of writing paper from her kimono sleeve, tore it into narrow strips, and bound the wound on her forefinger.

2

The sun was high when the couple took to the streets, she under a light blue Western-style parasol, he donning a straw-colored panama. Their shapeless, wrinkled garments were devoid of bright hues; it was as if the blazing sunlight had bleached them of all color. The slovenly pair made their way meekly down the street in the intense heat, looking thoroughly beaten by the midday sun. Both their necks were flushed red, as if they had been pressed with a hot iron, and their white *tabi* were stained a pale red ocher by dust rising from the street.

The couple turned into an alleyway. Wind gusted through the narrow space under the eaves of houses. The ground was damp, as if it lay at the bottom of a depression. In the dark, earthen-floored entrance to a house opposite the well, a woman sat weaving at her loom, a soiled towel wound around her neck. The couple ascended a flight of stone steps at the alley's far end. From the top of the steps, Yūko walked over to a low fence and gazed across the Sumida River at the Mukōjima Embankment.

Both river and embankment, seemingly weary of the heat, threw off a golden light and yet begrudged any sign of life. Yūko noticed black smoke hovering over the houses below, their tin roofs repelling the rays of a summer sun that beat down on every corner. Squinting in the glare, she redirected her gaze toward the shade. There, standing on a stepping stone, Akiji was eyeing a young apprentice geisha from behind as she pulled on a rope in front of a shrine, making the bell attached to it ring out with a clatter.

The interior of Matsuchiyama Shōden Temple's main hall was dimly lit, as if shrouded by a black curtain. Here and there, silver altar vessels exuded a faint white radiance, at once mysterious and evocative. In their midst, candles atop a massive circular stand cast their flickering light high and low, left and right, throughout the hall, as if calling down a curse on the sweltering heat. The unceasing quiver of the faintly glowing flames recalled the glint in the eyes of a fasting priest intent on his austerities.

Yūko could make out the figures of two or three other people in the hall.

The couple left the temple by way of the main stone staircase. The sun-baked street below was utterly deprived of shade. Yūko felt as if she were being grilled on a copperplate. Her eyes stung, and her lungs hurt. She held her parasol close to shade her body.

I have to leave him now. I just have to. Yūko turned the same thought over and over again in her mind. *I need to get away from this man. I need to be alone for a while and think carefully about what happened last night. . . .* Her mind was racing, but she could not bring herself to say a word to him. She felt physically constrained, as though her hands and feet were in shackles.

"Look at her tremble. She's a study in hesitation. She can't say a word to me and just lets herself be led about under this hot sun. How far is she going to tag along?"—*He doesn't have to say it, but that is surely what he's thinking.* Yūko dabbed the sweat on her forehead.

The apprentice geisha whom the couple had seen at the shrine overtook them and hurriedly walked past. Yūko's eyes were drawn to the nape of the girl's slender neck, visible from beneath her painted, bright vermilion Japanese parasol. The girl's neck, tilted forward and extending well beyond her pulled-back collar, was eerily translucent. The hem of her navy-blue silk gossamer kimono, dyed in a coarse, feathered-arrow splash pattern, revealed her stark white *tabi*-less feet with every step. Her purple Hakata obi was tied snugly in a shell knot, the long end pointed up.

Yūko gazed wistfully into the blinding glare at this lovely, virginal figure whose long, sheer kimono sleeves nearly touched the ground.

How she envied the girl! She, meanwhile, felt her body—in a state unchanged from the previous night—being mercilessly exposed under the infernal sun; it emitted, she was sure, a foul odor reminiscent of rotting fish. She desperately wished that someone would pluck her body off the street and heave it aside.

The couple continued their walk in silence. Reaching the end of a wide street, they turned down a narrow lane.

The ground in front of a shaved-ice shop, a reed screen and a red wind chime hanging in the door, had been wet down. Yūko could see right into another house: a woman wearing nothing but a sleeveless undergarment that exposed her dark limbs was giving a child lessons in *Gidayū*-style chanting. The smell of rancid oil wafted toward her from a low-roofed knick knack shop nearby. Akiji, who was several steps in front of her, cut behind a noodle shop and headed for the park.

Under the harsh sunlight, the glossy, lacquer-red Amida Hall appeared to take on the dull color of earthenware. The dragon-headed Kannon fountain behind the temple was completely dry. Not even a trickle of water flowed from it. Peering up at the Kannon goddess's bronze torso, perched high on its pedestal and baking in the heat, Yūko could feel her own hair being singed by the blazing sun.

A group of women sauntered by, their faces painted white and all wearing splash-patterned *yukata* dyed a deep blue and tied with red obis. The hems of their robes, clinging to their perspiring feet, flapped open occasionally as they walked to reveal bright red undergarments. They were followed by a man fanning himself and wearing only a light mesh under-robe, his sleeves hitched above his shoulders. Many other people were gathered about the waterless fountain.

They all eyed the couple intently. Akiji looked down, obviously ill at ease. Yūko had to admit that the low esteem in which everyone apparently held them fairly matched the dismal view she had of herself. *Well, then, let them gawk at me all they want. So my flesh is tainted—that shouldn't shock the likes of them!*

Once again, Akiji walked on ahead. Yūko felt the urge to fling herself at something or to utter something peevish. She had no desire whatsoever to speak to the man she was with.

They made their way past a crowd of people knotted in front of Hanayashiki Amusement Park and found themselves at the entrance to a small, makeshift theater specializing in acrobats who performed tricks while balanced on rubber balls.

"Let's have a look."

Akiji darted inside, not waiting for an answer. Yūko followed in silence.

The balcony, perched high up in the little theater, was very dark. Its wooden pillars, cushions, and thin rush matting were all damp to the touch, telling of the great number of people who had previously lounged on them and left their sweat.

Five or six people were sprinkled about the balcony. All were engrossed in the performance below, their hands clutching the railing, as if they would never again be witness to such an act. Akiji, having found himself a comfortable-looking spot on the matting, slipped a thin cushion under his knees. He glanced back at Yūko and smiled.

A hand bell similar to the kind used in temple services rang out, and a boy dressed in a flesh-colored upper garment announced the next performance in a low, thick voice. Each slight upward or downward movement of the advertising banner hanging outside the theater obscured the upturned faces of the people standing in its shadow and caused the stage to darken a bit. Four or five young girls in tight-fitting, dark pink upper garments appeared on stage, their hair in small gingko-leaf–style coiffures, their ruddy faces made up with thick white powder, their hands tucked under their arms. Each stood atop a large rubber ball and proceeded to roll it across the stage while holding a braided, red-and-white hoop.

The girls moved their hoops from leg to arm and then over the shoulder to the other arm, all while rolling the balls underfoot. The sight of the skin behind their tiny ears, all caked with white makeup powder, filled Yūko with sadness. She retreated to a box seat in the rear of the balcony and removed a fan from her sash.

The folding fan with its lacquered ribs gave off a warm, wistful fragrance as she waved it in front of her. Each slight upward movement of the banner outside revealed an intense midday sun beating down on everything, from the heads of the crowd nearby to the pond in the distance. Yūko noticed the young female and adult male performers stare blankly at the crowd outside between acts: the languor permeating the dimly lit theater was palpable.

Her attention was now drawn to a young girl onstage dressed in a pair of wide-legged trousers made of satin, dyed a deep turquoise blue and worn over her long-sleeved kimono. The girl's thick hair, done up in a low Shimada, was decorated with a lavender silk scarf in a dappled fawn-skin pattern.

Lying face up on a stand, the girl twirled an umbrella on her toes. Pure white forearm guards were strapped to her slender wrists. The long sleeves of her kimono were draped over both sides of the stand. The girl spread the umbrella open with her feet, balanced its edge on her toes, and spun it around like a pinwheel. Her leggings were also pure white. So were her small *tabi*. Occasionally, the pleats of her satin trousers, part of a man's formal attire, would fall into disarray, and the long sleeves of her kimono would tremble. When that happened, a samisen in the orchestra offstage would strike up a plaintive, syncopated melody, alternately taut and slack, that made Yūko's breast tug with emotion.

After dismounting from the stand, the girl bowed to the audience with a winsome smile and immediately retreated backstage. The hairpiece in her Shimada had come undone. Yūko could still see the pattern of the girl's long-sleeved kimono in her mind's eye. Akiji, like the rest of the audience upstairs, clung to the railing and eyed the stage below. Yūko stared intently at his slender neck. Onstage, another girl was balancing a stack of small wooden buckets on her feet; a young boy appeared from the rainwater barrel that had been placed atop them. Yet another girl performed an assortment of tricks with a hidden water hose. Still more children performed similar acts, one after the other.

Yūko, utterly weary of it all, felt as though her body would soon dissolve in its own sweat. She dimly recalled that she had been grieving and that she ought to be grieving still. "Oh, who cares?" she felt like shouting. "Let happen what may!" No matter how deeply mired she was in despair, however, she could make out, on the far side of her depression, distant human forms. Yūko gazed fondly at the performers in the makeshift theater. And those turquoise-blue satin trousers—she simply could not rid her mind of them.

The cycle of performances had run its course. Akiji made no move to leave, however, even though the program was about to be repeated. Seemingly overcome by drowsiness, he let his head drop onto his folded arms resting on the balcony railing. Yūko could only stare silently at the figure before her. She, too, felt herself drifting into a dream world, in search of something that eluded her grasp, and sensed her own head sinking—into a vision of that girl's tiny white face and her bright red sleeve cords fanning out in all directions, growing larger as they moved.

Occasionally, a wave of sultry, pungent air brushed against her and drifted away. Scattered, languid applause rang out dully from the earthen floor below. It was then that she noticed a sharp rustling sound, as of something flapping its wings right next to her ear.

Yūko felt her drooping eyelids snap open. She stood up and looked behind her but saw nothing.

Her head still turned back, she eyed the balcony from its sooty pillars down to the flimsy, grime-caked mats. There, on one of the rear panels, she spied something moving. It was black and resembled the tailfin of a large fish. Utterly still, she studied the thing's movements. When it stopped moving, she pinned it down with her fan. Dragging the fan across the wall, she watched the black thing slowly emerge from between the panels. When she had moved her fan about a foot, its form took shape: the wing of a bat.

Yūko dropped her fan and dashed to Akiji's side. Akiji, still on his cushion, paid her no heed. Feeling her blood run cold, she cast another glance at the rear panels. The black wing was gone. Pale yellow light from what must have been the setting sun seeped through an adjacent crack.

The two of them left the theater. It was evening: there were now people in the crowd wearing undyed *yukata* and looking as cool as deep pools of water. Akiji walked on ahead, silent as before. Yūko realized that she had grown faint with hunger. *I'll steal away from him without a word*. Her sweat-laden kimono felt dreadfully uncomfortable, clinging to the skin behind her knees as she walked.

"How far *is* this woman going to tag along?"

Yes, that's what he's thinking. I can tell from the way he acts.

When he finally spoke, however, all he said was, "We should get a bite to eat."

"I want to leave now."

"Leave?"

"Yes."

The man walked on in silence. They traversed a bridge over the pond to an island in the middle and perched themselves as if by prior arrangement on the stools of a stall near the bank serving shaved ice. The shrubbery in front of them dripped with the water that had been sprinkled on it. The couple remained glued to their seats, seemingly without a thought of going anywhere else.

By sundown, an evening crowd had emerged, washed clean of sweat and wearing neatly creased *yukata*. The couple, meanwhile, their bodies wilted by a day's worth of sweat, made their way past Niō Gate to Umamichi Boulevard and finally to the Sumida River. From a gravel landing on the riverbank, they watched the dusk gather over the flowing water.

If only he would take me in his arms and sweep me away—it doesn't matter where.

Yūko leaned against a post on the landing, lost in thought.

The bat is sucking the lifeblood out of that poor girl dressed in men's satin trousers. Sucking the very life out of her. . . .

The man took her hand, startling her from her reverie. It was then she realized that the strip of writing paper she had wrapped around her forefinger had fallen off. A raw, fishlike odor assailed her nostrils.

THE VOW

Translated by Edward Fowler

SEIKO APPEARED at my door this morning, a single bag in her hand, after having suddenly left her husband's house. She tells me that she will never go back there again. The following is her story.

****

Yesterday my husband and I made an excursion to Kōnodai.

This is where we'd once spent the day three years ago, before we were married. It was the beginning of summer then, and the fireflies were already out in Ichikawa. We were intoxicated by our newfound delight in caressing the other's shoulder or hair, a delight that sent the blood pulsing through our veins and communicated itself to each of our hearts. At the place where we dined, we watched several women, their faces painted white, entertaining some soldiers and bantering with them. We felt as if our tender affection had been sullied by brackish water, and we silently resolved to uphold our love. We left Ichikawa toward evening, after we'd amused ourselves chasing fireflies.

Recalling the pleasant time we'd had before, we decided to spend another day there, now that we were a couple, and embarked on our excursion.

We arrived at Ichikawa. As we passed by a tea stand in front of the station, I felt a giddy pleasure that made my skin tingle with excitement.

When we were here last, I had gotten a young waitress—she would have been only about sixteen—to fetch three fireflies for me from a grassy area behind the stand. This time, however, when I peered over the boxes of sweets stacked on the counter, I didn't see anyone who looked like her.

"This place makes me sick."

My husband blurted out the words as we walked down the street.

No matter what I laid my eyes on, it seemed to wink back at me invitingly and conjure up some tender emotion lodged in the pleats of memory. I could feel with my whole body the warmth of my lover's hand as it held mine on that day long ago. Silently, I cast on my companion the occasional, innocent glance of a woman once flushed with youthful love. And so when he uttered the words he did, just as I was becoming absorbed in reverie, I felt as though its object were being snapped from my grasp and placed out of reach.

"But it all comes back to me, you know," I said in my sweetest voice, in an effort to endear myself to him. Indeed, I did everything possible to pry the nostalgia loose from his heart—even tilting my head coyly—but all to no avail. He seemed unmoved and said nothing.

Staring at the shadows cast on the ground by a mild sun, I walked on in pursuit of a bee in flight and sensed in its umber hue the waning spring. The man beside me now seemed utterly different from the man with whom I had once fallen in love. I yearned for the gentle countenance of that lover of old. . . .

As my lover, he used to tell me that he grew sick with worry about my pale skin being burnt to a crisp under the summer sun whenever we walked outdoors, as we were doing now. When the sun's hot rays beat down and left me panting, my lover would knit his brow in distress. . . . The man I am married to, however, merely walked on ahead, his arms casually folded in front of him. We headed toward the temple on Mama Hill.

Presently, we reached a shrine dedicated to the maiden Tekona. After reading a poem in her memory engraved on a stone, we ascended the stairs leading up to the shrine itself. My husband stepped right inside. It was then that I noticed a strikingly handsome young monk, about sixteen years old with very fair skin, sitting next to an older woman who was serving tea. The woman was saying something to the monk.

I scrutinized the boy's beautiful face. He had limpid eyes and a lovely mouth, the sort you might see on a Kabuki actor making his grand entrance down the *hanamichi* to the main stage.

"Please come in."

The boy monk bowed to me respectfully as he spoke. I remained where I was. At that very moment, my husband, who had been viewing the shrine's interior, noticed the monk saying something to me and rushed up to the serving table as though he had caught us in the midst of foul play.

I did not enter the shrine. The interior was filthy, and I had no desire to soil my *tabi*. Just then, the monk brought out a booklet of writing paper folded in half and asked me for a contribution. There was something unusual about this young monk. I soon realized that he was retarded: he had the oddest way of speaking, he garbled his words, and he managed to express only half the things he was trying to say. The old woman at his side would volunteer comments in an attempt to supplement his speech. My husband, too, noticed what was going on and listened to the monk for some time.

When the monk learned that we were from Tokyo, he told us that his sister worked as a geisha in the Karasumori quarter of Shimbashi. He used to go see her from time to time but eventually stopped because she kept scolding him for visiting her. Both siblings were born here. The more I looked at him, the lovelier his face became. What a pretty geisha his sister must be, I thought. I was utterly fascinated by this pair: the elder sister who worked as a geisha and the retarded younger brother who served tea at this shrine. I stared at length at the monk with the lovely face and soiled cloak.

The old woman teased the monk about obtaining a bride. The monk said nothing and merely smiled at my husband. We made a small offering and proceeded up the slope to the temple proper. I talked incessantly about the gorgeous young monk.

"Were you blushing back there at the shrine?" my husband asked me. We were standing at the offering box in front of the temple's main hall. I hadn't the faintest idea what he meant and said nothing. Then he told me that the monk had eyed me with a smile and said, "Her face is bright red!"

True, I had stood at the shrine entrance utterly captivated by the monk's good looks, but I recalled feeling neither arousal nor shame—nothing, in fact, that would have caused me to blush. Perhaps my husband had mistaken the monk's invitation to enter the shrine for something else. When I offered this explanation, however, he became incensed.

"There's something wrong with your hearing!" he growled. From then on, he was in a foul mood and maintained a stern silence no matter what I said.

Eventually, he told me he wanted to go straight home. We were descending the stone steps that led up to the temple.

I was distraught. This was the place where we'd once whispered sweet nothings to each other! We had come here again today, our sleeves touching, in order to recapture our love; yet now we found ourselves unable to look each other in the eye.

Although the trees and the sky above stirred fond recollections in the depths of my heart, neither of us had dared give voice to them. . . . Yet even at the risk of renewing the sad realization of a waning affection, of time forever lost, I still yearned to indulge the heady memory of that first love, in the shade of the very trees where I had originally experienced it. I wanted nothing so much as to extend a warm hand to the man with me now.

That such a petty misunderstanding would anger him and cause him to lose all interest was for me a matter of unspeakable grief. I explained to him at length how I felt and even attempted an apology. It did no good.

He refused to listen to a thing I said and insisted on leaving. I cried. When I did so, I realized that he had become quite loathsome to me. To think that he had once been my lover! I was furious. I loathed the unseen force in him that seemed intent now on shattering my sweet illusion.

"Why would I have any reason to loiter near the shrine entrance blushing?" I asked myself. This man, who could do nothing but grumble irritably, was utterly loathsome. I just stood there, on a path by a field of young barley rippling in the breeze, wiping away the tears that now streamed down my face.

"Let's make up and enjoy ourselves here for the rest of the day," I said, attempting to placate him. "Please, let's try." I was straining to control my emotions.

"No!" he snapped, practically flinging the word at me.

I felt very agitated. Crying loudly, I could feel myself about to sink to the ground in a heap. I am in the habit of poking at my husband impulsively with my hand whenever he gets into one of his stubborn moods. Now, too, this habit got the better of me. No sooner did I place my hand on his chest than I began pushing him as hard as I could.

"What do you think you're doing?!"

"Don't you see? I'm offering you an apology. Why can't you just accept it? Why must you lose your temper at the slightest provocation? Where do you think we are? You're so unfeeling!"

"Don't you dare say that!" he bellowed, exploding at me in an uncontrollable rage.

Here we were in this special place, and I yearned to be intoxicated by the memory of a dazzling affair that had so brightened a part of our lives. I resolved to do whatever was necessary to restore his mood. Shedding tears of vexation, I poked at him incessantly.

Just then, an itinerant peddler selling knick-knacks happened to pass by. After he had gone ahead a little way, he turned around and stared at us.

"Stop it, will you? You're making a scene."

"Am I? Then why don't we at least try to have a good time, the way we were supposed to do in the first place? If you can't do that, then please go home by yourself. I don't want to leave just yet."

"Suit yourself," he said and hurried on ahead.

I had been standing beside a hedge of Chinese hawthorn and tearing off one leaf after another, crying all the while. To think that such cold, heartless words as these were coming out of the mouth of the man who used to be my lover! Even supposing I had acted imprudently at the shrine, for him to hurl abuse at me in a place laden with such fond memories was almost too much to bear. That he could willfully crush the memory of my love in that headstrong way of his enraged me, and I wanted to lash out any way I could.

We returned to the train station without exchanging another word. Once there, I managed to collect myself and simply gazed at the faces of people gathered inside. I tried to start a friendly conversation with him, but it was no use; he maintained a stubborn silence and made no reply.

It was still light when we reached the house.

I felt out of sorts and washed my hair. After we had finished our dinner, he spoke to me at last.

"What is it about your manner that rubs me the wrong way?" His tone of voice was rough-edged and utterly without humor. "Everything you do irritates me no end."

I said nothing and simply maintained a meek silence before him. Then he started in all over again about the incident at the Mama shrine.

He said he was damned if he could understand why the words he took to be "Her face is red" sounded to me like "Please come in." And why hadn't I entered the shrine together with him to take a look around? Why did I have to be so willful?

What he said gave me pause. Am I obliged to bend my character in accordance with this man's every whim, just because there is something about it he doesn't like? Must I cower before him in every instance and take pains not to offend him just because my manner happens to rub him the wrong way?

Whatever revulsion my manner might provoke in others, at least it is something I can call my own. So it is with my character. It, too, is my very own, repulsive or hateful though it may be to others. For him of all people to dictate how I should behave was insulting in the extreme.

"What is it to you if he *did* say that I was blushing?" I snapped at him shrilly. "There is no end to the shame I feel on your account."

"You mean you don't feel ashamed when someone like him says you are blushing?" he snapped right back.

Well, what if I *had* blushed? Or if that handsome, retarded monk had said with a smile that I had? What was so shameful about that? The reason was beyond me. And so I argued, point by point.

"The fact remains I find your manner distasteful. I really do. You are a despicable woman."

The expression he wore when he spat out those words! Sinister creases were etched around his eyes, and his sneer cast a dark, grim shadow around his tightly closed mouth. . . . His cheekbones were so prominent that nothing, not even a hammer, seemed capable of smoothing them down. All his features were so sharp that his countenance seemingly lacked even a single soft line. I could only stare at him in amazement.

We had been living together as a couple for a year or so, but never before had I witnessed an expression that provoked in me such contempt. Could this man truly have been my lover? To think that this was the countenance of the man with whom I'd formed a spiritual bond—a bond that enabled our flesh and blood to mingle and made love blossom anew, adding a rich luster to our lives—overwhelmed me with an indescribable sadness.

"I simply cannot get along with you," he said. "Everything about you irritates me. . . . We'll get a divorce, that's what we'll do."

"We don't get along. . . . I can't to do a thing when someone like you is around. . . . I feel myself becoming totally worthless. . . ." These were the sorts of things he had said to me in the past. When I asked him why he felt that way, he never gave me a straight answer. He would merely say his piece and then become lost in thought.

"We'll get a divorce": this was something I had never heard him say before. The words startled me—so much so, in fact, that they refused to take clear shape in my mind, however often I repeated them to myself. I couldn't imagine how the feelings he harbored toward me would lead him to ask for a divorce. What I do know is that his talk of separating— in effect of abandoning me—took me completely by surprise.

"Why do you want a divorce?" I pressed him for a reply.

"I just don't like you," he said, lowering his eyes.

My breast was overcome by a flood of emotion, cold and constricting. All I could do was grit my teeth and stare at him for the longest time.

"Won't you agree to a divorce?" His voice seemed unnaturally composed.

"Why should I?" I pressed him again, staring at him blankly. "After all . . ."

I thought of appealing to the love we had for each other but then checked myself. Instead, I asked him, "Are you really capable of leaving me?"

"I just want to break it off," he said calmly, as if this were the only possible answer.

"Are you telling me this in all seriousness? You're not joking?" I found myself grabbing the sleeve of his kimono as I spoke.

"I'm very serious. I just want to get away from you. If you don't leave, then I will."

By uttering these words, he had taken the ultimate step. I felt as though I'd lost the initiative. Indeed, it annoyed me that he would be the first to fall out of love and break off our relationship.

"What are you saying? Now that I've faded from your affections, you don't want me so much as to appear in front of you anymore, and that's why we should split up?"

"It's not that. I'm not saying we should separate because my love for you is gone."

"Why, that's the strangest thing I've ever heard!"

"It doesn't matter whether you understand or not. Everything will be fine if we just go our separate ways."

"But I don't want to."

As soon as I had uttered these words, however, tears of frustration welled up uncontrollably in my eyes. I tried to say something, but the tears kept getting in the way and made my voice quaver. I don't know how many times I gulped down my tears and choked on my own sobs. All I could do was to stare at my husband, the tears streaming down my cheeks.

He, too, was silent for a while.

"You're just being cowardly!" I began to rail at him. "If you still love me as you say you do, then why don't you just kill me off instead of abandoning me? You want to keep me at a distance and make sure that whatever love you have left simply fades away. Really, how spineless can you get?"

I argued my case relentlessly and refused to let up. "You're afraid of me, aren't you? What exactly are you afraid of?"

He was always saying that I was the cause of constant strain. There was something about my manner, he claimed, that bordered on the licentious and led me to throw myself at any man in front of me; it made him recoil in disgust. In order to counter the strain, he resorted to berating me. "You make me sick," he would say. Yes, it's true. I positively loathed his cowardliness. It was so unmanly.

"Well, if you really feel such strain, then why not simply yield to it? Why must you harbor such a grudge toward someone you claim to love or at least claim to have loved in the past? That grudge has caused you to humiliate me many times over. Surely you realize how humiliating it is for me to hear you talk about a divorce."

At that point, I burst into tears.

"The fact is I don't love you at all," he said after a while. I detected the glint of cold indifference in his eyes. "How could I love a woman whom I can't bear the thought of being with? I'm sick of you, and that's why I'm saying we should split up."

At that moment, I felt the blood boil in my veins. *I'll kill that man. Yes, I'll kill him—that's all that matters.* . . . Murderous thoughts swept over me like a tempest. I glared at his face so intently that my eyeballs might as well have rained blood on him.

"I will not have you leaving me. I'm still in love with you!"

This is what I told him, even though something in me made me mock my own words. My pride had been sorely wounded, and yet I still couldn't bring myself to say to him, as he had said to me, "I don't love you at all. Let's split up." My words to him did, in fact, bespeak my true feelings. Yet having to express myself as I did with a complement of tears and displays of sincerity was distasteful to me. Thus, even as I confessed to him, "I'm still in love with you," I cursed my unnatural attachment.

"I can't accept it when you talk about divorce without good reason," I said. "So go ahead and kill me. I hope you're man enough. . . . That's how strong my love is for you."

"I hate that kind of argument," he retorted. "I really hate it. How can you logically compare the strength of one person's love to another's? You say you want me to kill you? I'd be only too happy to. But it's silly to do so when I have no affection for you whatsoever. I value my own life too much."

He let out a dry laugh. "If talk about a divorce really upsets you that much, then you can make amends by apologizing for everything that's happened since this morning. Next, you can make a vow never again to go against my word. If you do that, then I'll forgive you."

I had never heard such nonsense. "How mean of you!" I wanted to scream.

"I have nothing to apologize for," I said. "I will not apologize. Why must I apologize? I'd rather be killed than forced to make an apology to you!"

"Then it's settled. We'll split up. I can't stand it any longer. I really can't!"

"Why must you insist on separating?"

He stood up and made as if to leave. I grabbed the front of his half-cloak and held it fast.

"You're the one who is putting *me* off!" I said. "Which one of us brought up this insufferable matter in the first place? Which one, I ask?"

That is when he hit me.

"Why did you hit me? What crime did I commit to deserve this?"

I must have looked wild-eyed with anger. "Just who do you think you are?" I screamed, venting in a single phrase all the confused emotions that had accumulated in my breast.

My scream grew hoarse and turned into a sob.

At this, my husband proceeded to kick my vanity dresser and break the glass in the mirror. The magazine I then threw at him hit the electric light and smashed the bulb. Grabbing his hair so tightly that it seemed to loosen from his scalp, I attempted to drag him about the tatami mats, now strewn with glass shards. I kept slapping him all over with the hollow of my hand until the joints in my palm seemed to crumble. Each time I slapped him, however, his rough hands pummeled me with ever greater fury.

"Say you're sorry!" he shrieked, jabbing at my bony shoulder. "Say you're sorry!"

Thrusting his long, pointed chin forward and glaring at me with the coarsest of expressions, he wagged his head at me in rhythm with his harsh words. Hot tears as thick as blood flowed from my eyes and stung my cheeks.

"What the hell for?" I fairly spat out the words. "I wasn't born into this world to apologize to the likes of you!"

Feeling utterly defiant, I hurled the most abusive language I could think of at him.

My left sleeve had split at the seam and dangled limply to the floor. I hadn't put my hair up after washing it that evening, and it was now a tangled mess, what with his pulling at it and my flailing about. Locks of hair hung over my eyes and ears like so many spider legs. They clung to my face and neck with a rank, sultry warmth that only drove me into greater frenzy. I hurled anything and everything within my grasp. In return, he kicked me on the shoulder blade so hard that I thought my body had shattered.

"Either I kill you or you kill me," I shouted. "I won't stop until one of us dies!"

If a sharp knife had lain within my grasp at that moment, I feel certain that I would have run it through him. If I could just pierce his flesh with a single thrust of some sharp object, then all the mounting emotions I felt—my own fit of temper along with the shame and disgust I felt toward a man who would beat me and force me to apologize—would have dissipated, I was sure. That failing, I would have just as soon be killed—be defeated once and for all by this man. Far better for me at least that one of us emerge the victor in a fight to the death than to prolong a tedious argument in which I was continually berated and beaten and put to shame.

I really saw no way for my anger to subside until the final blow had been struck. My breathing became so labored that I grew faint. Occasionally, I succeeded in grabbing the hem of his kimono, and when I did so I clutched it with all my might and hurriedly struck at him again and again.

"That's enough!"

He wrestled me to the floor with brute force.

"I swear I'm going to kill you. Kill you, I say!"

I yelled at him in a voice that had gone completely hoarse.

"Very well then," he said calmly, "let's go outside."

On the way out, we passed our young maid, who was slumped in a heap on the floor and appeared to be crying. I continued marching outside, but he called me to a halt.

"Wait—don't go out looking like a madwoman! Why don't you at least do something with your hair?"

"Who cares about my hair? I'm serious—I won't stop until one of us kills the other!"

My voice trembled like a taut wire. Out I went, my hair a mess and pieces of cotton wadding coming out of my sleeve.

It was pitch dark outside. There was no one on the street. A single lamp flickered in front of a house several doors down. Someone was playing the koto quietly in the house opposite our garden. My husband said something to the maid and then came out himself.

"You really are mad. What if you get stopped by the police? This is a public street, you know!"

When I heard these gutless words, a chilly wave of derision passed through me and doused the flames of passion.

"For me, there is no inside or outside. I don't give a damn whether people on the street see me or call me insane. I just want to kill you or be killed by you. That's all I care about!"

"Come now, don't be so petty," he said in a soothing voice. He was trying to placate me.

These last words finally brought me to my senses. It was as if the dark blood that had churned wildly through my brain had receded into the marrow. At the same time, his words made me realize just what sort of person he was.

"How can you talk about being petty? I can't begin to gauge the magnitude of the problem. Haven't you just told me you want a divorce?"

"That's right. But let's get hold of ourselves and think this through carefully."

"What is there to think about? Nothing, I should say. I shall kill you, or you shall kill me. I won't have it any other way. You are quite the coward, aren't you? Why did you want us to step out of the house?"

"Stop talking nonsense!" he hissed and started to walk away.

"I am not talking nonsense! You had your wits about you when you said you wanted to split up. I have my wits about me now."

"Suit yourself, then."

No sooner had he uttered these words than he darted to his right and disappeared. I chased after him as far as the main road only to lose sight of him; I could not even hear his footsteps. I stood there motionless for a time.

I was standing atop a weather-beaten bluff that fell away sharply. Train tracks ran along the base of the bluff below. A coal fire burning in the nearby station cast a pale wreath of crimson around the area, like a naked candle spreading its dim, flickering light into the surrounding darkness. The sky looked overcast; not a single star shone. The faint, quavering notes of the koto next door played about the hem of my skirt.

My heart braced itself against the inevitable wave of sorrow. My emotions were so spent that they could not endure even the warm breeze that wafted across the darkness and caressed my skin. It is in times like these, no doubt, that people think of killing themselves; I was so exhausted that I could barely stand up after the beating I'd taken, a beating that had drained my muscles of all strength. I felt my nerves go completely slack; it was as though my hands, long bound together, had suddenly been untied. It was difficult even to think. All that was left of my emotions was the empty feeling of misery and despair that had lodged itself in my breast. I slumped to the ground. The sight of my kimono torn at the seam made me utterly despondent; my life surely resembled those pieces of shredded cotton that dangled from the sleeve. I knelt there on the ground for some time.

"We'll get a divorce."

This thought, which had been lurking in the murky depths of my heart, gradually took on a distinct hue and eventually permeated my entire being with a serene sadness. Cradling the torn sleeve in my arm, I stepped back inside his house.

The tatami room was just as it had been before: in a complete shambles. All the young maid had done was to replace the light bulb; now she just sat there below it with a blank expression on her face. I don't know what she was thinking, but she made no attempt to clean up the mess. As soon as I entered the room, however, she clutched the skirt of my kimono and burst into tears.

I entered my own room and in the course of things started to gather together my belongings. I asked the maid to help me change my kimono. It was then I decided never to mend the torn sleeve, and I had the maid fold the kimono up just as it was and put it away.

The bouquet of anemone adorning my low writing table was a medley of color—lavender, white, and red—and looked all the more beautiful in the dim light. I sat there calmly on my crimson Yūzen cushion— the same cushion on which I used to rest my languid body after my bath while awaiting my husband's return, cheeks in hands, my elbows resting on the table. As I fixed my gaze on the flowers' gentle, soothing hues, my breast heaved with emotion, and the tears overflowed my eyelids, drop by burning drop.

I could not help reflecting on the love that had once been.

Our wedding took place after a series of complicated negotiations between his parents and mine. Plans for marriage went forward only because my elder sister intervened. If we were to split up under the present circumstances, I could never return to my own family. If I tried to return, they would probably get some busybody to intercede and force me to come back here.

"I want a divorce." Having heard him say these words, the idea of prostrating myself before my husband and begging him to retract them was abhorrent to me. No, my feelings for him hadn't died out completely, even now that I was no longer at his side. But once he'd declared his desire to separate, I had no intention of going back to him again—none whatsoever! It hardly mattered if my lingering affection still entwined itself around him. Ever since he let the word "divorce" escape his lips, I could think only of the precariousness of my position as a woman who had been shamed.

Where to go after I left this house? I mulled over even such trivial matters as this. I could leave here this very night—but whither? I couldn't very well go to my sister's house.

My nerves, which at one point had gone slack, seemed to revive; they were now as taut as ever. I shut my eyes to the problem of where to go and concentrated instead on gathering together those personal items I might easily take with me.

Still he did not come home.

I packed a small bag and set it to one side. I went about my preparations intent on leaving before his return. Placing a hand mirror on the vanity, I proceeded to comb my hair.

Still he did not come home.

I simply had to see him one more time, I realized. And what would I tell him once I had done so?

"I shall give you your divorce." That is what I wished to tell him, perfectly composed, right to his face.

It was already past midnight. I had the maid lock up the house and told her to retire. Leaning against my low writing table, I waited for his footsteps to reverberate in the entranceway.

A broken mirror: how strange that my vanity mirror, shattering as it did, would portend such a sad train of events. I stared at the crack running diagonally across the glass. When we were first married, my husband, enthralled by the large mirror I had installed in my room, would sit down in front of it and gaze into it. He also enjoyed standing next to me and watching me make myself up, especially as I nimbly worked my eyebrow brush. I would have him place one kind of flower or another in the long, thin-stemmed vase decorating the vanity. He took pleasure in that sort of thing. We'd look at our faces reflected together in the glass. Now this mirror, having broken in two, seemingly foretold our fate as a couple.

More than once, I had endured the brunt of his fury. Whenever I caught a cold, he never bothered to comfort me. Instead, he would blurt out gruffly, "Why did you go and catch a cold, anyway?" I hated his petty grumbling.

Lost in such thoughts, I whiled away the hours in anticipation of his return. I felt my senses being sucked into the ticking sound of the clock sitting on the wall shelf. Looking at the hand inching across the face, I recalled the previous times I waited impatiently for his return. Formerly, when my husband was late coming home, I would place my finger on the hand and track its movements, as if it were a crawling insect.

The pain radiating from my backbone around to my arms now flared up in earnest; I felt as though I was being jabbed with the butt end of a pole. Enveloped in the pleasant warmth of the charcoal brazier in my room and feeling the effects of the pain and fatigue as I leaned against my writing table, I began to feel feverish. I dozed off but woke up again immediately.

I looked at the clock. It was now past two in the morning. Still he had not returned. Having nodded off for a moment, my nerves had grown less taut, and I felt less anxious. Let happen what may. "Say you're sorry!" If he asked it of me, well, I would do so, obediently, out of a desire to exchange warm and friendly smiles with him once again. I wanted to give my weary heart over to his gentle words. I could not attain a state of equanimity, physically or spiritually, without seeing him again. It was so very hard not seeing him. If, when I clung to him, he would just say to me, "I'm sorry about what happened!" then I could return to my former lightheartedness and become excited about anything I heard or saw. I'd let myself succumb to happy tears of nostalgia and bury my face in his chest. . . .

Such were my thoughts. My husband hadn't once come home as late as two o'clock during the entire time we've been married. I pictured him wandering the streets aimlessly in the middle of the night, hands tucked in his robe, and was overcome with unspeakable distress. "Forgive me. It was entirely my fault." If I were to say this and then prostrate myself before him, he would surely beam with joy. This was the beautiful scene I envisaged, of kneeling before my husband, my hands outstretched toward him. . . .

I stepped into his study, seized by the desire to be in his room. I pulled open the drawer to his writing desk, traced my hand along his bookshelves, and clasped to my breast his beloved figurine cast in the image of Salammbō. Then I leaned up against the desk and imagined myself in his embrace.

Still he did not come home.

Where on earth could he be? I racked my brain for an answer.

He could not possibly be walking about alone at this late hour. That would mean he was staying overnight at a friend's house—except that he had no close friend on whom he might impose. Where could he have gone, then? I couldn't help thinking that he might be standing right outside the gate and refusing to come in out of spite.

I stepped out of the house and opened the gate. The terrifying nocturnal darkness pressed in on my eyes; I saw no sign of anyone. I shut the gate and stood for the longest time on the stone steps leading to the house. A wind had risen—when I'm not sure—and was rattling the shutters violently. By the light of the front door, I could see blossoms falling like so many specks of dust from the cherry tree by the gate. . . .

He did not return until morning. I waited for him until dawn. It seemed like forever. The bag I'd packed the night before—what an odd lump of reality it contained—I could just make it out, sitting below the window in the dim but ever-increasing light. . . .

"Good morning," he said upon his return. I looked up at his face as though I hadn't laid eyes on it for years. There was a bright, fresh luster to his complexion that suggested he'd taken a bath. He toyed with a toothpick between his teeth. I detected the smell of alcohol on this breath.

"What shall we do about the matter we'd talked about last night?" I said before he had a chance to speak. "You said you wanted a divorce, and I've been waiting here ready to do as you decide."

"Well, then, let's go ahead with it." So saying, he went straight to his room without uttering another word. I left his house immediately after that.

****

Such was her story. "I'll never return to my husband's side again," Seiko vowed. I wonder how long she intends to stay with me upstairs.

NOTES

1. Hasegawa Kei, "Kaisetsu," in *Tamura Toshiko*, ed. Hasegawa Kei, *Sakka no jiden*, ed. Saeki Shōichi and Matsumoto Ken'ichi, vol. 87 (Tokyo: Nihon tosho sentā, 1999), p. 259.

2. Setouchi Harumi argues that Tamura was Japan's first self-supporting female professional writer. See, for example, Setouchi Harumi, *Tamura Toshiko* (Tokyo: Kōdansha, 1993), p. 457; and Setouchi Harumi, "Tamura Toshiko no koto," in *Josei sakka jūsan'nin ten*, ed. Okuno Takeo, Kōno Toshirō, and Yasumasa Masao (Tokyo: Kindai Nihonbungakukan, 1988), p. 35. A casual glance at the available chronologies (*nenpu*), on which this essay has relied extensively, suggests that the most important period in Tamura's career as a

writer was the period between 1910 and 1915, which is to say the last few years of Meiji and the first few years of Taishō.

3. Setouchi, *Tamura Toshiko*, p. 18.

4. Sakai Morinosuke, "Tamura Toshiko," in *Nihon kindai bungaku daijiten*, ed. Nihon Kindai Bungakkan (Tokyo: Kōdansha, 1977), 2:372. Specific note is made of "Jo ni kaete jinseijō no shizenshugi o ronzu," the celebrated preface to a collection of essays Hōgetsu published in 1909.

5. The chronology of the marriage is uncertain. Setouchi Harumi (*Tamura Toshiko*, p. 445) dates the union to 1920; Fukutani Sachiko dates it a year earlier ("Nenpu," in *Meiji joryū bungaku shū*, ed. Shioda Ryōhei, in vol. 82 of *Meiji bungaku zenshū* [Tokyo: Chikuma Shobō, 1965], 2:435; Sakai Morinosuke to 1921 or 1922 ("Tamura Toshiko," p. 372); and Hasegawa Kei to 1923 (*Tamura Toshiko*, p. 255).

6. Abe Tomoji, Hotta Yoshie, Kubota Mantarō, Kusano Shimpei, and Takeda Taijun all made Toshiko's acquaintance in China, and several wrote about their meetings with her. See, for example, Abe Tomoji, "Kaei: Inaka e no tegami," *Bungakkai* 3, no. 4 (June 1949): 24–33.

7. See, for example, Hasegawa Kei, "Sakuhin kanshō," in *Tanpen josei bungaku kindai*, ed. Imai Yasuko, Yabu Teiko, and Watanabe Sumiko (Tokyo: Ōfūsha, 1992), p. 52.

8. Mama, a hill overlooking Kōnodai (a district in what is now the city of Ichikawa, Chiba Prefecture, east of Tokyo), is the site of an ancient legend that tells of the maiden Tekona (or Tegona), who was courted by two (or more) lovers and ends up drowning herself rather than having to choose between (among) them. The legend is the subject of several verses in the *Man'yōshū*, the great eighth-century poetic anthology.

9. One such suggestion can be found in Donald Keene's cursory dismissal of women's writing (with the exception of Higuchi Ichiyō and partial exception of the early Tamura Toshiko), not only of the Meiji period but of the entire modern era before World War II. See Donald Keene, *Dawn to the West: Japanese Literature in the Modern Era* (New York: Holt, Rinehart, and Winston, 1984), pp. 1113–1115.

10. The source texts used for these translations are from Setouchi Jakuchō, Odagiri Hideo, and Kusano Shimpei, eds., *Tamura Toshiko sakuhinshū* (Tokyo: Orijin shuppan sentā, 1987), pp. 187–199 (Lifeblood) and 239–264 (The Vow). Grateful acknowledgment is made to Kumakura Chiyuki and Ōno Yōko for their help with terms related to clothing and popular culture in the stories translated here and to the UC Irvine Humanities Center for a research grant that supported the translations.

FURTHER READING

BIBLIOGRAPHIES

Ericson, Joan E., and Midori McKeon. "Selected Bibliography of Japanese Women's Writing." In *The Woman's Hand: Gender and Theory in Japanese Women's Writing*, ed. Paul Gordon Schalow and Janet A. Walker, pp. 461–493. Stanford: Stanford University Press, 1996.

Mamola, Claire Zebroski. *Japanese Women's Writings in English Translation: An Annotated Bibliography*. 2 vols. New York: Garland, 1989, 1992.

GENERAL RESOURCES

English

Bardsley, Jan. *The Bluestockings of Japan: New Women's Fiction and Essays from Seitō, 1911–1916*. Ann Arbor: Center for Japanese Studies, University of Michigan, 2006.

———. "*Seitō* and the Resurgence of Writing by Women." In *The Columbia Companion to Modern East Asian Literature*. ed. Joshua S. Mostow, Kirk A. Denton, Bruce Fulton, Sharalyn Orbaugh, pp. 93–98. New York: Columbia University Press, 2003.

Bernstein, Gail Lee, ed. *Recreating Japanese Women, 1600–1945*. Berkeley: University of California Press, 1991.

Brownstein, Michael. "*Jogaku Zasshi* and the Founding of *Bungakukai*." *Monumenta Nipponica* 35, no. 3 (1980): 319–336.

Copeland, Rebecca. *Lost Leaves: Women Writers of Meiji Japan.* Honolulu: University of Hawai'i Press, 2000.

———. "The Meiji Woman Writer 'Amidst a Forest of Beards.'" *Harvard Journal of Asiatic Studies* 57, no. 2 (1997): 383–418.

———. "Meiji Women Writers." In *The Columbia Companion to Modern East Asian Literature*, ed. Joshua S. Mostow, Kirk A. Denton, Bruce Fulton, Sharalyn Orbaugh, pp. 69–73. New York: Columbia University Press, 2003.

Ericson, Joan E. "The Origins of the Concept of Women's Literature." In *The Woman's Hand: Gender and Theory in Japanese Women's Writing*, ed. Paul Gordon Schalow and Janet A. Walker, pp. 74–115. Stanford: Stanford University Press, 1996.

———. *Be A Woman: Hayashi Fumiko and Modern Japanese Women's Literature.* Honolulu: University of Hawai'i Press, 1997.

Gatten, Aileen, and Anthony Hood Chambers, eds. *New Leaves: Studies and Translations of Japanese Literature in Honor of Edward Seidensticker.* Ann Arbor: Center for Japanese Studies, University of Michigan, 1993.

Hane, Mikiso. *Reflections on the Way to the Gallows: Rebel Women in Prewar Japan.* Berkeley: University of California Press, 1988.

Harrison, Marianne Mariko. *The Rise of the Woman Novelist in Meiji Japan.* Ann Arbor: University of Michigan Dissertation Services, 1994.

Hastings, Sally. "The Empress' New Clothes and Japanese Women, 1868–1912." *The Historian* 55, no. 4 (Summer 1993): 677–692.

Keene, Donald. *World Within Walls: Japanese Literature of the Pre-Modern Era, 1600–1897.* New York: Holt, Rinehart, and Winston, 1976.

———. *Dawn to the West: Japanese Literature in the Modern Era.* Vol. 1, *Fiction.* New York: Holt, Rinehart, and Winston, 1984.

Lewell, John. *Modern Japanese Novelists: A Biographical Dictionary.* New York: Kodansha International, 1993.

Loftus, Ronald. *Telling Lives: Women's Self-Writing in Modern Japan.* Honolulu: University of Hawai'i Press, 2004.

Mackie, Vera. *Feminism in Modern Japan.* Cambridge: Cambridge University Press, 2003.

Marran, Christine. "'Poison Woman': Takahashi Oden and the Spectacle of Female Deviance in Early Meiji." *U.S.-Japan Women's Journal*, no. 9 (1995): 93–110.

Monnet, Livia. "In the Beginning Woman Was the Sun: Autobiographies of Modern Japanese Women Writers." *Japan Forum* 1, nos. 1–2 (1989): 55–57, 197–223.

Mertz, John Pierre. *Novel Japan: Spaces of Nationhood in Early Meiji Narrative, 1870-88.* Michigan Monographs in Japanese Studies, no. 48. Ann Arbor: Center for Japanese Studies, University of Michigan, 2003.

Mulhern, Chieko I., ed. *Japanese Women Writers: A Bio-critical Sourcebook.* Westport, Conn.: Greenwood, 1994.

Rose, Barbara. *Tsuda Umeko and Women's Education in Japan.* New Haven: Yale University Press, 1992.

Sakaki, Atsuko. "Sliding Door: Women in the Heterosocial Literary Field of Early Modern Japan." *U.S.-Japan Women's Journal,* no. 17 (1999): 3–38.

Sato, Barbara. *The New Japanese Woman: Modernity, Media, and Women in Interwar Japan.* Durham, N.C.: Duke University Press, 2003.

Sievers, Sharon. *Flowers in Salt: The Beginnings of Feminist Consciousness in Modern Japan.* Stanford: Stanford University Press, 1983.

Tanaka, Yukiko. *Women Writers of Meiji and Taishō Japan: Their Lives, Works, and Critical Reception,* 1868–1926. Jefferson, N.C.: McFarland, 2000.

Terazawa Yuki. "The State, Midwives, and Reproductive Surveillance in Late Nineteenth- and Early Twentieth-Century Japan." *U.S.-Japan Women's Journal,* no. 24 (September 2003): 66.

Uno, Kathleen. "The Death of 'Good Wife, Wise Mother'?" In *Postwar Japan as History,* ed. Andrew Gordon, pp. 293–324. Berkeley: University of California Press, 1993.

Japanese

Higuchi Ichiyō and Itō Sei. *Higuchi Ichiyō shū: Fu Meiji joryū bungaku.* Vol. 10 of *Nihon gendai bungaku zenshū.* Tokyo: Kōdansha, 1962.

Higuchi Ichiyō and Izumi Kyōka. *Higuchi Ichiyō, Meiji joryū bungaku, Izumi Kyōka shū.* Tokyo: Chikuma shobō, 1972.

Imai Yasuko, Yabu Teiko, and Watanabe Sumiko, eds., *Tanpen josei bungaku kindai.* Tokyo:Ōfūsha, 1992.

Inoue Teruko. "Jogaku no shisō no keisei to tenkai." *Tōdai shinbun kenkyūjo kiyō,* no. 17 (1968): 35–62.

Itagaki Naoko. *Meiji, Taishō, Shōwa joryū bungaku.* Tokyo: Ōfūsha, 1967.

Kataoka Yoshikazu. *Kindai bungaku nyūmon: Kataoka Yoshikazu chosaku shū.* Vol. 10. Tokyo: Chūō kōron, 1980.

Murakami Nobuhiko. *Meiji josei shi.* Vol. 2. Tokyo: Riron sha, 1970.

Nobeji Kiyoe. " 'Jogakusei,' 'hakuhyō *Jogaku zasshi*' ron—*Jogaku zasshi* no nagare no naka wo mite." *Bungaku* 4, no. 47 (1979): 15–27.

Seki Reiko. *Kataru onnatachi no jidai: Ichiyō to Meiji josei hyōgen.* Tokyo: Shin'yōsha, 1997.

Shioda Ryōhei, ed. *Meiji joryū bungaku shū.* Vol. 2. Vol. 82 of *Meiji bungaku zenshū.* Tokyo: Chikuma shobō, 1965.

——. *Meiji joryū bungaku shū.* Vol. 1. Vol. 81 of *Meiji bungaku zenshū.* Tokyo: Chi-kuma shobō, 1966.

——. *Meiji joryū sakka ron.* Tokyo: Nara shobō, 1965.

——. *Shintei Meiji joryū sakka ron.* Tokyo: Bunsendō shuppan, 1983.

Sōma Kokkō. *Meiji shōki no sanjosei.* Tokyo: Kosei kaku, 1940.

Takada Chinami, Nakagawa Shigemi, and Nakayama Kazuko, eds. *Josei sakka shū. Shin Nihon koten bungaku taikei,* no. 23. Tokyo: Iwanami shoten, 2002.

Wada Shigejirō. *Meiji zenki joryū sakuhinron—Higuchi Ichiyō to sono zengo.* Tokyo: Ōfūsha, 1989.

Watanabe Sumiko. *Nihon kindai josei bungakuron: Yami wo hiraku.* Kyoto: Sekai shisōsha, 1998.

HASEGAWA SHIGURE

English

Kano, Ayako. *Acting Like a Woman in Modern Japan: Theater, Gender, and National-ism.* New York: Palgrave, 2001.

Japanese

Hasegawa Shigure. *Hasegawa Shigure zenshū.* 5 vols. Tokyo: Fuji shuppan, 1993.

Ikuta Hanayo. *Ichiyō to Shigure—denki: Higuchi Ichiyō/Hasegawa Shigure denki sōsho.* Tokyo: Ōzorasha, 1992.

Iwahashi Kunie. *Hyōden: Hasegawa Shigure.* Tokyo: Chikuma shobō, 1993.

Ogata Akiko, *Nyonin geijutsu no sekai—Hasegawa Shigure to sono shūhen.* Tokyo: Domesu shuppan, 1980.

——. *Kaguyaku no jidai—Hasegawa Shigure to sono shūhen.* Tokyo: Domesu shup-pan, 1993.

HIGUCHI ICHIYŌ

English

Compernolle, Timothy J. Van. "Happiness Foreclosed: Sentimentalism, the Suf-fering Heroine, and Social Critique in Higuchi Ichiyō's 'Jūsan'ya.'" *Journal of Japanese Studies* 30, no. 2 (2004): 353–381.

Danly, Robert. *In the Shade of Spring Leaves: The Life and Writings of Higuchi Ichiyō, A Woman of Letters in Meiji Japan.* New Haven: Yale University Press,

1981. [Contains translations of *Yamizakura* (*Flowers at Dusk*), *Yuki no hi* (*A Snowy Day*), *Koto no ne* (*The Sound of the Koto*), *Yamiyo* (*Encounters on a Dark Night*), *Ōtsugomori* (*On the Last Day of the Year*), *Nigorie* (*Troubled Waters*), *Jūsan'ya* (*The Thirteenth Night*), *Takekurabe* (*Child's Play*), and *Wakare-michi* (*Separate Ways*).]

Kamei, Hideo. "The Structure of Rage: The Polyphonic Fiction of Higuchi Ichiyō." Trans. Joshua Young. In *Transformations of Sensibility: The Phenomenology of Meiji Literature*, ed. Michael Bourdaghs, pp. 111–133. Ann Arbor: Center for Japanese Studies, University of Michigan, 2002.

——. "*Shinjū* as Misdeed: Love Suicides in Higuchi Ichiyō and Chikamatsu Monzaemon." Trans. Lewis Harrington. In *Transformations of Sensibility: The Phenomenology of Meiji Literature*, ed. Michael Bourdaghs, pp. 135–158. Ann Arbor: Center for Japanese Studies, University of Michigan, 2002.

Keene, Donald. "The Diary of Higuchi Ichiyō." In *Modern Japanese Diaries: The Japanese at Home and Abroad as Revealed Through Their Diaries*, pp. 284–303. New York: Henry Holt, 1995.

Lewell, John. "Higuchi Ichiyō." In *Modern Japanese Novelists: A Biographical Dictionary*. New York: Kodansha America, 1993.

Maeda, Ai. "Their Time as Children: A Study of Higuchi Ichiyō's 'Growing Up.'" Trans. Edward Fowler. *Text and the City: Essays on Japanese Modernity*, ed. James Fujii, pp. 109–143. Durham, N.C.: Duke University Press, 2004.

Millett, Christine M. "Inverted Classical Allusions and Higuchi Ichiyo's Literary Technique in 'Takekurabe.'" *U.S.-Japan Women's Journal*, no. 14 (1998): 3–26.

Mitsutani, Margaret. "Higuchi Ichiyō: A Literature of Her Own." *Comparative Literature Studies* 22, no. 1 (Spring 1985): 53–66.

Nishikawa, Yūko. "Diaries as Gendered Texts." In *Women and Class in Japanese History*, ed. Hitomi Tonomura, A. Walthall, and H. Walita, pp. 241–256. Ann Arbor: Center for Japanese Studies, University of Michigan, 1999.

Orbaugh, Sharalyn. "Higuchi Ichiyō and Neoclassical Modernism." *The Columbia Companion to Modern East Asian Literature*, ed. Joshua Mostow, pp. 79–83. New York: Columbia University Press, 2003.

Sherif, Ann. "Ichiyō." In *Modern Japanese Writers*, ed. Jay Rubin, pp. 121–133. Scribner Writers Series. New York: Scribner's, 2001.

Takagi, Kiyoko. "Religion in the Life of Higuchi Ichiyō." *Japanese Journal of Religious Studies* 10, nos. 2 and 3 (1983): 123–147.

Tanaka, Hisako. "Higuchi Ichiyō." *Monumenta Nipponica* 12, no. 3/4 (1956): 171–194.

Ueda, Makoto. "Higuchi Ichiyō: 'Growing Up.'" In *Approaches to the Modern Japanese Short Story*, ed. Thomas Swann and Kinya Tsuruta, pp. 73–80. Tokyo: Waseda University Press, 1982.

Vernon, Victoria. "Between Two Worlds: Higuchi Ichiyō's 'Takekurabe.'" In *Daughters of the Moon: Wish, Will, and Social Constraint in Fiction by Modern*

Japanese Women, pp. 35–68. Berkeley: Institute of East Asian Studies, University of California, 1988.

Japanese

Gotō Seki. *Shōnin to shite no Higuchi Ichiyō*. Tokyo: Senshūsha, 1987.

Higuchi Ichiyō. *Gendaigo-yaku Higuchi Ichiyō*. 5 vols. Tokyo: Kawade shobō shinsha, 1996–1997.

——. *Higuchi Ichiyō shū*. Ed. Kan Satoko and Seki Reiko. *Shin Nihon koten bungaku taikei: Meiji-hen*, ed. Nakano Mitsutoshi, no. 24. Tokyo: Iwanami shoten, 2001.

——. *Higuchi Ichiyō zenshū*. 4 vols. [vols. 3 and 4 each consist of two separate books, published in different years]. Tokyo: Chikuma shobō, 1974, 1976, 1978, 1981, 1994.

——. *Kanzen gendaigo-yaku Higuchi Ichiyō nikki*. Trans. Takahashi Kazuhiko (into modern Japanese). Tokyo: Adoree, 1993.

——. *Nikki: Jō* and *ge*. Books 1 and 2. Ed. Shioda Ryōhei, Wada Yoshie, and Higuchi Etsu. In vol. 3 of *Higuchi Ichiyō zenshū*. Tokyo: Chikuma shobō, 1976 and 1978.

——. *Zenshū Higuchi Ichiyō*. 4 vols. Tokyo: Shōgakukan, 1996.

Higuchi Ichiyō Kenkyūkai, ed. *Ronshū Higuchi Ichiyō*. Tokyo: Ōfū, 1996.

Inoue Hisashi, ed. *Higuchi Ichiyō ni kiku*. Tokyo: Bungei shunjū, 2003.

Iwami Teruyo, ed. *Higuchi Ichiyō jiten*. Tokyo: Ōfū, 1996.

Kimura Masayuki, ed. *Higuchi Ichiyō to gendai*. Tokyo: Kanrin shobō, 2005.

Kitani Kimie. *Higuchi Ichiyō to jūsan-nin no otoko tachi*. Tokyo: Seishun shuppansha, 2004.

"Higuchi Ichiyō: Nikki no ryōbun, sōsaku no toposu" [collection of critical essays]. *Kokubungaku kaishaku to kyōzai no kenkyū* 49, no. 9 (August 2004): 6–137.

Maeda Ai. *Higuchi Ichiyō no sekai*. Tokyo: Heibonsha, 1978.

——, ed. *Higuchi Ichiyō*. *Shinchō Nihon bungaku arubamu*. Tokyo: Shinchōsha, 1985.

Masuda Mizuko. *Higuchi Ichiyō*. *Josei sakka hyōden*, no. 1. Tokyo: Shintensha, 1998.

Nagata Ryūtarō. *Sazanami nikki: Higuchi Ichiyō no sekai*. Tokyo: Nagata shobō, 2005.

Nihon Bungaku Kyōkai and Shin Feminizumu-hihyō no Kai, eds. *Higuchi Ichiyō wo yominaosu*. Tokyo: Gakugei shorin, 1994.

Nishio Yoshihito. *Zenshaku Ichiyō nikki*. 3 vols. Tokyo: Ōfūsha, 1976.

Ōoka Makoto, Takahashi Hideo, and Miyoshi Yukio, ser. eds. *Higuchi Ichiyō*. *Gunzō Nihon no sakka*, no. 3. Tokyo: Shōgakukan, 1993.

Sakura Momoko. *Chibi Maruko-chan no Higuchi Ichiyō (manten jinbutsu-den)*. Tokyo: Shūeisha, 2004.

Sawada Akiko. *Ichiyō den: Higuchi Natsuko no shōgai*. Tokyo: Shin Nihon shuppansha, 2005.

Seki Reiko. *Ane no chikara*. Tokyo: Chikuma shobō, 1993.

———. *Higuchi Ichiyō: Kataru onna-tachi no jidai: Ichiyō to Meiji josei hyōgen*. Tokyo: Shin'yōsha, 1997.

———. *Higuchi Ichiyō wo yomu*. Tokyo: Iwanami shoten, 1992.

Seki Ryōichi. *Higuchi Ichiyō: Kōshō to shiron*. Tokyo: Yūseidō, 1980.

Shioda Ryōhei. *Higuchi Ichiyō kenkyū*. Tokyo: Chūō kōronsha, 1975.

Setouchi Jakuchō. *Hono'o kooru: Higuchi Ichiyō no koi*. Tokyo: Shōgakkan bunko, 2004.

Shirasaki Shōichirō. *Higuchi Ichiyō nikki no sekai*. Tokyo: Chōeisha, 2005.

Tanaka Yūko. *Higuchi Ichiyō: "Iyada!" to iu*. Tokyo: Shūeisha, 2004.

Wada Yoshie, ed. *Higuchi Ichiyō dokuhon: Sono shōgai to sakuhin*. Tokyo: Gakken, 1958.

———. *Ichiyō no nikki*. Tokyo: Fukutake shoten, 1983.

———, ed. *Higuchi Ichiyō*. Nihon bungaku arubamu, no. 3. Tokyo: Chikuma shobō, 1974.

———Yamada Yūsaku. *Higuchi Ichiyō*. *Sakka no jiden*, no. 22. Tokyo: Nihon tosho sentā, 1995.

KISHIDA TOSHIKO

English

Nakajima, Shōen. "To My Fellow Sisters." Trans. Rebecca Copeland and Aiko Okamoto MacPhail. In *An Anthology of Meiji Literature*, ed. Robert Campbell, Charles Inouye, and Sumie Jones. Honolulu: University of Hawai'i Press, forthcoming.

Sievers, Sharon. "Feminist Criticism in Japanese Politics in the 1880s: The Experience of Kishida Toshiko." *Signs: Journal of Women in Culture and Society* 6, no. 4 (Summer 1981): 602–616.

Japanese

Itōya Toshio. *Josei kaihō no senkushatachi: Nakajima Toshiko to Fukuda Hideko*. Tokyo: Shimizu shoin, 1975.

Nishikawa Yūko. *Hana no imōto: Kishida Toshiko den*. Tokyo: Shinchōsha, 1986.

KITADA USURAI

Japanese

Kitada Usurai and Kajita Hanko. *Usurai ikō*. Tokyo: Shun'yōdō, 1901.

Kiyoto Fukuda. *Meiji shōnen bungakushū*. Tokyo: Chikuma shobō, 1970.

Noguchi Kōichi. "Nihonbashi sodachi no Kitada Usurai." *www.city.chuo.tokyo.jp/koho/130115/sano115.html* (accessed October 21, 2005).

Shōwa Joshi Daigaku Kindai Bungaku Kenkyūshitsu, ed. "Kitada Usurai." In *Kindai bungaku kenkyū sōsho*, 4:371–409. Tokyo: Shōwa Joshi Daigaku Kōyōkai, 1956.

Todoroki Eiko. *Kitada Usurai kenkyū*. Tokyo: Sōbunsha shuppan, 1984.

MEIJI WOMEN POETS

English and French

Beichman, Janine. "Akiko Goes to Paris: The European Poems." *Journal of the Association of Teachers of Japanese* 25, no. 1 (1991): 123–145.

———. *Embracing the Firebird: Yosano Akiko and the Birth of the Female Voice in Modern Japanese Poetry*. Honolulu: University of Hawai'i Press, 2002.

———. "Yosano Akiko: Return to the Female." *Japan Quarterly* 37, no. 2 (April–June 1990): 204–228.

Cranston, Edwin A. "Carmine-Purple: A Translation of 'Enji-Murasaki,' the First Ninety-Eight Poems of Yosano Akiko's *Midaregami*." *Journal of the Association of Teachers of Japanese* 25, no. 1 (1991): 91–112.

Dodane, Claire. *Yosano Akiko: Poète de la passion et figure de proue du féminisme japonais*. Paris: Publications Orientalistes de France, 2000.

Goldstein, Sanford, and Seishi Shinoda, trans. *Tangled Hair: Selected Tanka from Midaregami*. Rutland, Vt.: Tuttle, 1987. Rev. ed: Boston: Cheng and Tsui, 2002.

Hamill, Sam, and Keiko Matsui Gibson, trans. *River of Stars: Selected Poems of Yosano Akiko*. Boston: Shambhala, 1996.

Larson, Phyllis Hyland. "Yosano Akiko and the Re-Creation of the Female Self: An Autogynography." *Journal of the Association of Teachers of Japanese* (special issue, "Yosano Akiko [1878–1942]," ed. Laurel Rasplica Rodd) 25, no. 1 (April 1991): 11–26.

Morton, Leith. "The Canonization of Yosano Akiko's *Midaregami*." *Japanese Studies* 20, no. 3 (December 2000): 237–254.

———. "Akiko, Tomiko and Hiroshi: Tanka as Conversation in Fin-de-siècle Japan." *Japanese Studies: Bulletin of the Japanese Studies Association of Australia* (Adelaide, S.A.) 14, no. 3 (December 1994): 35–49.

———. "The Concept of Romantic Love in the *Taiyō* Magazine, 1895–1905." *Japan Review: Bulletin of the International Research Center for Japanese Studies* (Kyoto), no. 8 (1997): 79–103.

O'Brien, James. "A Few Strands of Tangled Hair." *Journal of the Association of Teachers of Japanese* 25, no. 1 (1991): 113–122.

Rabson, Steve. "Yosano Akiko: To Give One's Life or Not—A Question of Which War." In *Righteous Cause or Tragic Folly*, pp. 107–143. Ann Arbor: Center for Japanese Studies, University of Michigan, 1998.

Rexroth, Kenneth, and Ikuko Atsumi. *Women Poets of Japan*. New York: New Directions, 1982.

Rodd, Laurel Rasplica. " 'On Poetry,' by Yosano Akiko, with a Selection of Her Poems." In *New Leaves: Studies and Translations of Japanese Literature in Honor of Edward Seidensticker*, ed. Aileen Gatten and Anthony Hood Chambers, pp. 235–246. Ann Arbor: Center for Japanese Studies, University of Michigan. 1993.

———. "Yosano Akiko and the Bunkagakuin: 'Educating Free Individuals.' " *Journal of the Association of Teachers of Japanese* 25, no. 1 (1991): 75–90.

———. "Yosano Akiko and the Taishō Debate over the 'New Woman.' " In *Recreating Japanese Women, 1600–1945*, ed. Gail Lee Bernstein, pp. 175–198. Berkeley: University of California Press, 1991.

———. "Yosano Akiko on Poetic Inspiration." In *The Distant Isle: Studies and Translations of Japanese Literature in Honor of Robert H. Brower*, ed. Thomas Hare, Robert Borgen, and Sharalyn Orbaugh, pp. 409–425. Ann Arbor: Center for Japanese Studies, University of Michigan, 1996.

Rowley, G. G. *Yosano Akiko and The Tale of Genji*. Ann Arbor: Center for Japanese Studies, University of Michigan, 2000.

Stevens, John. *Lotus Moon: The Poetry of the Buddhist Nun Rengetsu*. New York: Weatherhill, 1994.

Tanaka, Mitsuko. "Unsealing Yamakawa Tomiko's Tanka: Construction of Tomiko's Gendered Image in Contrast to Akiko's." In *Japanese Poeticity and Narrativity Revisited*, ed. Eiji Sekine, pp. 219–236. Proceedings of the Association for Japanese Literary Studies, vol. 4. West Lafayette, Ind.: Association for Japanese Literary Studies, 2003.

Ueda, Makoto. "Yosano Akiko." In *Modern Japanese Poets and the Nature of Literature*, pp. 53–94. Stanford: Stanford University Press, 1983.

Walthall, Anne. *The Weak Body of a Useless Woman: Matsuo Taseko and the Meiji Restoration*. Chicago: University of Chicago Press, 1998.

Japanese

Akashi Toshiyo. *Myōjō no chihō kajin kō*. Tokyo: Kasama shoin, 1979.

Akatsuka Yukio. *Yosano Akiko kenkyū—Meiji no seishun*. Tokyo: Gakugei shorin, 1990.

————. *Yosano Akiko kenkyū—Meiji, Taishō soshite Shōwa e.* Tokyo: Gakugei shorin, 1994.

Kōuchi Nobuko. *Yosano Akiko to shūhen no hitobito—jānarizumu to no kakawari wo chūshin ni.* Tokyo: Sōjusha, 1998.

Nakagawa Hachiyō. *Yosano Akiko ni manabu—kōfuku ni naru josei to jendā no kyozetsu.* Tokyo: Gurafusha, 2005.

Naoki Kōjirō. *Yamakawa Tomiko to Yosano Akiko.* Tokyo: Hanawa shobō, 1996.

Nishio Yoshihito. *Akiko, Tomiko: Meiji no atarashii onna—ai to bungaku.* Tokyo: Yūhikaku shuppan sābisu, 1986.

Shirasaki Shōichirō. *Yamakawa Tomiko to Meiji kadan.* Tokyo: Yoshikawa hirobumikan, 1996.

Takenishi Hiroko. *Yamakawa Tomiko—Myōjō no utabito.* Tokyo: Kōdansha, 1985.

Watanabe Seiko. *Yosano Akiko: Josei sakka hyōden shiroīzu.* Tokyo: Shintensha, 1999.

Yamakawa Kikue. *Kogane no kugi o utta hito.* Tokyo: Kōdansha, 1985.

Yanesen Kōbō, ed. *Higuchi Ichiyō kashū shū.* Tokyo: Yanese kōbō, 2001.

Yosano Akiko. *Teihon Yosano Akiko zenshū.* Tokyo: Kōdansha, 1980.

MIYAKE KAHO

Japanese

Ishibashi Ningetsu. "Yabu no uguisu no saihyō." *Kokumin no tomo*, August 1888, pp. 34–36.

Ishibashi Shian. "Yabu no uguisu no saihyō wo yomu." *Kokumin no tomo*, August 1888, pp. 35–37.

Katada Fujio. "*Yabu no uguisu*, Ichiyō, Tōsui." *Kokugo to kokubungaku*, August 1934: 258–261.

Miyake Kaho. "Omoide no hitobito." *Fujin kōron*, April 1939: 106–122.

————. *Yabu no uguisu.* In *Gendai Nihon bungaku taikei*, vol. 5. Tokyo: Chikuma shobō, 1972.

Miyamoto Yuriko. "*Yabu no uguisu.*" In *Gendai Nihon bungaku taikei*, vol. 5. Tokyo: Chikuma shobō, 1972.

Seki Ryōichi. "*Yabu no uguisu.*" *Kokubungaku* 13, no. 5 (1968): 17–20.

MIZUNO SENKO

Japanese

Arishima Takeo. "Mizuno Senko-shi no sakuhin ni tsuite." *www.aozora.gr.jp/ cards/000025/card214.html* (accessed May 10 2004).

Igarashi Rantei. "Hyōden Mizuno Senko." *Gakuen* 294 (1 June 1964): 51–52.

Imai Kuniko. "Mizuno Senko-san no omoide." In *Meiji joryū bungaku shū,* ed. Shioda Ryōhei, pp. 2:399–405. Vol. 82 of *Meiji bungaku zenshū.* Tokyo: Chikuma shobō, 1965.

Mizuno Senko. *Mizuno Senko shū.* Vol. 10 of *Sōsho Seitō no onnatachi.* Tokyo: Fuji shuppan, 1986.

——. *Mizuno Senko yonpen.* Tokyo: Editoriaru dezain kenkyūsha, 2000.

Saitō Minako. *Ninshin shōsetsu.* Tokyo: Chikuma shobō, 1997.

Takeda Fusako. *Mizuno Senko: Richi no hahaoya naru watakushi no kokoro.* Tokyo: Domesu shuppan, 1995.

Tayama Katai. *Katai shūhen sakka no shokan shū.* Tatebayashi-shi: Tatebayashi-shi kyōiku iinkai bunka shinkōka, 1995.

——. "O-Tei-san no shū no mae ni." *page.frcctt.com/Schuricht/oteisan.htm* (accessed May 10 2004).

NOGAMI YAEKO

English

Enomoto, Yoshiko. "*Machiko* and *Pride and Prejudice*." *Comparative Literature Studies* 28, no. 3 (1991): 245–258.

Hogan, Eleanor J. "Beyond Influence: The Literary Sisterhood of Nogami Yaeko and Jane Austen." *U.S.-Japan Women's Journal,* no. 28, forthcoming.

——. "Marriage and Women as Intertext in the Works of Nogami Yaeko and Jane Austen." Ph.D. diss., Washington University, 2001.

——. "When Art Does *not* Represent Life: Nogami Yaeko and the Marriage Question." *Women's Studies: An Interdisciplinary Journal* 33, no. 4 (2004): 381–398.

McClain, Yoko. "A Writer as Steady as a Cow." *Journal of the Association of Teachers of Japanese* 17, no. 2 (1982): 153–172.

Nakamura, Mariko. "Novelists of Integrity: Nogami Yaeko and Kaga Otohiko." *Japanese Studies* 20, no. 2 (2000): 141–157.

Nogami Yaeko. "New Life." Trans. Jan Bardsley. In *The Bluestockings of Japan: New Women's Fiction and Essays from Seitō, 1911–1916,* ed. Jan Bardsley. Ann Arbor; Center for Japanese Studies, University of Michigan, forthcoming.

——. "Birdhouses." Trans. and intro. Juliet Winters Carpenter. In *New Leaves,* ed. Aileen Gatten and Anthony Hood Chambers, pp. 223–234. Ann Arbor: Center for Japanese Studies, University of Michigan, 1993.

——. "The Full Moon." Trans. Kyoko Iriye Selden. In *Japanese Women Writers: Twentieth Century Short Fiction,* ed. Noriko Mizuta Lippit and Kyoko Iriye Selden, pp. 22–43. Armonk, N.Y.: M. E. Sharpe, 1991.

——. "*The Neptune*"; "*The Foxes.*" Trans. Ryōzō Matsumoto. Tokyo: Kenyūsha, 1957.

———. "The Story of a Missing Leg." Trans. and intro. Yukiko Tanaka. In *To Live and to Write: Selections by Japanese Women Writers*, 1913–1938, ed. Yukiko Tanaka, pp. 145–158. Seattle: Seal, 1987.

Japanese

Inagaki Nobuko. *Nogami Yaeko nikki o yomu.* Tokyo: Meiji shoin, 2003.

———. *Nogami Yaeko nikki wo yomu: Meiro kansei made. Sengo.* 2 vols. Tokyo: Meiji sho'in, 2005.

Nakamura Tomoko. *Ningen Nogami Yaeko: "Nogami Yaeko nikki" kara.* Tokyo: Shisho no kagakusha, 1994.

Nogami Yaeko. "Tsuma to haha to sakka no tōitsu ni ikita jinsei." *Nogami Yaeko zenshū*, supp. 2, pp. 119–136. Tokyo: Iwanami shoten, 1982.

———. "Sakka ni kiku." *Nogami Yaeko zenshū*, 21:381–395. Tokyo: Iwanami shoten, 1981.

———. *Nogami Yaeko zenshū.* 26 vols. Tokyo: Iwanami shoten, 1980–1982.

———. *Nogami Yaeko zenshū. Dai II-ki.* 31 vols. Tokyo: Iwanami shoten, 1986–1991.

Sakasai Hisako. *Nogami Yaeko.* Tokyo: Miraisha, 1992.

Senuma Shigeki. *Nogami Yaeko no sekai.* Tokyo: Iwanami shoten, 1984.

Sugekawa Noriyoshi. *Nogami Yaeko.* Tokyo: Nihon tosho sentā, 1997.

Watanabe Sumiko. *Nogami Yaeko kenkyū.* Tokyo: Yagi shoten, 1969.

———. *Nogami Yaeko no bungaku.* Tokyo: Ōfūsha, 1984.

SHIMIZU SHIKIN

English and German

Copeland, Rebecca. "Broken Rings and Broken Brushes: The Broken Dreams of a Modern Murasaki." *GA/ZOKU Dynamics in Japanese Literature: Proceedings of the Midwest Association for Japanese Literary Studies* 3 (1997): 242–260.

———. "Shimizu Shikin's 'The Broken Ring': A Narrative of Female Awakening." *Review of Japanese Culture and Society* 6 (December 1994): 38–47.

Jaschke, Renate. "Das buraku-Problem in der japanischen Literatur am Beispiel der Erzählungen von Tokuda Shusei und Shimizu Shikin." In *Japanstudien. Band 5/1993. Jahrbuch des Deutschen Instituts für Japanstudien der Philipp-Franz-von-Siebold-Stiftung*, pp. 389–427. Munich: Iudicium, 1994.

Jennison, Rebecca. "Approaching Difference: A Reading of Selected Texts by Shimizu Shikin." Master's thesis, Cornell University, 1990.

———. "Equality and Difference: The Shifting Terms of Discourse in Selected Essays by Shimizu Shikin." *Journal of Kyoto Seika University*, no. 8 (1995): 93–106.

———. "Narrative Strategies in Shimizu Shikin's 'The Broken Ring.'" *Journal of Kyoto Seika University*, no. 3 (1992): 18–36.

Wellhaeusser, Nadja, trans. "Shimizu Toyoko: Warum duerfen Frauen nicht an politischen Versammlungen teilnehmen? (1890)." In *Anbauten Umbauten. Beiträge zur Japan-Forschung*, ed. Wolfgang Seifert and Asa-Bettina Wuthenow, pp. 371–384. Munich: Iudicium, 2003.

Winston, Leslie. "The Voice of Sex and the Sex of Voice in Higuchi Ichiyō and Shimizu Shikin." In *Drifting Clouds of Language: Textuality, Linguistic Theory, and Literary Studies in Contemporary Japan*, ed. Michael Bourdaghs. Ann Arbor: Center for Japanese Studies, University of Michigan, forthcoming.

Japanese

Egusa Mitsuko. "Shimizu Toyoko: Shikin to Higuchi Ichiyō no aida—Fujime Yuki *Sei no rekishigaku* wo hojosen to shite." *Bunkyō daigaku kokubun*, no. 33 (March 2004): 33–45.

——. "Shimizu Toyoko/Shikin (1), Joken no jidai." *Bunkyō daigaku bungakuku kiyō* 17, no. 1 (2003): 1–21.

——. "Shimizu Toyoko/Shikin (2), Joken to ai." *Bunkyō daigaku bungakubu kiyō* 17, no. 2 (2004): 65–91.

Kitada Sachie. "Onna no 'watashi katari'—Shimizu Shikin 'Koware yubiwa.'" In *Feminizumu hihyō e no shōtai*, ed. Ogata Akiko, Iwabuchi Hiroko, Kitada Sachie, and Kōra Rumiko, pp. 13–37. Tokyo: Gakugei shorin, 1995.

Komashaku Kimi. "Shikin shōron—Joseigakuteki na apurōchi." In Kozai Shikin, *Shikin zenshū*, ed. Kozai Yoshishige, pp. 583–609. Tokyo: Sōdo bunka, 1983.

Kozai Yoshishige. "Meiji no onna—Shimizu Shikin no koto." In Kozai Shikin, *Shikin zenshū*, ed. Kozai Yoshishige, pp. 550–565. Tokyo: Sōdo bunka, 1983.

Morioka Sukeyuki. "Shimizu Shikin 'Imin Gakuen' ni tsuite." *Koperu*, no. 149 (1990): 7–15.

Murakami Nobuhiko. "Shimizu Toyoko." In *Meiji josei shi: Joken to ie*, vol. 2, part 1. Tokyo: Rironsha, 1970.

Nagamatsu Fusako. "Josei sakka ni totte no Meiji—Shimizu Shikin no baai." *Bulletin of Hōsei University Graduate School*, no. 5 (1980): 39–57.

Nagao Masako. "Shimizu Shikin to 'Imin gakuen' (1)." *Kyōto burakushi kenkyūjo hō*, no. 28 (April 1980): 1–4.

——. "Shimizu Shikin to 'Imin gakuen' (2)." *Kyōto burakushi kenkyūjo hō*, no. 29 (May 1980): 1–3.

——. "Shimizu Shikin to 'Imin gakuen' (3)." *Kyōto burakushi kenkyūjo hō*, no. 31 (July 1980): 1–5.

Okanishi Ano. "Shimizu Shikin 'Koware yubiwa' ron—sono kontei to naru mono." *Doshisha joshi daigaku daigakuin, bungaku kenkyūka kiyō*, no. 3 (2003): 25–40.

Sasabuchi Tomoichi. "Shimizu Shikin ron." In *Meiji Taishō bungaku no bunseki*, pp. 120–134. Tokyo: Meiji shoin, 1969.

Shimizu Shikin. *Shikin ẓenshū.* Tokyo: Sōdo bunka, 1983.

Takeda Kiyoko. "Shimizu Shikin—Kirisuto kyō to jiyū minken to no aida." *Risō,* no. 8 (1959): 56–67.

Tanabe Yusuke. "Shishōsetsu no genryū (tokushū): Meiji ki ni miru shishōsetsu– Shimizu Shikin 'Koware yubiwa.'" *Shishōsetsu kenkyū,* no. 2 (2001): 40–41.

Tanaka Mitsuko. "Shikin no ichi to 'Koware yubiwa' no kigōsei—'kowasu' gensetsu e no kataku to sabarutan e no manazashi." *Review of Gender and Women's Studies* 3, no. 1 (2000): 179–200.

Watanabe Sumiko. "Shimizu Shikin, 'Koware yubiwa.'" *Nihon bungaku* 3 (1980): 74–80.

Yamaguchi Reiko. *Naite aisuru shimai ni tsugu—Kōẓai Shikin no shōgai.* Tokyo: Sōdo bunka, 1977.

TAMURA TOSHIKO

English

Ericson, Joan, ed. Special issue on Tamura Toshiko, *U.S.-Japan Women's Journal,* no. 28 (2005).

Larson, Phyllis Hyland. "Re-reading Tamura Toshiko: a Failed New Woman?" In *Revisionism in Japanese Literary Studies. Proceedings of the Midwest Association for Japanese Literary Studies* 2, ed. Eiji Sekine, pp. 253–267. West Lafayette, Ind.: Midwest Association for Japanese Literary Studies, 1996.

Sokolsky, Anne. "No Place to Call Home: Negotiating the 'Third Space' for Returned Japanese Americans in Tamura Toshiko's 'Bubetsu' (Scorn)." *Japan Review: Bulletin of the International Research Center for Japanese Studies* (Kyoto), no.17 (2005): 121–148.

Tamura Toshiko. "Glory." Trans. Yukiko Tanaka. In *To Live and to Write: Selections by Japanese Women Writers,* 1913–1938, ed. Yukiko Tanaka, pp. 19–38. Seattle: Seal, 1987.

——. "A Woman Writer." Trans. Yukiko Tanaka. In *To Live and to Write: Selections by Japanese Women Writers,* 1913–1938, ed. Yukiko Tanaka, pp. 11–18. Seattle: Seal, 1987.

Tanaka, Yukiko. "Tamura Toshiko." In *To Live and to Write: Selections by Japanese Women Writers,* 1913–1938, ed. Yukiko Tanaka, pp. 5–10. Seattle: Seal, 1987.

Yonogi, Reiko. "Desire for Autonomy and Connection: Tamura Toshiko's Female Characters." In *The Outsider Within: Ten Essays on Modern Japanese Women Writers,* ed. Tomoko Kuribayashi and Mizuho Terasawa, pp. 3–18. Lanham, Md.: University Press of America, 2002.

Wu, Peichen. "Performing Gender along the Lesbian Continuum: the Politics of Sexual Identity in the Seitō Society." *U.S.-Japan Women's Journal*, no. 22 (2002): 64–86.

Japanese

Abe Tomoji. "Kaei: Inaka e no tegami." *Bungakkai* 3, no. 4 (June 1949): 24–33.

Hasegawa Kei. "Sakuhin kanshō." *Tanpen josei bungaku kindai*, ed. Imai Yasuko, Yabu Teiko, and Watanabe Sumiko, pp. 51–54. Tokyo: Ōfūsha, 1992.

——, ed. *Tamura Toshiko. Sakka no jiden*, ed. Saeki Shōichi and Matsumoto Ken'ichi, no. 87. Tokyo: Nihon tosho sentā, 1999.

Sakai Morinosuke. "Tamura Toshiko." In *Nihon kindai bungaku daijiten*, ed. Nihon Kindai Bungakkan, 2:371–373. Tokyo. Kōdansha, 1977.

Setouchi Harumi. *Tamura Toshiko*. Tokyo: Kōdansha, 1993.

——. "Tamura Toshiko no koto." In *Josei sakka jūsan'nin ten*, ed. Okuno Takeo, Kōno Toshirō, and Yasumasa Masao, pp. 35–38. Tokyo: Kindai Nihonbungaku-kan, 1988.

TAZAWA INABUNE

Japanese

Itō Seiko. *Hono'o no joryū sakka Tazawa Inabune*. Tokyo: Tōyō shoin, 1979.

Matsuzaka Toshio. *Tazawa Inabune—sakuhin no kiseki*. Tsuruoka: Tōhoku shuppan kikaku, 1996.

——. "Tazawa Inabune sobyō—sono hito to bungaku." In *Josei: seikatsu to bunka, Yamagata Joshi Tanki Daigaku sōritsu 20-shūnen kinen ronshū*, ed. Yamagata Joshi Tanki Daigaku, pp. 85–101. Yamagata: Tomizawa Gakuen Yamagata Joshi Tanki Daigaku, 1987.

Ōno Shigeo. *Ronkō Tazawa Inabune*. Tokyo: Seishidō, 1986.

Tazawa Inabune and Hosoya Masatake. *Tazawa Inabune kenkyū shiryō*. Akita: Mumyōsha shuppan, 2001.

——. *Tazawa Inabune sakuhinshū*. Akita: Mumyōsha shuppan, 1996.

——. *Tazawa Inabune zenshū*. Tsuruoka: Tōhoku shuppan kikaku, 1988.

Tsuruoka Shiritsu Toshokan, ed. *Aru Meiji no seishin: Tazawa Inabune joshi ni tsuite*. Tsuruoka: Tsuruoka Shiritsu Toshokan, 1964.

CONTRIBUTORS

TOMOKO AOYAMA is a senior lecturer of Japanese at the University of Queensland, Australia. Her publications include "The Cooking Man in Modern Japanese Literature" (2003), "Childhood Reimagined: The Memoirs of Ōgai's Children" (2003), "A Room Sweet as Honey: Father-Daughter Love in Mori Mari" (2001), and "The Love That Poisons: Japanese Parody and the New Literacy" (1994).

CAROLE CAVANAUGH is a professor of Japanese studies at Middlebury College in Vermont. Her publications include *Word and Image in Japanese Cinema* (2001), edited with Dennis Washburn.

REBECCA COPELAND is a professor of Japanese literature at Washington University in St. Louis, Missouri. Her published works include *Woman Critiqued: Translated Essays on Japanese Women's Writing* (2006); *The Father-Daughter Plot: Japanese Literary Women and the Law of the Father* (2001), edited with Dr. Esperanza Ramirez-Christensen; *Lost Leaves: Women Writers of Meiji Japan* (2000); and *The Sound of the Wind: The Life and Works of Uno Chiyo* (1992).

EDWARD FOWLER teaches Japanese literature and film at the University of California, Irvine. He is the translator of *A Man with No Talents: Memoirs of a Tokyo Day Laborer*, by Ōyama Shirō (2005), and author of *San'ya Blues: Laboring Life in Contemporary Tokyo* (1996) and *The Rhetoric of Confession: Shishōsetsu in Early Twentieth-Century Japanese Fiction* (1988).

BARBARA HARTLEY is a lecturer of Asian studies and Japanese studies at the University of Queensland, Australia. Her recent articles include "Writing the Body of the Mother: Narrative Moments in Tsushima Yūko, Ariyoshi Sawako and Enchi Fumiko" (2003). Currently she is researching images of the body in the work of Shiraki Shizu (1895–1919), Takeda Taijun (1912–1976), and selected Korean Japanese writers.

ELEANOR J. HOGAN is an associate professor of Japanese language and literature at Gettysburg College in Pennsylvania. She is also the cochair of the new Department of Asian Studies. Her articles include "When Art Does *not* Represent Life: Nogami Yaeko and the Marriage Question" (2004) and "Beyond Influence: The Literary Sisterhood of Nogami Yaeko and Jane Austen" (forthcoming). Hogan's research interests cover Nogami Yaeko, influence and intertextuality, women's writing, and Japanese science fiction.

REBECCA JENNISON is a professor of gender studies and literature in the Department of Humanities at Kyoto Seika University. She has published articles on the work of Shimizu Shikin and Morisaki Kazue and curated three exhibitions of work by contemporary women artists. Her recent articles included "The 'Shaman' and the 'Fox' in the Art of Tomiyama Taeko" (2003).

AIKO OKAMOTO MACPHAIL is an adjunct assistant professor in the French and Italian department at Indiana University. She has a general interest in women's writing and theory in the Heian Period. Her publications include "In Search of the Absolute Origin: Hermeneutics of Language in Ogyū Sorai" (2004), "From the Pages of Classics to Fantastic Tales: Kyokutei Bakin and the Seven Rules of Fiction" (2003), and "Interacting Signs in the Genji Scrolls," in *The Pictured Word*, ed. Martin Heusser (1998).

MIDORI YONEZAWA MORRIS is Luce Junior Professor of Japanese Language and Culture at Gettysburg College in Pennsylvania. Her specialty is sociolinguistics, and among her publications is "Influence of Vowel Devoicing on Dialect Judgments by Japanese Speakers" (2002). Another article, written with Dennis R. Preston, entitled "Japanese Vowel Devoicing: Regional Caricature and Perception," is forthcoming.

KYŌKO ŌMORI is an assistant professor of Japanese language and literature at Hamilton College in upstate New York. Her publications include translations of Mizukami Tsutomu's "One Night With Mother" (2006) and Tani Jōji's "The Shanghaied Man" (2005) and articles entitled "*Shinseinen*, the Contract, and Vernacular Modernism" (2004) and "'Merican-Jap and Modernity: Tani Jōji's Popular Negotiation of the Foreign" (2002). She is currently working on a book titled *Detecting Modanizumu: Shinseinen Magazine, Detective Fiction, and the Culture of Japanese Vernacular Modernism*, 1920–1950.

MELEK ORTABASI is an assistant professor of comparative literature at Hamilton College in upstate New York. Her publications include "Sketching Out the Critical Tradition: Yanagita Kunio and the Reappraisal of Realism" (2003), "The I-Novel" (2001), and "Fictional Fantasy or Historical Fact? The Search for Japanese Identity in Miyazaki Hayao's *Mononokehime*" (2000). Ortabasi's research interests, besides Meiji women writers, include Japanese film and popular culture, as well as translation theory. She is currently working on a book about ethnologist Yanagita Kunio (1875–1962).

LAUREL RASPLICA RODD is a professor of Japanese and comparative literature at the University of Colorado at Boulder. In addition to publications and translations of classical Japanese *waka*, she has published numerous articles on the twentieth-century poet Yosano Akiko, including "Yosano Akiko and Nationalism" (1998), "Yosano Akiko on Poetic Inspiration" (1996), "Yosano Akiko's 'On Poetry'" (1993), "Yosano Akiko and the Bunkagakuin: 'Creating Free Individuals'" (1991), and "Yosano Akiko and the Japanese Women's Movement in the Taishō Era" (1991).

YUKIKO TANAKA received her doctoral degree in Comparative Literature from UCLA in 1977. She is the author of *Women Writers of Meiji and Taishō Japan* (2000) as well as *Contemporary Portraits of Japanese Women* (1995). She edited and translated *Unmapped Territories: New Women's Fiction from Japan* (1991), *To Live and to Write: Stories of Japanese Women Writers* (1987), and *This Kind of Woman: Ten Stories by Japanese Women Writers*, 1960–1976 (1982). More recently, she has translated Kojima Nobuo's *Embracing Family* (2005).

INDEX

Names of the Meiji women writers featured as well as the works included in this anthology are indexed where they occur outside their respective chapters. Titles of other works by featured authors are indexed everywhere they occur. The Meiji-era works themselves are not indexed.

CPSIA information can be obtained
at www.ICGtesting.com
Printed in the USA
LVHW041524181118
597560LV00012B/618/P